Regulatory Reform

Regulation of Economic Activity

General Editors, Nancy L. Rose and Richard Schmalensee, MIT Sloan School of Management

Regulatory Reform:
Economic Analysis and British Experience

Mark Armstrong, Simon Cowan, and John Vickers

The MIT Press
Cambridge, Massachusetts
London, England

Second printing, 1995
© 1994 Massachusetts Institute of Technology

All rights reserved. No part of this book may be reproduced in any form by any electronic or mechanical means (including photocopying, recording, or information storage and retrieval) without permission in writing from the publisher.

This book was set in Times Roman by Asco Trade Typesetting Ltd., Hong Kong and was printed and bound in the United States of America.

Library of Congress Cataloging-in-Publication Data

Armstrong, Mark.
  Regulatory reform: economic analysis and British experience / Mark Armstrong, Simon Cowan, and John Vickers.
     p.   cm.—(Regulation of economic activity; 20)
  Includes bibliographical references and index.
  ISBN 0-262-01143-3
1. Industry and state—Great Britain. 2. Trade regulation—Great Britain.
3. Deregulation—Great Britain. 4. Government ownership—Great Britain.
5. Privatization—Great Britain. 6. Public utilities—Great Britain.
I. Cowan, Simon. II. Vickers, John, 1958–   . III. Title. IV. Series.
HD3616.G72A76   1994
338.941—dc20   94-8884
                                                                    CIP

Contents

List of Tables and Figures

Tables

Figures

Series Foreword

Government regulation of economic activity in the United States has changed dramatically in this century, radically transforming the economic roles of government and business as well as relations between them. Economic regulation of prices and conditions of service was first applied to transportation and public utilities and was later extended to energy, health care, and other sectors. In the early 1970s explosive growth occurred in social regulation, focusing on workplace safety, environmental preservation, consumer protection, and related goals. Regulatory reform has occupied a prominent place on the agendas of recent administrations, and considerable economic deregulation and other reform has occurred. But the U.S. economy remains highly regulated, and the aims, methods, and results of many regulatory programs remain controversial.

The purpose of the Regulation of Economic Activity series is to inform the ongoing debate on regulatory policy by making significant and relevant research available to both scholars and policymakers. Books in this series present new insights into individual agencies, programs, and regulated sectors, as well as important economic, political, and administrative aspects of the regulatory process that cut across those boundaries.

Historically industries that have been subjected to economic regulation in the United States have more commonly been government-owned in other nations. In the 1980s, however, the comprehensive privatization program of the Thatcher government in the United Kingdom replaced government ownership by economic regulation in a number of important sectors. New regulatory institutions were created, and new forms of regulation (in particular, price caps) were employed. In this book Mark Armstrong, Simon Cowan, and John Vickers provide a clear and careful analysis of this important experience. In the first part of this book, they present an accessible and insightful overview of the policy implications of recent theoretical work on optimal regulatory institutions and policies. They then employ this analytical framework in analyses of the U.K. experience with price cap regulation in general and of postprivatization developments in telecommunications, gas, electricity, and water supply.

This important book should be of interest to scholars and policymakers concerned with the industries on which Armstrong, Cowan, and Vickers concentrate. It is also essential reading for those interested in price cap regulation or in the design of regulatory institutions and policies. It has been used with considerable success as supplementary reading in an advanced course on regulatory economics at MIT.

Nancy L. Rose and Richard Schmalensee

Preface

This book stems from a project on the Regulation of Firms with Market Power that was funded by the U.K. Economic and Social Research Council (grant W102251008) and the Office of Fair Trading. We are very grateful for their financial support.

Thanks are due to many individuals for helpful comments and suggestions on draft chapters, including Chris Bolt, Martin Cave, David Elliott, Sir Christopher Foster, Richard Green, David Harbord, Dieter Helm, Stephen Littlechild, Geoffrey Myers, David Newbery, Tim Polack, Andrew Powell, Catherine Price, Howard Smith, Michael Waterson, and the anonymous reviewers of The MIT Press. More generally we wish to acknowledge the influence and help of Jean-Jacques Laffont, Jean Tirole, and of university colleagues, including Christopher Harris, Donald Hay, Paul Klemperer, Meg Meyer, Jim Mirrlees, Derek Morris, and Steve Nickell. The views expressed in this book are, however, ours alone and should certainly not be taken to reflect the views of the individuals and funding bodies to whom we are indebted. Likewise responsibility for all errors and omissions rests entirely with us. In chapters 6 to 10 we have attempted to describe British experience with regulatory reform up to the end of 1993, but events keep happening and brief postscripts have been added to chapters 7 and 9 to note some major developments early in 1994.

We are also most grateful to Philipp von Hagen and Dominic Webb for their valuable research assistance; to Candy Watts and Caroline Wise for their secretarial expertise; and to Dana Andrus and Terry Vaughn for the smooth efficiency of The MIT Press. Finally, we thank our respective universities and colleges for the fine environment that they provide.

Mark Armstrong
Faculty of Economics,
and Gonville and Caius College
Cambridge, England

John Vickers
Institute of Economics and Statistics,
and All Souls College
Oxford, England

Simon Cowan
Institute of Economics and Statistics,
and Worcester College
Oxford, England

March 1994

Regulatory Reform

1

Introduction

How to regulate firms with market power is one of the central questions for industrial policy. It is a question to which the answers given by policy-makers in many countries have altered considerably in the last decade or so, and change is continuing. It is also a question that is illuminated by recently developed methods for analyzing the economics of industrial organization and incentives. In this book we set out an analytical framework for studying the main issues in regulatory reform, and we apply the analysis to four utility industries—telecommunications, gas, electricity and water supply.

In Britain all those industries were state-owned monopolies ten years ago, but now they are in private hands, and subject to competition at least in parts. In the process of regulatory reform, markets have been liberalized, industries have been restructured, and new regulatory methods and institutions have been created. The dramatic and comprehensive nature of these reforms means that the utility industries in Britain make a particularly interesting and instructive case study, but there are a number of parallels elsewhere.

Modern regulatory reform began in the United States in the 1970s, notably in telecommunications, airlines, trucking, and financial services.[1] Deregulation has also occurred in oil and gas and in the railway industry. For the purposes of this book, however, of most significance is the 1984 break up of AT&T, following an antitrust suit brought by the U.S. Department of Justice ten years earlier. The AT&T case raised the fundamental question whether effective regulation of an integrated monopolist can coexist with conditions for effective and undistorted competition in industries that contain both naturally monopolistic and potentially competitive activities, or whether structural separation between these activities is necessary. The latter course was chosen, and AT&T was divested of its more naturally monopolistic regional network operations.[2]

Regulatory reform is now in progress worldwide, most importantly, of course, in Eastern Europe and the former Soviet Union. Among the other

---

1. See Winston's (1993) survey of deregulation in the United States.
2. See section 7.3.

OECD countries,[3] Japan has pursued far-reaching policies of regulatory reform, often in conjunction with privatization: the telecommunications industry has been extensively liberalized, and in 1987 Japanese National Railways was split to form seven separate companies. Radical measures of deregulation, privatization and public sector reform have been implemented in New Zealand. In Western Europe there are reform initiatives in many countries, and also at European Community level. As part of its single-market program the EC has issued directives to promote harmonization and liberalization of network access, for example, in telecommunications, energy, and railways.[4] As well as structural reform and liberalization, methods of conduct regulation are also changing. Following the introduction of RPI $-$ X regulation in Britain in the mid-1980s, there have been moves, for example, in U.S. telecommunications, away from rate-of-return regulation toward price caps for monopoly control.

In part II of this book, we focus on the telecommunications, gas, electricity, and water industries. All four have naturally monopolistic network activities that require regulation—local telecommunications, gas pipelines, electricity grids, and water and sewerage infrastructure—and common policy questions, for example, concerning separation between network provision and the supply of services, arise in each. In other respects, however, there is considerable diversity between the industries, not only in respect of technological and economic characteristics but also in terms of the regulatory reform policies adopted in Britain. All four industries were privatized and underwent regulatory reform at least a few years ago, so there is some experience to report. Rail and post are network industries where some similar (and some different) policy issues arise, but regulatory reform has not yet been implemented—at the time of writing it is about to happen in rail and is under consideration for the postal service in Britain. Much of the analysis that follows, and some of the lessons from experience, have potential application in those industries and others, including broadcasting and elsewhere in the transport sector. Indeed the liberalized utility industries are of interest for competition policy in general, since they provide fertile ground for a rich variety of monopolistic and anticompetitive practices.

We make no attempt to explain in full why it is in recent years that methods of regulating firms with market power have been undergoing

---

3. See OECD (1992) for a survey of regulatory reform in these countries to the end of 1990.
4. See Henry (1993).

such change. A number of interacting economic, political, and technological factors have been at work. In telecommunications, for example, technological change and demand growth have significantly diminished the domain of natural monopoly and enlarged the potential for competitive market forces. At a general level there has been a reassessment of the importance of regulatory failure relative to market failure. However, as British experience shows, regulatory reform is certainly not a simple matter of having more competition and less regulation. Indeed that is why "regulatory reform" rather than "deregulation" appears in the title of the book.

Analytical Framework

No industries are exactly alike in their economic characteristics, but the utilities, and some other industries, have important elements in common. In particular, they each combine (1) naturally monopolistic activities, such as transmission networks, and (2) potentially competitive activities, such as the provision of services over the networks, which may or may not actually be competitive, for which access to activities of type 1 is an essential ingredient.

Thus in telecommunications, activities of type 1 include local fixed-link network services, for the short term at least, and those of type 2 include many long-distance services. In gas and electricity, type 1 activities include transmission and distribution, and those of type 2 include production/generation and supply, at least to larger users. In railways, type 1 activities include the infrastructure of track, signaling systems and stations, but train services might come within type 2. The water industry, however, has very few activities of type 2.

Public policy toward an industry of this kind involves answering a number of questions.

1. *Vertical integration.* Is the firm in the naturally monopolistic activities (firm *M*, say) allowed also to operate in the potentially competitive activities?

2. *Liberalization.* Does *M* have an exclusive right to operate in the potentially competitive sector, and hence enjoy a monopoly over the whole industry, or is there free entry? In the event of liberalization, should entry be restricted, assisted, or neither?

3. *Horizontal structure.* If firm *M* does operate in the potentially competitive activities, should its assets there be broken up into competing units?

4. *Regional structure.* In the natural monopoly activities, is firm *M* a nationwide monopolist, or is there a separate natural monopolist in each geographical region?

5. *Product price regulation.* Which of the products supplied by the industry have their consumer prices regulated, and what form does such regulation take?

6. *Access price regulation.* On what terms can other firms in the industry obtain access to the natural monopoly services of firm *M*?

7. *Regulation of nonprice behavior.* How does regulation apply to nonprice aspects of conduct by firm *M* and others in the industry, for example, service quality and compliance with environmental policy requirements?

The first four of these questions concern structure. The simplest structure of all—*vertically integrated monopoly*—is shown in figure 1.1. Firm *M* is the only operator in both activities, so there is no question of access pricing to rivals, but all consumer prices need to be regulated. It is supposed that some of the naturally monopolistic products and services are supplied directly to consumers (in "market 1") as well as being an intermediate product for producers. Local network services in telecommunications are an example. Products and services that require inputs that could in principle be supplied competitively are sold to consumers in "market 2". Broadly speaking, vertically integrated monopoly was the situation of all the utility industries in Britain before 1980—they had statutory monopolies over virtually all aspects of their business. Of course they were state owned as well, and regulation was implicit rather than explicit as now.

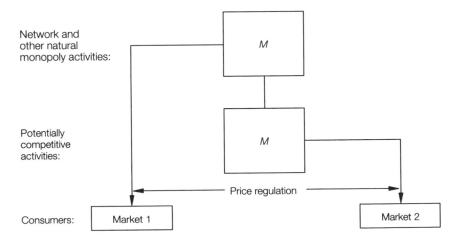

Figure 1.1 Vertically integrated monopoly

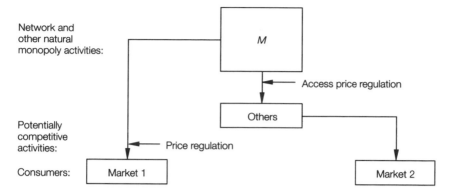

Figure 1.2 Vertical separation

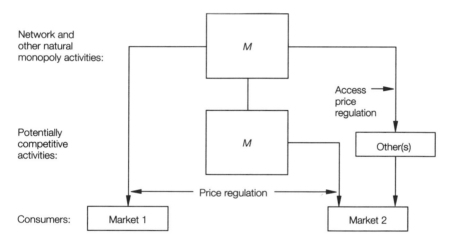

Figure 1.3 Vertical integration with liberalization

A very different structure is *vertical separation*, as shown in figure 1.2. Firm *M* is confined to the natural monopoly activities, whose prices are regulated, and there is competition elsewhere. A move from vertically integrated monopoly to vertical separation would entail the divestiture of *M*'s potentially competitive activities, perhaps horizontal breakup, and liberalization. Vertical separation does not do away with the need for access price regulation, but the rival firms are on an equal footing in the sense that none is linked by ownership with firm *M*.

This is not so in the hybrid case of *vertical integration and liberalization*, as shown in figure 1.3, where there is obviously an asymmetry between firm *M* and its rivals. The asymmetry may require that all *M*'s prices continue to be regulated, even in potentially competitive activities. Whether it distorts competition depends very much upon the regulation of access terms.

Oversimplifying somewhat, British Telecom was privatized on the hybrid model, British Gas was privatized effectively as a vertically integrated monopolist, and vertical separation was adopted for the electricity supply industry. Thus a variety of approaches has been used in the British utilities, and as we will explain, there have also been trends in policy— broadly speaking toward separation—over time.

Plan of the Book

The book is in two parts, which deal respectively with analytical issues and industry case studies. The first part is organized around the analytical framework sketched above; see figure 1.4. Chapters 2 and 3 are about monopoly regulation. For the most part they abstract from competitive and "vertical" questions, and the focus is on the monopolistic activities (or all activities in the integrated monopoly case). Some sections of these two chapters are marked by asterisks; these sections contain more technical material and may be omitted without loss of continuity. Chapter 2 begins by reviewing the market failure rationales for regulation, notably monopoly power. The economics of regulation would be a relatively simple

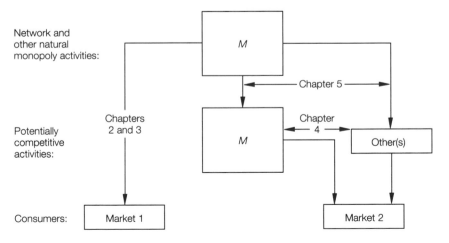

Figure 1.4 Analytical framework

matter if regulators were omniscient, benevolent, and able to precommit future policy, but in practice there are problems arising from asymmetric information, policy credibility, and the danger of "capture." The basic static issues are discussed in chapter 2, while more complex multiproduct and dynamic aspects are covered chapter 3.

Policy toward competition and liberalization is the subject of chapter 4. Except in contestable markets theory, which we argue is of limited relevance for policy toward the utility industries, competition is a more or less imperfect mechanism, and the question is how it compares with the imperfect alternative of regulation. The possibility that liberalization can result in excess entry or "cream-skimming" is discussed, but the informational and incentive advantages of competition are emphasized. Incumbent advantages and strategic entry deterrence in the utility industries may make liberalization ineffective without procompetitive regulation, and there is the question of whether to give assistance to entrants. The chapter also considers the possibility of franchising monopoly rights, and some interactions between competition and regulation: liberalization can help or hinder regulation, and regulation can distort competition.

Whereas chapter 4 concerns purely "horizontal" competition, "vertical" relationships between monopolistic and competitive activities, which are of central importance in the utility industries, are analyzed in chapter 5. First, we abstract from regulatory issues and consider how integration can affect productive efficiency, and how it may serve inefficient anticompetitive purposes. Then some principles of optimal access pricing are reviewed. Depending on competitive circumstances, these may vary according to whether or not firm M is vertically integrated. Finally, there is some analysis and broader discussion of the fundamental question of vertical separation versus integration. This question is inevitably difficult, for it involves a combination of a number of the competitive and regulatory issues that have gone before.

The second part of the book begins, in chapter 6, by describing and assessing the form of price cap regulation known as RPI $-$ X, which has been a rather novel and distinctive element of regulatory reform in Britain, and the subject of much international attention. The industry case studies —telecommunications, gas, electricity, and water—follow in chapters 7 to 10. In each of them we describe the economic characteristics of the industry (natural monopoly elements, other market failures, etc.), the broad policy options, the choices between those options made in Britain, and lessons from the resulting experience. While conditions in these industries can be related to the analytical framework sketched above, each also has important economic characteristics of its own which we consider. Thus, for example, environmental questions are particularly important in the electricity and water industries.

The final chapter contains conclusions about developments in regulatory policy toward industry structure, liberalization and price control, lessons to be drawn from British experience, and some challenges for the future. We also comment on the new institutions of regulation.

Regulatory Reform and Privatization

It is obviously no coincidence that many of the regulatory reforms discussed in this book happened in conjunction with privatization. The transfer to private ownership of firms with substantial market power necessitated new regulatory arrangements and was naturally the occasion for a review of the competitive structure of the industries concerned. However, this book is not directly about privatization.

The economic analysis of privatization has a number of aspects.[5] There are questions about the process of transferring ownership—technique of sale, pricing of shares, revenues raised, effect on share ownership, and so on—and there is the fundamental question: How does ownership matter for performance? For competitive industries free of significant market failures, theory and evidence both support the conclusion that private ownership is more efficient than public ownership, but the answer is less straightforward for industries such as the utilities.

In industries with market power and/or other market failures, irrespective of ownership or ownership change, incentives for efficiency depend critically on the regimes of competition and regulation in which the industries operate. These regimes and their reform are crucial in determining how ownership matters, how well privatization succeeds in its efficiency aims, and more generally how well the industries perform, whether under public or private ownership.

In sum, incentives for efficiency depend jointly on ownership, competition, and regulation. This book is about the reform of competitive and regulatory frameworks, but the analysis nevertheless has numerous implications for privatization, which is often part of the process of regulatory reform in any event.

---

5. See Vickers and Yarrow (1988) and Foster (1992), for example.

I

ANALYTICAL FRAMEWORK

2

Monopoly Regulation: Static Analysis

For most parts of the economy monopoly regulation has no role to play. The interests of firms and of society more or less coincide in many markets: a firm in competition with other firms will attempt to reduce its costs, increase the quality of its output (or offer a lower quality for a lower price if that is preferred by consumers), or introduce new products in order to gain competitive advantage over other firms. These effects will in turn tend to increase welfare overall. Loosely speaking, firms in most markets make profits by giving consumers what they want to buy, and competitive profit seeking is good for consumers' well-being.

There are, however, several reasons why markets can fail to operate in this beneficial way. Such market failures in some cases can be so severe as to merit regulation despite its attendant costs. Broadly speaking, there are three classes of market failure, and these may be termed problems of asymmetric information, problems of externalities, and problems of monopoly power.

Markets can fail when firms offer goods or services with characteristics about which consumers are in some way uncertain before purchase. One class of examples are markets for information, for instance, about the financial state of quoted companies. Consumers of this information have no way of knowing the quality of this information before purchase and must therefore trust the seller to some degree. Consumers of legal and medical services also fall into this category; indeed the very reason people usually obtain the services of a lawyer or doctor is to obtain advice from someone who is better informed than they are themselves. Since it is hard to ascertain the quality of a lawyer or doctor from a single meeting, it seems sensible to require these professions to have some kind of minimum level of qualification to enter the profession in order to stop "quacks" from preying on ill-informed consumers (see Leland 1979). Similarly consumers cannot directly observe whether a particular new drug is safe and effective unless all new drugs are required to be licensed by a testing authority; cars and other complicated mechanical goods are required to satisfy certain minimum safety conditions, and the managers of most financial funds are required to follow rules when making their investment decisions. Of course there are many aspects of this information problem that are not subject to external control: for instance, a buyer typically will not be able to be certain in advance how long a new car will last. Markets with asymmetric information that are unregulated were first analyzed by Akerlof (1970) who looked at the case of the secondhand car market. He showed that the presence of asymmetric information about the quality of cars can sometimes result in complete market failure—no trades may take place even though many mutually beneficial trades are possible. External regulation will not always be needed in order to curb such problems, however, since devices such as warranties will directly insure the buyer against the unlucky purchase of a low-quality item and, in addition, could act as a signal of the item's quality at the time of purchase. Also we would expect reputational effects to ameliorate the adverse effects of asymmetric information to a significant degree (see Allen 1984).

Externalities often are a potent source of market failure. When the behavior of a firm affects other firms or people (for reasons other than price effects) in either a positive or negative way, then there may be scope for regulatory action to improve the welfare of all agents concerned. If the generation of electricity using a fossil fuel also produces acid rain, then this imposes a direct cost on others that is not borne by the firm, and the result is more pollution than is efficient. Regulators could impose on firms either a ceiling on emissions or a tax per unit of emissions in order to reduce the level of pollution to a more efficient level. Similarly, if water and sewerage companies were permitted simply to dump sewage directly into rivers or the sea, then bathers and the general natural environment would suffer and this cost is not faced by the firm. (Environmental regulation, itself a large subject, is not analyzed in the first part of this book, but aspects of it are discussed in chapters 9 and 10.) An example of a positive externality occurs in telephone networks. Existing subscribers to a network benefit from the addition of further subscribers to the network because of the increased possibilities for communication. However, the pricing policy of an unregulated telecommunications firm would equate the marginal cost of subscription with the revenue obtained from the marginal subscribers, and would not take direct account of the benefit to the inframarginal subscribers. One possible remedy might be for the government to subsidize the costs of providing additional telephone lines. This network externality also has implications for the development of competition in the telecommunications industry: a small rival to a larger incumbent network operator has a tremendous disadvantage in attracting customers because, even if it is more efficient and can offer lower call charges, its potential customers realize that they will be able to call only a small fraction of those they could call using the incumbent's network. The small rival will most likely stay small unless the incumbent firm is required to provide interconnection between the two networks.

The final class of market failure—and the class with which we will be concerned most in this book—is that of market power, which exists when the market in question suffers from ineffective competition (actual or potential). At the extreme the market is supplied by a single firm, protected by barriers to entry, which in the absence of regulation would face no check on the prices it could charge except for its consumers' willingness to pay for its products. In the utility industries most consumers would be prepared to pay a great deal for the firms' outputs (demand elasticities are low), and the unregulated monopoly could charge prices that would result in a dramatically inefficient allocation of resources. As discussed below, the most efficient use of resources usually involves consumers facing a price equal to the marginal cost of supplying the product, and a price in excess of this results in a loss of welfare, or *allocative inefficiency*. Since the profit-maximizing monopolist will set price above the level of marginal cost, there is a clear benefit in finding ways to reduce this allocative inefficiency. The problem of prices diverging from costs is not the only problem that comes with market power, and monopolies neither have sufficient incentives to cut their costs where possible, nor may they be as quick to introduce new products as firms acting in competitive markets. This results in *productive inefficiency*. These dynamic effects could be at least as important as deadweight loss considerations.

Broadly, there are two alternative ways to curb the problem of market power: to introduce regulation in some form to prevent the firm from charging the prices it would like, or to find ways (if possible) to introduce more competition into the market. The second option is the subject of chapter 4, and it suffices here to note that the interrelations between competition and regulation are complex and sometimes conflicting. For instance, requiring a firm to charge a low price might benefit consumers in the short term but inhibit entry to the consumers' detriment in the longer term. As well as bringing price close to marginal cost, competition normally gives firms good dynamic incentives for cost reduction and innovation, and if regulation is chosen as the principal means to contain the excesses of market power, then some care should be taken to ensure that it too gives the firm good incentives.

In an ideal world the regulator of a firm would be omniscient, benevolent, and have ample powers of precommitment. The information available to the regulator—concerning consumer demand, the firm's costs, and possibilities for cost reduction, for example—would then in no way be inferior to that known to the firm, the regulator would choose to act as the "high custodian of the public interest" and would have the means to commit to any dynamic regulatory contract. In section 2.1 we examine this benchmark case. This includes discussions on marginal cost pricing, average cost pricing, two-part tariffs, nonlinear tariffs, and possibilities for cost reduction. In sections 2.2 and 2.3 we relax the assumption that the regulator knows as much about industry conditions as the firm. In this case the regulator must take into account the firm's monopoly of information on some aspects of the industry and should try to design regulation to give the firm some *incentives* to set prices and costs efficiently. In section 2.2 we allow the regulator to have the authority to make monetary transfers to or from the firm, whereas in section 2.3 regulation must rely on price alone to provide incentives. Finally, section 2.4 contains some concluding comments. In the next chapter we consider, as well as multiproduct issues, the effect of relaxing the further assumptions that the regulator is benevolent and able to commit to future regulatory policy.

2.1   Regulation with Symmetric Information: Benchmark Case

2.1.1   Marginal Cost Pricing

The most familiar pricing principle is that of marginal cost pricing. Suppose, as we do throughout this chapter, that the firm produces only a single product and does so for only a single period in time.[1] If a consumer faces a price per unit of the firm's output that differs from the firm's marginal cost of producing one more unit, then both the firm and the consumer could be made better off by appropriately changing the quantity produced in return for a transfer of money. For instance, if price exceeded marginal cost—as is the case with unregulated monopoly—then both parties would benefit if the firm produced a further unit of the good in return for a payment somewhere between price and cost. Thus the only efficient allocation of the firm's output (in the sense that neither the firm nor the consumer can simultaneously be made better off by changing the

---

1. We use a partial equilibrium framework throughout. The validity of the implicit assumptions behind this approach are discussed below.

allocation) involves the consumer paying a price for his or her marginal unit equal to the cost of producing that unit. In particular, if the firm offers a price to all consumers that equals marginal cost, then output is efficiently allocated. Let $C(Q)$ be the firm's cost of producing a total output Q, and let $C'(Q)$ denote the firm's marginal cost. Then, if aggregate demand at price P is $Q(P)$, there is efficient marginal cost pricing at price P^* if $P^* = C'(Q(P^*))$.

There are two caveats to this rule. If there are externalities in the production or consumption of the good, then the cost function $C(Q)$ should be modified to reflect *total* costs in producing Q, rather than just the costs faced by the firm. For instance, if it costs an electricity generating firm $C(Q)$ to produce Q kilowatt hours of electricity, but in addition harms the environment by an estimated $D(Q)$ (measured in terms of money), then total costs are $C(Q) + D(Q)$, and efficient pricing involves setting price equal to the total marginal cost $C'(Q) + D'(Q)$.[2] Second, if there are other distortions in the economy, then it is not always best to use marginal cost pricing in a particular market. If the regulated firm's output is used as an input by other firms (as is the case with all utility industries) and if these upstream firms do not operate in competitive markets, then it might be desirable to set price below marginal cost in order to counterbalance the price/cost markup practiced by these other firms (see section 5.2 below).

Unfortunately, there is the problem with marginal cost pricing in industries like the utilities that it may entail the firm making a loss. For instance, if the firm has a constant variable cost per unit of c and faces fixed overheads of K, so that $C(Q) = cQ + K$, then marginal cost pricing would set P equal to c, which would result in the firm making a loss equal to K. More generally, whenever the firm has increasing returns to scale so that its average cost $C(Q)/Q$ decreases with its output Q, then marginal cost pricing necessarily will result in revenues failing to cover costs. Many industries do not exhibit severe increasing returns to scale, and in the normal course of events we would expect competition to push price approximately down to marginal cost and for firms to continue to break even. However, many regulated industries—including those discussed in part II of this book—are regulated precisely because they suffer from problems of monopoly power caused in part by elements of increasing returns to scale, and for such industries marginal cost pricing offers no

---

2. In this example, the relationship between pollution and output is fixed. In practice an important concern is efficiently to reduce pollution per unit of output; see section 9.4.4.

simple solution to the regulatory problem. Of course the shortfall in profit caused by marginal cost pricing could be covered by a direct subsidy to the firm out of public funds, but since there is no way of generating these funds other than by causing distortions elsewhere in the economy, this policy itself has problems.

As a general rule regulators are simply not permitted either to tax or to subsidize the firms they regulate,[3] and in sections 2.1.2 to 2.1.4 we examine the best method of regulating the firm subject to the proviso that the price or tariff that the firm charges should cover the firm's costs.

2.1.2   Average Cost Pricing

We have seen that first-best regulation generally involves setting price equal to marginal cost, but that for firms with increasing returns to scale, such pricing will result in the firm making a loss. Here we show that setting the firm's price equal to average cost is best in terms of overall welfare subject to the constraint that the firm break even.

First, we must make explicit our welfare criterion. We suppose that the regulator's objective is to maximize welfare as given by the expression

$$W(P) = V(P) + \alpha\pi(P), \tag{2.1}$$

where P is the price charged by the firm and α is a constant lying between zero and one. Since this is going to be the measure of welfare we use throughout this book, expression (2.1) deserves some explanation. Here $V(P)$ is consumer surplus at price P so that $V(P)$ is the area under the demand curve $Q(\cdot)$. It satisfies $V'(P) = -Q(P)$, where V' is the derivative of V: the reduction in consumer welfare resulting from a small price increase is equal to the quantity demanded by consumers multiplied by the price increase. Consumer surplus is a standard measure of consumer welfare, but it does have some well-known drawbacks. It is strictly valid only when there are no income effects so that changes in income do not result in changes in demand for the good. However, for small changes in price, $V(P)$ provides an approximate measure of consumer welfare.[4] A second problem arises from that fact that all the utility industries produce

---

3. We will come back to this point in section 2.3, among other places. One rationale for why regulators cannot use transfers as a regulatory instrument might be that doing so would give them too much discretion and could leave them vulnerable to "capture"; see section 3.7.

4. For more on the conditions under which $V(P)$ is a good measure of consumer utility, see Willig (1976).

goods that are used as inputs by other firms. Unless all of these down-stream firms operate in competitive markets, there are further reasons why the measure $V(P)$ is imperfect.

An implicit assumption in taking $V(P)$ as the measure of consumer welfare is that the regulator regards a pound in the hand of one consumer to be just as valuable as a pound in the hand of any other consumer, in other words, that the marginal utility of income is constant across consumers. With an ideal tax/benefit system this might be true, but in cases where the system is imperfect, there is the question of whether the regulator should take into account imperfections in the government's redistributive efforts when framing regulatory policy. In theory and with an idealized regulator, it is hard to see to how the answer to this question can be other than yes. In practice, however, it seems likely that the regulation of private firms is a tool ill-suited for redistributive policy, and we will ignore differences in the marginal utility of income across consumers when discussing theoretical aspects of regulation. However, in part II of the book, we will see that distributional concerns have played a part in regulatory policy in Britain.

The profit of the firm $\pi(P)$ is given by $PQ(P) - C(Q(P))$. Instead of simply adding together producer and consumer surplus, in many cases it seems more appropriate to add a *weighted* sum of consumer and profit, and so the weight α is included in (2.1). A reason why we might wish to place less weight on profit than on consumer surplus (to take $\alpha < 1$) is that, since shareholders tend to be wealthier than general consumers, a welfare criterion with some distributional concern should value a pound in the hand of a typical consumer more than a pound in the hand of a typical shareholder.[5] Alternatively, if, as in the utilities, the fraction of shareholders that are resident outside the country is greater than the fraction of consumers of regulated services that are foreign, then a smaller fraction of profits should count toward welfare if it is defined in nationalistic terms.

An important point to stress about the welfare criterion (2.1) is that the only distributional concern is between consumers and the firm. This approach is taken by Baron and Myerson (1982), for example. More

---

5. Of course this conflicts with our earlier assumption about marginal utility being constant across the population. Alternatively, taking a more "political" viewpoint we could see the regulator as mediating a bargain between consumers and shareholders of the firm over their shares of the gains from trade, with α representing the relative weakness of shareholders in the process.

generally, we could explicitly introduce government into the welfare criterion. It would be appropriate to do this if lump-sum transfers from consumers to the government had positive social value, for example, because of the ability to reduce distortionary taxation elsewhere in the economy. This "social cost of public funds" approach is taken by Laffont and Tirole (1993). While there are differences between these two complementary welfare criteria, they have in common the central point that there exists a conflict between *efficiency* and *distribution* (or rent extraction; see section 2.2).

The regulator's problem is to choose P^* in order to maximize $W(P)$ in (2.1) subject to the constraint that $[PQ(P) - C(Q(P))] \geq 0$. This has a simple solution in the case where the firm has increasing returns to scale (where average cost $C(Q)/Q$ decreases with output Q), the case that is most relevant when considering the utilities. In this case the optimal price P^* is equal to average cost (whatever the value of α): $P^* = C(Q(P^*))/Q(P^*)$. With increasing returns this price is uniquely defined and is the lowest price for which the firm does not make a loss. Average cost pricing is optimal subject to the break-even constraint when there are increasing returns because, if $P > C(Q(P))/Q(P)$, the firm makes a strictly positive profit and a small price reduction would not result in the firm making a loss. Whenever welfare is written as in (2.1) and price exceeds marginal cost, then welfare is increased by moving price down toward marginal cost. (The resulting increase in consumer surplus will more than match the weighted loss in profits.) Provided that the firm has increasing returns, price being greater than average cost implies price is greater than marginal cost. Therefore, if price exceeds average cost, welfare could be increased by a price reduction that allows the firm to break even, and so it must be optimal to require the firm to charge a price equal to average cost.

Setting price equal to average cost reflects the compromise between a desire for allocative efficiency—setting price near to marginal cost—and the need for the firm to break even. We next see how these conflicting aims can be better resolved.

2.1.3 Two-Part Tariffs

The preceding section considered how best to regulate a firm if consumers are offered a tariff in which the price for each unit of the product is the same, that is, when the firm offers a *linear* tariff. In many cases it is possible to increase welfare by choosing tariffs in which the price a consumer faces for a unit of the product varies with the quantity chosen, that is, when the firm offers *nonlinear* tariffs. A common class of nonlinear tariffs are *two-part tariffs* which require a consumer to pay a fixed charge A in order to buy any quantity of the product and in addition a marginal price P per unit (so that the charge for the first unit of the product is $A + P$ and for all subsequent units the charge is P). Therefore, if a quantity $q > 0$ is consumed, the total charge is

$$T(q) = A + Pq. \tag{2.2}$$

Two-part tariffs are often used in the utility industries: in the telecommunications, gas, and electricity supply industries consumers pay a quarterly fixed charge in addition to a charge per unit used; in the water industry many households in Britain face an extreme kind of two-part tariff in which the marginal charge is zero and the charge is independent of the quantity consumed. For economic analyses of two-part tariffs, see Oi (1971), Varian (1989), and Wilson (1993).

The simplest way to see how nonlinear tariffs can improve upon simple linear tariffs is to suppose that all consumers are identical and so can be regarded as a single consumer with surplus function $V(P)$. The problem we consider here is how to choose the two-part tariff so as to maximize welfare subject to (1) the firm breaking even and (2) the consumer being willing to participate in the market. The total consumer surplus obtained from the tariff (2.2) is $V(P) - A$, and so this second constraint requires that $V(P) - A \geq 0$. Welfare is $V(P) - A + \alpha[A + R(Q(P)) - C(Q(P))]$, and it is optimal to set the marginal price P^* equal to marginal cost $C'(Q(P^*))$ and to make up for any shortfall in profits by means of the fixed charge A. For instance, if the firm's cost function is of the form $C(Q) = cQ + K$, then it will be optimal to set the two-part tariff with $A^* = K$ and $P^* = c$ (provided that $K < V(c)$), regardless of the form of the demand function and the value of α. In this case the optimal two-part tariff results in the first-best allocation with price equal to marginal cost, an allocation that gives the consumer a higher level of surplus than does average cost pricing. The addition of the fixed charge A^* allows price to be set equal to marginal cost, while covering the firm's fixed costs.

When consumers are heterogeneous, this argument could break down because those who are prepared to pay relatively little for consuming the product would drop out of the market with the introduction of a uniform fixed charge sufficient to cover the loss the firm makes with marginal cost pricing. This is inefficient in so far as consumers would be prepared to pay a price at least equal to marginal cost for some units of the product. On the other hand, it would be desirable to continue to charge a marginal price equal to marginal cost for allocative efficiency reasons. Typically in such cases it will be optimal to set marginal price somewhat above marginal cost with a correspondingly lower fixed charge in order to balance these two opposing effects.

This dilemma—between a desire to keep low-demand consumers in the market (for efficiency and possibly for distributional reasons) and to make all consumers face a tariff with marginal price close to marginal cost—can be resolved to some extent by tariffs of a more general form than two-part tariffs. Consumers could be offered the choice between two tariff schemes —say, a two-part tariff with a low fixed charge and higher usage charge aimed at the low-demand end of the market together with a tariff with a higher fixed and lower usage charges for the consumers who wish for larger quantities of the product. In fact it is not hard to show that if, in addition to a linear tariff with price greater than marginal cost, the firm offers consumers the choice of using a two-part tariff with price equal to marginal cost and a sufficiently high fixed charge, then no consumer can be made worse off (everyone still has the option of using the old tariff) and both the firm and some sufficiently high-demand consumers are made strictly better off.[6] In the next section we consider tariffs in which the marginal price for a unit of the product is allowed to vary *continuously* with the quantity purchased.

*2.1.4 Nonlinear Tariffs

The analysis of general nonlinear tariffs in this section is of interest in its own right, but in addition it involves techniques that will be useful later in the book. This section is somewhat more technical, and it can safely be skipped by the general reader. The main points are that the welfare-maximizing nonlinear tariff will most likely involve the firm offering consumers *quantity discounts*, that is to say, a tariff for which the charge for an additional unit of the product decreases with the total quantity purchased by a consumer.

We have seen that if all consumers were identical, then two-part tariffs would provide the ideal solution. However, consumers usually do differ substantially, not least because of income inequality, and the regulator should allow for this heterogeneity when deciding which tariff the firm should offer. One way that consumer differences can be modeled is to

---

6. For a discussion of the Pareto improvements made possible by these "optional two-part tariffs," see Willig (1978) and also section 3.3 below. Ordover and Panzar (1980) show that if the firm produces an intermediate product and sells to an industry that is only imperfectly competitive, then it may not be possible to find Pareto-improving nonlinear tariffs.

introduce a taste parameter θ that varies across consumers.[7] A consumer with tastes given by θ gains utility of $\theta u(q) - T(q)$ from consuming the quantity q for a charge of $T(q)$, where $u(\cdot)$ is a concave function such that $u(0) = 0$. Thus a higher value of θ means that a consumer has stronger tastes for the product. The crucial assumption is that the firm cannot distinguish one type of consumer from another, and therefore each consumer must be offered the same tariff $T(q)$.[8] Suppose that the number of each type of consumer is given by the distribution function $F(\theta)$, so that the fraction of consumers who have a type parameter less than θ is $F(\theta)$. The lowest and highest possible type are, respectively, $\underline{\theta}$ and $\bar{\theta}$ so that $F(\underline{\theta}) = 0$ and $F(\bar{\theta}) = 1$. The taste parameter θ is assumed to be continuously distributed so that there is a density function $f(\theta)$ that satisfies $f(\theta) = F'(\theta)$. The problem is to design the nonlinear tariff $T^*(q)$ that maximizes welfare subject to the constraint that the firm at least breaks even.

Given a tariff $T(q)$ the type θ consumer will choose the quantity $q(\theta)$ (possibly zero) that maximizes utility $\theta u(q) - T(q)$ and will therefore attain a surplus of

$$v(\theta) \equiv \theta u(q(\theta)) - T(q(\theta)). \tag{2.3}$$

The first-order condition for $q(\theta)$ to be the optimal choice for the type θ consumer is

$$\theta u'(q(\theta)) - T'(q(\theta)) = 0. \tag{2.4}$$

Since consumers cannot be compelled to consume if they do not wish to, any tariff T must satisfy $T(0) \leq 0$. In this case $v(\cdot)$ as defined in (2.3) is nonnegative and increasing in θ, so consumers with stronger tastes for the product attain a higher level of surplus. In addition, by differentiating (2.3) and substituting (2.4) into the expression for the derivative, it can be seen that the surplus function $v(\cdot)$ has the "envelope" property

$$v'(\theta) = u(q(\theta)). \tag{2.5}$$

From (2.3) the firm's revenue from the type θ consumer is

$$T(q(\theta)) = \theta u(q(\theta)) - v(\theta). \tag{2.6}$$

---

7. The following description is *not* technically rigorous. For more detail, and for a thorough analysis of the whole topic of nonlinear pricing, see Wilson (1993).

8. It may be that there are observable characteristics that are correlated with a consumer's strength of demand for the good. Examples might be the number of people in the household, age, or income. However, it is often impossible or unacceptable to base a tariff on such factors.

The first stage in solving for the optimal tariff is to calculate the firm's profit when the tariff T is offered. For simplicity, let the firm have the cost function $C(Q) = cQ + K$. Given the consumer demand function $q(\theta)$ that satisfies (2.4), the total profit using the tariff T is

$$\pi(T) = \int [T(q(\theta)) - cq(\theta)]f(\theta)\,d\theta - K,$$

where integration is between $\underline{\theta}$ and $\bar{\theta}$, or using (2.6),

$$\pi(T) = \int [\theta u(q(\theta)) - v(\theta) - cq(\theta)]f(\theta)\,d\theta - K. \tag{2.7}$$

It would be convenient to rewrite this expression only in terms of the demand function $q(\theta)$; to do this, we need to eliminate the term in $v(\theta)$. However, using (2.5) and the fact that $f(\theta) = F'(\theta)$, we can integrate this expression by parts to obtain

$$\int v(\theta)f(\theta)\,d\theta = v(\underline{\theta}) + \int u(q(\theta))[1 - F(\theta)]\,d\theta. \tag{2.8}$$

By substituting this expression into (2.7), we see that total profit may be written as

$$\pi(T) = \int \{[\theta u(q(\theta)) - cq(\theta)]f(\theta) - u(q(\theta))[1 - F(\theta)]\}\,d\theta - v(\underline{\theta}) - K. \tag{2.9}$$

Total consumer surplus with the tariff T is $V(T) = \int v(\theta)f(\theta)\,d\theta$, which is given by (2.8). Using the welfare criterion (2.1), the problem is to choose the function T in order to maximize

$$W(T) = V(T) + \alpha\pi(T) \quad \text{subject to} \quad \pi(T) \geq 0.$$

Writing $\lambda \geq 0$ for the Lagrange multiplier corresponding to the constraint that profit be nonnegative, from (2.8) and (2.9) the regulator should set $v^*(\underline{\theta})$ and the function $q^*(\theta)$ in order to maximize

$$(1 - \alpha)v(\underline{\theta}) + \int \{(1 - \alpha)u(q(\theta))[1 - F(\theta)] + \alpha[\theta u(q(\theta)) - cq(\theta)]f(\theta)\}\,d\theta$$

$$- \alpha K + \lambda \left[\int \{[\theta u(q(\theta)) - cq(\theta)]f(\theta) - u(q(\theta)) \right.$$

$$\left. \times [1 - F(\theta)]\}\,d\theta - v(\underline{\theta}) - K \right]. \tag{2.10}$$

The constraints are that $v(\theta) \geq 0$ (that all consumers have a nonnegative surplus) and $q(\theta) \geq 0$. The multiplier λ is chosen so that the resulting profit is zero. There are then two cases to consider, depending on whether the lowest type has strictly positive or zero utility.

Case 1: $v^*(\underline{\theta}) > 0$ Since welfare in (2.10) is linear in $v(\underline{\theta})$ and $v^*(\underline{\theta})$ is chosen to maximize (2.10), it is necessary that $\lambda = 1 - \alpha$. In this case (2.10) implies that $q^*(\theta)$ is always chosen to maximize $\theta u(q) - cq$. The optimal tariff is therefore a two-part tariff of the form $T(q) = K + cq$, and the fixed costs are low enough to satisfy

$$K < \max\{\theta u(q) - cq | q \geq 0\}. \tag{2.11}$$

Therefore, provided that condition (2.11) holds the two-part tariff of section 2.1.3 will be optimal because nobody is driven from the market: even consumers with the weakest tastes for the product are willing to pay a large enough fixed charge to cover the firm's fixed costs. All consumers are efficiently served in the sense that they face a marginal price equal to marginal cost.

Case 2: $v^*(\underline{\theta}) = 0$ This is the more important case. If condition (2.11) does not hold, then the two-part tariff of section 2.1.3 is no longer able to cover the fixed costs of the firm, and matters become more complex. In this case (2.10) implies that the optimal $q^*(\theta)$ should maximize

$$u(q)\left[\theta - \left(1 - \frac{1}{\alpha + \lambda}\right)\frac{1 - F(\theta)}{f(\theta)}\right] - cq. \tag{2.12}$$

If setting $v^*(\underline{\theta}) = 0$ maximizes welfare in (2.10), it must be the case that $\lambda > 1 - \alpha$ so that $[1 - 1/(\alpha + \lambda)] > 0$ in the above. Setting $\theta = \bar{\theta}$ in (2.12) implies that $q^*(\bar{\theta})$ maximizes $u(q) - cq$ and that therefore those consumers with the strongest tastes for the product are served efficiently. All other consumers are served with a lower quantity than would be efficient with full information. Writing $p(q) \equiv T'(q)$ to be the marginal price of the qth unit of the product with the tariff T, we see from (2.4) it follows that $p(q(\theta)) = \theta u'(q(\theta))$ for all θ. Therefore (2.12) implies that

$$p^*(q^*(\theta)) = \frac{c}{1 - [1 - 1/(\alpha + \lambda)][1 - F(\theta)]/\theta f(\theta)}, \tag{2.13}$$

where $p^*(\cdot)$ is the optimal marginal price schedule. Provided that the distribution for θ satisfies

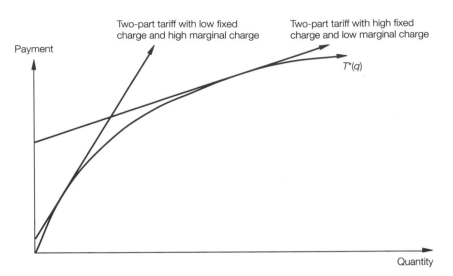

Figure 2.1   Implementing the optimal nonlinear tariff by means of a menu of two-part tariffs

$$\frac{1 - F(\theta)}{\theta f(\theta)} \quad \text{is decreasing in} \quad \theta,$$

$p^*(q)$ as given in (2.13) is a decreasing function of q. Many commonly used distributions for the parameter θ do satisfy this condition. In other words, the welfare-maximizing tariff involves the marginal price decreasing with the quantity purchased: it is optimal to offer quantity discounts for the firm's output.

An alternative way to think about nonlinear pricing with quantity discounts is that instead of the firm offering the single tariff $T^*(q)$, it offers consumers a choice from a *menu* of two-part tariffs (see figure 2.1). This menu would give consumers the option of trading off a high fixed charge and low usage charge against a low fixed charge and higher usage charge. The discussion above shows that in a wide variety of circumstances it is optimal for the firm to offer such a menu of two-part tariffs.

2.1.5   Cost Reduction

In most cases it is unrealistic to suppose that costs of a regulated firm are simply exogenous. Indeed a central concern of regulation is to provide good incentives for cost efficiency. By investing more effort, firms are generally able to reduce costs. In such cases the hypothetical omniscient regulator should control two things: price and the level of cost-reducing activity.

It is convenient to subsume all cost-reducing activities into the catchall term *effort*. Specifically, following Laffont and Tirole (1986), suppose that the firm expends effort at level e. Then the constant marginal cost of the firm is $c_0 - e$, where c_0 is the zero-effort cost level; the firm's fixed cost is given by $\psi(e)$, where ψ is an increasing and convex function. In this setting, how should price and cost reduction be chosen so as to maximize welfare? For simplicity, consider the case where the firm offers a single two-part tariff (2.2) and all consumers are identical. Then by exactly the argument used in section 2.1.3, the usage charge should again be set equal to marginal cost: $P^* = c_0 - e$ for any given effort level e. The fixed charge should just cover the fixed cost $\psi(e)$ so that profits are exactly zero. Under this regime consumer surplus is $V(c_0 - e) - \psi(e)$, and e^*, the optimal level of cost-reducing effort, should be chosen to maximize this expression. This implies that e^* satisfies

$$Q(P^*) = \psi'(e^*), \tag{2.14}$$

where $P^* = c_0 - e^*$. This is intuitive: if Q is the quantity produced then it must be optimal to choose effort so as to minimize total cost $(c_0 - e)Q + \psi(e)$, which implies (2.14). Thus in this first-best world there is allocative efficiency (marginal price equals marginal cost) and productive efficiency (total cost is minimized).

When consumers are not all alike, we again have the problem that setting marginal price equal to marginal cost may require a fixed charge high enough to drive low-demand consumers from the market and that as a result a marginal price in excess of marginal cost will prove optimal. Just as before, though, it remains optimal for there to be productive efficiency. Whatever price P^* is chosen, the optimal effort level will minimize total costs and so satisfy (2.14).

2.1.6 Discussion

So far we have discussed optimal regulation for the case where the firm and the regulator are equally well informed about conditions in the industry. The regulator's task here is quite straightforward: given what is known about the industry, the regulator simply calculates the optimal prices and level of cost-reducing effort for the firm and instructs the firm to implement this solution. The first-best price is equal to marginal cost. However, for the broad class of cost functions that have increasing returns to scale, marginal cost pricing necessarily results in the firm running at a loss. While this loss could be funded out of general government revenue, this would itself entail further distortions elsewhere in the economy. Therefore, as a rough way of avoiding these further distortions and also for reasons discussed in section 3.7, we imposed the constraint that only those prices that enable the firm to break even can be considered by the regulator.

We considered progressively more elaborate tariffs, ranging from simple linear tariffs, through to two-part tariffs and general nonlinear tariffs. The optimal linear tariff when the firm must break even is average cost pricing, and with scale economies the result is a degree of allocative inefficiency. The use of a two-part tariff enables price to be brought closer to marginal cost by imposing a fixed charge on consumers that helps to cover the firm's losses, but except in the unrealistic case where all consumers have the same tastes, there usually remains some inefficiency because some low-demand consumers are excluded from the market. Still higher levels of consumer welfare can be obtained by using a general nonlinear tariff, which normally takes the form of offering quantity discounts. Quantity discounts are a way of having the benefits of a two-part tariff with marginal price close to marginal cost for those customers with strong tastes for the product, while offering low-demand customers a tariff with a lower fixed charge. As a result fewer customers are excluded from the market and allocative efficiency is greater.

Finally, we considered the possibilities for cost reduction. Again, unless all consumers are alike, there remains a degree of allocative inefficiency because of the break-even constraint. But it is always optimal for there to be perfect productive efficiency so that total costs (including effort costs) are minimized. In the next section we move toward greater realism by relaxing the assumption that the regulator is as well informed as the firm about the firm's costs and effort level.

2.2 The Problem of Asymmetric Information

In the preceding discussion on nonlinear pricing, we encountered an example of an information problem: the inability of both regulator and firm to distinguish between consumers with weak preferences for the product from those with stronger preferences. This meant that it was best to offer consumers a nonlinear tariff that induced consumers to sort themselves into high- and low-demand groups. The resulting allocation is inferior to the first-best case of full information (which would involve all consumers being served at marginal cost) but better than offering a simple linear tariff that covered the firm's costs.

The information problem of most importance in the modern economics of regulation, however, concerns the asymmetry of information between the regulator and the firm. The firm typically is better informed than the regulator about (1) the cost and demand conditions in the industry and (2) its actions, for example, its level of cost-reducing effort. Using the language of the principal/agent paradigm, the former are problems of *hidden information* (or *adverse selection*), and the latter are problems of *hidden action* (or *moral hazard*). It may be, for instance, that BT has better estimates for the cost of converting various parts of its network to fiber-optic cable than the regulator, or that a water supplier has a better idea about carriage costs between two points in the distribution network than the regulator. As Weitzman (1978, 684) notes, "In most cases even the managers and engineers most closely associated with production will be unable to precisely specify beforehand the cheapest way to generate various hypothetical output levels. Because they are yet further removed from the production process, the regulators are likely to be vaguer still about a firm's cost function." Particular cases of hidden action in the context of utilities include the regulator being unable accurately to judge the effort electricity suppliers take to ensure that their power is obtained at minimum cost, or whether sewerage companies are being sufficiently zealous in preventing river pollution.

The most important problem of hidden action in the regulatory context, however, is the unobservability of the firm's cost-reducing effort and the consequent risk of managerial slack, and in this respect regulators are in a similar position to the shareholders of large firms. Indeed managers of a regulated private firm act as agents to two principals, the regulator and the body of shareholders, and these principals have quite different objectives that they would like the manager to pursue.[9] (Both principals can agree that the manager should try to reduce the firm's costs, but their interests diverge when it comes to the pricing policies they would like to see implemented.) It is common, when discussing regulation as a principal/agent relationship, to ignore the fact that there are monitoring problems for shareholders as well as the regulator and to view the manager as

9. For an analysis of the principal/agent problem when there is more than one principal, see Stole (1991).

simply maximizing the total profits of the firm (taking into account effort costs). While this assumption considerably simplifies the economic analysis of the information problem in regulation—and for this reason we will continue to use it—it does ignore one aspect of the overall problem.

If information asymmetries are present, then the kind of regulation considered in section 2.1 is no longer feasible. If the regulator does not accurately know costs, then marginal cost pricing becomes more problematic (although not impossible as we see in section 2.2.1).[10] If the firm's effort level is unobservable by the regulator, then the firm cannot simply be instructed to undertake a desirable level of effort, and the firm must be given an *incentive* to reduce its costs. Regulatory schemes that encourage the firm to reveal private information about its cost and demand conditions at the same time as encouraging it to undertake desirable cost-reducing activity will prove superior to the form of regulation in section 2.1 where the firm was simply instructed to offer a fixed price or tariff. In this section we examine how the various forms of asymmetric information can be incorporated into the framework of section 2.1. Typically we will see that the regulator faces a three-way trade-off among (1) allocative efficiency, where marginal price is kept close to marginal cost, (2) productive efficiency, where the firm's costs are kept as low as possible, and (3) minimizing the adverse distributional effect of the excess profits of the firm due to its informational advantage.

2.2.1 Regulation in the Absence of Distributional Concerns

Here we ignore distributional concerns and show how this greatly simplifies the problem, at least when consumer demand is known by both parties. Indeed, as observed by Loeb and Magat (1979), for this special case the informational asymmetries have no deleterious welfare effect.

By ignoring distributional concerns we mean that the regulator is interested in maximizing the simple sum of consumer surplus and profit: $\alpha = 1$ in (2.1). Suppose that the firm's total cost (including effort costs) in producing output level Q is $C(Q, e)$, where e is the level of cost-reducing effort by the firm. The regulator can here be assumed to know nothing about the

---

10. Of course, as the above quote from Weitzman indicates, it may well be that managers also do not possess perfect information about the detailed costs of running their businesses, but regulatory problems arise when the regulator is *less* well informed about costs than the manager rather than when both sides have equal but imperfect information. That is, it is the *asymmetry* of information that matters.

function $C(Q, e)$, nor is the regulator able to observe the actual cost C or effort e. The price P, the demand function $Q(P)$, and consumer surplus function $V(P)$ are, however, observable. In this setting, then, the regulator's informational problems lie entirely with the firm rather than with uncertainty about consumer demand.

The regulatory mechanism proposed by Loeb and Magat is very simple: for each price P offered by the firm, the regulator allows the firm to keep all the revenue $PQ(P)$ and in addition gives the firm a lump-sum transfer equal to the entire consumer surplus $V(P)$. In this case the firm's profit (including the transfer) if price P is offered is $V(P) + PQ(P) - C(Q(P), e)$, which is simply social welfare as defined in (2.1) with $\alpha = 1$. The firm's private objectives coincide precisely with the regulator's objectives, and the firm will choose P^* and e^* to maximize welfare. In particular, price will equal marginal cost, and effort will be chosen to minimize total cost given the output level. Therefore there is full allocative and productive efficiency. The efficient running of the firm can costlessly be delegated to the firm itself. This decentralization result means that the fact that so much information is unavailable to the regulator is not at all detrimental to social welfare.

This mechanism poses some obvious problems in practice, however.[11] The demand function is required to be known with certainty, whereas in most practical situations it can only be estimated, with the firm typically possessing more accurate information about demand than the regulator. More seriously, in the scheme as stated, consumers are left with none of the gains from trade. Loeb and Magat suggest that a way to alleviate this distributional problem is to auction the right to the monopoly franchise among competing firms. This option together with its drawbacks is discussed in chapter 4. Alternatively, the regulator could give the firm $V(P) - K$ instead of the entire surplus $V(P)$, where K is some positive constant. Then, provided the firm continues to find it profitable to carry on production, this constant has no effect on incentives. The first-best is still attained, and consumers retain K consumer surplus. The problem of course is how to choose the size of K. If K is set too high, there is the risk that the firm will not be able to make a profit and will shut down in cases where production is desirable. The regulator has to take a view about which levels of costs are probable and which are not, and the scheme loses its simple

---

11. See Sharkey (1979).

appeal.[12] In any case, if distributional concerns are relevant (when $\alpha < 1$), we will see below that the Loeb-Magat scheme—even when modified in this manner—is not optimal, and departures from either allocative or productive efficiency are desirable.

The next two sections on optimal regulation with hidden information and hidden action are again more technical in nature, and some readers may prefer to skip to the subsequent discussion of the analysis in section 2.2.4.

*2.2.2   Regulation with Hidden Information

There are two kinds of information asymmetries: those of hidden information and those of hidden action. In the former the firm possesses superior information than the regulator about its environment but has no way of altering this environment. In the latter the firm is able to influence its environment by expending effort, but this effort level is not observable by the regulator. Here we examine regulation in the presence of hidden information about costs and demand.

The problem of designing the optimal regulatory scheme when the firm's costs are unobservable was analyzed by Baron and Myerson (1982). Just as with the Loeb and Magat model, demand conditions are accurately known by all parties. Suppose that θ is the constant unit cost of production for the firm and that there is no fixed cost (little would be altered if there were, so long as it is known; Baron and Myerson do the general case). The parameter θ is unobserved by the regulator, although the regulator has a view on the likelihood of the various outcomes of θ, which is summarized by the density function $f(\theta)$ with support $[\underline{\theta}, \overline{\theta}]$. It may be that the regulator has commissioned auditor's reports or engineering studies on the firm and so has what it regards as a fairly precise estimate for θ; in such cases $f(\theta)$ should be taken to represent any residual uncertainty about costs. The cost level θ is assumed to be exogenous, so there is no scope for any cost reduction on the part of the firm.

---

12. Sappington and Sibley (1988) propose a dynamic variant of the Loeb-Magat scheme, which they call the *incremental surplus subsidy* scheme. In each period t the firm keeps its current profit $P_t Q(P_t) - C(Q(P_t))$ plus a lump-sum transfer equal to the increase in consumer surplus in this period over the previous period, $V(P_t) - V(P_{t-1})$, less the previous period's profit $P_{t-1} Q(P_{t-1}) - C(Q(P_{t-1}))$. In this case the firm makes a positive rent in its first period of operation, but from that point on it prices at marginal cost and receives just enough of a subsidy to break even.

The regulatory regime has the following form: if the firm chooses the price P, it is allowed to keep its revenues $PQ(P)$ and is given the lump-sum transfer $T(P)$ (which could be positive or negative). This transfer schedule $T(P)$ is the tool used by the regulator to try to induce the firm to set price P close to marginal cost θ at the same time as trying to minimize the firm's profits. (A special case of this was the Loeb-Magat mechanism where $T(P)$ was set equal to $V(P)$.)

The analysis required to find the optimal schedule $T^*(P)$ is very similar to that of the optimal nonlinear tariff discussed in section 2.1.4, and so we will be brief. Here the cost parameter θ and transfer schedule $T(\cdot)$ play analogous roles to the demand parameter θ and nonlinear tariff $T(\cdot)$ there. Given the transfer schedule $T(P)$, the firm with unit cost θ chooses its price $P(\theta)$ in order to maximize $(P - \theta)Q(P) + T(P)$ and as a result makes a profit of $\pi(\theta) = (P(\theta) - \theta)Q(P(\theta)) + T(P(\theta))$. The profit function $\pi(\theta)$ plays the role of $v(\theta)$ in section 2.1.4, and it satisfies the envelope condition $\pi'(\theta) = -Q(P(\theta))$. Integrating by parts, and since $\pi(\bar{\theta}) = 0$, we can write expected profit in terms of the firm's pricing strategy $P(\theta)$ as

$$\int \pi(\theta)f(\theta)\,d\theta = \int Q(P(\theta))F(\theta)\,d\theta.$$

Therefore the firm always makes a positive expected profit, and this profit is solely due to its superior information on its costs. Total welfare can then be written as

$$W = \int \{[V(P(\theta)) + (P(\theta) - \theta)Q(P(\theta))]f(\theta) - (1 - \alpha)Q(P(\theta))F(\theta)\}\,d\theta,$$

$$(2.15)$$

where $F(\theta)$ is the distribution function for the cost parameter θ. Maximizing (2.15) pointwise with respect to $P(\theta)$ implies that the optimal price function is

$$P^*(\theta) = \theta + (1 - \alpha)\frac{F(\theta)}{f(\theta)}. \qquad (2.16)$$

(The optimal transfer schedule $T^*(P)$ is then chosen in such a way as to ensure that the price $P^*(\theta)$ in (2.16) is actually chosen by the firm with cost θ.) If $\alpha = 1$, this formula implies that price equals marginal cost, so we have confirmed the optimality of the Loeb-Magat scheme when distributional concerns are irrelevant. When $\alpha < 1$, however, and except for the case where the firm has the lowest possible cost $\theta = \underline{\theta}$, price exceeds marginal cost $\underline{\theta}$. The greater the importance that is attached to distributional concerns—lower α—the greater is the degree of allocative inefficiency at the optimum.[13]

The reason why there is a degree of allocative inefficiency at the informationally constrained optimum is as follows. Expected profit, given the firm's pricing strategy $P(\theta)$, is $\int Q(P(\theta))F(\theta)\,d\theta$, and so increasing the price function $P(\theta)$ reduces this profit. Because of distributional concerns, profits are bad for welfare, and it is optimal to trade some allocative efficiency in order to get a reduction in adverse distributional effects.

An example may help to fix ideas. (A similar example was analyzed by Baron and Myerson, and we will also use this example later in chapter 4.) Let the demand function be linear, $Q(P) = 1 - P$, which implies that the consumer surplus function is $V(P) = \frac{1}{2}(1 - P)^2$. Suppose that unit cost θ is uniformly distributed on the interval $[0, b]$ so that $F(\theta) = \theta/b$ and $f(\theta) = 1/b$. Then (2.16) implies that the optimal price function is $P^*(\theta) = (2 - \alpha)\theta$ so that the price/cost markup $P^*(\theta)/\theta$ is constant over the various costs θ and is decreasing in the parameter α. To avoid complications, we need to have $P^*(\theta) \le 1$ for all possible θ, which requires that $b \le 1/(2 - \alpha)$. Then substituting $P^*(\theta)$ into (2.15) implies that expected total welfare with optimal regulation is $\frac{1}{6}[b^2(2 - \alpha)^2 - 3b(2 - \alpha) + 3]$. The expected full information, first-best welfare level, obtained by pricing at marginal cost and giving the firm zero profit, is $\frac{1}{6}(b^2 - 3b + 3)$. Therefore we can write the expected loss resulting from the asymmetric information as

$$L = \tfrac{1}{6}b(1 - \alpha)[3 - b(3 - \alpha)]. \tag{2.17}$$

This loss vanishes if (1) $\alpha = 1$ so that distributional concerns are irrelevant and we can use the Loeb-Magat mechanism, or (2) $b = 0$ when there is no asymmetric information (the regulator knows for certain that the firm's cost is zero).

Instead of the firm having private information about its cost level, we could imagine that it was the demand function about which it was better

---

13. The main issue we have glossed over here is whether the price function $P^*(\theta)$ in (2.16) can in fact be induced by means of a suitable subsidy function $T^*(P)$. It turns out that this can be done if and only if $P^*(\theta)$ is increasing in θ. From (2.16) an easily sufficient condition for this to occur is if $F(\theta)/f(\theta)$ is increasing in θ. This "hazard rate condition" is used repeatedly in rigorous treatments of the asymmetric information problem in regulation (for more detail, see Baron and Myerson 1982).

informed. For instance, the firm could have a particular cost function known by both parties, but the demand function with the parameter θ is $Q(P, \theta)$. Riordan (1984) and Lewis and Sappington (1988) have examined the question of how to regulate a firm with superior information about demand, and the analysis proceeds much as the solution above to the Baron and Myerson model. It turns out, however, that in many cases the regulator can obtain the first-best outcome, even when distributional concerns are present. For instance, if the firm has a known and constant unit cost of c, then it is clear that by requiring the firm to charge the price $P^* = c$, the regulator is doing precisely what would be optimal if the demand function were known. (The principle that marginal cost pricing is optimal does not depend on knowing the demand curve.) More generally, Lewis and Sappington show that whenever marginal cost is nondecreasing, the first-best can be imposed. However, when the firm has increasing returns, the case of more interest for utility regulation, the informational asymmetry does have an impact and the first-best cannot be attained. In this case the best that the regulator can do is to set a fixed price and a fixed transfer to the firm.

*2.2.3   Regulation with Hidden Action

Here we examine a simple version of a model of Laffont and Tirole (1986) which is complementary to that of Baron and Myerson.[14] Unit costs are assumed now to be observable, but the firm is able to reduce these costs by expending effort, effort that is not observed by the regulator. In detail, unit cost is constant and given by $c = \theta - e$, where θ is again a random term (not observed by the regulator but known by the firm) giving the no-effort cost level and $e \geq 0$ is the effort of the firm. Effort e results in a cost $\psi(e)$ to the firm, where ψ is increasing and convex (so that $\psi'' > 0$). The cost parameter θ is believed by the regulator to be distributed according to the density function $f(\theta)$. Thus this model contains elements of both hidden information and hidden action, and the regulator is unable to

---

14. As explained above, Laffont and Tirole's model differs from the version described here in two respects. Their social welfare function is the simple unweighted sum of consumer and producer surplus (i.e., with $\alpha = 1$), and in addition they assume a cost is involved in making transfers to the firm (this is the "shadow cost of public funds"). This means that, although the analysis and insights are very much as given here because of the basic trade-off between efficiency and distribution, some of their formulas differ from those in this section and in section 3.2.

deduce whether observing a low realization of c is due to good luck (low θ) or high effort. In fact, instead of focusing on the effort level e, it is more convenient to consider the type θ firm as choosing the cost c and thereby incurring an effort cost of $\psi(\theta - c)$.

The regulator here can base regulation on two observables—price and cost—and so the regulator can give the firm a lump-sum transfer of $T(P, c)$, conditional on both price and cost, if the firm chooses P and c. Again the analysis is very similar to that in section 2.1.4. Faced with the transfer schedule T, the type θ firm chooses price $P(\theta)$ and cost $c(\theta)$ in order to maximize $(P - c)Q(P) - \psi(\theta - c) + T(P, c)$, in which case it makes a total profit of

$$\pi(\theta) = [P(\theta) - c(\theta)]Q(P(\theta)) - \psi(\theta - c(\theta)) + T(P(\theta), c(\theta)).$$

This profit function π is decreasing in θ and satisfies the envelope condition $\pi'(\theta) = -\psi'(\theta - c(\theta))$. Again, using this envelope condition to integrate by parts, we can write total welfare in terms of the two functions $P(\theta)$ and $c(\theta)$ as

$$W = \int \{[V(P(\theta)) + [P(\theta) - c(\theta)]Q(P(\theta)) - \psi(\theta - c(\theta))]f(\theta)$$

$$- (1 - \alpha)\psi'(\theta - c(\theta))F(\theta)\} \, d\theta, \qquad (2.18)$$

where $F(\theta)$ is the distribution function for the cost parameter θ. Maximizing (2.18) pointwise with respect to both $P(\theta)$ and $c(\theta)$ implies that the following expressions for optimal price $P^*(\theta)$ and effort $e^*(\theta)$ hold:

$$P^*(\theta) = c^*(\theta), \qquad (2.19a)$$

$$\psi'(e^*(\theta)) + (1 - \alpha)\frac{F(\theta)}{f(\theta)}\psi''(e^*(\theta)) = Q(P^*(\theta)). \qquad (2.19b)$$

(Here c^* and e^* are related by $c^*(\theta) = \theta - e^*(\theta)$.) Equation (2.19a) states that price always equals marginal cost, and so there is allocative efficiency at the optimum. Also, if $\alpha = 1$, then condition (2.19b) reduces to the first-best condition (2.14), and there is productive efficiency (again confirming the optimality of the Loeb-Magat scheme in the absence of distributional concerns). When $\alpha < 1$, (2.19b) shows that except for the lowest-cost type firm $\underline{\theta}$ (when $F(\underline{\theta}) = 0$), $\psi'(e^*(\theta)) < Q(P^*(\theta))$. Clearly there is insufficient effort provided for the level of output $Q(P^*(\theta))$, and total costs are *not* minimized. Thus the information problem means that it is optimal for there to be a degree of productive inefficiency, with greater emphasis on distributional concerns—a lower α—involving greater inefficiency (and hence, by (2.19a), also a higher price).[15]

There is a degree of productive inefficiency at the informationally constrained optimum because the relationship between effort and profit given by the envelope condition $\pi'(\theta) = -\psi'(e(\theta))$ implies that expected profit can be written in terms of the firm's effort function $e(\theta)$ as

$$\int \pi(\theta)f(\theta)\,d\theta = \int \psi'(e(\theta))F(\theta)\,d\theta.$$

Since $\psi'(e)$ is increasing in e, this means that a higher value of the effort function $e(\cdot)$ results in greater profits for the firm. Because of distributional concerns, profits are bad for welfare, and it is optimal to trade some productive efficiency in order to obtain a reduction in the firm's rents.

As in section 2.1.4, an alternative way to think about implementing the incentive scheme is to use a menu of linear contracts. Since (2.19a) implies that price will be set equal to observed cost, optimal regulation involves the firm being granted the transfer $T^*(c)$ if its unit cost is observed to be c, in which case the price is set equal to this cost. In a wide variety of cases the optimal effort function $e^*(\theta)$ is decreasing in θ, and it can be shown that this implies that the optimal transfer schedule $T^*(c)$ is convex (and decreasing) in c.[16] A convex function can be represented as the "upper envelope" of a menu of linear cost sharing rules of the form $a(b) - bc$, where the parameter b is chosen by the firm having observed θ. In other words, having observed its private information θ, the firm chooses a particular linear cost-sharing rule given by $b(\theta)$, where in the event that its cost is observed to be c it receives a transfer equal to $a(b(\theta)) - b(\theta)c$. Naturally the function $a(b)$ is increasing in b, so more responsiveness to cost (high b) is rewarded by a higher fixed payment $a(b)$; see figure 2.2.

---

15. As in section 2.2.2, in this derivation of the optimal price and effort rule we have not considered whether the functions in (2.19) can be induced by a suitable subsidy function $T^*(P, c)$. It turns out that this can be done if $c^*(\theta)$ is increasing in θ. By differentiating (2.19b), we find that an easily sufficient condition for this to occur is if $F(\theta)/f(\theta)$ is increasing in θ and the third derivative of ψ is positive. Then, if this condition holds (after some algebraic manipulation), effort $e^*(\theta)$ can be shown to be decreasing in θ. (For more detail, see Laffont and Tirole 1993, secs. 1.4, 2.4.)

16. Since $c^*(\theta)$ is chosen to maximize the firm's profit $T^*(c) - \psi(\theta - c)$, it is given by the condition $(T^*)'(c^*(\theta)) + \psi'(e^*(\theta)) = 0$. Therefore differentiating this expression implies that $(T^*)''$ has the same sign as $-(e^*)'/(c^*)'$, which is positive since e^* is decreasing and c^* is increasing in θ.

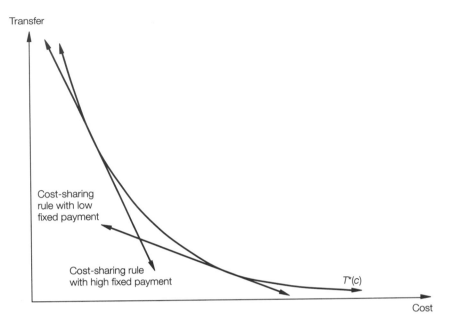

Transfer

Cost-sharing
rule with low
fixed payment

Cost-sharing rule
with high fixed payment

$T^*(c)$

Cost

Figure 2.2 Implementing the optimal transfer schedule by means of a menu of cost-sharing rules

In this model, then, the effect of asymmetric information is to make it optimal to deviate from productive rather allocative efficiency: the regulator observes the cost level, asks the firm to set its price equal to this cost, and then gives the firm a transfer that decreases with cost. It is this dependence of the firm's transfer on observed cost that induces the firm to exert a degree of effort, albeit at a suboptimal level compared to the first-best case. The fact that there is allocative efficiency can be expressed as saying that it is optimal to have full "cost passthrough," in the sense that observed costs are fully passed on to consumers. Note, however, that this depends crucially on the ability to give cost-reduction incentives by means of lump-sum transfers.

2.2.4 Discussion

It is only in the last decade or so that information has been analyzed explicitly in the regulation problem, but now it has assumed a central importance in the economics of regulation (e.g., see its prominence in Laffont and Tirole's 1993 book). If the firm does not possess better information about industry conditions than the regulator, and if there are no other regulatory failures, then the monopoly problem can be solved simply by instructing the firm to carry out whatever is calculated to be the socially optimal plan. Indeed, in such a case, the benevolent regulator could simply run the firm. In reality the firm is much better informed about many aspects of the running of the firm than the regulator, and so the problem is to design regulatory regimes that motivate the firm to use its superior information for general benefit rather than to increase its own monopoly rents.

In Baron and Myerson's model the regulator cannot observe the firm's cost level, there is no role for cost reduction and hence no possibility of productive inefficiency; the regulator faces a trade-off between attaining allocative efficiency and minimizing adverse distributional effects. Allocative efficiency is certainly a feasible option (by implementing the Loeb-Magat mechanism), but this entails too great a distributional cost. To reduce this distributional cost it is optimal to set price above marginal cost to some degree. In the Laffont and Tirole model the firm's cost is observable, but the firm can lower its costs by expending effort, and the regulator then faces a three-way trade-off between allocative efficiency, distributional effects, and productive efficiency. In the simple form we described, the way this is settled is to set price equal to marginal cost and to use the lump-sum transfer to provide the firm's incentives for cost reduction. Because of the unobservability of effort, this can be done only imperfectly, and the firm is left with excess profits due to its monopoly of information and produces at a cost greater than the minimum possible. In this setting the information problem results in the firm underinvesting in cost-reducing activity.

It is important to appreciate the purpose of the two models of regulation of Baron and Myerson and of Laffont and Tirole. The regulator of any real single-product firm (assuming there were any such firms) will not find an explicit solution to the regulatory problem by reading these papers. While these models of asymmetric information represent a significant improvement in realism over the benchmark case of section 2.1, they are not intended to capture all relevant aspects of reality. Subsuming all the firm's private information into just one or two variables (θ and e in the models) presents a very simplified version of actual informational asymmetries. For instance, in the models as we have described them the regulator knows for certain that the firm has a constant unit cost and is merely uncertain about the level of this cost. Why would a regulator not entertain doubts about the *shape* of the cost function? Why is the regulator uncertain about the cost function but perfectly informed about consumer demand? The amount of private information built into the models seems too small compared with the problems actual regulators face. One way partially to overcome this problem might be to introduce more parameters to represent the firm's private information. The regulator, for instance, might suppose that the firm's cost function is approximately quadratic or cubic but does not know the precise coefficients of the polynomial. Or we could simultaneously have both demand and cost uncertainty. However, the analysis required for analyzing such models is significantly more complex than the models presented here, and the optimal regulatory schemes have been obtained only for special cases and with great effort. We will return to this point when we discuss the regulation of multiproduct firms in section 3.2.

The models considered here should be regarded as guides for our intuition and as sources of insights rather than as solutions to an actual regulatory problem. The central implication of the "new economics of regulation" is that the more information about industry conditions the regulator possesses, the better can be the result (at least in the absence of other regulatory failures). For instance, if there are impediments that prevent regulators from obtaining important data from a firm, this could well work against the proper functioning of effective regulation. Or the regulator might find it beneficial to investigate a firm's costs, even if this itself involves a cost, in order to reduce the asymmetry of information (see Baron and Besanko 1984).

The purpose of part I of this book is not just to examine fully optimal regulation in theoretical models but to analyze the properties of regulatory schemes used in practice. For instance, it is only rarely the case that regulators themselves have the power to make lump-sum transfers or offer "menus" of contracts, and when these policy tools are not available, the schemes outlined above—schemes that make full use of lump-sum transfers—are not feasible. Joskow and Schmalensee (1986) in their survey of electricity regulation in the United States observe that "to our knowledge, no state statute permits commissions directly to fine or subsidize utilities subject to their jurisdiction. Rather, it is the methods used to determine prices that provide incentives, either good or bad, to regulated firms." While it is true in the settings we have discussed that regulation would be improved by granting regulators powers to make transfers, there are reasons that lie outside the formal models that may preclude their use. (We will discuss this point more fully in section 3.7.) Ideally we would have a grand model that jointly explained (1) the absence of transfers, and (2) optimal regulation subject to (1).[17] But that is too ambitious for present purposes. It therefore seems worth considering what constitutes "good" regulation when prices alone are used as the principal means of controlling firms.[18] This is the subject of the next section.

2.3 Price Regulation

Suppose that the government is commissioning a new project—say, a rail link—from a firm. This project will cost an uncertain amount, but the cost can be affected by the firm exerting effort. The government has a choice: it can offer a contract to carry out the project in return for a particular fixed price, an offer the firm either accepts or refuses, or it can offer to pay a price that depends in some way upon the final cost of the project. In the former case the government bears no risk in the price it will pay, the firm has every incentive to minimize total cost, but it may turn out that the government pays significantly more than cost for the project. At the other extreme, the government could simply contract to pay whatever the project eventually costs. In this case the government is uncertain what the price will eventually be, price is in line with cost, the firm makes no abnormal profits, but the firm has no incentive to undertake any cost-reducing measures. Intermediate contracts, which pay the firm more than some reference price if cost turns out to be particularly high or allow the government to claw back some of the offered price if cost is low, have incentive and efficiency effects that lie between these extremes. Exactly the same dilemma exists when regulating utilities, and in the following we consider both linear incentive schemes and fully optimal incentive schemes.

2.3.1 Linear Pricing Rules
Suppose that the firm is just as described in section 2.2.3, so marginal cost is constant for the firm and given by $c = \theta - e$, where θ is private information to the firm and e is the effort of the firm (which again incurs a cost

---

17. This approach is taken by in Laffont and Tirole (1991).
18. This approach, which leaves unexplained why transfers are ruled out, can be criticized as ad hoc. But we believe that it is nevertheless a useful complement to approaches that assume, contrary to what is observed, that transfers are available. Indeed it is debatable which is the more ad hoc.

$\psi(e)$). Cost c is observable by the regulator. Demand is assumed to inelastic in this example, so let $Q = 1$. If the regulator is unable to make lump-sum transfers, then the only tool at the regulator's disposal is to make the allowed price depend in some way on cost: $P = P(c)$. Fixed price regulation would involve the regulator offering the price $P(c) \equiv \bar{P}$ regardless of what c is observed to be. If all types of firms are to be willing to participate in the regulatory process, then this fixed price must be set high enough so that the maximum value over all effort levels e of $\bar{P} - (\bar{\theta} - e) - \psi(e)$ is nonnegative, where $\bar{\theta}$ is the worst possible type of firm. If this is ensured, then it is clear that all firms with cost parameter $\theta < \bar{\theta}$ will make a strictly positive profit and there will be adverse distributional effects. In addition price will often deviate significantly from cost. On the other hand, for each type of firm the optimal level of effort will be chosen to minimize costs $(\theta - e) + \psi(e)$, and there is full productive efficiency. Alternatively, if price is set always to equal cost so that $P(c) = c$, then it is clear that $e = 0$ and $P = c = \theta$. The firm makes no profit, and there is allocative efficiency but no cost-reducing effort and thus productive inefficiency. Intermediate between these cases are linear price rules of the form

$$P(c) = \bar{P} + (1 - \rho)c, \qquad (2.20)$$

where $0 \leq \rho \leq 1$ is a parameter that determines the sensitivity of price to cost. Thus some degree of cost uncertainty is permitted to be passed through to consumers, though the firm also bears some of the loss if costs turn out to be high (unless $\rho = 0$).

A simple model in which we can explicitly calculate the optimal level of cost passthrough goes as follows:[19] Demand is inelastic and equal to 1 at all prices, and the cost of effort is given by the function $\psi(e) = e^2/2$. In contrast to the Laffont and Tirole model, suppose now that the firm's effort decision is taken *before* the realization of the cost parameter θ is known.[20] Because of this the firm faces some risk on its profit, and we

---

19. A similar model is discussed in Milgrom and Roberts (1992, ch. 7). This question has also been examined in Schmalensee (1989), and his model is analyzed further in Gasmi et al. (1992).

20. We will use a variant of the following model in section 3.4 below. Readers familiar with the principal/agent literature will recognize that the first-best outcome is feasible in this situation using a "shifting support" argument. If e^* is the level of effort in the first-best outcome and $\bar{\theta}$ is the maximum possible level of θ, then by granting the firm a very low price whenever $c > \bar{\theta} - e^*$, the firm will choose the effort level $e = e^*$. In the following we look for the best *linear* price rule, which rules out this sort of forcing contract. In some other settings where the support does not shift, though, linear schemes are in fact fully optimal; see Holmstrom and Milgrom (1987).

suppose that it is risk-averse, in the sense that its utility function is given by $E[\pi] - \gamma/2\,\text{var}[\pi]$, where $E[\pi]$ is the expected value of profit, $\text{var}[\pi]$ is the variance of profit, and γ is a parameter that measures the degree of risk aversion. (This "mean/variance" method of describing the firm's attitude toward risk is chosen because it is particularly simple to analyze.) The problem considered here is to find which among the family of price rules of the form (2.20) is optimal. With such a rule the firm's profit with effort level e is $\bar{P} - \rho(\theta - e) - e^2/2$, and hence its utility is

$$\bar{P} - \rho(\mu - e) - \frac{e^2}{2} - \frac{\gamma\rho^2\sigma^2}{2},$$

where μ is the mean of θ and σ^2 is the variance of θ. Therefore the utility-maximizing effort level for the firm is $e^* = \rho$, and we see that making price more sensitive to cost in (2.20)—by taking a lower value for ρ—results in the firm choosing a lower effort level. Substituting $e^* = \rho$ into the above expression gives the firm's maximum utility as

$$\bar{P} - \rho(\mu - \rho) - \frac{\rho^2}{2} - \frac{\gamma\rho^2\sigma^2}{2}, \tag{2.21}$$

where we suppose that this utility must be greater than some reservation utility π_0 if the firm is to be willing to go into production. Consumers are risk-neutral and the regulator wishes to minimize expected total expenditure $\bar{P} + (1 - \rho)(\mu - \rho)$ subject to the participation constraint $\bar{P} - \rho(\mu - \rho) - \rho^2/2 - \gamma\rho^2\sigma^2/2 \geq \pi_0$. While the reference price $\bar{P}$ will depend on the reservation utility level of the firm, the optimal amount of cost passthrough will not and can be calculated to be given by

$$\rho^* = \frac{1}{1 + \gamma\sigma^2}. \tag{2.22}$$

Therefore (2.22) implies that a pure price cap is optimal ($\rho^* = 1$) if either the firm is risk-neutral or there is no uncertainty (γ or σ^2 is zero). The regulator should make price more sensitive to cost if (1) the firm is more risk-averse (higher γ) or (2) there is more uncertainty about costs (higher σ^2). If consumers are also risk-averse, in the sense that they dislike uncertainty in price, considerations of risk sharing will enter the analysis. The more risk-averse consumers are, the lower will be the optimal degree of passthrough, other things being equal.

The form of regulation given by (2.20) can usefully be compared to the first-best regime in which the regulator *can* observe and control the effort level of the firm. In this case the optimal effort level can be shown to be

$e* = 1$, and the regulator should then give the firm a price $\bar{P} + c$ so that there is full cost passthrough ($\bar{P}$ being set so that the firm achieves its reservation utility). In other words, the firm should be fully insured against uncertainty in its costs. Compared to this case, then, in a second-best world where effort is not observable, there is insufficient effort (effort is $\rho* < 1$) and inadequate insurance for the firm. The reason is that prices are required to perform two tasks: to give incentives to supply cost-reducing effort and to insure the risk-averse firm against cost uncertainty. Unfortunately, these two tasks work in opposite directions and the way to increase effort is to offer less insurance. Because of these conflicting aims there is a trade-off between incentives and insurance, and the optimum point on that trade-off is given by (2.22).

*2.3.2 Fully Optimal Pricing Rules

The above discussion considered only incentive schemes that were linear. It is natural to ask what the optimal *nonlinear* price function $P*(c)$ is like. For a general demand function $Q(P)$ this problem is quite difficult.[21] However, if we continue with the assumption of inelastic demand, we can use the analysis described in section 2.2.3 to answer this question. Therefore suppose that the firm's technology is as given in section 2.2.3, and return to the assumption that the firm's choice of effort is made *after* it observes θ. If transfers were allowed then, because demand is inelastic, the firm only cares about its total revenue $P + T$. So the fact that the regulator is not permitted to offer transfers makes no real difference. We can deduce that the equation governing the optimal level of effort is still (2.19b):

$$\psi'(e*(\theta)) + (1 - \alpha)\frac{F(\theta)}{f(\theta)}\psi''(e*(\theta)) = 1. \tag{2.23}$$

Again, unless $\alpha = 1$, there is a degree of productive inefficiency. The first-order condition for $c*(\theta)$ to be the profit-maximizing choice of cost for the type θ firm is $[P'(c*(\theta)) - 1] + \psi'(e*(\theta)) = 0$, so the optimal price function $P*(c)$ satisfies

$$(P*)'(c*(\theta)) = (1 - \alpha)\frac{F(\theta)}{f(\theta)}\psi''(e*(\theta)). \tag{2.24}$$

If $\alpha = 1$ so that distributional concerns are absent, expression (2.24) implies that $P*(c) \equiv \bar{P}$ for some constant $\bar{P}$ and that a (high) fixed price is optimal. In this case there is full productive efficiency. However, if $\alpha < 1$,

---

21. For more on this, see Laffont and Tirole (1993, sec. 2.7).

then $(P^*)'(c) > 0$, so price should be responsive to cost to at least some degree. Because of this there is a degree of productive inefficiency.

In the special case where $\psi(e) = e^2/2$ and θ is uniformly distributed on the interval $[0, b]$, (2.24) simplifies to

$$(P^*)'(c) = \frac{1 - \alpha}{2 - \alpha}(1 + c).$$ (2.25)

Thus the optimal degree of cost passthrough, given by $(P^*)'(c)$, in this example is not constant across all levels of cost and is decreasing in the weight placed on profits α.

2.3.3 Discussion

This section has considered two models of price regulation. In the first we made the ad hoc, but simplifying, assumption that only linear pricing rules could be used. The firm made its effort choice before any uncertainty concerning costs was resolved. This was to highlight the effect of cost passthrough on the risk borne by the regulated firm. It was shown that a higher degree of risk aversion for the firm implied a greater degree of cost passthrough than should be allowed. In the second model we returned to the assumption that the firm chose its effort after observing the cost function to discuss the *optimal* level of cost passthrough. In this case the firm faced no risk, so the degree of the firm's risk aversion was irrelevant. Demand was taken to be inelastic for analytical convenience. If the regulator was not concerned with distributional issues ($\alpha = 1$), then a pure price cap was seen to be optimal and no cost passthrough was allowed. This is just a special case of the Loeb-Magat scheme. If the regulator was concerned to keep informational rents down ($\alpha < 1$), then a degree of cost passthrough was always optimal.

When demand is not inelastic, however, allocative efficiency becomes an issue, and the fact that the regulator cannot use the instrument of lump-sum transfers complicates the problem considerably. In section 2.2.3 it was seen that price was used to obtain allocative efficiency and that the transfer was used to give the firm an incentive to cut costs and increase productive efficiency. When transfers are not available, price is involved with the attempt to achieve both of these tasks. Allocative efficiency is not possible because prices must cover the firm's effort cost $\psi(e)$ as well as the unit cost c. If price is made very sensitive to costs—a kind of cost-plus or rate-of-return regulation—the result will be inefficient production. Pure price cap regulation, a form of regulation that recently has been more popular, does induce productive efficiency, but it has the twin drawbacks that price may be significantly out of line with costs and that the firm may make exceptional profits.

2.4 Conclusions

The purpose of this chapter has been to provide a brief and selective survey of modern theories of regulation. The setting is kept as simple as possible: the regulated firm produces a single product at a single point in time, and there are no competitive threats. Moreover the regulator is taken to act purely benevolently. The role of regulation is to prevent the monopoly from setting its price too far above cost and to encourage sufficient cost-reducing activity.

In section 2.1 we examined the benchmark case where regulator and firm were equally well informed about conditions in the industry. In this case optimal regulation involves setting price equal to marginal cost in order to obtain allocative efficiency. For firms with increasing returns, however, this policy requires a lump-sum subsidy to the firm to prevent it operating at a loss. If such subsidies are ruled out, there is the additional constraint that prices should be sufficiently high to cover all costs, with the result that there should be average rather than marginal cost pricing. A greater degree of allocative efficiency could be attained if the firm offers more complex tariffs—either two-part or general nonlinear tariffs. Two-part tariffs have the advantage that (marginal) prices are no longer required to cover all costs, and a fixed charge can be used to make up any shortfall in profits. However, this fixed charge will cause low-demand consumers to drop out of the market, which is bad for allocative efficiency. General nonlinear tariffs or optional two-part tariffs can overcome this problem to some extent by allowing high-demand customers to be served at price close to marginal cost (while paying a substantial fixed charge) at the same time as low-demand customers pay a price well above marginal cost (while paying little or no fixed charge). Thus allocative efficiency is not sacrificed too much as a result of the firm's break-even constraint. As such the device can ameliorate to some extent the problem caused by the asymmetry of information between the regulator and consumers.

Similar tactics are effective when there is asymmetric information between the regulator and firm about industry conditions concerning, for instance, the firm's cost or effort levels. This information problem lies at the heart of modern theories of regulation. When the firm possesses private information, say, about its unit cost, then a good regulatory scheme should discriminate between firms with differing unit costs. However, because firms with different costs must be offered the same contract, the firm's monopoly of information entails that low-cost firms will make monopoly rents on this information. It was shown that there is a trade-off between the aims of allocative efficiency—price close to marginal cost—and of minimizing these informational rents which, for distributional reasons, reduce overall welfare. As result it is generally optimal to set price above marginal cost. When the firm can reduce its costs by expending effort, the effort level being unobservable by the regulator, the third issue of productive efficiency arises. In the formal model it was seen that allocative efficiency is attained, but a degree of productive efficiency is sacrificed to reduce undesirable monopoly rents.

These optimal regulatory schemes make heavy use of lump-sum transfers to the firm and menus of two-part tariffs. Since actual regulators rarely have the authority to make such transfers—possibly for good reason as we will discuss in section 3.7—we considered how best to regulate a monopoly using prices alone. Roughly this is the question of the appropriate level of cost passthrough: given that cost is determined both by exogenous factors and the effort level of the firm, both of which are unobservable to the regulator, how sensitive should price be to the final cost level? If price accurately reflects actual observed costs, which is one possible representation of rate-of-return regulation, then allocative efficiency is nearly attained and there are no excessive profits, but the firm has only weak incentives to act to reduce costs. When the price is fixed at some predetermined level, a kind of pure price cap regulation, then these benefits and problems are reversed. In almost all cases it was seen that good price regulation should lie intermediately between these polar extremes, with more cost uncertainty and greater risk aversion on the part of the firm implying that a greater proportion of costs should be passed on to consumers.

In the next chapter some of the rather restrictive assumptions made here are relaxed. In particular, the analysis is extended to the case where the firm makes several products and production takes place over time. This raises the problem of policy credibility. In addition we consider some implications of the danger of regulatory capture.

3

Monopoly Regulation: Multiproduct and Dynamic Issues

The previous chapter looked at regulation in a very special setting: the regulated firm produced only a single product and for only a single period. This enabled us to focus on certain issues that apply to all regulated firms—the principles of efficient pricing, and regulatory regimes that give firms with private information good incentives to bring price into line with costs and to engage in cost-reducing activities without giving firms too great a profit from their monopoly on information—in a simple framework without the distractions of other factors. In this chapter we extend our analysis to include these factors, and consider firms that produce more than one product and at more than one point in time. The fact that regulation takes place in a dynamic setting raises the issue of regulatory credibility and commitment, something that leads to the possibility of underinvestment on the part of the regulated firm. In addition we consider the possibility that the regulator may not always act in a purely benevolent manner, and ask how the regulator as well as the firm can be given good incentives to act in a socially desirable way.

The plan of the chapter is as follows. In sections 3.1 to 3.4 we consider multiproduct regulation in a static framework. First, the benchmark case of full information is analyzed, and this includes two-part tariffs and peak-load pricing as special cases. Next, more complex multiproduct tariffs designed to discriminate between differing consumers are discussed. In sections 3.2 and 3.3 we extend the analysis to the situation where the firm possesses private information, and ask how a multiproduct firm can be given incentives to set prices close to marginal costs and to undertake socially desirable cost-reducing expenditures. In 3.2 we allow the regulator to make lump-sum transfers to or from the firm, whereas in 3.3 we consider the possibly more realistic case where the regulator has no such power and look at the properties of a variety of commonly used forms of price regulation. In section 3.4 we see what happens if the regulated industry is regionally separated (something that often is or could be the case in network utilities), and how this affects the information available to the regulator and the form of the regulatory regime. In sections 3.5 and 3.6 time is introduced into the analysis. The issue of regulatory lag as an incentive mechanism is discussed, some forms of dynamic multiproduct regulation are considered, and the problem of policy credibility and consequent underinvestment by the regulated firm is introduced. Finally, in section 3.7 the possible problem of "capture"—collusion between the regulator and the regulated firm—is discussed.

3.1   Regulating a Multiproduct Monopoly: Benchmark Case

Just as in chapter 2, initially we examine desirable methods of regulating a firm in a setting in which problems concerning information about industry conditions are absent. These principles provide the benchmark with which we will compare regulation in more complex settings.

Few real firms produce just one product. Certainly none of the utility industries does so. A telecommunications firm typically offers a great number of distinct products: a call from Oxford to London at 10:00 in the morning is a different product, with different demand characteristics, from a call from Oxford to Cambridge at the same time, and also a different product from a call from Oxford to London at 8:00 in the evening. Moreover there are many telecommunications products other than simple telephone calls, including electronic mail, mobile communications, directory inquiries, and telecommunications apparatus. Superficially the gas, water, and electricity supply industries provide a more homogeneous range of products than does a telecommunications firm, but in addition to the time-of-day and time-of-year differentiation of their main products, these firms supply many different products to their large industrial customers, products that differ along dimensions such as whether the supply is interruptible and the customer's required maximum demand. In Britain the gas and electricity suppliers also engage in the retailing of the various household items that use these energy sources. Water companies supply clean water and dispose of dirty water and many different kinds of industrial waste that require different treatment techniques; in addition they may offer various consulting services to other firms. Of course not all of these services are covered by regulation, but the examples show that the economics of multiproduct firms is crucial to the understanding of the regulatory problem in practice.

The various markets in which the multiproduct firm operates require different regulatory approaches: there may be markets where the firm faces vigorous and effective competition and for which regulation may be thought unnecessary; some markets could be potentially competitive but without some procompetitive action by the regulator—regulation *for* competition—would remain monopolized by the incumbent firm, and in some markets competition, even if it could be brought about, might be undesirable because of strong increasing returns to scale in the technology. In the latter case the regulator needs to constrain the firm's prices and to provide incentives for the firm to become more efficient. The next two chapters examine how competition and regulation interact, but here we confine attention to the regulation of multiproduct firms that face no competition in any of the markets in question.

3.1.1 Marginal Cost Pricing and Natural Monopoly

Marginal cost pricing continues to be optimal in the multiproduct case for exactly the same reason as in the single-product case: if a consumer faces a price for an additional unit of one of the firm's outputs that differs from the firm's marginal cost of producing it, then both parties could be made better off by changing the quantity produced in return for a transfer of money. Therefore the only (linear) prices that are efficient are equal to the firm's marginal costs. Suppose that the firm makes n products, which we label from 1 to n, and that it incurs a cost of $C(\mathbf{Q})$ in producing the vector of outputs $\mathbf{Q} = (Q_1, \ldots, Q_n)$. Here and throughout the analysis let C_i denote the marginal cost of producing one more unit of product i, so that $C_i \equiv \partial C / \partial Q_i$. (In general C_i is a function of the entire quantity vector $\mathbf{Q}$.) Suppose that when the firm's vector of prices is $\mathbf{P} = (P_1, \ldots, P_n)$ aggregate consumer demand is the vector $\mathbf{Q}(\mathbf{P}) = (Q_1(\mathbf{P}), \ldots, Q_n(\mathbf{P}))$. Then using this notation there is marginal cost pricing with the price vector $\mathbf{P}^*$ if $P_i^* = C_i(\mathbf{Q}(\mathbf{P}^*))$ for each i.

Just as with the single-product case there is the important possibility that marginal cost pricing will lead to the firm being unable to break even. If the firm has a constant variable unit cost of c_i in producing product i but also has a fixed cost of K so that $C(\mathbf{Q}) = \sum_{i=1}^{n} c_i Q_i + K$, then marginal cost pricing would entail setting $P_i = c_i$, and the firm would make an overall loss of K. In the single-product case we saw that any firm with increasing returns to scale would make a loss under marginal cost pricing. However, when the firm produces more than one product the notion of "increasing returns" is less clear-cut. In the single-product case a cost function C was said to have increasing returns if the average cost of production $C(Q)/Q$ decreases with output Q. A possible multiproduct version of this is the condition

$$C_i(\mathbf{Q}) \quad \text{is decreasing in} \quad Q_j \quad \text{for each } i \text{ and } j, \tag{3.1}$$

so the marginal cost of making one more unit of a product is a (weakly) decreasing function not only of the quantity produced of that product but of the quantities produced of the other products as well. Whenever the cost function C satisfies (3.1), it is straightforward to show that pricing at marginal cost will not allow the firm to cover its costs.

Condition (3.1) is related to the concept of natural monopoly, a term used frequently in discussions about regulation. An industry is said to be a *natural monopoly* if it is cheaper to produce a given vector of outputs $\mathbf{Q}$ using one firm than by spreading production over several firms (each having the same cost function) or, more formally, if the industry cost function $C(\mathbf{Q})$ is *subadditive*:

$$C\left(\sum_{j=1}^{m} \mathbf{Q}_j \right) \leq \sum_{j=1}^{m} C(\mathbf{Q}_j) \quad \text{for any set of output vectors} \quad \mathbf{Q}_1, \ldots, \mathbf{Q}_m. \quad (3.2)$$

It is easy to check that the example above where $C(\mathbf{Q}) = \sum_{i=1}^{n} c_i Q_i + K$ is subadditive because the fixed cost K is incurred m times rather than just once. Condition (3.1) is a stronger condition than the natural monopoly condition (3.2), in the sense that any cost function satisfying (3.1) can be shown also to satisfy (3.2).

It should be emphasized that the definition of natural monopoly is in terms of the technological structure of the industry, and it is quite distinct from the question of whether there is an *actual* monopoly in the industry. An industry that does not have natural monopoly cost conditions could nevertheless be monopolized, for instance, if a firm has somehow managed to deter entry or if it has been awarded an exclusive franchise. Alternatively there may be several firms operating in an industry that is characterized by natural monopoly conditions. An additional caveat to the definition of natural monopoly is that it takes the cost function to be exogenous. In a second-best world where firms do not always produce at minimum cost, there is the possibility that two firms, operating in an apparently naturally monopolistic industry, might produce the total industry output at lower cost than a single firm. An actual monopoly might undertake only limited cost-reducing activity, and the introduction of competition could induce it to produce more efficiently, with the result that total costs could be lowered.[1]

---

1. For more on multiproduct cost functions and the theory of natural monopoly, see Panzar (1989) and Sharkey (1982).

3.1.2 Ramsey Pricing

If marginal cost pricing does not cover the regulated firm's costs, and if lump-sum subsidies from the regulator to the firm are ruled out, then the regulator must find a way to cover the firm's costs by means of some tariff. Just as in the single-product case we can consider tariffs of increasing complexity—linear prices, two-part tariffs, and general nonlinear tariffs. The problem of finding the best linear prices—first solved by Frank Ramsey in 1927, and analyzed further by Boiteux (1956) and Baumol and Bradford (1970), among many others—involves the regulator choosing the vector of prices that maximizes social welfare subject to the constraint that the firm not make a loss. If marginal cost pricing does not cover the firm's costs, there must be price/cost markups (though in some markets these could be negative), and the question is: What determines the optimal pattern of markups?

Total welfare is again defined to be a weighted sum of consumer surplus and firm profit. Consumer surplus $V(\mathbf{P})$ is now a function of the vector of prices $\mathbf{P} = (P_1, \ldots, P_n)$. This surplus function satisfies $\partial V(\mathbf{P})/\partial P_i = -Q_i(\mathbf{P})$, so the loss of consumer welfare given a small price change is approximately described by the change in the total cost of buying the old output vector. Write $\pi(\mathbf{P})$ for the firm's profit when prices are $\mathbf{P}$, so $\pi(\mathbf{P}) \equiv \sum_{i=1}^{n} P_i Q_i(\mathbf{P}) - C(\mathbf{Q}(\mathbf{P}))$. Therefore the Ramsey problem is to maximize $V(\mathbf{P}) + \alpha\pi(\mathbf{P})$ subject to $\pi(\mathbf{P}) \geq 0$. Since in all interesting cases the profit constraint will bind at the optimum, we can simplify this to the problem of maximizing consumer surplus $V(\mathbf{P})$ subject to the firm breaking even (i.e., the solution does not depend on the weight α placed on profit); see figure 3.1. This problem has the optimal prices $\mathbf{P}^*$ satisfying the first-order conditions

$$\lambda Q_i(\mathbf{P}^*) = -\sum_j [P_j - C_j(\mathbf{Q}(\mathbf{P}^*))] \frac{\partial Q_j}{\partial P_i}(\mathbf{P}^*) \qquad \text{for each } i, \qquad (3.3)$$

where $\lambda \geq 0$ is chosen so that the resulting prices satisfy the zero profit condition $\pi(\mathbf{P}^*) = 0$. The prices that solve this problem are termed *Ramsey prices*. This formula for the welfare-maximizing prices is similar to that for the unregulated profit-maximizing prices except for the presence of the constant factor λ, the so-called Ramsey number. It is a necessary (but not sufficient) condition for there to be pricing below marginal cost in one or more markets that some of the products be complements (in the sense that $\partial Q_j/\partial P_i < 0$ for some $i \neq j$).

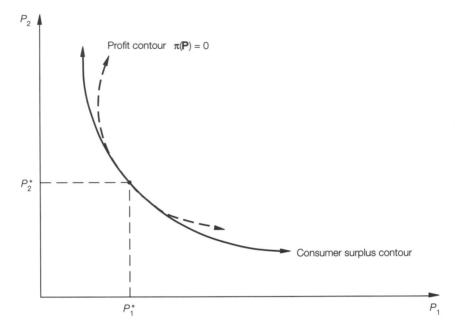

Figure 3.1   First-order conditions for Ramsey prices

In the special case where consumer demands are independent—there are no cross-price effects—this rather complicated formula reduces to the familiar inverse-eiasticity rule for optimal price/marginal cost markups

$$\frac{P_i^* - C_i}{P_i^*} = \frac{\lambda}{\eta_i},$$ (3.4)

where $\eta_i \equiv -P_i(\partial Q_i/\partial P_i)/Q_i$ is the elasticity of demand for product i. In other words, price should be closer to marginal cost in markets where demand is more sensitive to price. In particular, even if marginal cost is the same for all products, it will generally be optimal to price products in different markets differently, so third-degree price discrimination is optimal for consumers overall when the firm must cover its costs.

Another special case occurs when the demand for one of the products is very inelastic, in which case the Ramsey formulas (3.3) can be shown to imply that at the optimum the other products should have prices almost equal to marginal cost and the price for the inelastic product should be set high enough to cover any resulting shortfall in the firm's profits. Note that Ramsey pricing does *not* require that common costs be "allocated" in any sense to individual products. On the cost side it is *marginal* not average costs that matter, and in addition demand factors are part of the optimal price calculation.[2] We next look at some special cases of Ramsey pricing with particular interest for the utility industries, namely two-part tariffs and peak-load pricing.

Two-Part Tariffs As with the single-product case, the introduction of a fixed charge for the right to consume any of the firm's products can improve upon straightforward linear prices, since it enables marginal prices to become closer to marginal costs while helping to cover the firm's fixed costs. We can use the Ramsey framework to analyze optimal two-part tariffs for a multiproduct firm. Suppose that the firm offers a two-part tariff of the form $T(\mathbf{q}) = A + \sum P_i q_i$, where $\mathbf{q} = (q_1, \ldots, q_n)$ is the vector of quantities chosen by the consumer. (Here and elsewhere in the chapter all sums are for $i = 1, \ldots, n$.) Such tariffs are offered by telecommunications suppliers (where A is the line rental charge) and by electricity and gas suppliers (where A is the standing charge). It is useful to define another abstract "product", called *access*, of which a consumer must first purchase one unit at price A before any actual products may be purchased. For any particular consumer the quantity of access chosen will be either zero or one, depending on whether or not the consumer joins the market. Summed over the whole population of consumers we can write the total demand for access—the number of consumers who decide to participate in the market—as $N(A, \mathbf{P})$. If the number of consumers is large, then N can be thought of as a continuous variable. In most instances we expect the number who participate to be sensitive to both the price of access A and the vector of prices $\mathbf{P}$, so some marginal consumers will leave the market if either the access price or any of the usage prices increase. The vector of total demands for the firm's actual products, $\mathbf{Q}(A, \mathbf{P})$, will be sensitive to both A and $\mathbf{P}$. Access will be complementary with each of the actual products, since an increase in P_i will cause N to decrease and an increase in A will cause each Q_i to decrease (given the standing assumption that there are no income effects). Let $C(N, \mathbf{Q})$ be the cost function of the firm. Cost depends on the number of consumers served N in addition to the total output Q (e.g., a utility must lay pipes or cables to a house in order to be able to offer any service to that house).

---

2. The question of when Ramsey prices *are* "subsidy free" in the sense of the contestability literature is examined in Baumol et al. (1982). The question of subsidy-free pricing is considered further in chapter 4.

Now we can simply use the Ramsey formulas (3.3), this time with $n + 1$ products (including access), to find the optimal two-part tariff given by the $n + 1$ charges $A^*, P_1{}^*, \ldots, P_n{}^*$. Since N and each Q_i are complementary, there is a possibility that the optimal access price A^* *could* be below the marginal cost of access (or indeed that a usage charge could be below its marginal cost). On the other hand, if demand for access is rather inelastic —as we would expect if the products, like electricity or water, are essential —then as discussed above, (3.3) implies that the usage charges $P_i{}^*$ should approximate marginal costs and that the fixed charge should be set high enough to cover any shortfall in profits. In effect, this is just the argument of section 2.1.3 that if a high fixed charge does not drive people from the network, the first-best outcome can be obtained by setting usage charges equal to marginal costs and recovering any resulting shortfall in the firm's profit by means of a suitable fixed charge.

Pricing with Capacity Constraints   Each of the utility industries faces demand that fluctuates systematically over the day, the week, and the year: Businesses usually demand services only during working hours, domestic customers tend to demand more services outside office hours, in Britain there is a higher demand for gas and electricity during the winter months, people travelling to work either by road or rail tend to do so at certain times of the day, and so on. Typically the bulk of a utility's capital costs are incurred when constructing sufficient capacity to meet the peak demands. For instance, once a high-capacity telephone link has been made between the United States and Britain, the marginal cost of a call is effectively zero as long as the channel has spare capacity.

Suppose that there are only two relevant time periods, peak and off-peak, with deterministic demand functions given by $Q_1(P_1)$ and $Q_2(P_2)$, respectively. (Later we discuss the case where demands have a random component.) For simplicity we suppose there are no cross-price effects and that $Q_2(P_2) < Q_1(P_1)$ for all relevant prices P_1 and P_2. (This second condition ensures that there is no ambiguity as to which of the periods is the "peak" period.[3]) Let the cost function of serving demands (Q_1, Q_2) be $C(Q_1, Q_2)$. Then the optimal prices are given by the Ramsey formulas (3.4). The marginal cost of providing the peak service, C_1, is much greater than

---

3. In the utilities matters are rarely this simple. While it is true that in aggregate BT carries more calls per minute in peak periods than off-peak periods, this probably is not true everywhere. For instance, an exchange in a suburban area with few businesses faces a peak in the early evening rather than midday.

C_2, the marginal cost of the off-peak service, because the construction of additional capacity is required whereas the capacity needed for Q_1 could meet an increase in Q_2.[4] Because of this expression (3.4) implies that the optimal time-of-day pattern of prices is such that P_1 is greater P_2 (unless for some reason the off-peak demand elasticity η_2 is *much* lower than the peak elasticity η_1). The peak price is higher in order to discourage the more costly peak-time usage. If, as seems likely, there *are* cross-price effects between peak and off-peak demand—we expect that the two products are rather close substitutes—then the optimal prices are given implicitly by (3.3). (For more on the peak-load pricing problem, see Berg and Tschirhart 1988; Brown and Sibley 1986, and Wilson 1993, ch. 11.)

In many cases demands fluctuate randomly as well as systematically. Typically capacity in utility networks is fixed in the short term (e.g., a year), yet the demand for services through the network varies in the short term in a way that is not fully predictable. For example, on a particularly cold winter's day there will be a larger demand for heating than would be the case for the average cold day. One solution to this problem might be for the utility to offer more complicated "real time" tariffs where the price of the service at any time reacts continuously in an attempt to equalize demand with capacity at all times. However, for this to be possible, it would be necessary for consumers to be aware of the price at all times, say, by a display on the phone or electricity meter, something that itself would require heavy investment and other costs.[5]

More realistically, suppose that the firm is constrained to offer stable and predictable prices. Then there is a trade-off: if enough capacity is built to satisfy only the average demand, then some demand will go unsatisfied whenever there is an unusual peak. If, on the other hand, enough capacity is built to satisfy all conceivable demand, there will be no rationing,

---

4. Matters are a little more complex than this in the electricity generation industry. There are a variety of generating technologies, ranging from nuclear power to gas turbines, and these have different cost characteristics. Nuclear power has relatively low usage cost but large sunk costs, whereas the cost of using a gas turbine is high but the plant requires less capital outlay. Because of this the average cost per kWh of using nuclear energy is lower than gas if the plant is on continuously, but the average cost of using gas is lower if the plant is used only intermittently. Therefore the efficient mix of technology is to have nuclear plants running continuously and to switch on the gas stations for the extra supply needed for peak periods. For more on peak-load pricing with diverse technologies, see Crew and Kleindorfer (1976).

5. For a theoretical analysis of real time pricing, see Bohn et al. (1984). It seems possible that utilities can benefit by offering companies with particularly large and variable demands such real time tariffs. In Britain the price paid to electricity generators varies by the half-hour to equalize supply and demand (see chapter 9).

though capacity construction costs will be much higher. The choice is between a cheap and unreliable service or an expensive and reliable service, and the possibilities in between. An important extra complication occurs when the available capacity at any given time is itself uncertain (e.g., the case with electricity generation). In practice, various utilities have chosen a fairly wide range of options: within Britain there is only a small chance of a fixed-link telephone call failing to get through to its destination, but it is more common for mobile calls to be blocked; in the electricity supply industry, if demand exceeds capacity, there are power losses, and therefore the emphasis there tends to be on a reliable service.

When demand is stochastic, the optimal set of prices and capacity level will depend on how damaging rationing is, and this can be quantified by assigning a "shadow" price for each unit of the product for which demand exceeds supply. In the electricity supply industry in Britain, this price is termed the *value of lost load*. The higher the value of lost load, the more important is the reliability of the service, and there will generally be a higher level of capacity at the optimum. The cost of rationing—the value of lost load—depends on the precise nature of rationing in the event of demand exceeding supply, the two main possibilities being *random* rationing (where all customers have an equal chance of being supplied) and *efficient* rationing (where the customers with the highest valuation for the service are served first). Clearly in the former case the value of lost load is greater, since some customers with a high valuation for the service will not be served.[6]

If a particular telephone route is full so that some calls are being blocked, then it seems unreasonable to think that anything other than random rationing will occur.[7] In other utilities, however, there are ways to make rationing more efficient, and it is desirable to use such methods as far as possible, since the value of lost load decreases and a lower level of capacity is needed. One way to do this is to use the form of price discrimination known as *priority pricing* (see Wilson 1993, ch. 10, for an analysis). It involves the firm giving customers (usually its large customers) a *menu* of choices over the reliability of the service they wish to have, with the more reliable service being more expensive. For instance, British Gas of-

---

6. For some analysis of peak-load pricing in the presence of uncertainty, see Berg ar Tschirhart (1988) and Kleindorfer and Fernando (1993).

7. However, it is likely that those blocked customers with greater need to make the c keep redialing and so will be probably get through more quickly than other custom will result in partially efficient rationing, but at a cost.

fers its larger customers a choice between a *firm* service—where supply is more or less guaranteed—and an *interruptible* service—where the customer accepts that at certain times the service may be cut off. Naturally the former is more expensive, and hence those customers who value the service most (e.g., because they have no alternative fuel source) will choose the firm service. Therefore in the event that demand exceeds supply for gas, British Gas will shut off the service to its interruptible customers first, and the resulting rationing scheme will be roughly efficient.[8]

3.1.3 More Complex Multiproduct Tariffs

In section 2.1.4 we discussed the benefits of nonlinear tariffs in the context of a single-product firm and showed that in many cases welfare could be improved by tariffs that offer quantity discounts rather than linear or two-part tariffs. In the multiproduct context more possibilities arise. As well as making the price for a unit of one product decrease with the number units of that product purchased, price can be related to the number of units of *other* products purchased. For instance, in the telecommunications context it is certainly feasible to make the cost of a local call depend on the number of long-distance telephone calls a customer makes. Indeed BT has recently introduced quantity discounts on customers' bills, so that if a customer's quarterly bill is more than £100 a 10% discount is granted. Since the telephone bill is the sum of a customer's charges for local, long-distance, and international calls (among other items), such a quantity discount implies that the marginal charge for one type of call is a decreasing function of the quantities of other types of calls made. Another complex tariff is offered by the electricity supply companies in France, where the marginal charge for peak-time electricity for certain industrial customers depends upon how much off-peak electricity a customer uses.

An interesting question, then, is whether introducing such cross-dependencies would result in improvements in welfare and, if so, what form they should take. Armstrong (1993b) analyzes this problem assuming

---

8. The optimal pricing of firm and interruptible services can also be analyzed within the basic Ramsey framework. Let P_f and P_i be the prices for the firm and the interruptible services respectively, and let the two demand functions be $Q_f(P_f, P_i)$ and $Q_i(P_f, P_i)$. (There must be cross-price effects in this case because one product is of a higher quality than the other, and so if $P_f < P_i$, we must have $Q_i(P_f, P_i) = 0$.) Let C_f and C_i the respective marginal costs of supplying another unit of the firm service and the interruptible service, and, as with peak-load pricing, we expect C_f to be substantially greater than C_i because supply an extra unit of the firm service will require capacity expansion. Then the optimal prices are given by (3.3) above.

that consumers have utility functions given by the natural multiproduct extension of those considered in section 2.1.4. More precisely, if there are n products, a consumer with parameters $\theta_1, \ldots, \theta_n$ who consumes the quantities $q_1, \ldots, q_n$ of the various products, gains utility

$$\sum_{i=1}^{n} \theta_i u_i(q_i) - T(q_1, \ldots, q_n),$$

where $T(q_1, \ldots, q_n)$ is the payment a consumer must make to consume these quantities. Therefore the parameter θ_i represents the consumer's taste for the ith product.

In a class of cases the firm should make the charge for consuming a bundle of quantities depend (in some nonlinear way) only on the firm's total cost of producing that bundle. So, if the firm has a constant marginal cost c_i for the production of the ith product, then the profit-maximizing and welfare-maximizing nonlinear tariffs are both of the form

$$T(q_1, \ldots, q_n) = T\left(\sum_{i=1}^{n} c_i q_i \right).$$

Within this class of cases the firm makes the marginal price for one product decrease with the quantities of the other chosen, so a natural kind of quantity discount is often optimal also in the multiproduct setting.[9]

3.1.4   Discussion

If the regulator is well informed, benevolent, and has the ability to make lump-sum transfers to the regulated multiproduct firm, the result will be marginal cost pricing in each of the firm's products. Lump-sum transfers are required, since pricing at marginal cost will not cover total costs when, as seems likely in the utility industries, the firm has economies of scale and scope. If such transfers are not possible, then Ramsey pricing will be the result of optimal regulation. To solve for these optimal prices, the regulator needs to know accurately consumer demand as well the cost function of the firm. In the case where consumer demands are independent, a simple test suffices to show if prices are optimal: the price/cost markup divided by the demand elasticity should be constant across all products.

Ramsey prices appear rarely to be implemented. Indeed aspects of utility pricing often fail to reflect rather obvious cost differences across

9. For some other progress in this area, see Wilson (1993, ch. 12–14), who uses these techniques to analyze the optimal multiproduct nonlinear tariff for bulk electricity customers.

markets (let alone the demand factors that are also involved in Ramsey pricing). For instance, in Britain the charge for being connected to the telephone network does not depend on whether the user lives in a rural or urban area, despite the fact that providing a rural service is typically more expensive than an urban service. Similarly the charge for sending a letter within the country does not vary with the distance it travels or from where the letter was sent. Another way in which actual pricing policy does not sufficiently reflect costs is the comparative rarity of peak-load pricing. Even though the demand for gas is far higher in winter than summer, British Gas charges smaller customers exactly the same in each season, and as a result it presumably has greater capacity requirements than is optimal.

What considerations might justify such departures from efficient pricing? One possible justification could be the simplicity of uniform tariffs, but this seems unconvincing, since the existing tariffs are relatively complex in any case. (For instance, people are used to paying different charges for different destinations when they send their letters abroad, as well as paying different charges for different weights of letter, and peak-load pricing is well accepted in telecommunications.) A more likely rationale involves some notion of "fairness" among consumers so that the regulator views it as unfair, or politically unacceptable, to make different consumers face different prices for the "same" product. However, the theory of Ramsey pricing implies that the loss that some consumers would suffer in the move away from a uniform pricing policy would be more than compensated by the gains enjoyed by the others, at least when consumer surplus is taken as the measure of overall consumer welfare. In any case it is not clear what is "fair" about charging two consumers the same for a product whose supply to one consumer uses more scarce economic resources than supply to the other.

As well as this notion of fairness, a crucial reason why Ramsey prices are rarely seen in practice is the enormous informational requirements concerning demand and costs needed to implement the policy. As reported in Laffont and Tirole (1993, 200–202), not even when Boiteux—one of the pioneers of the theory of Ramsey pricing—was in charge of Électricité de France was Ramsey pricing attempted. Instead, the simpler "Allais" doctrine of *uniformly* increasing prices above marginal costs (rather than basing the markup on demand elasticities) was adopted, a policy that requires little in the way of demand information (although such a policy would still require that prices reflect costs).[10] In the following sections we extend the insights and analysis of Ramsey pricing to allow for this last point, and we also consider how to give the multiproduct firm good incentives to increase its productive efficiency.

*3.2 The Problem of Asymmetric Information: the Multiproduct Case

In this section we briefly give an account of how the discussion of single-product regulation with asymmetric information in section 2.2 can be extended to a multiproduct setting. It is assumed here that lump-sum transfers are possible. It is clear that the Loeb-Magat solution to the regulation problem when distributional concerns are irrelevant ($\alpha = 1$) applies equally to a multiproduct firm. The firm should be given a lump-sum transfer equal to $V(\mathbf{P})$ if it charges the vector of prices $\mathbf{P}$, and the result will be perfect allocative and productive efficiency. In addition, however, the firm will most likely obtain a large rent due to its informational advantage, and when the regulator attaches less weight to profits in the welfare function, this scheme again will not be optimal.

3.2.1 Regulation with Hidden Information

Suppose, then, that the firm's profit is less valuable socially than consumer surplus ($\alpha < 1$). Sappington (1983) analyzes one multiproduct extension to the Baron and Myerson model discussed in section 2.2.2. The model has no possibilities for cost reduction, and the firm with exogenous scalar cost parameter θ has the multiproduct cost function $C(\theta, \mathbf{Q})$, where $\mathbf{Q}$ is the vector of total outputs of the firm. Much the same techniques apply as used in section 2.2.2, and similar implications result.

One special feature of this way of modeling the problem of how to regulate a multiproduct firm with hidden information is the assumption that there is only a single parameter of cost uncertainty. This means that the firm's n marginal costs, $C_1(\theta), \ldots, C_n(\theta)$, are all perfectly correlated with each other, and there are no shocks or uncertainties specific to particular products. For example, a rather natural multiproduct cost function that does not fit into this framework is

---

10. This in some ways parallels policy on commodity taxation. In theory different goods should face a different rate of indirect taxation, but because of the formidable informational requirements needed to calculate these different rates, most governments impose a common tax rate across a broad class of goods.

$$C(\theta, \mathbf{Q}) = \sum_{i=1}^{n} \theta_i Q_i. \tag{3.6}$$

Here θ_i is the constant unit cost of producing product i, so there are n scalar parameters, $\theta_1, \ldots, \theta_n$, each of each is allowed to vary independently of the others. Armstrong (1993a) considers the optimal form of regulation when the firm's costs take the form (3.6) and when the vector of unit costs θ is not observable by the regulator. Within a class of cases it is optimal to set the price/cost markup to be constant across products (although this markup depends on the parameters θ):

$$\frac{P_i - \theta_i}{\theta_i} \equiv h(\theta) \qquad \text{for all } i \text{ and for some function } h.$$

(In other words, a form of the Allais doctrine is the optimal policy in this model.) The optimal transfer from the regulator to the firm is an increasing function of the total consumer surplus $V(\mathbf{P})$, so the optimal transfer schedule here bears some resemblance to the Loeb-Magat scheme that gave the firm the entire consumer surplus. Again, though, whenever the regulator places less weight on producer than consumer surplus, there is a trade-off between allocative efficiency and distributional concerns, and the result is that prices will deviate from marginal costs in order to diminish the informational rent of the firm.

3.2.2　Regulation with Hidden Action

Laffont and Tirole (1993, ch. 3) provide an analysis of optimal regulation of a multiproduct firm that possesses private information concerning its cost function and the level of cost-reducing effort undertaken, but total cost is observable. As in the single-product case of section 2.2.3, there is a trade-off between the objective of productive efficiency and the distributional aim of limiting the firm's profit. The information asymmetry prevents the simultaneous achievement of both objectives.

Using the same notation as section 2.2.3, suppose that the firm's multiproduct cost function is $C(\theta, e, \mathbf{Q})$, where θ is a scalar parameter that is exogenous to the firm, e is the level of cost reducing activity by the firm, and $\mathbf{Q}$ is the vector of total outputs of the firm. Let us focus on the simple case where this cost function can be written in the special form

$$C = C(\beta(\theta, e), \mathbf{Q}) \tag{3.7}$$

so that θ and e are aggregated together in the cost function using the function β. (In section 2.2.3 we examined the case $C(\theta, e, Q) = (\theta - e)Q$

which is obviously of this form. For technical reasons, it is convenient to aggregate both the information asymmetries together into a single parameter β.) Suppose that C is increasing in β and that the function β is increasing in θ and, because effort reduces total costs, decreasing in e. Effort level e costs the firm $\psi(e)$. In fact it is easier to concentrate on the parameter β than e, and to write $E(\beta, \theta)$ as the effort level e needed to obtain β given the exogenous parameter θ (i.e., $E(\beta(e, \theta), \theta) \equiv e$). The regulator is able to observe output $\mathbf{Q}$ and total cost $C(\beta, \mathbf{Q})$, and hence can deduce the variable $\beta(\theta, e)$, but not θ or e individually. The regulatory scheme involves the regulator offering the firm a subsidy $T(\beta, \mathbf{Q})$ if the firm obtains β and produces outputs $\mathbf{Q}$. Given this subsidy schedule, the firm with cost parameter θ chooses $\beta(\theta)$ and $\mathbf{Q}(\theta)$ in order to maximize

$$\sum P_i(\mathbf{Q})Q_i - C(\beta, \mathbf{Q}) - \psi(E(\beta, \theta)) + T(\beta, \mathbf{Q}).$$

Then, by exactly the same method as used in the previous chapter, given our welfare criterion,[11] we can show that when the cost parameter is θ the optimal prices $P_i^*(\theta)$ and effort level $e^*(\theta)$ satisfy

$$P_i^*(\theta) = C_i^*(\theta) \qquad \text{for } i = 1, \ldots, n, \tag{3.8a}$$

$$\psi' + (1 - \alpha)\frac{F(\theta)}{f(\theta)}\left\{\psi''E_\theta + \frac{\psi'E_{\beta\theta}}{E_\beta}\right\} + C_e = 0, \tag{3.8b}$$

where we have used subscripts to denote partial derivatives and $C_i^*(\theta)$ is the marginal cost of producing product i when the cost parameter is θ and effort is $e^*(\theta)$. In the single-product case this reduces to equation (2.19b) in chapter 2 because $E_\theta = 1$, $E_{\beta\theta} = 0$, and $C_e = -Q$. Since E_θ is positive, the term in brackets $\{\cdot\}$ is positive provided that $E_{\beta\theta} \leq 0$. In this case (3.8b) implies that $\psi' + C_e < 0$, so there is underinvestment in effort. (The first-best optimal effort level is given by $\psi' + C_e = 0$.) Just as in the single-product case, unless $\alpha = 1$, optimal regulation entails marginal cost pricing but suboptimal effort supplied by the firm.

This is Laffont and Tirole's "incentive-pricing dichotomy": *prices* are used to obtain allocative efficiency (price is set equal to marginal cost), while the *transfer* is used to give incentives for the firm to reduce its

---

11. Recall that our welfare criterion is different from Laffont and Tirole's, in that we place a different weight on producer than consumer surplus but assume that government transfers have no social cost; Laffont and Tirole simply add producer and consumer surplus together but assume that any transfers require extra distortions elsewhere in the economy and hence incur a social cost. This means that, while the principles are the same in each case, our formulas (3.8) look different from those in Laffont and Tirole (1993).

costs.[12] Since the firm possesses private information about its costs (the parameter θ), these incentives are imperfect. Effort is undersupplied relative to the symmetric information case, and the firm makes strictly positive profits from its monopoly on information. Thus the optimal trade-off involves some productive inefficiency, some distributional inefficiency but perfect allocative efficiency.

Laffont and Tirole show that this kind of model—which again represents the private information as single scalar parameters—can neatly be adapted in some cases to incorporate both the effort e and the cost parameter θ being multidimensional. Suppose that the unit cost of product i is constant and equal to $\beta_i(\theta_i, e_i)$, where θ_i is the exogenous cost parameter and e_i is the effort level specific to product i. The cost of supplying the effort levels e_i is just $\psi(\sum e_i)$. We can write the cost function for a given level of *total* effort e as

$$C(\theta, e, \mathbf{Q}) = \min \sum_{i=1}^{n} \beta_i(\theta_i, e_i) Q_i$$

subject to $\displaystyle\sum_{i=1}^{n} e_i = e.$ (3.9)

This procedure effectively means that effort can again be considered as a scalar variable. What is more surprising is that in some cases (depending on the functional forms for β_i) the cost function C in (3.9) turns out to have the form

$$C(\theta, e, \mathbf{Q}) = C(\beta(\Lambda(\theta), e), \mathbf{Q})$$ (3.10)

for some functions β and Λ. In using Λ, the n parameters θ_i are aggregated in the cost function (see Laffont and Tirole 1993, sec. 3.8.2). But (3.10) has the same form as (3.7) except that θ is replaced by the scalar variable $\Lambda(\theta)$, so equations (3.8) will continue to hold except that f and F refer to the distribution of Λ rather than θ.

3.2.3 Discussion

Despite the more complicated analysis, the basic principles of optimal regulation under asymmetric information when lump-sum transfers are possible is essentially the same in the multiproduct as in the single-product case. With the models of hidden information there is no possibility for cost

---

12. Laffont and Tirole (1993, sec. 3.6) also show that when the cost function is not of the form of (3.7), then the incentive-pricing dichotomy does *not* hold, so prices should also be used to give the firm effort incentives.

reduction (so productive efficiency is not an issue), and the regulator faces a trade-off between allocative efficiency—the vector of prices being close to the vector of marginal costs—and the reduction of the distributional loss due to the firm profiting from its monopoly of information. Unless the regulator is indifferent to distributional concerns, it is optimal to deviate from marginal cost pricing in order to drive down profits. In Laffont and Tirole's model the regulator can observe the firm's costs but is unable to determined whether low costs are due to luck (a low value of θ) or design (a high level of effort e). Provided that the incentive dichotomy condition (3.7) holds, optimal regulation settles the three-way conflict among allocative efficiency, productive efficiency, and distributional concerns by setting the vector of prices equal to marginal costs and using transfers from the regulator to the firm to bring about a degree of productive efficiency (which occurs at the cost of increasing the firm's informational rent).

3.3 Price Regulation: the Multiproduct Case

In this section we suppose that the regulator does not have the authority to make lump-sum transfers to the multiproduct firm and so must rely on prices alone to try to perform three tasks: to attain allocative and productive efficiency, and to keep informational rents to a minimum. As discussed in section 3.1.2, the multiproduct framework can encompass two-part pricing as well as straightforward linear pricing, and in the following we can, if we wish, consider one of the products to be "access" and its corresponding price to be the fixed charge in a two-part tariff. We look first at a version of a model of price regulation with hidden action which we introduced in section 2.3, and then we consider pure price cap regulation (without any cost passthrough).

3.3.1 Cost Passthrough

Here we suppose that there is a multiproduct firm facing an inelastic unit demand for each of its products. There are two products, and the cost of manufacturing the unit of product i is $c_i = \theta_i - e_i$, where the cost of effort e_i is $\psi(e_i) = e_i^2/2$ for each product. As in section 2.3, consider linear pricing rules

$$P(c_1, c_2) = \bar{P} + (1 - \rho_1)c_1 + (1 - \rho_2)c_2, \tag{3.11}$$

where $P(\mathbf{c})$ is the firm's total revenue if the cost vector is observed to be $\mathbf{c}$ and ρ_i is a parameter that determines the sensitivity of revenue to cost c_i.

For simplicity, consider the simplest case where the random cost parameters θ_i are symmetrically distributed. In particular, let $E[\theta_i] = \mu$, $\text{var}[\theta_i] = \sigma^2$, and if $i \neq j$, then $\text{cov}[\theta_i, \theta_j] = r\sigma^2$, where $\text{cov}[\theta_i, \theta_j]$ is the covariance of two distinct parameters θ_i, θ_j, and $0 \leq r \leq 1$ is a parameter that measures the degree of positive correlation between cost parameters.

Because everything is symmetric, the regulator will choose $\rho_1 = \rho_2$ in (3.11) and the price function will be of the form

$$P(\mathbf{c}) = \bar{P} + (1 - \rho)(c_1 + c_2). \tag{3.12}$$

The firm's payoff is again measured by $E[\pi] - \gamma/2\,\text{var}[\pi]$, and when the price function is given by (3.12), we have

$$E[\pi] = \bar{P} - \sum_{i=1}^{2} \rho(\mu - e_i) - \sum_{i=1}^{2} \tfrac{1}{2}e_i^2$$

$$\text{var}[\pi] = 2\sigma^2\rho^2(1 + r).$$

Therefore the firm will choose effort level $e_i = \rho$ for each product. The regulator is interested in minimizing the expected payment to the firm $P(\mathbf{c})$ subject to the firm attaining some minimum level of utility π_0. Just as in section 2.3, it is easily shown that the optimal passthrough parameter in (3.12) is given by

$$\rho^* = \frac{1}{1 + \gamma\sigma^2(1 + r)}. \tag{3.13}$$

Therefore revenue is more sensitive to cost (ρ^* is smaller) if the degree of positive correlation r is greater, this being because a higher degree of correlation between θ_1 and θ_2 implies that the firm faces a greater degree of aggregate uncertainty and so should receive a greater degree of insurance.

We will return to this model when we discuss yardstick competition below, and for reference later, here we calculate the maximum value of welfare (i.e., the minimized expected payment to the firm). The expected payment to the firm given ρ is

$$2(\mu - \rho) + \rho^2 + \rho^2\gamma\sigma^2(1 + r) + \pi_0,$$

and so with the choice of ρ^* given by (3.13) this payment has the value

$$L_{\text{int}} = 2\mu - \frac{1}{1 + \gamma\sigma^2(1 + r)} + \pi_0. \tag{3.14}$$

(Later we will compare this expected payment L_{int} with that obtained if there were two firms, each producing one of the products.) Note that consumers are made worse off and that total welfare is lower when there is higher correlation in costs, because the aggregate risk faced by the firm is greater.

3.3.2 Properties of Different Forms of Price Cap Regulation

In this section we abstract from problems of productive inefficiency, and take the firm's costs to be fixed.[13] However, these costs are not observable to the regulator (otherwise, Ramsey prices could be implemented as described in section 3.1.2). Also, for most of the price cap schemes discussed here, we will require little in the way of demand information. We discuss four different kinds of price caps: an "ideal" price cap that can induce a kind of Ramsey pricing, a price cap where the index of average prices has fixed weights, an average revenue price cap, and optional tariffs. In section 3.5.2 we will discuss dynamic aspects of price cap regulation.

An Ideal Price Cap   When deciding on the form of price regulation for a multiproduct monopolist, the first question is whether to have a separate price constraint for *each* of the firm's products, to have an overall constraint on some measure of the *average* of the prices charged by the firm, or—as an intermediate case—to have a constraint on the average of a subset of the firm's prices. This question has been debated on several occasions in Britain (see chapters 6 and 7 below). As discussed in section 4.3.3, the policy of having separate constraints has benefits regarding the nondeterrence of entry. For now, though, we abstract from such considerations and suppose that there is no possibility of competition in any market.

In the monopoly context it might be thought that an advantage of regulating individual prices is that uncertainty over relative prices is eliminated. For if the firm is free to charge whatever relative prices it chooses subject to a constraint on some measure of the average of its prices, uncertainty about individual prices would exist, and this for some reason may be undesirable.

The main argument for having a single constraint on an average price is that it gives the firm more freedom to respond to uncertainty in its costs. If, for example, the cost of product i turns out to be lower than expected in relation to the cost of product j, then for most forms of average price

---

13. The following is based on Armstrong and Vickers (1991) and Armstrong et al. (1992). See also Bradley and Price (1988) and Wilson (1993, sec. 5.2).

regulation the firm will tend to lower the price of i and increase the price of j compared with the situation of separate constraints. This (albeit very loose) tracking of cost by price in each market will tend to be beneficial for allocative efficiency. On the other hand, the firm's private incentives will not perfectly coincide with what is socially desirable, and particular forms of average price regulation will give the firm incentives to over- or under-price some products compared with what would be desirable in a first-best world.

However, and again in the monopoly context, it is simple to show that some forms of average price regulation do better than simply giving the firm a single set of prices that it must charge. Indeed suppose that the regulator gave the firm *no* choice over its prices, and forced it to charge P_i^0 for product i. Therefore total welfare with this form of regulation is $V(\mathbf{P}^0) + \alpha\pi(\mathbf{P}^0)$. Consider the following change in the regulatory regime: instead of having to offer the price vector $\mathbf{P}^0$, the firm can offer any vector of prices $\mathbf{P}$ that does not reduce consumer surplus, that is, the firm's allowed set of prices is

$$\{\mathbf{P} \mid V(\mathbf{P}) \geq V(\mathbf{P}^0)\}. \tag{3.15}$$

By construction, allowing the firm to choose from such a set of prices cannot make consumers in aggregate any worse off (although particular individuals may of course lose out), and in most cases the firm will be able to make a strictly greater profit by choosing some price vector different from the original $\mathbf{P}^0$ within this constraint. Therefore, allowing the firm some price flexibility, subject to constraints, is preferable to simply ordering the firm to offer some fixed-price vector. In fact the form of price regulation in (3.15) has another desirable property: since profit is maximized subject to consumers being guaranteed a certain level of surplus— a problem that is effectively the same as the Ramsey problem of section 3.1.2 where consumer surplus was maximized subject to the firm being guaranteed a certain level of profit (the tangency point between the iso-profit and iso-surplus curves is the same as in figure 3.1)—no matter what informational assumptions we make on the cost side, the Ramsey conditions (3.3) will be satisfied.

The form of price regulation given by (3.15) is of course not easily put into practice because of the unrealistic amount of information on the demand side that would be needed. (The function $V(\mathbf{P})$ needs to be accurately known.) We next examine the outcome—for consumers and the firm—of particular forms of price cap regulation that are less demanding of information.

Regulation with Fixed Weights   A general way of representing price cap regulation is to suppose that the firm is constrained that an index of its prices, $I(\mathbf{P})$, must not be greater than some cap $\overline{P}$ but is otherwise free to choose relative prices. (For instance, in the form of regulation given by (3.15), the index of prices was $I(\mathbf{P}) = V(\mathbf{P}^0)/V(\mathbf{P})$, and the price cap was $\overline{P} = 1$.) Which prices result from regulation will then depend on the firm's costs and the precise form of index $I(\mathbf{P})$ chosen. The firm will choose its vector of prices in order to

maximize $\pi(\mathbf{P})$ (3.16)

subject to $I(\mathbf{P}) \leq \overline{P}$.

Suppose that the regulator simply fixes the weights in the price index: $I(\mathbf{P}) = \sum_{i=1}^{n} \overline{w}_i P_i$ for some weights $\overline{w}_i$. As a particular case, consider the following scheme which is closely related to the above ideal price cap but is a little less demanding of information. Let $\mathbf{P}^0$ be a given reference price vector, as above, and suppose that the demands at these prices (but not necessarily at other prices) are known. Let the fixed weight $\overline{w}_i$ be given by the demand for product i when prices are $\mathbf{P}^0$ so that $\overline{w}_i = Q_i(\mathbf{P}^0)$. More precisely, suppose that the firm is allowed to choose any price vector $\mathbf{P}$ in the set

$$\left\{ \mathbf{P} \middle| \sum_{i=1}^{n} P_i Q_i(\mathbf{P}^0) \leq \sum_{i=1}^{n} P_i^0 Q_i(\mathbf{P}^0) \right\}.   (3.17)$$

It follows immediately that any prices in the set (3.17) are also in the set (3.15); that is to say, consumers are better off with any price vector $\mathbf{P}$ in the set (3.17) than with $\mathbf{P}^0$ (see figure 3.2).

Intuitively, with any price vector $\mathbf{P}$ in (3.17), consumers in aggregate can buy the bundle of products $\mathbf{Q}^0$ for a total cost no greater than they paid when prices were $\mathbf{P}^0$. Therefore they can consume $\mathbf{Q}^0$ as before and be at least as well off, and in general they will choose a different bundle and be strictly better off. Naturally the firm is also better off faced with constraint (3.17) than with the fixed price $\mathbf{P}^0$, since it has more alternatives available ($\mathbf{P}^0$ lies in the set (3.17)). Therefore the welfare effect of a move from regulation with fixed price $\mathbf{P}^0$ to average price regulation given by the fixed-weights regime (3.17) is unambiguously positive.

While permitting the firm to choose relative prices subject to an overall cap has these desirable welfare properties, the fixed-weights form of regulation still requires a good deal of demand information: to ensure that the firm satisfies the regulatory constraint (3.17), the regulator needs to know the outputs demanded at the hypothetical prices $\mathbf{P}^0$.

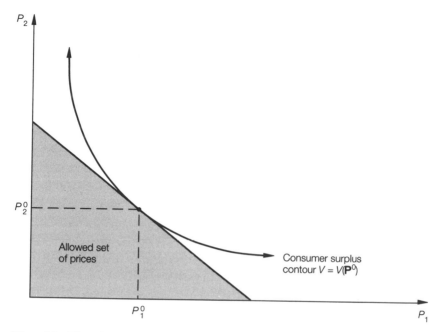

Figure 3.2 The price cap constraint with "fixed weights"

Average Revenue Regulation A form of average price regulation often used in practice is *average revenue* regulation, where the total revenue divided by total output—the average revenue—of the firm is constrained to be no greater than a price cap $\bar{P}$. Forms of average revenue regulation are used for British Gas, the British Airports Authority, and the electricity supply industry in Britain. This type of regulation is most appropriate in the context where the various products of the firm are commensurable, in the sense that the firm's costs depend only on the total output $\sum_{i=1}^{n} Q_i$ produced so that

$$C(Q_1,\ldots,Q_n) = C(Q),$$

where

$$Q \equiv \sum_{i=1}^{n} Q_i. \tag{3.18}$$

For instance, the firm might produce a single physical product (e.g., gas or electricity) but sell it in various geographical markets, and to various different types of customer (e.g., domestic or industrial). Alternatively, the firm might offer a nonlinear tariff to discriminate among different types of consumer.[14] When the firm's output are commensurable in the sense of (3.18), we can discuss the effects of price regulation in terms of *price discrimination*: Which kinds of price discrimination, if any, should be permitted?

When the firm operates in n markets, with average revenue regulation the firm is permitted to choose any price vector from the set

$$\left\{ \mathbf{P} \,\middle|\, \sum_{i=1}^{n} Q_i(\mathbf{P})P_i \leq \bar{P} \sum_{i=1}^{n} Q_i(\mathbf{P}) \right\}. \tag{3.19}$$

Unlike the fixed-weights regime (3.17), the weights in this price index are endogenous to the firm in that they depend on the prices set. Also average revenue regulation has the very important advantage over a fixed-weights cap that only observed consumer demands need to be known to implement the constraint, not hypothetical demands for some reference set of prices. (The demands $Q_i(\bar{\mathbf{P}})$, where $\bar{\mathbf{P}}$ is the vector of prices with each component equal to $\bar{P}$, do not play any role in (3.19).)

To take the analysis further, it is convenient to introduce the *revenue function*, $R(\cdot)$, where $R(Q)$ is defined to be the maximum possible revenue the firm can generate from selling the total quantity Q by whatever means it has at its disposal. There are two main cases of interest:

1. *Third-degree price discrimination.* In this case the firm operates in n markets and can charge a different price in each market. The demand function is $\mathbf{Q}(\mathbf{P})$, where $Q_i(\mathbf{P})$ is the quantity demanded in market i when the price vector is $\mathbf{P}$. Therefore, in this setting the revenue function is defined to be

$$R(Q) = \max \sum_{i=1}^{n} P_i Q_i(\mathbf{P})$$

$$\text{subject to} \quad \sum_{i=1}^{n} Q_i(\mathbf{P}) = Q; \tag{3.20}$$

in words, $R(Q)$ is the maximum revenue the firm can obtain by selling output Q using third-degree price discrimination.

---

14. An important case where the firm's products are commensurable in an intuitive sense but where (3.18) does *not* hold occurs when products are differentiated according to time of day and there is peak-load pricing. In section 3.1.2 we argued that capacity constraints implied that the marginal cost of providing peak service would greatly exceed that of the off-peak service, something which is not consistent with cost being a function simply of total output. This section on average revenue regulation, then, is not applicable to the peak-load pricing setting.

2. *Second-degree price discrimination.* Here the firm serves a single market in which there are consumers with (unobservable) differing tastes for its product (see section 2.1.4). It discriminates among customers with weak and strong preferences for its product by using a nonlinear tariff $T(q)$. In this case $R(Q)$ is defined to be the maximum revenue that the firm can obtain from the population of consumers by selling total quantity Q using a nonlinear tariff $T(q)$. Normally this revenue-maximizing nonlinear tariff will offer consumers quantity discounts.

These two kinds of price discrimination differ fundamentally in that with third-degree price discrimination the firm can observe the consumer's type and so can base the price directly on the observed type of the consumer (e.g., where the consumer is located, or whether they are a business or a domestic user), whereas with second-degree price discrimination this is not possible. However, once we have constructed the revenue function $R(Q)$, which incorporates whatever informational constraints are operating in the firm's market(s), we can ignore the distinction in what follows.

Under average revenue regulation the profit-maximizing regulated firm will choose its revenue R and total output Q in order to maximize $R - C(Q)$ subject to (1) the regulatory constraint $R \leq \bar{P}Q$ and (2) the feasibility constraint $R \leq R(Q)$. The solution to this problem typically involves the firm choosing its level of total output Q^* to satisfy $R(Q^*) = \bar{P}Q^*$ (which will usually determine Q^* uniquely) and then choosing the tariff that maximizes the revenue possible given this output. This entails that total output Q be maximized subject to the binding regulatory constraint.

It is instructive to compare this outcome with the no-discrimination alternative where all prices must equal $\bar{P}$. It can easily be shown that any price vector **P** for which the constraint (3.19) is *binding*—and if regulation is to have any bite, this constraint will bind—will result in consumers being made worse off compared with the uniform price $\bar{P}$. Intuitively, this is because when all prices are $\bar{P}$, consumers in aggregate can purchase the bundle **Q(P)** for the same total cost as when the prices are **P**, and as a result consumers must be at least as well off, and generally better off, with the nondiscriminatory prices $\bar{P}$ than with **P** (see figure 3.3).

As before, the firm is better off being given the freedom to discriminate. The overall welfare effect (i.e., the change in the weighted sum of consumer and producer surplus) of a move to discrimination is ambiguous, although if the weight on producer surplus α is small enough, discrimination will prove detrimental to overall welfare.

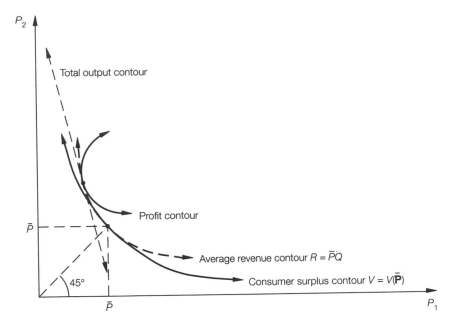

Figure 3.3 The effect of average revenue regulation

In the third-degree price discrimination case, one interesting question concerns the effect that average revenue regulation has on relative prices compared to efficient Ramsey prices. As discussed above, typically the firm will choose a set of prices that maximizes its total revenue subject to a total output constraint. In other words, the firm's prices solve (3.20) for some some total output Q^*. Suppose for simplicity that there are no cross-price effects in demand. If we assume an interior solution to (3.20), we obtain the following first-order conditions for prices:

$$P_i^* = \hat{\lambda}\left(\frac{\eta_i}{1 - \eta_i}\right),$$

where $\hat{\lambda}$ is a constant and η_i is the elasticity of demand for product i. If it is the case that $\eta_i < 1$ (something that usually holds in the utility industries), then $\hat{\lambda} > 0$ in the above expression. This contrasts strongly with the Ramsey formula (3.4) in that here prices are higher in the markets with more elastic demand instead of following an *inverse* elasticity rule.

Optional Tariffs A natural form of regulating price discrimination is to allow the firm to price discriminate as much as it wishes subject to the proviso that no consumer is made worse off compared with the regime of uniform pricing.[15] This is equivalent to the constraint that the firm should continue to offer consumers the *option* of using the uniform tariff if they choose or, alternatively, to the constraint that the firm cannot raise any price above the no-discrimination level.

In the context of second-degree price discrimination the uniform tariff is the linear tariff where the price for each unit of the product is $\bar{P}$. Under a regime of optional tariff regulation, the firm is permitted to offer any nonlinear tariff $T(q)$ subject to the constraint that $T(q) \leq \bar{P}q$ for all q. Suppose that the profit-maximizing *unregulated* nonlinear tariff is $T^*(q)$, with corresponding optimal marginal price schedule $p^*(q)$. With this form of regulation, and provided that the profit-maximizing tariff T^* involves quantity discounts, it can be shown that (1) the firm will choose to offer a marginal price schedule given by $p(q) = \min\{p^*(q), \bar{P}\}$, (2) no consumers are worse off if the firm is permitted to discriminate, (3) the firm and at least some consumers are strictly better off with discrimination, and (4) output increases. Clearly, compared with no discrimination, a regime of optional tariff regulation induces a higher level of welfare. However, it can be shown that the welfare comparison of regulation using optional tariffs against average regulation is ambiguous. Like average revenue regulation, the informational requirements to operate a regime of optional tariffs are minimal—all that needs checking is that whichever tariff is offered by the firm lies everywhere below the uniform tariff $T(q) = \bar{P}q$.

3.3.3 Discussion

In this section we have discussed the regulation of a multiproduct monopoly when transfers to the firm are ruled out. In section 3.3.1 we constructed a simple model with inelastic demand to consider the desirable degree of passthrough of costs. As we noted in section 2.3, cost passthrough has the twin tasks of providing good incentives for cost reduction—this can be ensured by making price insensitive to observed costs—as well as providing insurance to the risk-averse firm. The best way to trade off these conflicting aims was given by (3.13). Because a higher degree of correlation in costs increases the overall uncertainty faced by the firm, the price is made more sensitive to observed costs in order to give the firm greater insurance against adverse shocks to its costs.

---

15. See also Wilson (1993, sec. 5.2).

In section 3.3.2 we abstracted from considerations of providing adequate effort incentives to analyze the effects that the various forms of price cap regulation have on the *structure* of prices, and the welfare consequences of this for consumers and the firm. Apart from possible adverse effects on competition, there is no reason why the regulated firm should not be given at least some freedom in its choice of relative prices. For instance, compared to a regime where the firm is forced to offer a fixed set of prices, allowing the firm to offer any tariff that results in the same level of consumer surplus will increase welfare overall. Given that some form of average price regulation is desirable, the question remains as to which precise form of price cap should be chosen. The form of this cap is important for overall welfare. If, for instance, there are suitably chosen *fixed weights* in the price index, average price regulation will make consumers as a whole better off compared with giving the firm no discretion over relative prices, whereas the opposite is the case with average revenue regulation. Average revenue regulation, on the other hand, has the crucial advantage that only observed demands need to be known to calculate the price index. Any price cap that differs from the ideal cap (3.15) will cause the firm's pricing incentives to diverge from the regulator's. For instance, in contrast to Ramsey prices, a firm facing an average revenue cap will choose *higher* prices in its more elastic markets.

This choice of price cap raises the question: given a particular set of assumptions on what cost and demand information is available, what is the *optimal* form of the price cap? If the consumer surplus function were known accurately, one plausible candidate for the optimal price cap might be of the form (3.15) because it induces efficient Ramsey prices. Alternatively, although we have seen that average revenue regulation has some serious drawbacks, is there another price cap with the same minimal informational requirements as average revenue regulation that does better? Little theoretical work has been done in this area, and what determines the shape of an optimal price cap at present remains an open question. In particular, we do not know of any natural conditions that would guarantee the optimality of any of the price caps considered in this section.

3.4 Yardstick Competition

The central insight of the new regulatory economics that emphasizes incentives is the crucial importance of *information* in the regulatory process. If the regulator is uninformed about industry conditions, then regulation

—even *optimal* regulation—will leave firms with undesirable rents due to their monopoly on information. Yardstick competition is a way of regulating several regional monopolies so as to induce a form a competition via the regulatory mechanism that weakens individual firms' monopolies of information, and hence improves the terms of the trade-off between allocative, productive, and distributional efficiency. This is done by making the reward to one firm depend on its performance relative to that of other firms. For instance, in the United States Medicare's payment to a hospital for a course of treatment depends on the average cost of similar treatments in other hospitals (see Laffont and Tirole 1993, sec. 1.7). Such a scheme gives individual hospitals the incentive to cut costs to below the average level, and when all hospitals seek to do this, the average cost falls. As we discuss later in chapters 9 and 10, the regional structure of the electricity supply and water industries in Britain could allow yardstick competition between regional areas, although at present little *explicit* use has been made of this.

Consider this simple example which uses the same model of cost technology and firm behavior as described in section 3.3.1.[16] There are two firms operating in independent markets, and each firm produces just one unit of a product. The cost of the product for firm i is $c_i = \theta_i - e_i$. As before, we assume that the two parameters θ_1 and θ_2 are positively correlated, so for a given effort level the fact that one firm's observed cost is high implies that the second firm's cost is also likely to be high.

The regulator can observe each firm's cost, and it may make the price it offers to firm i for the unit of its product depend on both c_i *and* the other firm's cost c_j: $P_i = P_i(c_i, c_j)$. The reason why the regulator would want to do this is because one firm's cost is informative about the effort level of the second firm. To keep the problem simple, as we did in section 3.3.1, suppose that the regulator only considers price formulas that are *linear* in **c**:

$$P_i(c_i, c_j) = \bar{P} + (1 - \rho)c_i + \rho\kappa c_j, \tag{3.21}$$

---

16. For other analyses of yardstick competition as a method of regulation, see Demski and Sappington (1984) and Shleifer (1985). Both papers construct models in which the regulator can use yardstick competition to obtain the first-best level of welfare, so that the asymmetry of information is "competed away" by the two firms. In Demski and Sappington's model the firms possess private information about their costs, and there is no possibility of reducing these costs. Their model also has a number of special assumptions, including the firms' being risk neutral and being able to suffer possibly large losses ex post. More generally, for theoretical treatments of the benefits of using comparative measures of performance for a principal monitoring several agents, see Holmstrom (1982b), Nalebuff and Stiglitz (1983), and Mookherjee (1984).

where the parameters $\bar{P}$, ρ, and κ are to be determined. (Since everything is symmetric, the price rule for each firm is taken to be the same.) Our focus will be on the magnitudes of the parameters ρ, which is related to the level of (own) cost passthrough, and κ, which reflects the sensitivity of one firm's price to other firm's cost.

Given the pricing formula (3.21), the expectation and variance of profit for firm i in this example are equal to

$$E[\pi_i] = \bar{P} - \rho(\mu - e_i) + \rho\kappa(\mu - e_j) - \tfrac{1}{2}e_i^2,$$
$$\text{var}[\pi_i] = \rho^2\sigma^2[1 + \kappa^2 - 2\kappa r].$$

(3.22)

Therefore each firm will choose effort level $e^* = \rho$. Each firm's maximized expected utility, when facing the price rule (3.21), is

$$\bar{P} - \rho(1 - \kappa)(\mu - \rho) - \tfrac{1}{2}\rho^2 - \tfrac{1}{2}\gamma\rho^2\sigma^2[1 + \kappa^2 - 2\kappa r].$$

This is constrained to be no less than some reservation utility level π_1.

The regulator again wishes to minimize the sum of expected prices subject to the firms being willing to participate in the regime. Therefore, after substituting out $\bar{P}$ from the participation constraint the regulator should choose ρ^* and κ^* to be equal to

$$\rho^* = \frac{1}{1 + \gamma\sigma^2(1 - r^2)},$$

(3.23a)

$$\kappa^* = r.$$

(3.23b)

Since κ^* in (3.23b) is always nonnegative, the regulator should make a higher cost observation for one firm result in a higher price for the other firm. This is intuitive: for a given effort level, observing that firm i has a high cost indicates that the parameter θ_i is high and hence that θ_j is also likely to be high, in which case firm j should be compensated with a higher price. The greater is the degree of correlation r, the more sensitive one firm's price should be to the other's cost. In particular, if $r = 0$ so that there is no correlation between the two firms' uncertainty, then the regulator should set $\kappa^* = 0$, and the price for one firm should not depend at all on the other firm's cost. The reason for this is that one firm's cost then gives no information about the conditions faced by the other firm, and so including this cost in the other's price formula serves only to increase the risk for that firm with no compensating benefit. (In this case the expression for the optimal level of (own) cost passthrough (3.23a) reduces to that for the single firm case given by (2.22) in the previous chapter.) If the firms' costs are perfectly correlated ($r = 1$), then one firm's price should depend *only* on the other's cost, and the result is the first-best effort level $e^* = 1$ and there is full insurance for each firm against uncertainty.[17]

This example demonstrates that when there are several regional monopolies with private information that is correlated, the effectiveness of regulation is improved by the use of yardstick regulation rather than by regulating each firm independently (i.e., setting $\kappa = 0$ in (3.21)). The reason for this is that being able to observe a second firm's cost realization improves the precision with which the regulator can infer the effort level of a given firm from its own cost realization.

Under yardstick competition the expected total payment with the regulatory scheme in (3.21) is

$$2(\mu - \rho) + \rho^2 + \gamma\rho^2\sigma^2[1 + \kappa^2 - 2\kappa r] + 2\pi_1,$$

and so substituting from (3.23) means that the minimum expected payment to the two firms is

$$L_{\text{sep}} = 2\mu - \frac{1}{1 + \gamma\sigma^2(1 - r^2)} + 2\pi_1. \tag{3.24}$$

Notice that in contrast to the case of regional integration in (3.14), here the expected total payment *decreases* with the degree of correlation r: the more closely one firm's private information corresponds with the other's, the more effective is yardstick competition.

A natural question in this context is whether a given integrated firm should be broken up regionally in order to reduce the firm's monopoly of information and to take advantage of yardstick competition. By examining (3.14) and (3.24), we see that welfare under integration is decreasing in the correlation r and that welfare with regional separation is increasing with r. Therefore a greater degree of correlation in the firms' environments will, all else being equal, make regional separation relatively more desirable. More generally, there is a trade-off between the enhanced effectiveness of regulation when there are several firms and the possible loss of economies of scale or scope that breakup would involve.[18]

3.5 Dynamic Issues

So far we have been silent about dynamics in this discussion of regulation. In reality regulation is an ongoing process, and decisions that the firm and

---

17. This is essentially an instance of Shleifer's (1985) result.
18. For more on the trade-off between economies of scale and more effective regulation, see Auriol and Laffont (1992) and Dana (1993).

regulator made in the past affect the options available today and in the future. Moreover both parties make current decisions with an eye to what they expect future regulatory policy to be. This section and the next consider dynamic issues, including the use of regulatory lag to promote cost reduction, the use of past observations of the firm's behavior to influence present and future regulatory policy, and problems of regulatory commitment and credibility.

3.5.1 Regulatory Lag

Two aspects of the comparison between "price cap" and "rate-of-return" regulation are (1) the degree of cost passthrough (see section 2.3 and 3.3.1) and (2) the degree of discretion over pricing policy that is given to the firm (see section 3.3.2). Here we consider a third dimension: (3) the length of time between regulatory reviews.[19] Regulatory regimes are not fixed for all time. Industry conditions—involving costs, new products, and the extent of competition—are likely to evolve in ways that are not foreseen, and it will be beneficial to change the regime to meet the changing circumstances, namely to have regulatory reviews. Simplifying somewhat, under traditional rate-of-return regulation the firm's costs and profitability are examined by the regulator each time the firm files a new set of prices, a process that could be described as one of *continual* regulatory review. In contrast, the regulator may wish to commit to a particular regime for a preannounced period of time before the next review occurs, something that usually takes place with price cap regulation.

Suppose, for example, that the firm's costs change over time in a way that is affected by its effort level. Provided that the regulator has sufficient power to precommit future policy for any length of time, there is the option of fixing the firm's regulated price for a predetermined period, and then subsequently revising this price. At each review the regulator can observe the firm's current costs, and must ensure that the fixed price is high enough that the firm is prepared to continue with the regulatory process until the next review.[20] If there are frequent price reviews, then price tracks cost closely, and just as with the cost-plus regulation discussed in section 2.3, the incentives for cost reduction as a result are small. If the price is fixed for a long period, so that there is considerable "regula-

---

19. See Baumol and Klevorick (1970) and Armstrong et al. (1991).
20. If the firm's costs are not accurately observable, then the firm has an incentive either to misrepresent or artificially increase its costs in the lead up to a review in order to obtain more advantageous terms at that review (see section 3.5.3).

tory lag," then the incentives for productive efficiency are greater because the firm can keep any cost savings made for the duration of the regulatory period. (These incentives become less powerful as the end of the review period nears because the firm then keeps its cost savings only for a short time.) However, allocative efficiency may be adversely affected since cost movements over a long period of time will mean costs and prices diverge. The optimal amount of regulatory lag has to trade off the increasing incentive to invest in cost-reducing expenditures against the increased problem of allocative inefficiency and the possible high ex post profits that result from long lags.[21]

The length of regulatory lag is an important aspect of the difference between price cap and rate-of-return regulation. It is clearly a difference of degree rather than of kind. In this section we have mentioned some determinants of the optimal trade-off between allocative efficiency and incentives for dynamic productive efficiency, among other things. In chapter 6 we discuss how regulatory lag and the process of regulatory review are determined in practice in the British experience of $RPI - X$ price cap regulation.

3.5.2 Dynamic Price Cap Mechanisms

In this section we consider dynamic multiproduct regulation when the regulator cannot make lump-sum transfers to the firm. Unlike the discussion of section 3.5.1, we will largely ignore the effects regarding effort incentives and productive efficiency, and suppose that the firm's cost function is exogenous. This cost function is assumed, however, not to be known to the regulator, for otherwise a dynamic version of Ramsey pricing could be implemented.

Dynamic price cap regulation can generally be represented as the following. Time is measured by $t = 0, 1, 2, \ldots$, where t is the number of periods (e.g., years) since regulation began. In each period the firm produces n products, where the price of product i in period t is denoted P_i^t and the vector of prices at t is $\mathbf{P}^t$. In any period t the firm is allowed to choose a price vector $\mathbf{P}^t$ as long as an average price index $I^t(\mathbf{P}^t)$ is less than a cap $\bar{P}^t$. Here the index I^t and cap $\bar{P}^t$ are allowed to vary over time. In particular, they could be modified in the light of previous behavior of the firm. If this is the case, however, the regulator should recognize that the firm may

---

21. If in addition the firm is risk averse, then the insurance properties of short versus long lags will play a role. Since prices track costs more closely with short lags, better insurance against cost movements is obtained under rate-of-return-type regulation.

choose its current prices strategically to make its future price caps more favorable to it.

At the end of section 3.3.2 we noted that the general problem of *optimal* price cap regulation for multiproduct firms remains unresolved in a static, let alone dynamic setting. We will therefore analyze the properties of some simple examples of dynamic price caps.

The Vogelsang-Finsinger Mechanism   A central difference between the dynamic case and the static case of section 3.3.2 is that the regulator can learn about the firm's costs or demand conditions as time evolves. For instance, suppose that the firm has a per-period cost function $C(\mathbf{Q}^t)$ if it produces the vector of quantities $\mathbf{Q}^t$ in period t, and suppose that this cost function is stable over time. Even though the regulator does not know the function $C(\cdot)$, the actual costs incurred by the firm in the previous period, $C(\mathbf{Q}^{t-1})$, may be observable in period t.

Vogelsang and Finsinger (1979) propose an ingenious dynamic mechanism within this framework that has desirable long-run properties, albeit under some strong assumptions. The regulator observes both the total cost $C(\mathbf{Q}^{t-1})$ and the vector of outputs $\mathbf{Q}^{t-1}$ of the previous time period. The firm has a per-period cost function C that exhibits "decreasing ray average costs," that is, for $\lambda > 1$, $C(\lambda \mathbf{Q}) \leq \lambda C(\mathbf{Q})$. The firm is myopic (its discount factor is zero), and initially (at $t = 0$) it is making positive profits. In each period t, and given the observations from the previous period, the regulator requires that the firm's vector of prices $\mathbf{P}^t$ lies in the set

$$\left\{ \mathbf{P} \,\middle|\, \sum_{i=1}^{n} P_i Q_i^{t-1} \leq C(\mathbf{Q}^{t-1}) \right\}. \tag{3.25}$$

In words, the constraint requires that prices in period t should be such that with these prices the previous period's outputs should cost no more than that period's total observed costs (e.g., if the firm produces only one product, this constraint requires the current price to be no greater than the previous period's average cost). The assumption that the firm is myopic means that it chooses its current price vector $\mathbf{P}^t$ from the allowed set (3.25) in order to maximize its *current* period's profits, and ignores the effect its current choice $\mathbf{P}^t$ will have on the constraint (3.25) in subsequent periods and hence on its future profitability. In this case it can be shown that aggregate consumer surplus $V(\mathbf{P}^t)$ rises in each period. Vogelsang and Finsinger show further that in any long-run stationary equilibrium: (1) the firm's profit is zero and, (2), the necessary conditions for Ramsey pricing given by (3.3) hold. (It is straightforward to show that maximizing current profit subject to (3.25) gives first-order conditions which are the same as the Ramsey conditions (3.3) whenever $\mathbf{P}^t = \mathbf{P}^{t-1}$.)

Unfortunately, there are several problems with the Vogelsang-Finsinger mechanism that severely restrict its application. When the cost function does not have decreasing ray average costs, the scheme might result in the firm making a loss, and more important, the concept of a per-period cost function with no intertemporal linkages seems artificial (e.g., there is no durable capital in the model). Moreover it is unclear how the mechanism could cope with changes in technology or movements in factor prices affecting the firm's cost function. Finally, if the assumption of myopia is relaxed, then the firm can have an incentive to indulge in wasteful expenditures in order to relax future constraints. Indeed Sappington (1980) demonstrates that this problem of strategic waste might even reduce total welfare to below the unregulated monopoly level.[22]

Tariff Basket Regulation An alternative regulatory mechanism is the price cap scheme known as the *tariff basket* mechanism. Here no information on past costs is needed, and the regulator requires that the firm's price vector in period t lies in the set

$$\left\{ \mathbf{P} \,\middle|\, \sum_{i=1}^{n} P_i Q_i^{t-1} \leq \sum_{i=1}^{n} P_i^{t-1} Q_i^{t-1} \right\}. \tag{3.26}$$

Thus the firm's prices in period t must be such that, with these prices, the previous period's outputs cost consumers no more than they cost with the previous period's prices (i.e., constraint (3.26) requires that the Laspeyres price index be no greater than 1 in each period). Using the same argument as in section 3.3.2 on regulation with fixed weights, this form of regulation necessarily entails consumer surplus $V(\mathbf{P}^t)$ rising over time. The present scheme has fixed weights within the period, but, since one period's prices determine the next period's weights, the weights are endogenous over time. It can be shown that a nonmyopic firm maximizing the discounted value of its profits subject to (3.26) will set prices in a steady state that satisfy the Ramsey conditions (3.3) (see Vogelsang 1989). Intuitively, if prices in the steady state did not have the Ramsey property, then profits

---

22. For suggested improvements to the Vogelsang-Finsinger mechanism, both involving the regulator making lump-sum transfers to the firm, see Finsinger and Vogelsang (1982) and Hagerman (1990).

would not be maximized subject to the given consumer surplus level. The firm could then find prices that satisfy the tariff basket constraint and yield higher profits.

The tariff basket mechanism has an unambiguously positive effect on welfare relative to requiring the firm to keep its prices fixed at some initial level $\mathbf{P}^0$. Consumer surplus rises each period, and the present value of profits must exceed the present value of the profit stream with fixed prices, since the constraint (3.26) allows the firm always to choose the initial vector of prices $\mathbf{P}^0$ if it so wishes. Unlike the Vogelsang-Finsinger mechanism, the tariff basket price cap does not require the firm to return previous profits to consumers, so the price cap does not generate full allocative efficiency and does not eliminate the firm's rents over time. On the other hand, the tariff basket mechanism will encourage productive efficiency because costs are not mentioned in the constraint. Effort will be optimal given the prices that are set, and there will never be any wasteful expenditures.

Of course, as discussed in the previous section, in practice no system of regulation is set to last forever, and a regulator will inevitably take observed costs into account at a time of regulatory review. In such cases the regulatory scheme will be a mixture of the tariff basket and Vogelsang-Finsinger schemes.

In Britain versions of the tariff basket mechanism are used to cap the prices of BT and the water companies, although the constraint is modified to allow for "normal" productivity improvements by adding the factor X. In this case the constraint (3.26) becomes

$$\sum_{i=1}^{n} P_i^t Q_i^{t-1} \leq (1 - X) \sum_{i=1}^{n} P_i^{t-1} Q_i^{t-1}.$$

See chapter 6 for more details about how X is chosen in practice.

Average Revenue Regulation   Average revenue regulation clearly can be implemented in a dynamic context just as in the static context considered in section 3.3.2, with the constraint set (3.19) being set to hold in each period t. A practical issue is that total demands in period t, $\mathbf{Q}^t$, are not accurately known until the end of the period, whereas prices, loosely speaking, are set at the start of the period. Therefore, when particular prices are filed, it is not possible to check ex ante whether they will turn out to satisfy the average revenue constraint in that period. Because of this demands typically must be forecast for the coming year, and any in-accuracies that occur ex post are settled at the end of the period.

Perhaps to avoid this complication, an alternative dynamic average revenue scheme is used in the United States to regulate some services supplied by AT&T. Sappington and Sibley (1992) discuss a stylized version of this AT&T price cap which they call the "average revenue (lagged)" scheme. As in section 3.3.2 it works only for products that are commensurable, in which case the constraint is that in period t the price vector $\mathbf{P}^t$ is required to lie in the set

$$\left\{ \mathbf{P} \,\middle|\, \sum_{i=1}^{n} P_i Q_i^{t-1} \leq \sum_{i=1}^{n} \overline{P} Q_i^{t-1} \right\}, \tag{3.27}$$

where $\overline{P}$ is the per-period cap on average revenue. This is a dynamic version of average revenue regulation that uses the previous rather than the current period's quantities to define average revenue. As in section 3.1.2, two-part tariffs can be incorporated into this framework by interpreting one of the products as "access," with a corresponding price given by the fixed part of the two-part tariff. Sappington and Sibley show by example that when the firm sets a two-part tariff, the rebalancing between the fixed charge and the marginal price(s) can generate a decline in both consumer surplus and total welfare over time.

As with tariff basket regulation, in both Britain and the United States average revenue regulation is modified in practice to take account of expected productivity improvements and efficiency gains over time by means of an RPI $- X$ factor. In this case the per-period average revenue cap $\overline{P}$ is reduced in real percentage terms by the factor X.

3.5.3 Optimal Dynamic Regulation with Transfers

The above mechanisms were not optimal. For instance, the observation of the firm's choice of prices in one period presumably gives the regulator some information about costs, information that could be used to improve welfare in subsequent periods. It may be, for instance, that the firm sets its price for one product higher than the regulator expected, which could reveal the firm to have higher costs for that product than previously was thought. If, however, past choices by the firm *are* used to update the regulator's views on conditions in the industry, this raises the possibility that the firm will choose its present behavior strategically in order to obtain a more favorable regime in the future. For this reason it may be that social welfare would be greater ex ante if the regulator could commit *not* to use information revealed by the firm when deciding future policy. We will discuss this point in more detail in the next section, but we first consider a simple model.[23]

Here we describe a dynamic version of Baron and Myerson's model of hidden information in which the firm operates for two periods rather than just one. (The argument would be affected little if the firm produced for $T > 2$ periods.) The firm's unit cost θ, which is unobservable by the regulator, is assumed to be the same in each of the two periods. Depending on whether or not the regulator has the power to precommit to future strategy, there are two possibilities to consider: (1) the regulator commits to give the firm a single lump-sum transfer of $T(P^1, P^2)$ at the end of the two periods if the firm is observed to charge P^t in period t, or (2), the regulator gives the firm $T_1(P^1)$ in period 1 and then, in the light of the firm's choice in the first period, offers the firm the transfer schedule $T_2(P^1, P^2)$ in the second period, this schedule being designed to maximize welfare in the second period.

Since any policy followed under case 2 is feasible with the commitment case 1, it is simple to see that the level of welfare attainable under case 1 must be at least as great as in the no-commitment case 2. By using the analysis in section 2.2.2, it is possible to show for case 1 that the optimal schedule simply replicates the single-period optimal transfer schedule. So if $T^*(P)$ is the optimal transfer schedule in the single-period problem of section 2.2.2, then the optimal two-period schedule is given by $T^*(P^1)/\delta + T^*(P^2)$, where δ is the discount factor. In this case the type θ firm will choose $P^1(\theta)$ and $P^2(\theta)$ to maximize its present discounted profits

$$(P^1 - \theta)Q(P^1) + T^*(P^1) + \delta[(P^2 - \theta)Q(P^2) + T^*(P^2)]$$

and so will choose the same price in each period. This price is $P^*(\theta)$, the optimal price response function in the single-period case (given by (2.16)). In the commitment case, then, the optimum is just the single-period Baron and Myerson solution repeated over time.

In the no-commitment case 2, however, matters are more complex. The commitment outcome simply is not feasible if the regulator cannot commit not to use any information obtained in the first period to improve welfare in the second period. Indeed, if the type θ firm's first-period price

---

23. See Baron and Besanko (1987), Laffont and Tirole (1988b, 1993, ch. 9) and Baron (1989, sec. 6).

is given by the function $P^1 = P^*(\theta)$, from (2.16) we see that different types of firm generally choose different prices. In other words, by observing the firm choose the price $P^*(\theta)$, the regulator is able to infer that the firm has unit cost θ, in which case the optimal policy in the second period is to set price $P^2 = \theta$, to make no transfer to the firm, and hence to obtain the first-best outcome in the second period. Anticipating this future behavior, the firm will find it optimal to deviate from the price $P^1 = P^*(\theta)$ in the first period in order to obtain some positive profit in the second period. For instance, consider what happens if the type θ firm pretends to be the slightly higher cost firm $\theta + d\theta$ in the first period, so it chooses the price $P^1 = P^*(\theta + d\theta)$ rather than $P^*(\theta)$. From the optimality of $P^*(\theta)$ in the single-period case, it thereby makes only a second-order loss in the first period. But since the second-period price as a result will be $\theta + d\theta$ rather than θ, this strategy increases its profit by order $d\theta$ in the second period, and hence its total profit overall.[24] Therefore the commitment strategy is no longer incentive compatible, and the fact that the regulator is unable to make binding commitments results in a loss of welfare compared with the commitment case. This is an instance of the general phenomenon known as the *ratchet effect* (see also Freixas et al. 1985). Because the regulator cannot accurately observe the firm's costs at the end of the first period, the firm has an extra incentive to pretend to have higher costs than it really has in order to obtain a more favorable regime in the second period.[25]

3.6 The Problem of Commitment, Underinvestment, and Regulatory Risk

Whereas in the previous section the problem concerned the regulator's temptation to exploit revealed information, we now turn to the temptation that might exist for the regulator to exploit the sunk cost nature of the

---

24. The above argument demonstrates that in the welfare-maximizing, no-commitment policy there must be a degree of *pooling* in the first period, in the sense that different types of firm will find it optimal to choose the same price in the first period in order not to give the regulator too much information (Laffont and Tirole 1993, sec. 9.3).

25. The preceding discussion focused on the adverse selection information problem, but the ratchet effect can also be modeled in a moral hazard framework (see Milgrom and Roberts 1992, 232–36). If a firm can reduce its costs by expending effort, and if future prices depend upon present costs, then the firm has less incentive to reduce costs, and productive inefficiency will result. The Vogelsang-Finsinger mechanism, discussed in section 3.5.2, was an extreme way to make future prices depend on current costs, and Sappington (1980) showed that strategic behavior of the firm—the ratchet effect—can make this mechanism result in a lower level of welfare than unregulated monopoly.

firm's capital investments.[26] This is a serious problem for effective and efficient regulation, and we discuss it further in chapter 6.

A simple example suffices to illustrate the problem. A regulated firm is considering whether to undertake some major piece of capital construction which, if built, will last for a number of years. For instance, suppose that a water supply company is deciding whether to build a new reservoir. This reservoir has a fixed construction cost of K, and once built, the cost is sunk and has no other use. The reservoir supplies water at a constant unit cost of c. Suppose that the welfare-maximizing regulator chooses the price P for the company's water after the investment has been sunk. (This is a natural move order, since investment decisions typically are long term and irreversible; prices have no such inertia.) If the reservoir is built, the regulator chooses the price P to maximize welfare subject to the firm being prepared to continue with the regulatory process. The firm is prepared to continue provided that the price at least covers the firm's future *avoidable* costs, i.e., provided that $P \geq c$. Therefore the ex post optimal price is given by $P = c$, and the first-best outcome is attained.

However, before the investment is sunk, the firm will recognize that price will be set equal to marginal cost—a policy that will not cover the firm's avoidable costs when viewed from that point in time. The result is that if the firm chooses to construct the reservoir, it will make a loss of K. If the regulator truly is unable to resist setting price equal to marginal cost after the firm's investment has been sunk, the investment will not take place. Because the firm anticipates that welfare will be maximized ex post, welfare is reduced ex ante.

3.6.1 Overcoming the Commitment Problem

The preceding example shows that the fact that a regulator lacks the power to precommit to future policy could well give rise to underinvestment relative to the policy with commitment.[27] If in the example the

---

26. This problem of ex post opportunism is discussed in Williamson (1975). See further the discussion of its role in the analysis of integration between firms in section 5.1.1.

27. This contrasts with the early contribution of Averch and Johnson's (1962) analysis of overinvestment by the firm facing rate-of-return regulation. They showed that if in a static model the allowed rate of return exceeds the firm's cost of capital, then the firm has an incentive to expand its capital base beyond the extent that is efficient for the output level that it produces. However, in recent years focus has shifted to the danger of under- rather than overinvestment as the crucial problem, partly because of policy developments. One recent exception to this, however, is Besanko and Spulber (1992) who present a model with asymmetric information about costs. As above, the move order involves the firm making its

regulator *could* commit to a particular price in advance of the firm's investment decision, then it is clear that the optimal (linear) price should be the lowest price that covers the firm's total cost, so that there is average rather than marginal cost pricing. In effect, this means that the regulator commits to give the firm a "fair" rate of return on its investment. Greenwald (1984) provides a discussion of how such a commitment to a fair rate of return—sometimes a legal or constitutional requirement of regulation (albeit one open to various interpretations)—has the twin advantages of safeguarding investors against ex post opportunism and of giving the regulator flexibility to respond to changing circumstances.

However, while a guarantee that the firm makes a fair return on all its investments has good incentive properties for encouraging a high level of investment over time, it does have rather poor incentive effects in other respects. For instance, it entails that inefficient or unnecessary projects be rewarded at the same same rate as efficient projects. Because of this problem, judicial precedent for rate-of-return regulation in the United States requires the regulator to allow a fair return only on capital that is considered to be "used and useful."

Gilbert and Newbery (1988) examine the effect of this legal constraint on the regulator's behavior in a model in which there is uncertainty about demand. Consider this simplified version of their model. There are an infinite number of production periods, and the firm decides its level of capacity Q before the regulator sets the price in each period. Capital depreciates completely after one period, per-unit cost is c, and the cost of using capacity is zero. Demand in each period is inelastic and equal either to one unit or $1 - x$ units of the product provided that the price is no greater than one (demand is zero for larger prices). Without any judicial constraints binding regulatory behavior, it might be difficult for the regulator to commit credibly not to expropriate the firm, and the temptation to cheat might be too great to sustain an equilibrium of the infinite horizon game with efficient investment. Suppose, however, that the regulator is constrained by the courts (as is broadly the case in the United States) to allow a fair rate of return on "used and useful" assets. In the context of this

---

investment decision before the regulator decides the price, the regulator being unable to commit to any particular price response to the observed level of investment. The fact that the firm has private information about its costs means that the regulator is unable ex post to set price equal to average avoidable costs. The firm's investment decision acts as a signal of its type, and in some circumstances it turns out that this signaling effect overcomes the tendency toward underinvestment, and the firm will choose to invest *more* than is socially optimal.

model this means that in the high-demand state the firm is guaranteed a fair return on 1 unit of capacity, and in the low-demand state the firm obtains a fair return on $1 - x$ units of capacity. Under this rule the firm is not protected against ex post opportunism altogether, but some protection is offered.

Salant and Woroch (1992) show how a welfare-maximizing regulator might not wish to deviate from a pricing policy that results in a moderately efficient investment path (depending on parameter values) even when there is no constitutional guarantee that the firm should break even. Suppose again that there are an infinite number of periods of production, and let δ be the discount factor. Once invested, capital does not depreciate over time (which makes the risk of expropriation especially great). As above, the cost per unit of investment is c, there are no variable costs of production and demand in each period is inelastic and equal to one unit of the product provided the price is no greater than one, and demand is zero for larger prices. (There is no demand uncertainty in this model.) The regulator's objective is to maximize total consumer surplus over time. (Little would be changed if α, the weight on profits, were positive, as long as $\alpha < 1$.) At the start of each period the firm decides on its level of investment for that period, and then the regulator sets the price for that period. The regulator has no means of committing to a particular future pricing strategy (nor can the firm commit to a particular investment policy).

Suppose that the efficient level of capacity is $Q^* = 1$. (This is true provided that the cost of providing a unit of capacity c is less than the discounted flow of benefits, which is $\{1 + \delta + \delta^2 + \cdots\} = 1/(1 - \delta)$. Therefore assume that $c < 1/(1 - \delta)$ in what follows.) Write P_t for the price and Q_t for the level of capacity at time t so that the cost of the firm's investment just prior to time t is $c(Q_t - Q_{t-1})$. The firm will not choose to invest immediately in the efficient level of capacity Q^* because it foresees that, if it did so, the regulator will subsequently choose $P_t = 0$ for all time, and it would make a loss of c. (Recall that capacity is infinitely durable.) Moreover, if the capacity level ever reached Q^*, the regulator would subsequently set price equal to zero, and the firm would make a loss on its final piece of investment. Therefore we can deduce that there is no way that the efficient capacity level Q^* could ever actually be attained when there is no regulatory commitment.

However, consider the following time path for capacity

$$Q_t = 1 - \varepsilon^t, \tag{3.28}$$

where ε is some number (less than one) yet to be determined. With this path the capacity level is asymptotically efficient, and the speed of convergence is inversely related to the magnitude of ε. When can the path (3.28) credibly be implemented? Suppose that the regulator claims that prices will be set so that all investment made by the firm prior to a given production period will always be reimbursed within that period, that is, that $P_t Q_t = c(Q_t - Q_{t-1})$.[28] From (3.28) this time path of prices is given by

$$P_t = \frac{c(1 - \varepsilon)\varepsilon^{t-1}}{1 - \varepsilon^t}. \tag{3.29}$$

With this pricing policy, then, price falls asymptotically to zero over time. If the firm believes that the regulator will in fact carry out this pricing policy, then it is (just) in its interest to follow the investment policy (3.28).

Since the regulator cannot *commit* to pursue the policy (3.29), we must check that it is in its interest to do so. Consider the first period. Suppose that the firm has invested according to (3.28) so that the initial capacity level is $Q_1 = 1 - \varepsilon$. The regulator then has two options, either to cheat and set price equal to zero for all periods or to cooperate and set price $P_1 = c$ according to (3.29). (In fact it is not hard to see that if the regulator ever chooses to cheat, the cheating will occur in the first period.) With cheating, total discounted welfare is

$$(1 - \varepsilon)(1 + \delta + \delta^2 \ldots) = \frac{1 - \varepsilon}{1 - \delta},$$

whereas, if there is cooperation (for all time), total welfare is

$$\sum_{t=1}^{\infty} \delta^{t-1} Q_t(1 - P_t) = \frac{1}{1 - \delta} - \frac{\varepsilon + c(1 - \varepsilon)}{1 - \delta\varepsilon}.$$

Therefore, the pricing policy (3.29) is credible to the firm provided that the latter is greater than the former, that is, if

$$\varepsilon \geq \frac{c(1 - \delta)}{\delta}. \tag{3.30}$$

The closer δ is to one—the less discounting there is—the smaller ε can be implemented, and hence the quicker can be the convergence to the efficient point. The fact that the firm and regulator meet repeatedly means that

---

28. In Britain price regulation for the water industry (an industry in which ex post opportunism might be thought to be particularly great because asset lives are especially long) was set partly with a view to financing investment expenditure as it occurs.

although a degree of underinvestment always remains, in the limit the optimal level of capacity is achieved.[29]

3.6.2 Discussion

The simple model where a firm was considering whether or not to build a new reservoir, knowing that the regulator subsequently would choose the price, served to illustrate the danger of underinvestment when the regulator cannot precommit future policy. One possible way to overcome this problem is to give the firm some legal or constitutional right to earn a fair return on its investments (or at least those investments that are judged to have been prudent). In this regard much depends on the political, legal, and institutional framework, and much depends on the ways that a "fair" return and capital assets are measured. Salant and Woroch suggest a second and partial solution to this problem: if the firm and regulator meet repeatedly over a long period (and if capital does not come in too lumpy a form and can be spread over time), the regulator could agree to investment being done in stages, with the cost of each stage being met as soon as it is completed. Provided that condition (3.30) holds, the regulator has no incentive to deviate from this. A third possible way out of the credibility problem could involve the mechanism of regulatory *reputation*, where it may be in the interests of the regulator to build up a reputation for giving the firm a fair return on its investment in order to induce future efficient investment.

The problem of ex post opportunism discussed above involved the regulator exploiting the fact that the firm's investment was sunk and irreversible. There are several other sources of regulatory risk. Another concerns future policy toward liberalization in the industry. If a firm believes there is chance that there will be free and effective entry at some point in the future—entry, say, that forces it to set price equal to marginal cost—then the result might again be to remove the incentive for the firm to engage in sunk investment. A further source of risk is future changes in environmental policy. For instance, electricity generators might be wary of a future carbon tax. Another risk is the possibility that the regulated firm will be

---

29. As with repeated games generally, the possibility of cooperation is very sensitive to the assumption that the two parties meet *infinitely* often. If there are a known finite number of production periods and complete information, it is not hard to show that the only equilibrium is the firm never making any investment. If the game between regulator and firm is one of incomplete information, however, then reputation mechanisms might assist credibility, at least for some of the time.

subject to some kind of structural reorganization. For instance, we will see in chapter 5 below that it may be desirable to divest an integrated incumbent firm of its natural monopoly operations in order to facilitate greater competition in other areas (notably as occurred to AT&T, and might have happened to British Gas; see chapter 8). Finally, there is the risk that the firm may be (re)nationalized on unfair terms at some point in the future. Anticipation of this event, which could be caused by a change of government, would again lead to reduced investment on the part of the firm.[30] For a further discussion of regulatory risk and the way in which it might increase the regulated firm's cost of capital, see section 6.1.

3.7   The Problem of Regulatory Capture

In our benchmark model of regulation, the regulator was omniscient, had the power to precommit to policy, and had benevolent objectives. So far in this chapter we have discussed departures from the first two of these assumptions. We now consider the effect of the regulator acting in ways that are not always aligned to social welfare. Naturally this too will usually cause a reduction in the effectiveness of regulation.[31]

Ideally of course a regulator should act in the interests of society as a whole. Several authors, including Stigler (1971), Posner (1971, 1974), and Peltzman (1976), have questioned whether this is a realistic assumption and consider the possibility of *regulatory capture*, where the regulator instead acts in the interests of incumbents in the industry rather than those of consumers or potential entrants to the industry. For instance, it has been argued that prior to recent deregulation, the regulatory bodies for the telecommunications, airline, and trucking industries in the United States acted to restrict entry, with the result that prices were higher and

---

30. Each of these sources of regulatory risk might be eased if there were widespread ownership of the firm's shares, in which case a government would be wary of such expropriation.
31. However, it is just possible that one kind of regulatory failure might ease another. Salant (1991) considers the effect on welfare of former regulators obtaining appointments in the firms they previously regulated. The firm and regulators meet repeatedly over time, and the firm makes sunk-cost investments that expose it to the problem of ex post opportunism on the part of these regulators. All else being equal, this would lead to underinvestment and low profits for the firm. However, because the regulator will later be employed by the firm at a rate that depends on the profitability of the firm, this provides an incentive to the regulator not to engage in opportunistic behavior. The result is that the apparently corrupt practice of regulators later working for the firms that they regulate might conceivably—but not in our view in fact—serve to improve the level of investment and welfare.

choice was less than was the case after deregulation. This body of work focuses on who are the winners and losers in the regulatory process, associated rent seeking, and the incentives facing the regulators themselves to act for or against various groups in society.

When the prices of a regulated firm are set, the regulator must trade off the desires of consumers for low prices against that of the firm for high prices and high profits. In practice, regulators are given a relatively vague mandate and have a degree of discretion over policy. Indeed industry-specific regulators typically are employed because they have or will gain specialist knowledge of the industry, and in such cases it is natural for Parliament or Congress to delegate much decision making to them. Writers on capture suggest that regulators might use whatever discretion is at their disposal to favor whichever group brings the most pressure to bear on their decision making. In addition to straightforward bribery, regulated firms can and do offer former regulators lucrative appointments within the firm. So there is the danger that there may be implicit contracts of some kind between regulators and firms, stating that a generous regime now will be rewarded by generous remuneration when they are no longer public servants. Moreover managers of regulated firms tend to meet with regulators on a regular basis and to be a more coherent and better-organized lobbying group than consumers.

To counter the temptations to favor the industry interests, there should ideally be countervailing incentives for regulators to serve consumers. A theoretical way to do this might be to make their income depend in some way on consumer surplus, say. However, such performance-related pay suffers from the general problems of measuring consumer surplus, and anyway, the regulator is likely to be much better informed about its performance than the government. Instead, factors—such as promotion, status, and official recognition—that control the activity of public servants generally will probably be all that can be done.

Laffont and Tirole (1991, 1993, ch. 11) offer a formal model involving the possibility of capture that explains one reason why it is that regulators generally are not permitted to make lump-sum transfers to the firms they regulate. For much of this and the previous chapter we assumed that the regulator was unable to make such transfers, even though within the framework of the models this would have made regulation more effective, for instance, by making marginal cost pricing a feasible option. Intuitively this restriction of a regulator's set of policy tools seems to have something to do with the possibility of capture, in that it gives "too much" discretion to regulators, discretion that may be manipulated by the firm's ability to influence the process. However, on the surface it is not clear why it is that the ability of a regulator to make lump-sum transfers makes the process more susceptible to capture than the ability to set prices: Why should a regulator be constrained in the use of transfers rather than in the prices that may be charged? One natural reason might be that consumers are much more aware of high prices—because they themselves have to pay them—than high transfers that are taken out of general taxation revenue. In other words, consumers are better able to monitor a regulator's behavior if prices, not transfers, are the policy tool, and this may reduce the chance of capture.

Regulation in the Laffont and Tirole model works as follows: before the start of the actual regulatory process, an incomplete "constitution" for regulators is drafted by Parliament. The particular decision those drafting the rules have to make is whether or not to allow the regulator to make lump-sum transfers. The firm has private information concerning its fixed cost of operation, and this information is known also to the regulator. The regulator is assumed to act in the industry's interest if it is profitable to do so. In this instance, "capture" means the regulator reporting that the firm has higher costs than it in fact does, and if this occurs there is the possibility that the regulator will be found out (e.g., by consumer watchdogs) and punished. If the regulator behaves benevolently, it is clear that welfare is higher if lump-sum transfers are allowed, since in that case first-best marginal cost pricing is feasible. However, regulation with and without transfers involves different costs for preventing capture and gives the consumer watchdogs different monitoring incentives. Indeed, for certain parameter values of the model, these differing incentive effects can outweigh the allocative efficiency effects with the result that a ban on transfers could improve welfare overall.

This model illustrates a general point: if there is a risk of capture, it could be desirable to limit the discretion of the regulator (in the above model, the discretion to offer lump-sum transfers to the firm), not just to prevent the worst excesses of capture but also to reduce the incentive for the firm to expend wasteful resources on rent seeking. Another instance of a limit on regulatory conduct is the attempt by Congress (in the 1978 Ethics in Government Act) to prevent certain regulators from obtaining employment in the firms that they regulated for a number of years after their retirement from public service.

There are few strong conclusions that can be drawn from the literature on capture other than the need to give regulators as well as firms incentives and limits on authority to behave in a socially desirable way. The view embodied in most models of the regulatory process, which have the firm's managers solely pursuing profit and the regulator selflessly pursuing social good, is something of a caricature, albeit a rather illuminating one provided that wider issues are not lost from sight. Just as those running the firm may have aims wider than profit maximization, there is the danger that regulators could be tempted to act other than in the public interest, especially if they are encouraged to do so by the firm.

3.8   Conclusions

The purpose of this chapter has been to extend the analysis of chapter 2 to cases where the regulated firm makes more than one product and where production takes place over time. In addition we considered the effect on regulation of having more than one regulated firm and the problem of regulatory capture.

In section 3.1 we examined the benchmark case of symmetric information between firm and regulator concerning industry conditions. First-best regulation involves setting prices equal to marginal costs, but there is the familiar problem that such prices might not cover the firm's fixed costs. Therefore, unless lump-sum transfers are possible, marginal cost pricing is not an option for such industries. The prices that maximize social welfare subject to the constraint that the firm break even, Ramsey prices, involve price/marginal cost markups across the various products, the markups depending upon own-price and cross-price elasticities of demand. Typically prices exceed marginal costs. Two-part tariffs and peak-load pricing were discussed within this Ramsey framework.

Ramsey prices rarely are implemented in practice, however. Indeed prices of regulated utilities often fail to reflect basic cost differences from one customer to another, let alone the demand elasticity factors required for Ramsey pricing. One reason has to do with ex ante regulatory or political preferences for particular pricing structures—for instance, for geographically uniform prices—perhaps justified by a notion of fairness. Another reason why Ramsey prices are difficult to implement is that they require too much information about both demand and cost conditions in the industry.

Section 3.2 relaxed the assumption that the regulator is as well informed about cost conditions as the firm, and multiproduct extensions of the models of asymmetric information discussed in chapter 2 were examined. Just as with the single-product case, private information allows low cost firms to make rents from the regulatory process. Because of distributional concerns, it is desirable to keep these rents low. It is also desirable to maintain allocative and productive efficiency, and the regulatory problem is to design the regime in order to trade off the three factors optimally. In models of hidden information about costs (where productive efficiency is not an issue), it is optimal to have price/marginal cost markups to reduce the firm's rents, whereas in Laffont and Tirole's model with possibilities for cost reduction, in simple cases it is optimal to have allocative efficiency and to use the transfer purely to encourage cost-reducing effort on the part of the firm.

When transfers are not available, prices need to play the dual role of maintaining allocative efficiency *and* giving the firm incentives for cost reduction. In section 3.3 we discussed ways to regulate multiproduct firms using prices alone. After discussing the desirable extent of cost pass-through in a multiproduct firm, we analyzed some simple forms of price cap regulation. The main policy question in this context is how much and what form of discretion to give the firm over the prices it offers: Should the firm be instructed to offer some fixed price vector, for instance, or should only some index of its average price be controlled? Subject to the important proviso that there is no actual or potential competition in any of the firm's markets (see section 4.3), we argued that the firm should be given some leeway in setting its prices, the reason being that prices can then track costs, albeit loosely, which improves allocative efficiency. Given that this is the case, the question remains: How should the firm's average price be calculated? Different indexes of average price have differing consequences for welfare.

In section 3.4 we discussed yardstick competition when there are several regionally distinct firms in the same industry. Unless there is no correlation in the cost conditions from one region to another, we saw that regulation could be made more effective if the price one firm could charge is made to depend not only on that firm's costs but also on the costs of other firms. If other firms are observed to have low costs, this implies that the firm in question probably is also capable of obtaining low costs, and hence that the price for that firm should be low. The mechanism by which yardstick competition works is that it improves the precision of the regulator's information about firms and so helps prices stay in line with costs, at the same time giving firms incentives for cost reduction. The more closely the environment of one firm resembles another's, the more effective yardstick competition can be made to be.

Dynamics were introduced into the analysis in sections 3.5 and 3.6, and this brought the issue of policy credibility to the fore. If the regulator has sufficient authority to precommit future policy for some length of time ahead, it may be beneficial for the regulator to commit to a period of stable prices—regardless of how costs and profits evolve over the period—in order to give the firm an incentive to cut costs and so achieve greater profits. The benefits of this cost reduction are returned to consumers at the end of the regulatory period. The drawback of having too great a regulatory lag is that allocative efficiency is impaired if cost diverges from price. In section 3.5 we also considered some particular dynamic regulatory mechanisms and their effect on welfare over time. The Vogelsang-Finsinger mechanism has some attractive qualities but requires strong assumptions that limit its applicability. On the other hand, the "tariff basket" mechanism also has some attractive features— welfare increases over time and in the limit a form of Ramsey pricing is attained—and needs fewer assumptions but has the drawbacks that the firm ends up with (possibly large) rents and that cost and demand conditions are required to be stable over time. When the firm possesses private information about its costs, there is the possibility that the regulator might use past observations of the firm's behavior to update beliefs about costs, something that would improve welfare ex post. However, if the firm believes that the regulator will indeed do this, a ratchet effect operates, and the firm will try to hide some of its private information early on so as to earn high rents subsequently. The result is that welfare ex ante is improved if the regulator can commit *not* to use information revealed by the firm for future policy.

This principle—that the regulator being unable to precommit future policy acts to reduce welfare ex ante—holds in many different situations. In section 3.6 we saw that underinvestment was a danger when the regulator could not commit not to bring price down to some low level after a sunk-cost investment had been made (a policy which, ex post, could well be desirable). However, the fact that regulation takes place in a dynamic setting—the source of the credibility problem—in some circumstances can also help cure the underinvestment problem insofar as policy credibility and regulatory reputation can be built up over time.

Finally, in section 3.7 we raised the possibility that the regulator might not necessarily fit the possibly idealized picture of perfect benevolence. If there is a danger that the regulator will be persuaded to act in the regulated firm's interests, then constraints on regulatory discretion—for example, the inability to make lump-sum transfers to the firm—may be desirable. In the following two chapters the analysis is taken further to allow for competition in some or all of the regulated firm's markets.

4

Competition and Liberalization

Liberalization[1]—the removal of restrictions on competition—has been a major theme of public policy toward industry in many countries in recent years.[2] In the United States, liberalization in the airlines, trucking, financial services, and telecommunications industries began in the 1970s, but it was in the 1980s that liberalization became widespread. Various economic, technological, and political factors have motivated liberalization, and it has sometimes been related to policies of ownership reform. In Britain in particular, privatization and liberalization policies have interacted, sometimes in curious ways. In the utilities there have been important measures of liberalization in telecommunications (apparatus, network operation, and service provision), gas (supply to larger users), and electricity (generation and supply to larger users). These developments will be examined in later chapters.

Starting from a situation in which one firm has a protected monopoly in an activity that is potentially competitive, there are three broad policy questions. First, should legal barriers to entry be removed, and if so, is complete laissez-faire appropriate or should there be more limited licensing of one or two new entrants? Second, should the operations of the former monopolist be broken into separately owned competing units, or should it be left intact? Third, will liberalization do away with the need for regulation, and if not, how should competition and regulation policies be related to one another?

The aim of this chapter is to analyze some of the economic principles that are relevant for answering these questions. Just as monopoly regulation was viewed as an incentive mechanism in the last two chapters, the competitive process is regarded as an incentive mechanism here. Both mechanisms are more or less imperfect: there are market failures as well as regulatory failures. Competition is not always efficient and neither is it always effective.

---

1. The removal of restrictions on competition is often referred to as "deregulation." However, "deregulation" can also mean the removal of regulation (e.g., price control). To avoid confusion, we therefore use "liberalization" to mean the opening up of competition.
2. See OECD (1992). On the performance of deregulation in the United States, see Winston (1993).

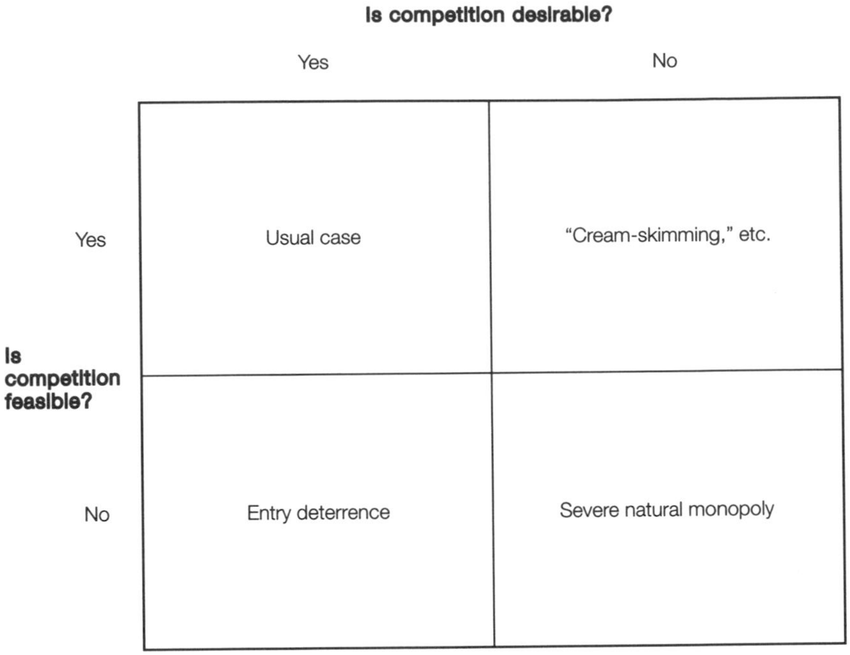

Is competition desirable?

	Yes	No
Yes	Usual case	"Cream-skimming," etc.
No	Entry deterrence	Severe natural monopoly

Is competition feasible?

Figure 4.1   The desirability and feasibility of competition

This last point is illustrated by figure 4.1, which distinguishes between the normative question of whether competition is desirable and the positive question of whether it is feasible. In most industries (top-left box) competition is certainly beneficial and circumstances are such that it flourishes naturally or at least with the safeguards of general competition policy. But this cannot be said of the utility industries, where competition problems exist in combination. In severe natural monopoly conditions (bottom-right box) competition is inefficient, and even if liberalization did occur, it is unlikely that any competition would come about. In these circumstances (analyzed in chapters 2 and 3) regulation has to be relied upon.

However, there are major parts of the utility industries, and indeed other industries, where competition is probably very desirable but where a dominant incumbent firm may thwart potential rivals by anticompetitive practices unless prevented from doing so (bottom-left box). In these cases laissez-faire does not imply effective competition, and there is an important role for procompetitive regulation (as distinct from monopoly regulation, e.g., price control). On the other hand it is sometimes claimed that there is a danger that liberalization will lead to too much competition (top-right box), for example, that "cream-skimming" of the most profitable business by entrants will undermine the sustainability of the business as a whole.

The chapter is organized as follows. The next two sections respectively concern the efficiency and the effectiveness of competition. Section 4.1 examines advantages and disadvantages of competition relative to the alternative of regulation, the contestable markets approach based on assumptions of "ultra-free" entry, trade-offs between allocative efficiency and cost efficiency when there are scale economies, and relationships between competition, information, and incentives.

The way that incumbent advantages may undermine the effectiveness of competition is the focus of section 4.2 on entry barriers. There is a distinction between entry barriers that arise from asymmetric opportunities (e.g., privileged incumbent access to particular inputs of production such as transmission networks) and those arising from strategic asymmetries (the incumbent's first-mover advantage). Both are important in the utility industries, and a question for liberalization policy is whether to assist entrants.

Section 4.3 analyzes some ways in which competition and regulation can interact, including franchising, the regulation of a dominant firm that faces a relatively small amount of competition, and multimarket interactions including the danger of regulation distorting competition. Finally, it should be noted this chapter concentrates on purely horizontal competition questions. Competition and regulation policy in vertically related industries is the subject of chapter 5.

4.1   Competition and Efficiency

4.1.1   A Basic Model of Liberalization

The desirability of competition depends on how it compares with the alternative of regulation. Monopoly regulation in the following setting was analyzed in section 2.2.2. The monopolist, firm M, has fixed cost K, which is a sunk cost, and marginal cost θ. The regulator, whose objective is the maximization of a weighted sum of consumer surplus and profit, cannot observe θ, which has prior distribution $F(\theta)$. This asymmetry of information is the source of regulatory failure: the regulator must compromise between allocative efficiency (price P close to marginal cost θ) and distributional efficiency (limiting the rent M gets from its monopoly of information). Productive efficiency is attained anyway because there are exogenously given natural monopoly cost conditions. The optimally regulated price exceeds marginal cost, thus compromising between allocative and distributional efficiency. To be precise, when transfers are possible, optimal regulation implies that

$$P^*(\theta) = \theta + (1 - \alpha)\frac{F(\theta)}{f(\theta)}, \tag{4.1}$$

where α is the weight on profit relative to consumer surplus in the welfare criterion. The asymmetry of information causes a welfare loss relative to the first best. If, for example, θ is uniformly distributed on $[0, b]$, where $b < 1/(2 - \alpha)$, and demand is linear ($P = 1 - Q$), then the expected welfare loss is

$$L = \tfrac{1}{6}b(1 - \alpha)[3 - b(3 - \alpha)]. \tag{4.2}$$

Suppose now that the industry is liberalized and that price control is also removed. Will effective competition happen, and if so will the result be better than regulated monopoly? To answer these questions, we need to specify the cost structures of rival firms and the nature of competitive interaction. Suppose first that all firms have the same technology as the incumbent firm, that there is common knowledge between firms (unlike the regulator) about cost conditions, and that there is Bertrand competition in the event of entry.

In these circumstances, *if* one or more firms enters to compete with firm M, competition will force price into line with marginal cost ($P = \theta$) whatever the level of θ, and there will be no positive profits. This outcome, which reflects the informational advantage of competition, combines allocative efficiency and distributional efficiency, but there is productive inefficiency because the fixed cost K is duplicated. In a sense this is the cost of overcoming the asymmetry of information that made regulation inefficient. Whether or not it is worth paying depends the size of K relative to the information asymmetry loss. In the example with uniformly distributed θ and linear demand, the comparison is between K and L as given in (4.2). With a high degree of natural monopoly, regulation will be superior to the competitive outcome, but if K is small in relation to the information asymmetry, competition will have the advantage.

However, the last paragraph began with a very big "if." In the circumstances described, no firm would actually want to enter to compete with firm M. The entry cost K would not be recouped by any positive profit because competition results in marginal cost pricing. Therefore liberalization would be ineffective: laissez-faire would lead not to competition but to unregulated monopoly. The fact that competition does not result from laissez-faire does not mean that it is unattainable. Rather, it requires assistance to come about. Thus a subsidy to cover the entry cost of a rival, which would cost K, could achieve the benefits of competition.

The basic model just described is very simplistic, but it serves to illustrate two general points. First, it exemplifies an informational advantage of competition: price is brought into line with cost without any regulator needing to know the level of cost. This point will be examined in other (e.g., non-Bertrand) settings below, and other kinds of informational advantages from competition will be discussed. Second, liberalization in the sense of laissez-faire is not a guarantee that competition will actually happen. Procompetitive policy measures may also be needed.

Finally, it should be noted that asymmetric information was the only source of regulatory failure in the basic model above. Monopoly regulation has further disadvantages relative to competition if there are regulatory commitment problems that cause underinvestment, or dangers of capture.

4.1.2 Contestability[3]

The theory of contestable markets is about the potency of *potential*, as distinct from actual, competition. In the example above, suppose that the fixed cost K is not sunk but recoverable in the event of exit from the industry. Then the possibility arises of "hit-and-run" entry: if any profit opportunity comes about, no matter how transitory, a rival can profitably enter the industry and undercut the incumbent and take away its business. The incumbent can prevent this only by behaving so that no such profit opportunities exist, which requires productive efficiency and average cost pricing (given uniform pricing). Subject to the constraint that profits cannot go negative, this outcome is welfare optimal—allocative efficiency is maximized subject to the break-even constraint without any duplication of fixed costs.

---

3. There is a large literature on the theory of contestable markets. For exposition and defense of the theory, see Baumol, Panzar, and Willig (1982), Baumol (1982), and Baumol and Willig (1986). Critical appraisals of the theory and its applicability include Brock (1983), Schwartz (1986), Shepherd, (1984), and Spence (1983). Some of their criticisms are discussed later in this chapter.

Indeed it is true generally, including in multiproduct settings (see below), that productive efficiency—at the level of the industry as well as each
firm—must hold at equilibrium in a contestable market and that there are
no supernormal profits. The price of each product cannot be less than its
marginal cost, and if two or more firms are active at equilibrium, then
prices must equal marginal costs. In short, the standard welfare properties
of allocative efficiency, productive efficiency and zero supernormal profits
all hold at equilibrium in a contestable market, and contestability provides a competitive benchmark which, unlike the conventional model of
perfect competition, does not require a vast number of small firms.

However, the applicability of the theory is seriously open to question.
For incumbent firms to be vulnerable to hit-and-run entry, there must not
only be symmetry between firms and *zero* sunk costs but also some positive interval between the entry of a new firm and the incumbent's price
response. It is not very natural to suppose that entry can happen faster
than the price response from the incumbent(s), but this is assumed in
contestability theory. Moreover, if the assumptions of the theory are relaxed a little—for example, if some small sunk costs are admitted—the
predictions of the theory can change a lot. This is the *nonrobustness* criticism. In the example above, if a small amount ε of the entry cost is sunk
and irrecoverable, and if the lag before Bertrand competition is provoked
by entry is of length τ, then the incumbent is safe from entry provided that
its profit flow does not exceed ε/τ. Even when ε is small, this ratio may be
large if τ is small also. Indeed the incumbent may be able to act as a pure
monopolist without attracting entry.

At this point it may seem that contestability theory has no relevance for
the utility industries because they have vast sunk costs. But this is not true
of all parts of the utilities. Sunk costs are a fundamental characteristic of
networks (telecommunications lines, gas pipelines, etc), but they are not
necessarily so important for the provision of services over networks
(value-added telecommunications services, gas supply to large users). And
the degree to which costs are sunk may depend in part on public policy.
For example, competition for operating franchises to provide services may
entail lower sunk costs than other forms of competition.

Quite apart from this, the proponents of contestability theory claim that
the theory may make its main contribution "as a guide for regulation,
rather than as an argument for its elimination" (Baumol and Willig 1986,
27). Consider a natural monopolist that supplies two products, where
demand is for one unit of each. Suppose that the cost of supplying either

one of these products in isolation—its *stand-alone* cost—is $C(1) = 3$, and that the cost of supplying them jointly is $C(2) = 4$. Thus there are economies of scope: joint supply is more efficient that separate supply. The *incremental* cost of each product is 1. How should the two products be priced?

If the industry were contestable, the force of potential competition would constrain the prices of the products to add up to $C(2) = 4$, and each price would have to be at least 1. In general prices between incremental and stand-alone costs do not attract entry even in a contestable market. Such prices are said to be "subsidy free." Since desirable welfare properties are known to hold in contestable markets, advocates of the theory recommend that regulated prices be constrained to lie between incremental and stand-alone costs also in markets that are not contestable—in short that regulation should simulate contestability.

There are two difficulties with this approach. First, there might be a very large range between incremental and stand-alone costs, especially if, as is typical in the utilities, there are large fixed costs common to the supply of a number of products. In the simple example above, the range is between 1 and 3. It would seem more straightforward to calculate optimal prices directly, rather than going the roundabout and indeterminate route of calculating what contestability would imply. The example with inelastic demands is a very special case in which optimal prices also happen to be indeterminate, but generally optimal prices are well defined. As shown in section 3.1.2 on Ramsey prices, which are optimal subject to the break-even constraint, optimal prices involve demand as well as cost information.[4] Given certain assumptions on costs and demand, Ramsey prices will not attract entry in a contestable market, and so meet the criterion in the last paragraph.

The second difficulty is the opposite of the first. Under some natural monopoly cost conditions, there exist *no* prices that will not attract entry, even though single firm supply is efficient. This is the problem of *non-sustainability* of natural monopoly (see Faulhaber 1975; Sharkey 1982, ch. 5). Extend the example above to three products, suppose that the cost of supplying the three products together is $C(3) = 6.5$, and continue to assume that $C(1) = 3$ and $C(2) = 4$. This industry has natural monopoly cost conditions because $C(3) = 6.5 < 7 = C(1) + C(2)$. But if the industry is contestable, entry is certain to occur. The three product prices charged

---

4. Ramsey prices therefore require more information, and this is a practical disadvantage.

by the natural monopolist must add up to 6.5. Otherwise, there will either be losses or entry by a three-product rival. It follows that the highest two of these prices must add up to at least $4\frac{1}{3}$. But this means that a two-product entrant, with costs of 4, can profitably enter and take away two-thirds of the incumbent's business, leaving it with a loss on the its remaining activity. This "cream-skimming" is a kind of inefficient entry.

Notwithstanding the logical possibility of this happening, we are doubtful whether it provides a good case for entry restrictions in the utility industries, which are not for the most part remotely contestable and where there is little evidence that cost conditions give rise to nonsustainability. Of more relevance is the possibility of nonsustainability induced by *policy* requirements. In the original two-product example, for instance, problems of cream-skimming might arise, depending on ease of entry, if the incumbent were required to supply one of the products at no charge (which would fail the contestability test). Then it would have to charge 4 for the other product in order to break even, and such pricing might attract inefficient entry. But if faced with the threat of entry, the firm would not actually find it optimal to charge 4. Suppose that a price of $(3 + \delta)$ would just forestall entry (perhaps $\delta = \varepsilon/\tau$ in the example given earlier in this section). Then the firm would do best to charge $3 + \delta$, which at least gives a profit of δ on the second product, although there is an overall loss of $1 - \delta$ because of the constrained price of the first product. There is no inefficient entry; rather, the problem is the enforced loss on the first product.

However, constraints on pricing *structure*, such as a requirement of uniform pricing (e.g., as exists geographically in postal services) may lead to nonsustainability and inefficient entry if costs differ substantially between products. We will return to the question of policy-induced nonsustainability in chapter 7—this question has been controversial in connection with telecommunications liberalization. Suffice it to say for the present that the danger of cream-skimming can be exaggerated, and where it exists, restrictions on competition are not necessarily the only answer.

4.1.3 Economies of Scale and the Excess Entry Question

Another kind of argument against promoting competition by liberalization or by breaking up a dominant incumbent firm into competing units is that cost advantages stemming from scale economies will be lost. (Similar arguments about the possible loss of economies of scope in the event of vertical divestiture will be examined in the next chapter.) Where scale economies are present, there is a trade-off—more competition is likely to improve allocative efficiency but at the expense of some productive efficiency. In this section we examine this trade-off.

We begin by explaining the *excess entry result*, the proposition that there is a tendency for there to be "too much" entry when there are scale economies, at least in homogeneous goods oligopoly models.[5] In addressing the question of whether there is likely to be excess or insufficient entry, it is useful to think in terms of the externalities that entry causes. When an additional firm enters a market, consumers will usually gain but incumbent firms will generally lose. It is not immediately obvious which way the net welfare effect will go, even assuming that profits and consumer surplus have equal welfare weight ($\alpha = 1$), as is assumed in this section.

Let $q(n)$ be output per firm when there are n firms in the industry, and let $C(q)$ be total cost per firm. (In the basic model above, $C(q) = K + \theta q$.) Firms are assumed to be symmetric. With n firms in the industry, welfare is

$$W(n) = U(nq(n)) - nC(q(n)), \tag{4.3}$$

where $U(Q)$ is gross consumer utility as a function of industry output.[6] Let $\hat{n}$ denote the "free entry equilibrium" number of firms, that is, the zero profit equilibrium number. The question is whether $W(\hat{n}) < W(\hat{n} - 1)$. If so, then free entry leads to excess entry in the sense that welfare would be higher if fewer than the equilibrium number entered. To evade integer problems,[7] let us treat n as a continuous variable and evaluate the sign of dW/dn at $n = \hat{n}$:

---

5. See von Weizsäcker (1980), Perry (1984), and especially Mankiw and Whinston (1986) and Suzumura and Kiyono (1987).

6. Welfare here is expressed in terms of the direct utility function $U(Q)$ because it is convenient to work with quantities, whereas in chapters 2 and 3 the indirect utility function $V(P)$ was used. The relationship between these equivalent approaches is that $U(Q(P)) = V(P) + PQ(P)$.

7. It is not really satisfactory to ignore integer issues in this way. For example, the optimal and equilibrium (integer) numbers of firms might coincide even though "equilibrium n" exceeds "optimal n" when n is treated as a continuous variable. In fact it is possible for the optimal number of firms to be one greater than the equilibrium number (see Mankiw and Whinston 1986). An important case of this occurs where no firm enters an industry in which it would be socially desirable for entry to occur. Note that in this case there is no negative business-stealing externality to offset the positive externality that entry brings to consumers. Apart from this case, however, the analysis that treats n as a continuous variable does not affect the general character of the argument and is a good way to illustrate the excess entry result.

$$\frac{dW}{dn} = (q + nq')U' - C - nq'C'$$

$$= (P - C')nq'. \tag{4.4}$$

The last expression is obtained by rearranging the first and using the facts that $U' = P$ and that $Pq = C$ at free entry equilibrium. Given that there are economies of scale it must be that $P > C'$. It then follows from (4.4) that W' has the sign of q'. Since output per firm typically decreases as the number of firms increases, it follows that there is a tendency to excess entry in those models. Equation (4.4) has a natural interpretation. At the margin the social value of an increment of output is $(P - C')$. The total output of incumbent firms changes by nq'. The marginal externality caused by entry is the product of these terms.

Does this result imply that *partial* liberalization—restricting the number of entrants—is a better policy than total liberalization? (This has been a central issue for telecommunications policy, as will be explained in chapter 7.) For a number of reasons we believe that it would be dangerous to draw any such conclusion. First, the result can be reversed if less weight is given to profits than to consumer surplus in the welfare criterion, because business stealing then matters less. If, for example, no weight is given to profits so that consumer interests are all that matter for welfare, then there is too little entry, provided only that total output is increasing in n, which is invariably the case.

Second, product differentiation introduces an added consumer benefit —that of greater product variety—which may overturn the result.[8] To see this, suppose that consumer utility U is a function of $\sum_i \phi(q_i)$, where ϕ is a strictly concave function such as $\phi(q) = q^\xi$ with $\xi < 1$. (In these terms the homogeneous goods case had $\phi(q) = q$, or $\xi = 1$.) This formulation captures consumer preference for variety: utility is higher with n firms each producing Q/n than with $n - 1$ firms each producing $Q/(n - 1)$, even though total output is the same in each case. Additional entry therefore increases variety, and this introduces a further source of positive externality. Assuming symmetry, we have

$$\frac{dW}{dn} = (\phi + n\phi'q')U' - C - nq'C'$$

$$= (P - C')nq' + \left[\frac{\phi}{q\phi'} - 1\right]C, \tag{4.5}$$

---

8. See Mankiw and Whinston (1986).

using the fact that $P = U'\phi'$. If $\phi(q) = q^\xi$, the term in square brackets is just $[1/\xi - 1]$. The second term in (4.5), which did not occur in (4.4), is positive. It may or may not be enough to outweigh the negative first term, depending, among other things, on the strength of consumers' preference for variety.

Third, policy intervention to curb entry might change the nature of product market interaction between firms. For example, Cournot behavior might be replaced by something more collusive. If they did affect the nature of competition, it seems likely that entry restrictions would make behavior more collusive rather than less so, in which case they would entail a welfare cost.

Fourth, intervention to limit the number of entrants would suffer from asymmetric information (and perhaps other types of regulatory failure). For example, suppose that $C(q) = \theta q + K$ and that θ is unknown to the regulator but common knowledge between firms. Let n^* be the number of firms that maximizes expected welfare $EW(n)$ subject to the asymmetric information constraint, taking as given the mode of product market interaction between firms, and let $\hat{n}(\theta)$ be the equilibrium number of firms under laissez-faire. Even if $\hat{n}(\theta)$ is larger than the (full information) optimal number of firms for all θ, it might still be true that expected welfare is greater with laissez-faire than with regulated entry—that is, $EW(\hat{n}(\theta)) > EW(n^*)$—because of the sensitivity of $\hat{n}$ to θ. More generally, it is sometimes illuminating to regard the competitive mechanism as equivalent to a well-informed agent whose objective is imperfectly aligned with social welfare, whereas a benign regulator is an imperfectly informed agent whose objective is perfectly aligned with welfare. Depending on the respective imperfections of objectives and information, free competition might be the better, albeit imperfect, alternative.

Fifth, the excess entry result was obtained assuming that cost conditions are exogenous and the same for all firms. This assumption excludes two of the most important benefits of competition—its effects on productive efficiency (1) at industry level by "selecting" more efficient firms from less efficient ones, and (2) within firms by improving incentives. These effects will be discussed shortly.

Sixth, there was no possibility of entry deterring behavior by incumbent firms in the model that yielded the excess entry result. Again this is because all firms in the model were assumed to be alike. In particular, entrants instantly became full-sized replicas of incumbents, with no need to build up capital over time. Entry deterrence in a richer setting will be examined in section 4.2.

As well as being important for policy toward entry conditions, the trade-off between competition and the exploitation of scale economies is central to policy regarding the (horizontal) breakup of erstwhile monopolists. Moreover policy toward horizontal breakup might affect incentives for entry and hence the efficiency of competitive outcomes in a liberalized regime. The breakup of the electricity generation monopoly in England and Wales in 1990 is a case in point (see further chapter 9). In some respects horizontal divestiture can usefully be viewed as the reverse of horizontal merger, a topic that has received a good deal of theoretical attention.

Farrell and Shapiro (1990), in their static Cournot analysis of horizontal merger in a homogeneous goods industry, find that while merger typically causes price to increase, the welfare consequences are ambiguous. In homogeneous-goods Cournot oligopoly, for a given level of industry output, increased concentration (as measured by the Herfindahl index, which is the sum of the squares of the market shares) is beneficial because larger firms have lower marginal costs than smaller firms, and it is therefore desirable for their market shares to increase at the expense of smaller firms. Indeed in Cournot oligopoly it may be desirable for small firms to be driven out of the market because the social value of their output is small, but they "steal" some business from their larger, more efficient rivals. The intuition here is similar to that for the Cournot excess entry result above, but with the added point about asymmetries between firms being due to differential efficiency.

Does this static Cournot analysis imply that horizontal divestiture is not such an attractive policy? We think not, for two main reasons. First, the breakup of a dominant incumbent and the competition between the resulting parts may well be good for industrial cost efficiency even within the terms of model described. For example, five competitors operating at a reasonably efficient scale could well achieve a better outcome than a dominant firm with an inefficient fringe of small firms. Indeed the competition resulting from divestiture could lead to their disappearance (or nonappearance). Second, it is open to question whether the static, homogeneous-goods Cournot model is appropriate for analyzing the question at hand. Farrell and Shapiro point out that their conclusions might not extend to industries with a substantial amount of product differentiation and that the maintained assumption of Cournot behavior does not allow for the realistic possibility that greater concentration will increase collusion between firms, which could lead to productive inefficiency (in terms of inefficient entry) as well as allocative inefficiency.

In addition, and perhaps most important, is the fact that static models of the kind reviewed in this section cannot address historical dynamic issues that are essential for understanding the current state of the utility industries. In telecommunications, for example, policy analysis would be very different if the asymmetry of market shares between BT and Mercury was entirely due to differential efficiency, rather than being largely the consequence of a history of protected monopoly. The tools of static oligopoly theory are useful for thinking about the utility industries (e.g., see the discussion of electricity generation in section 9.4.1), but they must be applied with care, and without losing sight of the historical dynamics. We will return to this theme when discussing entry barriers in section 4.2.

4.1.4   Competition, Information, and Incentives

In the models just described, as in most standard theory of industrial competition, costs are exogenous, and the chief benefit of competition is to improve allocative efficiency, albeit possibly at some cost in terms of productive efficiency. But, as has already been noted, many—perhaps most—of the benefits of competition have to do with productive efficiency rather than allocative efficiency, and they stem from the informational economy of the competitive process and the way that it creates incentives for static efficiency (the elimination of slack within firms and selection between firms) and dynamic efficiency (the discovery of new products and processes) over time. Though the importance of relationships between competition, information, and incentives has long been emphasized,[9] their formal analysis, both theoretical and empirical, is far from complete.

In this section we outline three aspects of the relationship between competition, information, and incentives—the way that competition selects more efficient firms from less efficient ones, its effect on effort incentives in situations of moral hazard, and dynamic competition to innovate.[10]

Competition and Selection[11]   Some firms are more efficient than others, contrary to the common modeling assumption that there is symmetry between firms, and an important determinant of overall efficiency is the share of production enjoyed by the most efficient. In so far as competition weeds out the inefficient, it has advantages over noncompetitive methods that lack the information to do so.

---

9. For example, in the writings of Hayek, Schumpeter, and Leibenstein.
10. For further discussion, see Vickers (1993) and the references therein.
11. Natural selection and evolutionary concepts of competition are not considered here.

The simplest setting in which competition plays a selecting role of this kind is an *auction*.[12] Consider, for example, an industry in which there is one unit of demand (unless price is very high), and suppose that there is an auction competition between n risk-neutral firms for the right to produce that unit, where firm i's production cost level θ_i is an independent random draw from some cost distribution $F(\theta)$ and private information. Let each firm's bid be the price at which it offers to produce. There are various forms of auction (English, Dutch, first-price, second-price), but in all of them the lowest cost firm will win the auction.[13] For example, if $F(\theta)$ is the uniform distribution on [0, 1], the expected cost of production is $1/(n + 1)$ and the expected price is $2/(n + 1)$. As n increases, both expected production cost and expected profit come down, and in the limit they approach zero. Any sunk fixed cost $K > 0$ of entering the competition must be considered too. However, there will not be excess entry if competition takes the form of a second-price auction, in which the winning (i.e., lowest price) bidder supplies at the second-lowest price (this is equivalent to Bertrand competition with common knowledge of costs after entry) because the private and social gains from entry are the same. By the revenue equivalence theorem, which applies in the circumstances assumed, this is also true in expected terms if competition is like a first-price auction, in which the winning bidder supplies at the lowest price bid (equivalent to Bertrand competition with private cost information).

If demand is elastic, there is in effect an auction where quantity is endogenous—quantity is higher the lower is the winning bid (Hansen 1988). If competition takes the form of a second-price auction, the expected price is again equal to the expected second-lowest cost, which is $2/(n + 1)$ in the uniform distribution example. The entry of an additional firm now creates a *positive* externality—the reverse of the excess entry result. An additional entrant gets zero revenue unless it is the lowest-cost firm, and in that event it does not appropriate all of the social benefit that its entry brings because output expands as price falls. (There are also social benefits, of which the entrant gets none, if the entrant is the second-lowest cost firm.) In the uniform distribution example, if competition takes the form of a first-price auction, and if demand is linear ($Q = 1 - P$), then equilibrium behavior for

12. The literature on auctions is vast. For a general survey, see McAfee and McMillan (1987), and in relation to regulation and procurement, see Laffont and Tirole (1993). Demsetz (1968) proposed that natural monopoly production rights could be auctioned; see section 4.3.1.
13. In the circumstances that have been assumed, the revenue equivalence theorem applies; see McAfee and McMillan (1987).

a firm with cost θ is to offer to supply at price $P(\theta) = \theta + (1 - \theta)/(n + 1)$. (This happens to be the price that would obtain with Cournot competition if all firms had cost level θ in this example.) Here competition has three advantages: as n increases, the expected price-cost margin diminishes, which is good for allocative efficiency; expected unit cost falls, which is good for productive efficiency; and expected profits fall, which is good for distributional efficiency. Entry does entail duplication of any fixed cost K, but again it can be shown that, in expected terms, entry yields a positive externality.

To summarize so far, we have looked at illustrative examples involving price competition as in auctions, in which competition has a selecting role. Allocative, productive, and distributional efficiency all increase as competition, as measured by the number of rival firms, increases. There may be duplication of entry costs, but from the point of view of welfare there was shown to be insufficient, rather than excess, entry.

Matters are less straightforward if there is Cournot competition between firms, instead of the Bertrand/auction type of competition that we have just been considering.[14] A property of Cournot competition, and many other types of oligopolistic competition, is that lower-cost firms have larger market shares than higher-cost firms: market shares and efficiency are positively correlated. The least efficient firms may not produce at all. As the number of firms increases, selection becomes tougher and average production cost falls. In the limit if there are no costs of entry, not only is there marginal cost pricing, but the marginal cost in question is the minimum possible marginal cost because of competitive selection. There may still be excess entry if fixed entry costs are significant, but this is not necessarily the case.[15] Asymmetries between firms modify the externalities caused by entry. For example, as well as "stealing business" from incumbent firms, the entrant may cause some "business shifting" from less efficient incumbents, who might even be induced to exit, to more efficient ones.

---

14. Palfrey (1985) analyzes a different connection between Cournot competition and auctions. Wilson (1977) showed that in "common value" auctions, as the number of bidders gets large, the wining bid converges to the true value of the object being sold, even though bidders do not communicate the partial private information that they have about the object's value. (By contrast, we have been considering "independent value" auctions.) Palfrey shows that a similar information aggregation property holds with Cournot behavior when firms have partial private information about demand: in the competitive limit there is allocative efficiency even though each firm has limited information. However, Vives (1988) shows that the competitive limit is not perfectly productively efficient if there are nonconstant returns to scale because marginal costs generally differ across firms.
15. See Vickers (1993).

These simple examples have illustrated how competition—even imperfect competition—can enhance productive efficiency at industry level via endogenous selection, and how the excess entry result can be modified once competition has a role in selection. Selection is not *optimal* when competition is imperfect—regulatory mechanisms involving auctions might be able to do better, at least in principle (see section 4.3.1)—but it seems possible that the benefits of competition relative to feasible regulatory alternatives may be understated if the role of competition in selection is ignored (e.g., by imposing symmetry assumptions when analyzing the excess entry question). In the absence of further analysis, however, these remarks must remain somewhat speculative.

Having considered how competition might bring productive efficiency gains at industry level by selecting between firms with exogenous costs, we now comment briefly on incentives for endogenous efficiency improvement.

Competition and Incentives   The fact that competition, by allowing performance comparisons, can enhance incentives for firms to cut costs has already been discussed in relation to yardstick regulation (in section 3.4). The basic idea is that "competitive markets provide a richer information base on which to write contracts" (Holmstrom and Tirole 1989, 96).[16] Competition, or more precisely comparability, allows better inferences to be made about the effort made by each agent, and so effort can be more effectively rewarded without imposing undue risk on the agent (see Holmstrom 1982b). For a given level of risk, comparability means that the agent can be given sharper incentives. Conversely, for given incentives, comparability allows risk reduction—there is a sense in which competition provides insurance. These properties hold very generally (at least in static settings[17]). Provided that the performance of agent j yields some information about the effort of agent i—loosely, that there is some correlation in the uncertainties faced by agents—it is optimal to base i's reward to some degree upon j's performance.[18] Precisely *how* to design optimal incentive

---

16. The relationship between competition and slack is more complicated if information about other firms is conveyed via product market competition. Hart (1983) and Scharfstein (1988) made different assumptions about managerial preferences and reached opposite conclusions.

17. In dynamic settings an important issue is whether or not incentives for future periods can be precommitted in advance. If not, there may be "ratchet effects" (see Milgrom and Roberts 1992, ch. 7), which will generally be influenced by relative performance comparisons.

18. Additional issues can arise in multi-task settings; see Holmstrom and Milgrom (1991).

schemes with an element of relative performance is difficult matter (again, see section 3.4). As well enabling more efficient managerial incentive schemes to be designed, competition can affect the *implicit* incentives that stem from managerial career concerns. Insofar as more competition improves the quality of inferences about performance made by participants in the managerial labor market, it will diminish managerial slack.[19]

Competition and Innovation   Incentives for investment to reduce costs and introduce new products and processes are of course a key determinant of industrial performance. There exists a large literature on relationships between competition and innovation (see Tirole 1988, ch. 10, for an introduction). One aspect of this question, which has parallels with the excess entry question discussed above, is whether, there is a tendency to "too much" or "too little" R&D competition. More competition may (or may not) lead to more rapid innovation, but it may entail more duplication of R&D efforts. There are trade-offs between positive externalities (to consumers and via spillovers between firms) and negative externalities (the equivalent of "business stealing" between firms).

Another aspect of the question is how competition and regulation compare in respect of dynamic efficiency incentives. Incentives for cost reduction under regulation were discussed in chapters 2 and 3 (sections 3.5.1 on regulatory lag and 3.6 on regulatory commitment are especially relevant in the present context). There is the possibility that socially efficient investment may be deterred because its benefits may before long be transferred by regulation to consumers rather than being enjoyed by the investing firm. Even if competition is imperfect in other respects, it may have the dynamic efficiency advantage that price becomes less sensitive to the firm's behavior than when endogenous regulatory changes are in prospect.[20]

4.1.5   Discussion
In this section we have looked at various relationships between competition and efficiency. In a perfectly contestable market, the forces of potential competition achieve maximum efficiency, but we expressed doubts about the applicability of contestable markets theory to the industries that we are concerned with. For the most part the competitive process is an

---

19. This can be shown in a version of Holmstrom's (1982a) dynamic model of implicit incentives.
20. See further Vickers (1991, especially sec. 3.3). The point that competition can reduce vulnerability to "holdup" will be discussed in another context in section 5.1.1.

imperfect mechanism, and the first question for policy toward liberalization and divestiture is how competition compares with the imperfect alternative of monopoly regulation. Many factors are relevant for this comparison, including those addressed in the previous two chapters, and in this chapter we have stressed the informational advantages and incentive effects of competition.

The second question for liberalization policy is whether there is a danger of too much competition, resulting in loss of scale economies, and hence whether competition should be "managed." Excess entry is indeed possible, but the case for entry restrictions on these grounds does not appear to be very strong, especially when the positive effects of competition upon the productive efficiency are taken into account. Cream-skimming is another reason sometimes put forward for entry restrictions. Where this danger exists, it is usually because of other distortions such as policy-induced cross-subsidies. The third question, to which we now turn, is whether desirable competition will fail to come about because of barriers to entry, thus creating a need for procompetitive regulatory policy.

4.2   Barriers to Entry

The removal of legal barriers to entry into an industry will not make it competitive if there are also economic barriers to entry. This point is of prime importance in the liberalized utility industries. Indeed they provide excellent case studies of the textbook situation of a dominant incumbent firm faced with potential entry.

4.2.1   Incumbent Advantages and Strategic Entry Deterrence
Several definitions of "entry barrier" exist (see Tirole 1988, ch. 8, and Gilbert's 1989 survey of the subject). A formal definition is unnecessary for our purposes, and we will say that entry barriers exist if incumbent firm(s) can persistently make supernormal profits by virtue of their incumbency without attracting entry.[21] This can happen only if there are asymmetries between incumbents and entrants, and it is useful to distinguish between two kinds:

---

21. Stigler defined entry barriers as costs that must be incurred by entrants but not by incumbents. This captures absolute asymmetries between firms but not asymmetries that result from first-mover advantage. The latter are of crucial importance in the deregulated utility industries.

1. Absolute asymmetries, for example, because of privileged access to crucial inputs to production.[22]

2. Strategic asymmetries, for example, first-mover advantages.

Note that neither of these asymmetries exists in a contestable market: the absolute case is ruled out by assumption, and the absence of sunk costs makes "history," and hence the strategic case, irrelevant. But both are very important in the utility industries. For example, in the period immediately after its privatization, British Gas had privileged access to North Sea gas supplies and pipeline transportation services, exclusive access to smaller customers, and considerable further advantages by virtue of being the incumbent.

There is a further distinction within strategic asymmetries. In an industry with large scale economies the incumbent may go unchallenged by entry for the simple reason that two firms cannot profitably coexist, without the incumbent needing to do anything more to dissuade potential entrants. This is the situation in parts of the utilities with severe natural monopoly cost conditions such as gas and electricity transmission and distribution, and water supply. Even if it were legal, entry would be *blockaded* by the underlying economic conditions, irrespective of the incumbent's behavior. With *strategic* entry deterrence, on the other hand, the incumbent deliberately acts to make the prospect of entry unattractive to potential rivals, for example, by investing in a high level of capacity to make a price war appear likely, or in a reputation for aggressive behavior with the same aim. As this last point suggests, strategic exit inducement and strategic entry deterrence are closely related. A particularly important kind of strategic entry deterrence, which links the two asymmetries, is incumbent anticompetitive behavior to induce cost asymmetries, for example, raising rivals' costs by denying them proper access to a vital transmission network (see chapter 5).

Whereas in some industries the advantages that accrue to the first-mover may be regarded, at least in part, as a just reward for the skill, industry, and foresight of the firm that won them—in R&D competition, for example—this is generally not so for the utilities. They owe their

---

22. If these inputs are traded on a competitive market, then their opportunity cost is the same for all firms, including the incumbent. In those circumstances the incumbent will earn a rent by virtue of owning the crucial inputs, but strictly speaking that will not by itself create a barrier to entry into the productive activity. In fact crucial inputs of this kind are not usually traded on competitive markets.

dominant positions not to successful innovation but to the inheritance of public monopoly. Dynamic incentive questions, which complicate the welfare analysis of entry barriers in cases where product market dominance has resulted from innovation, are therefore less applicable.[23]

A general survey of the literature on barriers to entry is obviously beyond our scope. Instead we will briefly describe some sources of incumbent advantages that are of particular relevance to the utility industries.

Sunk Costs   Many activities in the utility industries, including ones such as electricity generation and long-distance telecommunications that are not naturally monopolistic, are characterized by a high degree of sunk costs. This is important for entry conditions in two respects. First, the profitability of entry depends on the nature of competition *post*entry. It is entirely possible for entry to be profitable at the prices prevailing ex ante but unprofitable after the event because of the more intense competition triggered by entry. The more that entry costs are sunk, the greater is this possibility, because price competition is likely to be more severe when variable costs are lower. Second, irreversibility is a necessary condition for credible commitment by the incumbent firm, and hence for credibly manipulating expectations about the nature of postentry competition. Investing in a high level of capacity has already been mentioned in this regard.[24]

Needless to say, strategic investment to deter any entry is not always credible or the most profitable strategy for an incumbent monopolist (nor for incumbent duopolists or oligopolists, who may attempt to "free-ride" on each other's entry deterring efforts[25]). A degree of entry accommodation may be preferable for the incumbent(s), or inevitable anyway, for example, if capacity limits constrain entrants to be relatively small and if the incumbent(s) cannot engage in selective price discrimination against them.

Customer Inertia   Turning to the demand side, there can be major incumbent advantages in relation to customers. First, there is the marketing advantage that all consumers know of the incumbent because they used to

---

23. When the telephone was first invented, however, dynamic incentive questions were of course important; see Brock (1981) for an account of the development of the telecommunications industry.

24. See further Dixit (1980).

25. See Waldman (1987) on free-rider problems facing multiple incumbents seeking to deter entry.

have no choice but to buy from it. Mercury needs to advertise its presence in a way that British Telecom does not. Second, there may be costs of switching suppliers,[26] for example, the need to install a new gas or electricity meter or the need to change telephone number. Nonlinear pricing schemes involving quantity discounts can also give rise to switching costs. Third, if the entrant's product quality is uncertain, the incumbent may gain some advantage because of the costs—in terms of quality risk—faced by customers who switch suppliers. A similar risk might have existed when they first bought the incumbent's product, but then they were substituting out of marginal consumption whereas now they will typically be forgoing some consumer surplus from the incumbent's product.[27] Fourth, the incumbent may gain advantage from having a monopoly on complementary products. For example, a customer with non-BT telephone apparatus and domestic wiring may find that fault diagnosis and repair is more difficult than the customer whose equipment comes from the local network provider.

Although some of these incumbent advantages might be related to efficiency advantages (e.g., easier quality control in the example just mentioned might partly be a kind of scope economy), there is no doubt that entry barriers deriving from switching costs and other kinds of customer inertia are significant in the utility industries, especially for smaller customers.

Predatory Pricing[28]   Predatory behavior is behavior that would not be profitable but for its effect in inducing exit or deterring entry. Claims that such behavior is always irrational, and hence that predatory threats are always empty, have been refuted by game-theoretic analysis of the role of reputation when there is incomplete information.[29] It is therefore an open question whether predatory behavior, or the threat of it, is potentially a source of entry barriers in the utility industries. As far as predatory *pricing* is concerned, much depends on how the incumbent's pricing structure is regulated. If price discrimination is prohibited, then entrants might be shielded by a price "umbrella," and inefficient entry might be induced (as was mentioned above). On the other hand, some forms of price regulation, including some used in practice, may actually encourage "predatory"

26. See Klemperer (1987) for an analysis of markets in which consumers face switching costs.
27. See Schmalensee (1982).
28. See Tirole (1988, ch. 9) and the survey by Ordover and Saloner (1989).
29. See, for example, Milgrom and Roberts (1982).

pricing by allowing the forgone revenue to be recouped in the incumbent's more captive markets. We discuss this in more detail in section 4.3.3.

Input Market Issues Nonprice predatory behavior aimed at raising rivals' costs is perhaps more important still.[30] In particular, vertically integrated incumbent firms may be in a position to deny rivals fair access to essential inputs to production such as network access. The resulting danger of anticompetitive vertical foreclosure, and the consequent need for access price regulation, are discussed at length in the next chapter.

A related form of strategic entry deterrence involves long-term contracts with input suppliers (e.g., gas suppliers; see chapter 8). The desire to avoid competition that would dissipate some industry profits may give the incumbent an incentive not only to refuse to release existing contracts to rivals, but also to preempt new supplies. Moreover the incumbent might be able to deter input suppliers from dealing with its rivals if it remains their principal customer.

This has been a very selective account of some sources of incumbent advantage and possible entry-deterring behavior. The focus has been on issues relevant to the utility industries. In the same spirit we now ask whether entrants should be helped.

4.2.2 Assisting Entry

In view of the various incumbent advantages that exist in the utility industries, should potential entrants be given assistance? We take it for granted that entrants should be protected from anticompetitive behavior by the incumbent (see above). Additional assistance could take several forms, including the following:

1. Direct financial subsidy.
2. Relief from obligations placed on the incumbent.
3. Favorable restrictions on the incumbent's final product pricing.
4. Measures to reduce switching costs.
5. Limitations on further entry.
6. Favorable terms of interconnection to the incumbent's network infrastructure.

We will comment on points 1 through 5 in turn, but postpone point 6 until the next chapter on vertical relationships.

---

30. See Salop and Scheffman (1983, 1987).

First, however, it is important to review some principles. Proactive policy toward entry is called for if and only if there are significant beneficial *externalities* from entry. Much of the discussion earlier in the chapter bears on this point. For example, in the very basic Bertrand model of liberalization in section 4.1.1, entry had the positive externality of doing away with the need for regulation and its attendant costs. In particular, entry avoided the welfare loss L in equation (4.2), which arose because of the asymmetry of information between the regulator and the monopolist incumbent. Given the assumption of Bertrand competition, entry would occur only if all the sunk cost K was subsidized, and in the model this was socially beneficial if and only if $L > K$. Though extreme, this example does illustrate a coherent case for subsidizing entry to reduce the need for socially costly regulation.

In the basic excess entry model of section 4.1.3, on the other hand, entry caused a net negative externality because of business stealing, though we saw that this result could be overturned in richer models of competition with product differentiation or where selection and incentive considerations are relevant. However, these modeling approaches are static, and so cannot address dynamic aspects of competition, which intuitively seem to be a major part of the case for entry promotion. Just as "infant industry" arguments in trade policy are essentially dynamic, often having to do with temporary assistance while the benefits of learning by doing are achieved, the same is true of "infant firm" arguments in industrial policy. Unfortunately, dynamic oligopoly models with multidimensional state variables to represent evolving stocks of capital, goodwill, and so on, are not very well developed (but see Tirole 1988, sec. 8.6).

A very simple setting in which to pursue this point is a two-period Cournot duopoly model with learning by doing.[31] Whereas we have been describing situations where entry assistance may affect the number of firms, in the following setting the number of firms is fixed, and the issue is whether or not there is a case for assistance to influence the relative positions of firms. Suppose that there is a new entrant into a previously monopolized industry where learning effects are important. Current unit cost depends on accumulated output over time. The incumbent has already gained all the benefits of learning, but the entrant has not. Is there a case for subsidizing the entrant's first-period output in order to accelerate its learning, or are the benefits internalized by the entrant? To abstract

---

31. See the appendix to Neven and Vickers (1992) for more detail.

from first-period price effects, assume that intervention takes the form of a price-neutral subsidy to the entrant plus a tax on the incumbent's first-period output. Aside from its effects on government revenue, such intervention causes output-shifting from the incumbent to the entrant in both periods (in period 2 because of the entrant's lower unit cost) and a lower price in period 2 (for the same reason). This last effect is a positive benefit to consumers which the entrant does not fully appropriate, but the output shifting might be socially costly. Thus the trade-off is between foregone productive efficiency in the short term and greater competitiveness and allocative efficiency in the longer term.

From a theoretical point of view, then, it appears that subsidies to entry have ambiguous welfare effects. They might stimulate beneficial competition that would otherwise not exist, but they might distort competition and damage productive efficiency. In practice, however, subsidies to entry, at least direct subsidies, are usually not possible.[32] Regulators generally lack the power to make them, perhaps because of the dangers of capture and rent seeking. A more likely instrument of entry promotion is to exempt entrants from costly requirements placed on incumbent firms, which is a kind of indirect subsidy.

In discussing obligations placed on incumbent firms, it is important to distinguish between those that constrain the incumbent's pricing structure, for example, a requirement to provide universal service at a uniform price, and those that do not. It is not clear why the latter would positively assist entry—note the parallel with the discussion of cream-skimming in section 4.2.1. To take an extreme example, if BT was simply required to make a charitable donation of £10 million per annum, this by itself would neither help nor hinder its rivals because it would not change any relevant incentives at the margin. (Of course a similar requirement on potential rivals conditional upon entry would *hinder* entry.) Therefore entry assistance is more likely to come from obligations that affect the incumbent's pricing structure.

This brings us to point 3, which is discussed further in section 4.3.3. If an incumbent is required to provide universal service, and to do so at a uniform price, and if no such obligation is on placed on rivals, then powerful assistance to entry may be given. In such circumstances the Post Office's intra-London letter business, for example, would be an attractive tar-

---

32. Government subsidies to entrants are perhaps more common in international competition.

get for rivals in the event of total liberalization. As the discussion of cream-skimming showed, however, entry of this kind could be very inefficient—a rival considerably less efficient than the Post Office could profitably get a large market share in the hypothetical example. At best, restrictions on pricing structure seem a clumsy tool of entry assistance, especially when they result in cross-subsidies.[33] They are at the same time a hindrance to entry in the cross-subsidized market. (For example, they might shut out a rural postal firm that was more efficient than the Post Office.) As a general rule cross-subsidies are undesirable. The efficient solution is to relax requirements of uniform pricing, but this is not always feasible politically. In that case an explicit tax/subsidy scheme might have to accompany liberalization.

The way that the incumbent's prices are regulated can hinder entry. In section 4.3.3 we show how forms of average price regulation can distort competition by encouraging aggressive pricing in markets where the incumbent faces competitive threats. Price control should be framed in such a way that this does not happen. A more difficult issue is whether the level of prices (or price caps) should be set partly with a view to encouraging entry.[34] There are difficult intertemporal trade-offs: higher prices in the short term might lead to more entry and lower prices in the longer run. However, we believe that the links are too speculative to make a strong case for entry assistance by this means.

The way that switching costs can create barriers to entry was discussed above. Some switching costs, such as the information and effort needed to change supplier, are inevitable, but others can be reduced by regulatory intervention. For example, pro-incumbent biases in the telephone numbering system can be removed, and the installation of meters to facilitate competitive choices between rival utility companies could be promoted. However, such measures usually involve some cost. As always, the analysis of policy intervention must consider the externalities involved. In relation to metering, for example, these can be positive or negative, depending on the nature of competition between firms. If firms can price discriminate freely, then consumers' private incentives to install meters can exceed social incentives. If consumer j installs a meter, there is a negative externality

---

33. Incumbent price differentials that are apparently unrelated to cost differences might in some circumstances be evidence of predatory behavior and hence relevant to the protection of entrants from anticompetitive behavior. Of course such price differences are not necessarily bad—indeed Ramsey pricing generally entails them.

34. Or whether price should be left unregulated; see sections 9.4.1 and 9.4.2 on entry into the deregulated electricity generation industry in England and Wales.

to firms as a whole, because competition for that consumer's business intensifies, but other consumers do not benefit. If, on the other hand, individual price discrimination is not possible, then consumer j does benefit other consumers by installing a meter because competition generally is somewhat more vigorous, and the overall external effect can be positive, hence justifying intervention to encourage metering. More broadly, there is again the positive benefit that more effective competition can bring in reducing the need for costly regulation.

Protecting one or more entrants by raising barriers to the entry of others is on the face of it a curious way of assisting entry, and we mention it here only because the argument was used in justification of restrictions on entry into the British telecommunications industry in the 1980s (see chapter 7). The idea is that no entry might occur unless there is a guarantee against further entry, and that some competition is better than none. There are at least three problems with this argument (see also the discussion in section 4.1.3). First, if a second entrant would make the first entrant unprofitable, then why would the second entry occur, unless the second entrant were substantially more efficient than the first entrant, in which case its entry would seem to be desirable on productive efficiency grounds anyway? Second, barriers to further entry could well facilitate more collusive behavior. Third, the prime beneficiary of such a policy is likely to be the incumbent rather than the first entrant. Entry assistance, if desired, can surely be better targetted.

4.2.3 Discussion

Liberalization policies alone do not create conditions for effective and undistorted competition between an incumbent dominant firm and potential rivals. The incumbent may be protected by entry barriers arising from (1) absolute advantages over rival firms, (2) natural first-mover advantages, and (3) opportunities for strategic entry deterrence and/or credible threats of exit inducement. We have illustrated some of these possibilities as they relate to the utility industries under the headings of sunk costs, customer inertia, predatory pricing, and input market issues (which will be analyzed further in the next chapter).

So far as is possible, anticompetitive behavior under point 3 should be checked by procompetitive regulatory policy, especially toward vertically related activities controlled by the incumbent. However, there are well-known difficulties in determining when behavior is predatory, but at least it should be ensured that the structure of price regulation itself is not conducive to such behavior (see below). Other forms of entry assistance, including measures to reduce switching costs and relief from obligations placed on the incumbent, may be appropriate, depending on the circumstances, but it is hard to state general principles in this regard (partly because we do not have sharp theories of postentry dynamics).

Finally, although most of the discussion in this section has assumed that there is a single dominant incumbent, that will not be so if horizontal breakup has occurred. Aside from its advantages in terms of direct head-to-head competition, that might also make for entry conditions that are less vulnerable to anticompetitive distortion.

4.3 Competition and Regulation

Competition and regulation interact in various ways. Yardstick competition, which induces competition in cost reduction between regional monopolists, was examined in section 3.4. In this section we look at some other areas where competition and regulation are interrelated—franchising, regulation of a dominant firm that faces some competition, and cross-market links that arise when a multiproduct firm operates in both monopolistic and competitive markets. As subsequent chapters will illustrate, all these issues have been of considerable practical importance in the utility industries.

4.3.1 Franchising

Demsetz (1968) asked "Why regulate utilities?" and proposed instead that the right to operate a natural monopoly industry could simply be auctioned to the firm that offers to supply at the lowest price. This idea has been developed formally by Laffont and Tirole (1987) and Riordan and Sappington (1987), who analyze the optimal design of such an auction when firms have independent private information about cost conditions that is not available to the regulator. (The discussion of auctions in section 4.1.4 did not address this question of *optimal* auction design.) As in the pure monopoly case (see chapter 2), it is optimal for the regulator to auction not just one kind of contract but to offer a "menu" of contract types. By this means there is a degree of "self-selection" by firms that reveals information.

With optimal auction design, the effect of greater competition for the franchise is to reduce the rent obtained by the firm that wins the auction. The relationship between price and cost that results from the auction is unaffected by competition, and so is the same as if the winning firm were regulated as a pure monopolist. Thus with adverse selection as in the Baron-Myerson (1982) model, the price-cost relationship is still $P(\theta) = \theta + (1 - \alpha)F(\theta)/f(\theta)$. In Laffont and Tirole's auction model, which generalizes their (1986) monopoly regulation analysis, the relationship between effort and cost is just in the monopoly case, but competition leads to the franchise being won by the most efficient firm as well as to a reduction in rent obtained by that firm. The more competition there is, the greater is the expected efficiency of the winning firm, and hence the smaller is the distortion in effort incentives implied by optimal regulation. (Recall from chapter 2 that with optimal regulation the effort distortion is smaller for lower-cost firms and is zero with the most efficient type of firm.)

However, there are major practical problems with franchising in the utility industries that these models are not designed to address. Williamson (1976) made a number of powerful criticisms of the Demsetz scheme (see also Goldberg 1976). To work well, the scheme requires (1) that the franchise contract can be specified simply and completely, (2) that there is effective competition for the franchise not only when it is auctioned for the first time but on each occasion that it comes up for renewal, and (3) that if an incumbent franchisee is displaced by a rival, it receives proper compensation for transferable investments that it has made. While these assumptions may hold approximately for straightforward products that involve low sunk costs, as in the example of supplying license plates for taxis, they do not generally apply to the utility industries.

Consider a hypothetical auction of a monopoly franchise to supply telecommunications services throughout Britain for the next twenty-five years. A complete contract would need to specify pricing structures, quality levels, and so on, for every conceivable contingency. Unless it was crudely and inefficiently insensitive to future developments, for example, the evolution of costs, such a contract would be immensely complex and extremely difficult to write, monitor, and enforce. It would make much more sense to renegotiate some of the contract terms from time to time. Thus price controls could be reviewed every four or five years. Indeed it would be very hard for the government to commit not to vary some contract terms as events unfold. Much more likely, then, is some kind of incomplete contract that leaves a number of aspects to be resolved, perhaps according to agreed procedures, as time goes by. But this is effectively just what regulation involves—a continuing task of contract monitoring, enforcement, and renegotiation. Thus in circumstances of any complexity, franchising does not do away with the need for regulation.

A shorter-term contract, say, for five years of telecommunications services, might reduce the difficulties of contract specification and enforcement somewhat because fewer contingencies would have to be catered for, but problems of another kind are likely to result. In particular, the current incumbent may be deterred from making investments in long-lived industry-specific assets if the franchise is soon to be competed for again. Such assets are obviously very important in the utility industries, which have massive sunk investments in pipe and cable network infrastructure, for example. If a displaced incumbent could be accurately compensated for investments made during its tenure, without any adverse incentive effects, this underinvestment problem could be avoided, but that is hardly likely to be the case. Some investments activities are not readily measurable, and accounting measurements (e.g., of asset depreciation) contain inevitable arbitrariness from an economic point of view. Inaccurate valuation may distort competition between the incumbent and rivals in the next auction. Moreover, to the extent that cost-based approaches to asset valuation are used, the well-known incentive problems with cost-plus regulation will arise.

Further problems exist if the assets are not fully transferable between firms in the event that an incumbent is displaced by a rival. Investments in human capital, by training and learning by doing, are likely to be firm specific and nontransferable. If these are important, the incumbent will have a significant advantage over rivals, and bidding may not be effectively competitive.

Another kind of incumbent advantage that can jeopardize competition has to do with information. The value of a franchise is at least to some extent uncertain at the time of bidding. Important uncertainties, for example, concerning demand conditions, are common to the various bidders, but by virtue of incumbency, the current operator is likely to have superior information about them. As a result competitors to the incumbent suffer from an acute form of the "winner's curse" problem, which may lead to very cautious bidding by them and distort competition heavily in favor of the incumbent. If the incumbent has a much more accurate forecast of franchise value than rivals do, outbidding the incumbent indicates that the incumbent's (relatively accurate) information about the franchise was negative. Thus winning is in some ways a bad signal, and rivals will shade their bids accordingly. (This winner's curse problem exists when bidders have symmetric information too, but it is exacerbated by disparities in the precision of information available to different firms.)

Laffont and Tirole (1988a) ask whether the regulator should bias competition for or against the incumbent when a franchise is reauctioned, or whether bidding parity should be maintained. If investments are transferable in the event of the franchise changing hands but unobservable, then the incumbent should be favored. The case for pro-incumbent bias is that it ameliorates the underinvestment problem. If, on the other hand, investments are nontransferable, there is a case for favoring the rival, for reasons that have to do with minimizing profits (the regulator's cost information is improved by the revealed fact that the rival's cost level is low enough to win the auction). But, if important investments are nontransferable, the franchise is unlikely to change hands anyway, because the rival is at a considerable disadvantage. Laffont and Tirole therefore reach the pessimistic conclusion that where investments are important, the incumbent should be favored whenever it is not naturally protected by nontransferability. Either way, the prospects for effective competition are poor.

The conclusion to draw from this discussion is not that franchising is always impractical but rather that it works better in some circumstances than in others, and it tends to entail some degree of continuing regulation in any event. The analysis highlighted the importance of capital intensity, and this has implications for the design and scope of franchising. Consider franchising railway operations, which the British government is introducing (see Department of Transport 1992). The idea of franchising all British Rail's activities, including those relating to the sunk cost track infrastructure, would be hopelessly impractical for various reasons discussed above. Instead the plan is to franchise some rail *services*, with a separate authority responsible for the tracks. This kind of *operating* franchise may lose any synergies that exist between track and services, but it has advantages in terms of diminishing investment problems that might otherwise jeopardize competition. (Operating franchises of a similar kind are used in the water industry in France, with municipally owned capital infrastructure; see section 10.2.) Great difficulties—of contract specification, effectiveness of competition, and so on—still face the franchising of rail services, but at least they are not compounded by investment problems concerning the track infrastructure.

In sum, the answer to Demsetz's question "Why regulate utilities?" has several parts. Complexities of contract specification, monitoring, and enforcement mean that franchising will require some continuing regulatory involvement in any event. Auctioning the "regulatory contract" might nevertheless harness many of the information and incentive advantages of competition in some circumstances, especially for simply specified services that are not capital intensive. However, if investment in specific assets is important, as in major parts of the utilities, there is a serious danger either of underinvestment or of ineffective competition for franchises. Competitive bidding is therefore unlikely to be very useful for capital-intensive elements of natural monopoly industries, and its potential lies in less capital-intensive areas. Realization of that potential may require structural policies that distinguish between activities that have different capital intensities, as between the provision of network infrastructure and the supply of services over the network.

4.3.2   Effects of Competition on Regulation

When entry occurs in an industry that has been liberalized, price regulation often continues, at least for a period. For example, British Telecom has faced some competition from Mercury for a number of years and further liberalization is taking place, but price controls on BT are clearly essential in the foreseeable future, and indeed they have been strengthened over time (see chapter 7). The presence of product market competition can affect optimal regulation not only by its direct effect on the incentives of the dominant firm but also by influencing the information and opportunities of the regulator.

Since asymmetric information is a prime source of regulatory failure, competition can enhance the effectiveness of regulation by improving the information available for regulation. Caillaud (1991) analyzes regulation of a (single-product) dominant firm that faces some competition from a fringe of competitive producers who are not regulated. The regulator and the dominant firm are as in the Baron-Myerson model (see chapter 2). The presence of the fringe is doubly beneficial—the fringe may be able to produce more efficiently than the regulated firm, and it enables the information rents of the regulated firm to be diminished if there is correlation between cost levels.

In practice, competition and regulation usually interact in multiproduct industries. Laffont and Tirole (1990a, part II) extend their multiproduct monopoly model in which the regulator cannot observe effort to include various forms of competition. The effect of competition on optimal regulation depends, among other things, on the nature of product market competition, whether the competitors are regulated, and the welfare weight attached to their profits.[35]

If competitors are unregulated and their profits are distributionally costly, their presence may be undesirable inasmuch as it causes "leakage" of profits that could otherwise have been extracted from the regulated dominant firm. Competition may constrain regulatory opportunities in other respects too, as in Laffont and Tirole's (1990b) analysis of bypass and cream-skimming. For example, some pricing structures might be undermined by competitive entry. The possibility that in the event of complete liberalization, cream-skimming might undermine the system of nationwide postal services at a uniform price, which was mentioned in the discussion of nonsustainability of contestable markets, is an illustration of this general point.

In sum, most but not all of the effects of competition on regulation are positive. Although competition may limit regulatory opportunities in some circumstances, more generally it offers the possibility of more efficient sources of supply, it may further constrain incentives for monopolistic behavior, and it improves the information available for regulation.

4.3.3 Effects of Regulation on Competition

The most direct effect on competition of the regulation of the *level* of prices is that lower regulated prices harm competitors just as they harm the regulated firm. Tighter price controls on British Telecom mean that Mercury will have to charge lower prices too. It does not follow, however, that there is a case for lax regulation to promote competition because the prospects for competition more importantly depend on the position of competitors *relative* to the dominant firm, for example, whether or not they have good network access. This can be significantly influenced by the way that *relative* prices are regulated.

Suppose that the incumbent firm serves two markets and that there is some competition, at least potentially, in one of these, the other being captive. Suppose that the incumbent's costs are the same in each market,

---

35. For example, in the framework of section 3.1.2, if there is a price-taking fringe of firms with an upward-sloping supply curve, whose profits are distributionally costly, then pricing somewhat below marginal cost becomes optimal. The second-order loss in allocative efficiency is offset by a distributional gain as some fringe profit is tranferred to consumers. If there is a social cost of public funds (as in Laffont and Tirole 1990a), then the Ramsey elasticity formulas are modified by the presence of a competitive fringe. Similar points apply to access pricing; see section 5.2.2.

and consider the effect on competition of three different ways of regulating its price structure:

1. *Discrimination banned.* The incumbent must charge exactly the same price in each market, and this price must not exceed the regulated price cap $\bar{P}$.

2. *Average price regulation.* The average price charged by the incumbent must not exceed $\bar{P}$, but there is freedom to charge different prices in the two markets subject to that constraint.

3. *Separate caps.* Neither price must exceed $\bar{P}$, but there is freedom to charge different prices in the two markets subject to that pair of constraints.

Regime 1 may blunt the incumbent's incentive to compete. Suppose that $\bar{P}$ exceeds the incumbent's marginal cost c. If the incumbent reduces price below $\bar{P}$ in order to win custom in the competitive market, it loses revenue from customers in the captive market because the ban on price discrimination entails an equal price reduction for them. In effect this increases the incumbent's cost of serving the competitive market, and less efficient rivals, whose cost level exceeds c, may nevertheless succeed there.

Regime 2, on the other hand, can distort competition by making the incumbent excessively aggressive in the competitive market. As the incumbent reduces price to win custom in the competitive market, the fact that regulation applies to average revenue enables it to charge a higher price to customers in the captive market. This has the effect of artificially reducing the incumbent's cost of serving the competitive market. It is quite possible that pricing below marginal cost, which is often regarded as predatory pricing, could be induced by average revenue regulation. As a result competition from rivals may be thwarted even if they are more efficient than the incumbent. Only in regime 3 is the cross-market effect of regulation on competition neutral. This is an advantage of having separate caps, but a full welfare analysis must take account of other influences too (see Armstrong and Vickers 1993 for an examination of some of these).

In sum, the way that pricing structure is regulated can have an important influence upon the nature of competition faced by a multiproduct incumbent. In particular, regulating average revenue in a way that allows the incumbent complete freedom over price structure may have serious anticompetitive consequences. Quite apart from the issues discussed in chapter 3, competition reasons may argue against a policy of laissez-faire with respect to pricing structure.

Finally, it is important to mention the possibility that *potential* regulation might influence competition in (hitherto) unregulated industries. Consider, for example, an unregulated duopoly where tacit collusion is possible. If the probability that regulation will be introduced increases with the degree to which the firms collude to raise price, then the duopolists must strike a balance between high pricing to obtain short-term profits and moderating their pricing to forestall regulatory intervention that would jeopardize profits in the long run. A kind of limit pricing could result, with the aim of deterring the entry of the regulator rather than that of rival firms.[36] Indeed, insofar as the regulator was thought to regard the entry of rival firms as a sign of growing competition, the duopolists might not mind a degree of entry. We will return to the issue of potential regulation possibly affecting the nature of competition in a concentrated industry in section 9.4.1 below.

4.3.4   Discussion

There are important ways in which the effectiveness of regulation can be enhanced by harnessing competitive incentives. Competition, whether direct or indirect as with yardstick competition (see section 3.4 above), improves the information available for regulation and so has the potential to diminish a prime source of regulatory failure. Where competitive benchmarks exist, regulatory commitment may also be easier to achieve, with beneficial consequences for investment and cost-reduction incentives.

Franchising—auctioning the "regulatory contract"—can usefully exploit the informational advantages of competition in some circumstances, perhaps including parts of the utility industries. But in those industries as a whole, the scope for franchising is limited. Incumbent advantages, the small number of potential bidders, and the typically high degree of capital intensity mean that competition is likely to be ineffective or inefficient. Moreover the complexity of the industries is such that the inevitable problems of contract specification, monitoring, and enforcement imply that regulation will have to continue in any event.

However, competition and regulation can also combine in detrimental ways. On the one hand, competition can, in some circumstances, constrain regulatory opportunities, though it can be argued that such constraints are desirable more often than not. On the other hand, unless it is carefully

---

36. See Glazer and McMillan (1992).

framed, regulation can distort competition, either in favor of or against competitors to the incumbent dominant firm.

4.4 Conclusions

The case for policies of liberalization is not that competition is a perfect incentive system—generally it is not—but that in many circumstances it is better than the (also imperfect) alternative of regulated pure monopoly. As well as its benefits in terms of allocative efficiency, competition can have important productive efficiency advantages relating to information and incentives (albeit perhaps at some cost in terms of duplicating fixed costs). Thus it may overcome—more or less well—asymmetric information problems that limit the effectiveness of regulation. Other types of regulatory failure, concerning policy credibility and capture can also be avoided by the establishment of effective competition. These are important considerations for policy toward horizontal divestiture as well as toward liberalization.

In some respects, then, competition and monopoly regulation are potentially substitutes, but we have seen (and will see further in the industry chapters) that this is much too simplistic a view. First, desirable competition may be thwarted by incumbent advantages and strategic behavior unless there is firm procompetitive regulation to guard against anticompetitive conduct. Second, multimarket dominant incumbent firms typically face competitive threats in some markets but not in others. Unless it is carefully framed, the cross-market structure of regulation can distort competition, either for or against the incumbent. This is especially so when markets are vertically related.

5

Vertically Related Markets

Electricity generation, gas supply, long-distance telecommunications, and train services are all potentially competitive activities. But no one can compete effectively in them without proper access to essential related networks—for electricity and gas distribution, local telecommunications, and railway tracks—that are generally monopolized. But what is proper access? How to answer this *network access problem* is a fundamental question for policy toward the utility industries.

This problem, or rather set of problems, is shown in its essentials in figure 5.1. Firm M has a monopoly over the network activity, which we will assume to be subject to severe natural monopoly cost conditions. The vertically related activity—provision of services over the network—is not naturally monopolistic. Nevertheless, one policy option is to give firm M a monopoly, by law or de facto, over this activity too, making the whole industry a vertically integrated monopoly. This was precisely the policy toward the utility industries in Britain before 1980, and it remains the policy in many countries, albeit a decreasing number of them. The economics of regulating an integrated monopoly have already been covered in chapters 2 and 3.

The alternative, which has been adopted with varying degrees of success in Britain and elsewhere in recent years, is to deregulate the potentially competitive activities. Then there are two major questions. The question of *vertical structure* is whether to allow firm M into the deregulated sector, or whether to ring-fence it in the natural monopoly sector by a policy of vertical separation. If M starts off as a vertically integrated firm, then vertical separation entails divestiture, which is what happened to AT&T in the United States in 1984.

The question regarding *vertical conduct* is how to regulate the terms on which firm M gives network access to other firms. Should they, for example, have access at its marginal cost, or should they pay a contribution to the fixed costs of network provision? These questions arise whether or not there is vertical separation, but they are often more complex when vertical integration remains because of the asymmetry that exists between firm M and other firms. In particular, there is the problem that vertical integration may create the incentive and opportunity for anticompetitive behavior by firm M.

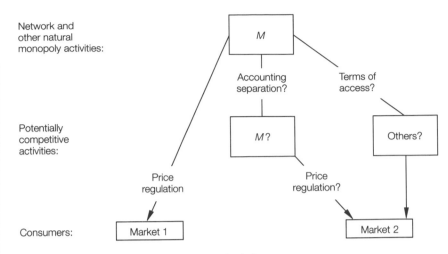

Figure 5.1 Vertically related markets: Some basic issues

The question whether or not vertical integration should be allowed has received a great deal of attention, but for the most part it has been examined without the monopolist being regulated. In the utility industries, regulation of the network monopolist is of course vital, but the general literature on vertical integration nevertheless contains many important insights. These are the subject of the next section, which looks at productive efficiency reasons for (and against) vertical integration, and at some dangers it may have for anticompetitive behavior. Section 5.2 is about the vertical conduct question and network access pricing in particular. The cases of vertical separation and vertical integration are both considered, and the overall comparison between them is made in section 5.3 on the vertical structure question.

The analysis could get very complicated because there are numerous factors that influence optimal policy toward vertical structure and conduct. The economic analysis of these issues is not yet fully developed, but some progress has been made. In an attempt to clarify *some* of the underlying economic principles, we will use a relatively simple analytical framework, but caution is needed in interpreting the significance of the results that emerge. Moreover some important aspects of network pricing will not be considered at all in this chapter because they are not intrinsically about vertically related markets. Thus network externalities between users, congestion problems arising from network capacity constraints, and spatial aspects of network pricing are discussed instead in the chapters on industries such as telecommunications and electricity where they are especially relevant.

5.1 Vertical Integration: Some Basic Issues

Before considering the pros and cons of vertical integration in the context of a regulated industry, there are some prior questions to be discussed, in particular, the effect that vertical structure may have on (1) productive efficiency and (2) anticompetitive behavior.

To fix ideas, we will conduct the discussion in this section in terms of two hypothetical companies that operate in a very simplified "electricity" industry. (For more real-world complexity, see chapter 9.) Firm G is a generator of electricity, possibly in competition with other generators, and firm M is a transmission/distribution monopolist.[1] The question is whether G and M should combine to form a single firm or keep separate. Which is the more profitable structure, and which is better in terms of social welfare?

5.1.1 Organizational Structure and Productive Efficiency
An important element of the question just posed has to do with productive efficiency: Will electricity be produced more efficiently with separation or integration? The choice between organizational forms is actually much wider than integration versus separation, hierarchy versus markets. There is a range of possibilities with pure spot market transactions or bargaining at one extreme, full integration at the other, and contractual arrangements of varying duration in between. Thus firms G and M might trade at arm's length only, respectively selling into and buying from a wholesale electricity market, they might have a supply contract for a period of years, or they might form a single company.

---

1. In reality, of course, electricity supply requires more than generation and transmission (see chapter 9), but it is convenient here to assume that there are two vertically related activities, not more. In terms of electricity supply technology, generation is "upstream" from transmission and distribution, whereas in figure 5.1 we depicted the natural monopoly network activity "upstream" from the potentially competitive activities. This is appropriate as a representation of the *economics* of the situation if, as in fact, firms in the competitive activities take network access terms as given. In the gas and electricity industries, some potentially competitive activities are upstream from the natural monopoly network and others (e.g., retail supply) are downstream, but the basic economic principles of network access pricing are best considered in the simpler setting of figure 5.1. To avoid confusion, we do not use the terms "upstream" and "downstream" in what follows.

The relationship between organizational form and productive efficiency is perhaps the most fundamental question in the theory of the firm, and one that raises deep issues. To give just the "technological" answer that integration is more efficient than separation if and only if there are economies of scope between the two activities simply restates the question. We must look for the underlying reasons why such economies do or do not exist. Coase (1937) proposed that attention be focused on the *transaction*, not technology, as the unit of analysis, and he argued that relative transactions costs determine whether transactions are carried out within firms or across markets. A number of authors have since examined various kinds of transactions cost; for example, see Williamson (1975) and the surveys by Holmstrom and Tirole (1989), and Perry (1989).

The Holdup Problem   An important advantage of integration over separation arises from the possibility of *holdup* involving asset-specific investments. Returning to our illustrative example, suppose that firm M is the only potential buyer of the electricity produced by firm G. Consider the situation before G has decided to build a power plant to serve M's needs. There are large sunk costs in electricity generation—power stations have little value in uses other than electricity generation. If G went ahead and built its plant without a contractual arrangement with M, it would be at M's mercy thereafter. For example, M might refuse to pay G more than just the operating costs (for fuel, labor, etc.) of electricity generation, leaving G unable to recover the bulk of its sunk capital costs. Anticipating this possibility, G might be deterred from investing in the power plant in the first place, to the detriment of all. Even if this did not happen, G might choose a less capital-intensive mode of production (e.g., gas instead of coal-fired plant) than it would have done otherwise. Conversely, if G is the only potential seller to M, then M might be wary of investing efficiently in transmission and distribution capital for fear that G might opportunistically exploit the situation ex post once the investment had been sunk.

Integration, or at least a long-term contract, between G and M can overcome the holdup problem. If the prices that M will pay for electricity, possibly indexed to exogenous factors such as the rate of inflation and the level of world oil prices, are fixed by contract before investments are sunk, then the scope for ex post opportunism is removed provided that the contract is enforceable. Likewise, integration removes the incentive for such behavior.

Note also that *competition* can improve matters. If G had a number of independent potential customers competing to buy its electricity, then none of them individually would be able to exploit G opportunistically. The investment by G would not be relation specific with M. Put another way, G's investment to supply M would involve a smaller degree of sunk cost in that situation because the power station could be used to supply other buyers instead.

Empirical evidence in support of the holdup problem as a determinant of organizational form comes from Joskow's (1987) study of coal-fired power stations, which are often built close to coal mines, for obvious efficiency reasons.[2] Unless there are competing suppliers of coal nearby, the owner of such a plant might be vulnerable to holdup by the mine owner in the form of a hike in coal prices once generating costs were sunk. This is formally the same as the problem between G and M above, the only difference being that the generator's problem here is with an input supplier rather than with a purchaser. Joskow found that longer-term contracts are more commonly found where generators have poorer alternative sources of coal supply available to them, which is what theory predicts.

Finally, note that the underinvestment problem associated with regulatory risk (see section 3.6) is essentially an instance of the holdup problem that we have been discussing. The risk is that the regulator, unable to commit his actions fully in advance, may alter price control or environmental policy ex post after the regulated firm has sunk costs in industry-specific investments. In short, the regulator might hold up producers. Unless this risk is overcome by credible commitments ex ante, efficient investment may be deterred. From this perspective, public ownership is like vertical integration between production and regulation, whereas with privatization these functions are separated.

Risk Sharing Another possible motivation for long-term contracts, as opposed to spot market dealings, between G and M is risk sharing.[3] Suppose, for example, that a large proportion of G's generation costs, including the capital costs, have been fixed in advance, and that M's revenues from customers are also fairly stable, perhaps because they have been

2. See also the empirical studies of vertical integration in the electricity supply industry by Kerkvliet (1991) and Kaserman and Mayo (1991).
3. For a detailed discussion of the economics of price stabilization, see Newbery and Stiglitz (1981).

determined by regulation. If G and M, respectively, sold to and bought from a wholesale electricity market or pool, they would both be exposed to volatility in the pool price. A long-term contract between G and M can offer mutual insurance because the outcome that is bad for G, namely a low pool price, is good for M, and vice versa for a high pool price.

Such a contract need not take the form of an agreement actually to supply electricity at a preagreed price, which is anyway technologically impossible in the case of electricity. It can instead be a purely financial arrangement whereby monetary payments are made between G and M according to the difference between the pool price and some agreed benchmark price. In principle, such arrangements could just as well exist between the electricity companies, on one hand, and third parties, on the other, for example, electricity contract brokers. (If a liquid market existed for contracts of this kind, investors themselves, rather than the firms' managers, could adopt contract positions to suit their own needs. There is an obvious analogy with foreign exchange cover.) This suggests that the risk-sharing motive per se is not an explanation for integration or long-term contracts between G and M. In addition there must be a reason why direct dealing between G and M is more efficient than independent transactions in a contract market, which takes us back to the question of relative transactions costs.

Incomplete Contracts and Property Rights   Although the holdup problem and risk sharing are two reasons (there are of course others) why it might be efficient for G and M not to transact entirely at arm's length, we have not really gone to the heart of the problem. First, a long-term contractual relationship is not the same as full integration between G and M in the sense of them being under common ownership. This raises the question of what exactly *is* ownership? Second, no efficiency arguments have so far been given *against* integration.

Recent theories of incomplete contract and property rights address these issues; see Grossman and Hart (1986) and Hart and Moore (1990). In a world where contracts were complete, in the sense of specifying what was to happen in every eventuality, ownership would not affect behavior at all because everything would be determined by the web of contracts. However, for various good reasons, we are in a world where contracts are incomplete—they leave all sorts of scope for discretionary behavior—and this is where ownership matters. Ownership of a piece of property, say, a generating plant, can be identified with the residual control rights over it—that is, the rights to decide what to do with the asset subject to what is already determined by contracts.

Some aspects of economic behavior, for example, investment in human capital, cannot easily be contracted. The distribution of property rights over related physical assets makes a big difference to incentives for non-contractable investment of this kind. The pattern of residual control rights determines bargaining power, and hence the division of surplus created by such investments. The holdup problem is a case in point. If the investment in generation and transmission equipment were noncontractable, then integrated ownership—and therefore integrated exercise of residual control rights—would be efficient.

In short the incomplete contracts approach to the theory of the firm identifies a firm as a collection of physical assets and views ownership in terms of residual control rights over those assets. Property rights affect incentives for noncontractable investments. When assets are complementary, integrated ownership can ameliorate holdup problems. When they are unrelated, on the other hand, separate ownership can reduce free-rider problems in relation to noncontractible investments. The incomplete contracts approach is of course much richer than this sketch suggests. It can embrace a great variety of organizational forms and has been extended to questions of financial structure. But the approach is in its early days, and it has not yet been fully developed as a theory of the large corporation. It nevertheless provides a valuable perspective on questions of integration within the utility industries, and on the relationship between firm and regulator, which can usefully be viewed as an incomplete "regulatory contract."

5.1.2 Vertical Integration and Foreclosure[4]

Having discussed possible effects of vertical integration on productive efficiency, we will now consider the effect it may have upon competition. Suppose, then, that firm G is one of a number of potentially competing generators. To abstract from regulatory issues, suppose initially that M is also unregulated. There appears to be the danger that if M is allowed to integrate with G, it will shut rival generators out of the market by means of prohibitive network access charges, and thereby extend its monopoly of transmission also to generation.

---

4. For a broader discussion, see Tirole (1988, ch. 4), which also includes analysis of issues that arise in manufacturer-retailer vertical relationships.

However, there are well-known counterarguments to this "extension of market power" hypothesis. First, monopoly profit from the industry can be extracted just once, and if M can get all that profit by appropriate transmission charges, then there is no reason to do with market power, as opposed to productive efficiency, for extending its activities into generation. Second, if G was not the most efficient generator, then it would seem that M could profitably contract for electricity supplies from a more efficient generator, in which case integration with G would occur only if it was the most efficient arrangement.

The first of these points is correct in a famous special case. Suppose that the two inputs are combined in fixed coefficients, that there are no economies of scope between the vertically related activities, that there are no vertical externalities, and that there are constant returns and perfect competition between symmetric firms in the competitive sector (i.e., "generation" in our example). Then it is indeed true that M can extract all the monopoly profit that there is to be had while remaining in the transmission activity alone. Let a be the price per unit of network access, let c be the unit cost of generation, and let P be the price of electricity to the final consumer. Given the assumption of perfect competition in generation, it will be the case that $P = a + c$. By the choice of a, firm M can bring about the $P = P^*$ that maximizes industry profit. None of that profit leaks to other firms—M gets all of it. And there is no productive inefficiency in this setting because there are no economies of scale or scope, input proportions are fixed, and firms are assumed to be symmetric.

It will be apparent, however, that this is a very special case, and the argument that there is no market power reason for vertical integration and foreclosure may not be robust. For example, if technology is such that input proportions are variable rather than fixed, then productive inefficiency will occur with vertical separation and linear access pricing, as generators substituted away from overpriced transmission. This will reduce industry profit below its maximum level and give M a profit incentive for vertical integration and foreclosure. In welfare terms that move has ambiguous effects because greater productive efficiency must be weighed against higher prices (M's market power having been diminished by the ability of firms in the competitive sector to substitute away from its input to some extent).

The reason for vertical integration and foreclosure that will be given most attention below is imperfect competition between firms in the competitive sector. From the point of view of profit, vertical integration and foreclosure is doubly profitable when there is imperfect competition. (It is assumed that all the other assumptions are in place, including symmetry, constant returns, and fixed coefficients.) First, it enables firm M to get the entire industry profit for itself. Without foreclosure it cannot stop some being obtained by other firms. Second, integration and foreclosure typically allows industry profit to be increased. This is because of the double markup problem with separation, which is a kind of vertical externality.

Assuming that there is uniform pricing of network access, the price of access a will exceed its marginal cost. With imperfect competition a further markup will be added: $P > a + c$. Therefore the final product price will contain two markups. The vertical externality is that, having set the access price a above the marginal cost of access, firm M would like demand for access to be maximized. But imperfect competition in the vertically related activity causes firms there somewhat to restrict output in order to increase their margins, which imposes a negative externality upon both M and consumers. Because of this double markup problem, the final price P generally exceeds the pure monopoly price P^*. Therefore consumers, as well as M, gain from vertical integration and foreclosure in this setting.

This argument rests, however, on the assumption that there is linear pricing of network access. If nonlinear pricing is feasible, all monopoly profit can be extracted even with vertical separation. (The same point applies to the input substitution case above.) With two-part pricing, for example, a can be set appropriately above the marginal cost of access so as to induce the profit-maximizing price P^*, and the fixed part of the pricing scheme can be set so as to channel all industry profit from the (imperfectly) competitive sector to firm M. Thus the double markup argument can be seen partly as a consequence of the assumed restriction on contracting possibilities when there is separation, in particular, the absence of nonlinear pricing, rather than being about vertical integration per se.

Imperfect competition and its associated price-cost markups are quite consistent with free entry and zero profits in the competitive sector if the assumption of constant returns is dropped. For example, if there is free entry and a fixed cost K in addition to the marginal cost c, then the gross profits from imperfect competition markups will be competed away by entry. A new factor then comes into the analysis—overall productive efficiency in the competitive sector. Vertical integration and foreclosure can save on duplication of the fixed cost K and convert it into profit for the monopolist M. This is effectively an instance of the excess entry result that obtains in homogeneous goods oligopoly models, which may be reversed when there is product differentiation, as discussed in section 4.1.3. When there are decreasing returns to scale in the competitive sector, however, vertical integration and foreclosure will tend to increase overall production costs.

Let us take stock of the discussion so far. It has been assumed that M has an *unregulated pure monopoly* over the network services that are an essential input for production and full *information* about industry conditions. We have compared the monopoly outcome under vertical integration and foreclosure with the monopoly outcome under vertical separation. In some circumstances, for example, constant returns to scale, fixed coefficients, symmetric firms, and perfect competition, the pure monopoly outcome can be implemented and M can extract all industry profit without entering the generation business. In other circumstances, for example, where competition entails wasteful duplication of fixed costs, vertical integration and foreclosure can promote welfare as well as profit: better efficient monopoly than inefficient monopoly.

But it is hardly surprising that vertical integration and foreclosure often has benign effects in the assumed circumstances. In the framework above, M had full information and a rich set of instruments, competition had little role to play in the promotion of efficiency, and regulation was absent. Policy analysis requires richer modeling of competition and regulation, and this may lead to a rather different perspective on the desirability of vertical integration and foreclosure.

First, let us relax the assumptions about full information and symmetry between firms. (We saw in section 4.1.4 the potential importance of the selecting role of competition in this context.) Suppose that demand is totally inelastic at one unit up to some reservation price level and that there are two generators G_1 and G_2, each with a cost level that is private information, drawn independently from some cost distribution. Assume that under vertical separation, that is, with M owning neither G_1 nor G_2, the generators bid for the right of access, or equivalently that M holds a competitive tender for generation services. A competition of this form will result in productive efficiency because the lowest cost generator will win the competition.

Now compare the situation when M is vertically integrated with G_1. In principle there is mutual advantage in achieving productive efficiency because, if G_2 is more efficient than G_1, the efficiency gain can be shared, thereby making all producers better off. But unless bargaining is costless, the asymmetry between G_1 and G_2 that vertical integration creates will lead to some chance of productive inefficiency. Despite this the expected joint profit of M and G_1 could very well be greater with integration than with separation because the asymmetry created by integration puts G_2 at a strategic disadvantage.

For example, suppose that bargaining takes the form of a take-it-or-leave-it offer by M to supply network access to G_2 at some fixed access price $\bar{a}$ (or equivalently an offer by M to buy generation services from G_2).[5] Productive efficiency requires that $\bar{a}$ be set so that G_2 will produce if and only if $c_2 < c_1$. In that case G_2 will make a profit $(c_1 - c_2)$ equal to its efficiency advantage in generation. However, it is not in M's interest to set $\bar{a}$ at this level because it can make more expected profit by setting $\bar{a}$ somewhat higher in order to have a chance of capturing some of any efficiency advantage that G_2 might have. Higher $\bar{a}$ increases M's share of G_2's efficiency advantage (if it has one) but also increases the probability that G_2 will not accept. The privately optimal compromise for M will be socially inefficient because the access price will preclude G_2 on some occasions when it is the more efficient generator.

A similar outcome occurs if, instead of M having the power to make a take-it-or leave-it offer, it is G_2 that offers generation services to M. Productive efficiency would require G_2 to offer a price of c_2 so that M would produce internally via G_1 if and only if $c_1 < c_2$, but offering to supply at c_2 would cause G_2 to make zero profit. It can get a positive expected profit by offering to supply at a somewhat higher price, which causes productive inefficiency with positive probability. This is quite consistent with M and G_1 making higher expected joint profits than they get with vertical separation.

These examples are of course no more than illustrations of how asymmetry of information combined with asymmetry of structure—G_1 being vertically integrated with M—can lead to inefficiency. Whereas vertical separation gives a "level playing field" and productive efficiency, with vertical integration there is a positive probability of inefficiency. Nevertheless, the network monopolist may well do better with integration than with separation. Thus private and social incentives can diverge. Asymmetric information can get in the way of (Coasian) efficiency.

Second, returning to the full information case, let us now relax the assumption that M has a pure monopoly over network services. Then

---

5. This argument is in the spirit of Aghion and Bolton's (1987) analysis of contracts as a barrier to entry.

there may be a new motive for vertical integration and foreclosure, namely the desire to thwart actual or potential network rivals. Let the original network provider be M_1, and suppose that it is threatened by the entry of a second network provider M_2. If M_1 preempts by acquiring both G_1 and G_2, and if this creates a credible commitment that neither of them will deal with M_2, then M_2 will not enter (or may exit if it is already in the market). This is a case of vertical integration and foreclosure maintaining or extending market power by its strategic effect on rival firms. A similar effect may be achieved even if M_1 acquires just G_1 because that may enhance G_2's potential market power in its dealings with M_2 to the point where M_2 can no longer enter (or remain in the market) profitably. This way of *raising rivals' costs* (see Salop and Scheffman 1983, 1987) by vertical merger has been analyzed by Ordover, Saloner and Salop (1990).

Hart and Tirole (1990), using the incomplete contracts approach of the recent property rights literature (see above), question whether a merger of M_1 and G_1 would by itself raise rivals' costs. If there is two-part pricing between M_2 and G_2, then the merger does not affect their marginal costs, and it may not be credible for the combined M_1 and G_1 to refuse to supply the other firms, since they can supply each other. But Hart and Tirole show that if, say, M_2 is relatively inefficient, then integration may indeed make refusal to supply credible, whereas it would not be otherwise because (unless constrained by an exclusive dealing contract) M_1 would have an incentive to sell some extra units to G_2. If M_1 owns G_1, then the incentive to sell to G_2 is much reduced, because the resulting competition from G_2, which would benefit consumers, would hurt the integrated M_1-G_1. In short, ownership changes incentives in such a way that foreclosure may happen. Hart and Tirole explore another motive for integration that arises when there are capacity constraints (see also Bolton and Whinston 1991, 1993). If, for example, transmission capacity is limited in the sense that a transmission company can serve just one generator, then a merger of M_1 and G_1 means that they will always trade together, but G_2 loses the opportunity to trade with M_1. This weakens the bargaining position of M_2, possibly to the point where it chooses to leave (or not enter) the industry.[6] This point can be related to the previous discussion of the holdup problem: the merger of M_1 and G_1 makes any sunk investment by G_2 more

---

6. This is similar in spirit to the effect examined by Ordover, Saloner, and Salop (1990), but it does not rely on an assumption that M_1 would not want to supply G_2. Capacity constraints mean that it cannot supply G_2.

vulnerable to holdup by M_2 once the alternative of dealing with M_1 disappears.

5.1.3 Discussion

From a general perspective vertical integration and vertical restraints can be viewed as having two main purposes: (1) overcoming externalities between the parties involved, and (2) creating strategic advantages with respect to third parties. The analysis in this section can be summarized from this perspective.

Included in point 1 are investment externalities when there is a danger of holdup, risk-sharing externalities, pricing externalities as with the double-markup problem, and nonprice externalities, for example, relating to product quality. Long-term contracts, let alone coownership, are not always necessary to deal with these externalities. In principle, markets can provide insurance and nonlinear pricing can remove double markups, for example. But missing markets and restrictions on feasible pricing schemes mean that long-term contracts may be the best practical solution. Because of inevitable contractual incompleteness, integration by ownership can dominate contracts. It is usually desirable for vertical externalities between firms to be overcome. Consumers tend not to benefit from them, as the double-markup problem illustrates. If integration enables economies of scope to be achieved, then consumers will benefit even if monopoly prevails. Overcoming vertical externalities, by itself, does nothing to extend market power from one activity to another.

Unfortunately, vertical integration and restraints have other purposes as well, which brings us to point 2. If endowed with full information and commitment power, and enough instruments of control, a monopolist in one activity would have nothing to gain from inefficiency in a vertically related activity because maximizing profit would entail maximizing efficiency. In particular, it would be neither privately nor socially desirable to exclude a more efficient competitor from the related activity. But reality does not accord with this theoretical benchmark case, and in practice there is much scope for divergence between private and social incentives. We saw above how vertical integration can enable the parties involved to capture some of the expected profits of rivals, and in a manner that damages productive efficiency. And we saw how it can make anticompetitive practices such as refusal to supply credible, thereby raising rivals' costs, perhaps to the point where rivals exit (or decide not to enter).

Strategic effects of this kind can certainly strengthen the market power of the integrated firm and lead to both allocative and productive inefficiency.

The most obvious shortcoming of analysis so far given our focus on the utility industries is the absence of regulation of network access prices. Before we return to the structural question of vertical integration versus separation in section 5.3, the next section is about this crucial aspect of conduct regulation.

5.2   Access Price Regulation

From now on it will be assumed that firm M has a pure monopoly of network operation and that its network monopoly is regulated. The question is how to set the terms on which other firms can have access to the network facilities. Should access be priced at marginal cost, or should a contribution be made to the fixed costs of network provision? On the other hand, could it be optimal to price access below marginal cost in order to offset the effects of price-cost markups due to imperfect competition? Is M's marginal cost in the competitive activity relevant? How do the answers to these questions depend on whether there is vertical separation or integration of firm M, and on whether M is regulated in the competitive sector?

To tackle these questions, we will adopt a step-by-step approach, starting from a very simple framework and then building up a richer picture. As with pure monopoly regulation (see chapters 2 and 3), we must specify the objectives, instruments, and information available to the regulator. For example, what welfare weight is attached to profits made by firms in the competitive activity, is nonlinear access pricing possible or must access prices be uniform, can final product prices be regulated, and what cost information does the regulator have? The nature of competition between firms if there is deregulation of the competitive sector must also be considered: for example, is competition Bertrand or Cournot, and is there free entry? In addition, from the vertical integration literature just reviewed, we know the significance of such matters as substitutability between inputs and possibilities for anticompetitive behavior.

For maximum simplicity, however, we will abstract from most of those factors and assume homogeneous goods and fixed coefficients technology. We will also assume that each firm has constant marginal costs. The discussion will be set in the following framework, which accords with that above and with earlier chapters: a is the price per unit of access, P is the final product price, $Q(P)$ is demand, θ is the marginal cost of access, F is the fixed cost of network provision, c_i is the marginal cost of firm i in the competitive sector, and K is the sunk cost of entry into that sector (sometimes K will be set equal to zero). Finally, the regulator's objective is to maximize the weighted average of consumer surplus and industry profit: $W = (V - T) + \alpha\Pi$, where V is the indirect utility function, T is the lump-sum transfer (if any) paid to firm M, Π is total industry profit, and α is a weight between zero and one. With cost symmetry between firms $(c_i = c)$ and with n firms in the competitive sector, we have

$$W = V(P) + [P(\theta) - (\theta + c)]Q(P) - (F + nK) - (1 - \alpha)\Pi. \qquad (5.1)$$

The first term in (5.1) is gross consumer surplus, the second term is product market revenue minus variable costs of production, the third term is fixed costs of production, and the final term is the distributional welfare loss from positive industry profits. In our base case it is assumed that regulation applies to a and T and that the regulator *knows* θ. (The relaxation of this strong informational assumption is discussed below.)

The nature of optimal access price regulation depends partly upon whether there is vertical separation or integration, and we consider the two cases in turn. The form of competition and regulation in the competitive sector is also important, and we consider both Bertrand and Cournot competition, in the latter case with and without free entry, and regulation of the final product market when there is vertical integration.

5.2.1 Vertical Separation

With vertical separation, if all firms in the competitive sector are symmetric $(c_i = c)$, then the final product price under Bertrand competition is simply $P = c + a$. (To be sustainable, Bertrand competition requires that $K = 0$ unless fixed costs are subsidized.) The first best outcome $P = \theta + c$ can be obtained by setting $a = \theta$ if transfers are allowed: break-even can be ensured by setting T equal to F, the fixed cost of network operation. If such transfers are not allowed, then average cost pricing of access, namely setting a so that $aQ(a + c) = F$, is optimal given the break-even constraint for firm M. If firms in the competitive sector are not necessarily symmetric —for example, if c_i is a random draw from some distribution of costs— then expected welfare will be maximized if access is priced a little below its marginal cost to offset the price-cost markup of the winning firm. But with

Bertrand competition, unless cost asymmetries are large, this markup is likely to be small, in which case marginal cost pricing of access is a good approximation to the first best.

With Cournot competition, however, there may well be a case for pricing access below its marginal cost in order to offset price-cost markups in the competitive sector. Suppose, for example, that the elasticity of demand is equal to one: $Q(P) = 1/P$ (this example will be discussed further below). With this functional form for the demand curve, industry profits at Cournot equilibrium are independent of the level of unit costs. In fact they are equal to $1/n - nK$, that is, $1/n^2 - K$ per firm, when there are n firms in the competitive sector. In this example, then, the choice of a does not affect the distributional loss from profits, the final term in (5.1). The final product price is given by $P = n(c + a)/(n - 1)$. If transfers are allowed, allocative efficiency $P = \theta + c$ can be achieved by setting $a = \theta - (\theta + c)/n$. This shows the subsidy necessary to offset Cournot markups in the competitive sector. The lump-sum transfer must cover the cost of this subsidy as well as the fixed cost F. In fact $T = F + 1/n$. Obviously access cannot be subsidized if lump-sum transfers are impossible.

This example illustrates a general point. With a fixed number of firms, the ability to make transfers, and full information, it is optimal to have allocative efficiency ($P = \theta + c$) irrespective of the particular demand curve. With imperfect competition in the competitive sector, it follows that $P > a + c$. Therefore it is optimal to have $a < \theta$ given the present assumptions.

Returning to the unit elastic demand example, suppose now that the number of firms n is determined endogenously by a free entry condition in the competitive sector. Assume that entry decisions are taken after the terms of access have been set. Ignoring integer problems, the free entry number of firms is given by the zero profit condition that $n = 1/k$, where $k \equiv \sqrt{K}$. Note that like profit in the fixed n case, this is independent of regulatory policy in this example. Therefore regulatory policy cannot affect the number of times that the fixed cost K is incurred. If lump-sum transfers are allowed, it is again optimal to induce allocative efficiency ($P = \theta + c$) by subsidizing access. This is achieved by setting $a = \theta - k(\theta + c)$, and the corresponding transfer is $T = F + k$.

In general, however, it is *not* true that profit in the competitive sector when there is a given number of firms, or the number of firms there under free entry, is independent of regulatory policy. With linear demand (e.g.,

$Q = 1 - P$), profits fall (or fewer firms enter) as the access price increases.[7]
In this case it is optimal to compromise between allocative efficiency and
curbing profits (or the number of times that fixed costs are incurred).
When n is determined endogenously by free entry, for example, it is optimal to set the price of access equal to its marginal cost ($a = \theta$), and this
induces $P = \theta + c + k$.[8] This strikes the optimal balance between allocative efficiency and curbing excess entry. However, recall from section 4.1
that the excess entry tendency that arises in homogeneous-goods oligopoly
with symmetric firms does not necessarily hold in other conditions, for
example, if there is sufficient product differentiation. Therefore curbing
entry will not necessarily be a reason for inducing some allocative inefficiency in those more general conditions.

In short, in this homogeneous-goods Cournot framework with free entry and the possibility of lump-sum transfers, there is a case for subsidizing
network access so as to offset oligopoly markups in the competitive sector.
But the terms of access are likely also to affect productive efficiency, in
particular, the extent of duplication of fixed costs, and this may be a
countervailing influence.

For n given exogenously, the terms of access have no effect on productive efficiency when firms are symmetric, but they are likely to affect the
profits and hence (depending on α) the distributional cost of profits in
welfare terms. In the special case of unit elastic demand ($Q = 1/P$), in
which profits are independent of access terms, this effect is neutral. But just
as in the free entry analysis, if $\alpha < 1$ and $-QP''/P' \equiv E < 2$, then it is
optimal to forgo a degree of allocative efficiency and have $P > c$ in order
to curb the distributional cost of oligopoly profits (but optimal P approaches c as n gets large). The fixed n and free entry cases are very similar
because oligopoly profits are the source of distributional loss in the former
and excess entry in the latter.

5.2.2 Vertical Integration

With vertical integration firms are no longer symmetrically placed. Irrespective of the level of the access price a, the direct cost of access for firm

---

7. In general, the sign of this effect depends on whether the elasticity of the slope of the
inverse demand curve $E \equiv -QP''/P'$ exceeds 2. With linear demand, $E = 0$ and profit falls as
a rises. With unit elastic demand, $E = 2$ and there is no effect. With general isoelastic demand, $P = Q^{-\varepsilon}$, $E = (\varepsilon + 1)$. On the importance of E in the analysis of Cournot oligopoly, see
Seade (1985).
8. More generally, with optimal regulation, $(a - \theta)$ has the same sign as $-E$, and $(P - c)$ has
the same sign as $(2 - E)$.

M's operations in the competitive sector is equal to the marginal cost of access θ, whereas for independent firms the cost of access is a. This might suggest that marginal cost pricing of access might be desirable to put firms on an equal footing. But that is not by itself a good argument, and there is a need for careful analysis that is sensitive to competitive and regulatory circumstances.

Regulated Product Market   Let us begin by supposing that as well as the access price being regulated, the final product price is fixed by regulation: $P = \bar{P}$, say. Let c_m be M's unit cost in the competitive activity, and assume that $K = 0$. Suppose that the regulator knows c_m but not the costs of rival firms. With P fixed, the access price has no effect on allocative efficiency. The access pricing rule that achieves productive efficiency is simply: $a = \bar{P} - c_m$. Rival i will be able profitably to undercut firm M in the competitive sector if and only if it is more efficient than M in that activity—that is, if and only if $c_i < \bar{P} - a$, which is equivalent to $c_i < c_m$.[9]

This pricing policy is an instance of the *efficient component pricing rule* (ECPR) due to Baumol (1983) and Willig (1979), and discussed by Baumol and Sidak (1994) in relation to railway and telecommunications network access pricing. The ECPR says that the price of access should equal the incremental cost to M of providing the access including any *opportunity cost* in terms of lost profit. In the example just described, M loses a unit of final product sales for each unit of access supplied to rivals—there is one-for-one displacement of business because the total quantity of access is fixed ($\bar{P}$ being set by regulation), and there are fixed coefficients in supply. Firm M would have made a profit of $(\bar{P} - c_m - \theta)$ on each of those units. Adding that opportunity cost to the direct marginal cost of access θ yields $a = P - c_m$.

Therefore the ECPR *is* a form of marginal cost pricing, where the cost involved includes the opportunity cost to M. This is true irrespective of the level of $\bar{P}$. Thus the ECPR provides a case for rivals being required to contribute to the fixed costs of network operation (see section 7.5.6 on the access deficit contributions issue in telecommunications).

---

9. Distributional considerations might call for a slight amendment of this rule. Suppose that M's profits have greater welfare weight than those of rival firms (e.g., because they can be extracted by the regulator via lump-sum transfers). Then there might be a case for setting a slightly *higher* than $\bar{P} - c_m$. This jeopardizes a small amount of productive efficiency but leads to an expected gain in distributional terms as some expected profits are transferred from rivals to M. A similar effect operates when the rivals are a competitive fringe with an upward-sloping supply curve.

An important assumption in this discussion was that $\bar{P}$ was *fixed* by regulation. A new factor enters the analysis if $\bar{P}$ is a price *cap* below which there is downward flexibility. If the cap has been set in accordance with allocative efficiency for firm M—that is, marginal cost pricing ($\bar{P} = \theta + c_m$) or average cost pricing if transfers are impossible—then the ECPR is still good. But suppose that $\bar{P}$ has been set at a significantly higher level. Then the ECPR, which is geared to productive efficiency, would entail significant losses of allocative and distributional efficiency. For example, in a contestable market, the final product price equals $\bar{P}$ or $P = a + c$, whichever is the lower. It is optimal to set access terms in this example in accordance with marginal cost pricing principles ($a = \theta$), or average cost pricing principles if transfers are impossible. That is consistent with the ECPR only if $\bar{P}$ has been set in accordance with the same principles. In this framework, then, the ECPR is an element of optimal price regulation, the desirability of which depends on the other element(s) being set optimally too and on the nature of product market competition.

The discussion has also assumed that all firms supply homogeneous products. If there is product differentiation, M's loss of final product sales as rivals are supplied with access will be at a rate less than one for one, and the opportunity cost of providing access will be correspondingly smaller. If, for example, rivals' products are totally independent from M's, then there is no opportunity cost of providing access, and it should be priced at direct marginal cost only. In intermediate cases, where products are substitutes but not perfect substitutes, access should be priced somewhere between $a = \theta$ and $a = \bar{P} - c_m$, given our other assumptions.

Unregulated Product Market Now consider the question of access pricing when the final product price is not regulated.[10] With Bertrand competition, homogeneous goods, and fixed coefficients technology, the principles of optimal access pricing are exactly the same as with vertical separation. In particular, "level-playing-field" arguments do not add to the case for pricing access at its marginal cost. This is because, although M's direct cost of providing access to rival firms is the underlying marginal

---

10. There is the question of why the regulator is not empowered to regulate the competitive sector too—it may appear ad hoc to confine regulation to the natural monopoly sector. However, given the fact that liberalization is often not accompanied by price and entry controls, it seems important to examine access pricing in the absence of regulation of the competitive sector even if we do not explain that absence. It is not hard to think of reasons outside the model discussed, notably regulatory failures, that could make full deregulation of the competitive sector optimal.

cost θ, the *opportunity* cost to M is the access price a, just as it is for independent firms in the competitive sector. (A similar point about opportunity cost was made in connection with the ECPR.) If the access price has been set at a and M undercuts a rival to supply final consumers, then M loses a times the amount of network access that the rival would have bought. Therefore, irrespective of the level of a, the opportunity cost of access is the same for all firms despite their apparent asymmetry when there is vertical integration. It is therefore optimal to set a as described at the beginning of section 5.2.1.

However, there is no automatic "level playing field" because of opportunity cost considerations, and hence there is no equivalence with the vertical separation case when there is Cournot competition (or any other form of competition in which the "conjectural variation" term is greater than -1). In that case M takes as given the output of rival firms. So its marginal cost of access is θ—there is no further opportunity cost because with Cournot behavior other firms do not reduce their output as a result—but the marginal cost for the rivals is a.

To investigate some consequences of this asymmetry, let us return to the earlier example with (otherwise) symmetric firms and free entry, but now suppose that one of the firms in the competitive sector is owned by firm M. What is the socially optimal access price in this setting? In the unit elastic demand example ($Q = 1/P$), the number of firms in the competitive sector is no longer independent of the access price when there is vertical integration: n is strictly decreasing in a. Therefore higher a reduces the duplication of fixed costs. Given the availability of lump-sum transfers, it turns out to be optimal to set $a = \theta - k^2(\theta + c)$, which induces $P = (1 + k)(\theta + c)$. Access is still subsidized, but to a lesser degree than under vertical separation. It is optimal to forgo some allocative efficiency ($P > \theta + c$) because higher a reduces the duplication of fixed costs when there is vertical integration, even in this example with unit elastic demand. In the linear demand example ($P = 1 - Q$), the number of firms n was decreasing in a even with vertical separation. It is more so when there is integration, and optimally regulated prices are higher as a result. In fact optimal regulation implies that $a = \theta + k$ and $P = \theta + c + 2k$ in the linear example. Both these prices are higher by k than in the case of vertical separation.

To summarize, in this Cournot example with symmetric firms, full information on the part of the regulator, and the availability of lump-sum transfers, there were two opposing reasons to depart from marginal cost pricing of access. The aim of inducing allocative efficiency—marginal cost pricing of the final product—gave a reason for subsidizing access in order to offset imperfect competition markups. However, account must also be taken of possible productive efficiency losses due to duplication of fixed costs with free entry (or distributional welfare losses associated with rival profits if the number of firms is fixed). We saw how it might therefore be optimal to forgo some allocative efficiency and induce $P > \theta + c$. This latter effect was stronger with integration than with separation, and optimally regulated prices were shown to be higher under integration for this reason in both the simple demand examples discussed.

5.2.3 Asymmetric Information

Assuming that the regulator has full information provides a useful benchmark case but, as explained in chapter 2, asymmetric information is an essential part of a good model of regulation. It would have been unduly complicated to start with a model of vertically related industries that combined both imperfect competition and asymmetric information, but now that the former has been discussed, it is time to ask what difference asymmetric information makes.

Adverse selection and moral hazard issues in regulation were considered in earlier chapters. The multiproduct analysis in chapter 3 is especially relevant because a setting with two vertically related industries can be regarded as a multiproduct example with the special feature that the intermediate product (access) and the final product supplied by M are substitutes, because if M charges a higher final product price, demand for access increases as rivals expand their supply of the final product. Laffont and Tirole (1990a sec. II.3, 1992) approach the question of access pricing from this perspective using their "hidden action" model of multiproduct monopoly regulation, in which the regulator can observe the level of costs but not the cost-reducing effort by the firm.

As in the analysis described in chapter 3, the question of optimal pricing can be separated from the question of cost-reduction incentives if the incentive-pricing dichotomy" property holds. If so—for example, if marginal costs are constant—then the principles of access pricing are essentially the same as with symmetric information provided that transfers are possible. The factors that determine optimal access pricing include (1) the welfare weight on competitor/fringe profits, (2) the nature of competition between firm M and its rivals (e.g., Cournot or price-taking fringe), (3) the elasticity of fringe supply in the price-taking case, (4) whether final product prices are regulated as well as the access price, and (5) whether lump-sum transfers are available.

Optimal access pricing in the framework described above, namely Cournot behavior with free entry, can be analyzed in the presence of asymmetric information as in Baron and Myerson's (1982) adverse selection model.[11] Optimal access prices, and the final product prices that they give rise to, have additional (positive) terms relating to informational rents. Recall that in the pure monopoly model (in chapter 2), the trade-off was between allocative efficiency, which argued for marginal cost pricing, and the desire to curb firm M's information rents. These factors are important also when the monopoly is vertically related to a deregulated activity, but there are additional considerations as well. They include M's desire to raise rivals' costs, oligopoly markups, and possibly excess entry (or profits) due to imperfect competition.

5.2.4 Discussion

Chapter 2 on integrated pure monopoly began with the familiar principle of marginal cost pricing, which is optimal given our welfare criterion when there are no information asymmetries and when lump-sum transfers are possible. Even with these simplifying assumptions, however, the principle of pricing access at marginal cost is not optimal in all circumstances, and neither is the principle that access prices be set so as to induce marginal cost pricing for the final product. This is because of distortions that can arise, for example, oligopoly markups in the competitive sector, which may lead to distributionally costly profits there or to productive inefficiency because of excess entry. (The Cournot example illustrated these points.) Departures from marginal cost pricing of access may therefore be desirable (but these may run into another kind of productive inefficiency if input substitution is possible).

Access pricing becomes more complicated when the network monopolist, firm M, is vertically integrated. If regulation determines the final product price as well as to the terms of access, then the efficient component pricing rule implies that the access price should be set so that rivals take M's custom if and only if that is productively efficient. For that to happen, if M loses one unit of final sales for each unit of access supplied to rivals, then the *difference* between the final product price and the access price should equal M's marginal costs in the *competitive* activity.

---

11. See Vickers (1992).

If competition determines the final product price, then the terms of network access can have a significant effect upon the nature of competition because of the asymmetry between firm M and its rivals in the competitive sector. On the one hand, there is the danger that high access prices will bias competition in favor of M, and on the other hand, there is the danger of inefficient entry. With Bertrand competition, homogeneous goods, and fixed coefficient technology, this problem does not arise because the *opportunity* cost of access is the same for all firms including M, but this is not true in general, for example, with Cournot competition. The Cournot example illustrated that the asymmetry between firm M and its rivals causes optimal access prices to be amended relative to the vertical separation case, again because of distributionally costly profits or excess entry. When regulation is constrained by information asymmetries, the desire to limit M's information rents becomes another factor in optimal access price regulation, just as it was in chapters 2 and 3.

Finally, there is an important point that has not so far been mentioned in this chapter—the promotion of competition by assisting entry (see section 4.2.2). The possibility of excess entry that existed in the simple theoretical models discussed above might be of much less relevance in practice than positive benefits of competition that were absent from those models. In recently liberalized industries, incumbent advantages and entry barriers are likely to be significant at least initially, especially if the incumbent is vertically integrated. There may well be a case for modifying access pricing rules to offset those incumbent advantages to some extent, and perhaps even to favor rivals so that competitive conditions becomes established. Among other things, this might reduce the need for direct regulation of the potentially competitive sector, and its attendant costs. Downward adjustment of access prices is a natural way to do this.

In sum, marginal cost pricing principles are relevant for access pricing, but subject to a number of qualifications, and in a way that is sensitive to opportunity costs and to structural, competitive, and regulatory conditions.

5.3 Separation versus Integration: Welfare Comparison

Having considered some of the main factors that influence optimal access pricing, in a variety of circumstances, under vertical separation and under vertical integration, it is now time for an overall welfare comparison of the two. We will confine attention initially to the homogeneous-goods, symmetric cost, fixed coefficients framework and look at both Bertrand and Cournot behavior, in the latter case focusing on the examples of unit elastic and linear demand. Some more general issues will be discussed in section 5.3.2.

5.3.1 Welfare Comparison in the Basic Framework

In the basic Bertrand model, it made no real difference whether or not M was integrated because its opportunity cost of access was the same as that of rival firms. For any level of a, production would occur by the most efficient means in any event. In this basic setting, then, the welfare comparison between separation and integration is neutral. Of course many other factors could influence the comparison—for example, if vertical integration altered technological opportunities, information conditions, or the instruments available to the regulator—and it would be affected if the assumptions of homogeneous goods and fixed coefficients technology were relaxed.

With Cournot competition, however, there are important differences between separation and integration even in our simple framework. The overall welfare comparison can go either way, as the two examples with free entry illustrate. With optimal access price regulation in the case of linear demand ($Q = 1 - P$), the final product price P exceeds marginal cost $\theta + c$ by $2k$ with integration compared with k with separation. Allocative efficiency, as measured by the welfare triangle loss, is therefore $\frac{3}{2}k^2$ higher with separation. But productive efficiency is poorer because there is more duplication of the fixed cost K ($\equiv k^2$) with separation. In fact, with optimal regulation in each case, there are two more firms, and so productive efficiency is lower by $2k^2$ with separation. In this example, then, integration has the overall welfare advantage, by $\frac{1}{2}k^2 = 2k^2 - \frac{3}{2}k^2$.

It should not be surprising that integration has the advantage in this case. Even with separation, excess entry considerations mean that it is not optimal to subsidize access in this example (in fact $a = \theta$). The outcome that is optimal with separation could have been brought about equally well with integration. (Integrated M effectively faces $a = \theta$ too.) Integration can achieve yet higher welfare than the maximum level attainable with separation. More generally, if optimal access price regulation involves premia rather than subsidies, then integration will be superior in this simple framework.

The same reasoning suggests that separation will be superior if, as in the unit elastic example, optimal regulation in the integrated case involves subsidizing access. Then, for a given level of a (which implies a corresponding level of P), separation is better because the same total output is produced at lower total cost (i.e., with fewer firms) than with integration.

In the overall welfare comparison for the unit elastic demand case, allocative efficiency is again higher with separation than with integration. Even though output is higher with separation, the number of firms is lower, and so productive efficiency is greater too. In fact welfare is higher with separation than with integration in this example by $[\log(1 + k) - k(1 - k)] > 0$.

It is not immediately obvious how asymmetric information affects the *relative* merits of vertical separation and integration. An important difference has to do with M's incentives to raise rivals' costs, which was discussed above in relation to vertical foreclosure. Other things being equal, M benefits as the access price is increased when there is vertical separation because its network profits rise. With integration, however, there is another kind of benefit to firm M: its rivals are disadvantaged by higher a and their market shares shrink, whereas M's market share and profits in the competitive sector increase correspondingly. Therefore, with asymmetric information, M may require more in the way of lump-sum transfer (at the margin) to discourage higher access prices when there is vertical integration. With separation this question of anticompetitive incentives obviously does not arise.[12]

It so happens that the overall welfare comparisons between integration and separation for the linear demand example and for the unit elastic demand example are the same when there is asymmetric information as when there is not, despite the fact that firm M obtains costly information rents (see Vickers 1992). With optimal regulation those rents are the same with integration as with separation, the greater incentive to raise rivals' costs being exactly offset by lower optimal output. Therefore the principles discussed in the full information setting are important (indeed in these examples decisive) when there is asymmetric information.

5.3.2 Discussion
The basic framework analyzed above was able to illuminate *some* aspects of the trade-off between vertical integration and separation, but it has obvious limitations. First, the assumptions about costs abstracted from

---

12. Another possible difference between integration and separation is that integration—or more generally diversification from monopoly activities into others—may itself worsen the asymmetry of information between regulator and firm, for example, if cost information from the two sets of activities becomes blurred. This is an important reason for having "separate accounts for separate businesses" in integrated utilities, and it has been an issue in diversification plans by water companies (see section 10.4.4). For a theoretical analysis of this point, see Braeutigam and Panzar (1989).

important issues such as economies of scope, input substitution, scale effects, endogeneity of costs, and asymmetries between firms. The last two of these seem particularly important because level-playing-field arguments for vertical separation cannot be addressed if it assumed from the outset that firms have symmetric and exogenous costs. Insofar as the benefits of competition and liberalization derive from incentives for productive efficiency (see section 4.1.4), a level playing field between firms may be important for their realization.

Second, the basic framework did not address some important concerns about anticompetitive behavior. When there is vertical integration, firm M has incentives to raise rivals' costs, which regulation may not be able to hold in check without cost. As mentioned above, this may create difficulties for access price regulation when there is asymmetric information between regulator and firm. In practice, other aspects of access terms are important too—the *quality* of access has been of continuing concern in telecommunications, for example (see further section 7.5.1). More generally, structural separation might improve the quality of information available for regulation.

Third, much (but not all) of our discussion was based on the assumption that the fixed cost of network provision could be financed by transfers independently of the (marginal) price of access. If, on the other hand, linear access prices are the only feasible way of financing those fixed costs, then vertical integration might imply a very asymmetric basis for competition, depending on the form of rivalry in the competitive sector.

5.4 Conclusions

Whether or not to apply policies of vertical separation to previously integrated monopolies is perhaps the most important question for structure regulation. How to set access prices and other terms of interconnection are key issues for conduct regulation and for the success of liberalization policies. In this chapter, by analyzing some simple models and by more general discussion, we have attempted to examine some of the main factors that bear on these questions.

This is no easy task because the analysis must combine elements from (1) the theory of the firm, (2) theories of vertical relationships, (3) theories of regulation, and (4) theories of the competitive process. We have seen in earlier chapters that elements 3 and 4 individually, never mind their combination with other factors, can be complex enough. Moreover second-best comparisons between imperfect institutional alternatives—vertical separation versus vertical integration in the present context—are always difficult and sensitive to assumptions, for example, concerning information and available instruments.

We began, abstracting from regulation, by reviewing some efficiency motivations for vertical relationships and integration, which mostly concerned the internalization of externalities between the parties, for example, relating to investment and transfer pricing. We then examined strategic motives for anticompetitive vertical foreclosure and their possible adverse consequences for both productive and allocative efficiency. Introducing regulation into the analysis, we examined factors that influence optimal access pricing, which can be especially complicated when there is vertical integration. The usual principles of marginal cost pricing (with proper account being taken of opportunity cost) are a useful guide, but their application requires careful interpretation and modification depending on competitive and regulatory circumstances. Finally, we commented on structural policy options in the light of the previous analysis.

Although this chapter has assumed that the potentially competitive sector of the industry is liberalized, it is appropriate to conclude by commenting on the choice between the *three* broad structural policy options set out in the introductory chapter: (1) vertically integrated monopoly, (2) vertical separation with liberalization, and (3) vertical integration with liberalization. At a general level three principal factors are relevant to the choice between these options: the extent of internal efficiencies arising from economies of scope, the danger that integration may distort competition and lose its efficiency benefits, and the effectiveness of conduct regulation.

If there are large economies of scope between the vertical related activities, then their combination might be significantly naturally monopolistic even if one of the activities by itself is not. In that case competition is likely to be ineffective or inefficient, in which case 1 will be the best option. The comparison between options 2 and 3 becomes relevant when that is not so.

If scope economies are known not to be significant, there is a case for separation (unless price regulation is easier when there is integration). If integration might yield significant scope economies, then ideally vertical conduct regulation—of interconnection terms, anticompetitive behavior, and so on—would be sufficient to establish conditions for effective competition without the need for structural separation. In many circumstances, however, it seems likely that the effects of integration on the firm's incentives and on the information available to the regulator might make the regulation of conduct, especially vertical conduct, harder. Measures of partial separation—separate accounts, separate subsidiaries, and so on— may or may not be able to ease this problem. If vertical conduct regulation is difficult and if the benefits of competition are thought to be substantial, then structural remedies even at some cost in terms of scope economies may deserve examination.

The purpose of the theoretical analysis in part I of this book has been to set out some of the main economic principles that are relevant for analyzing competition and regulatory policy in the utility industries. The rest of the book examines their application in the circumstances of four industries in particular—telecommunications, gas, electricity, and water —and describes the rich experience of regulatory reform in Britain. The varying policies toward structural reform in Britain's utility industries have been among the most interesting aspects of that experience.

II

BRITISH EXPERIENCE

6

RPI − *X* Price Cap Regulation

In part II of this book we apply the analytical framework developed in part I to assess regulatory reform in Britain. Chapters 7 to 10 present case studies of the telecommunications, gas, electricity, and water industries. In this chapter we describe and assess a key element of regulatory reform in Britain, the system of price cap regulation known as RPI − *X*. First applied to British Telecom (BT) in 1984, RPI − *X* regulation now exists for British Gas (BG), British Airports Authority (BAA), the regional water companies, and, in the electricity industry, the National Grid Company and the regional distribution and supply companies.[1] Almost fifty firms in Britain are subject to RPI − *X*, and the system has attracted considerable international interest.

We argued in part I that regulatory objectives usually include the promotion of allocative and productive efficiency, the minimization of informational rents, the avoidance of capture, and the development of credible commitment. In practice, the institutional and legal framework for regulation is an important determinant of regulatory objectives and instruments. When RPI − *X* was first proposed, it was claimed to be superior to alternatives such as rate-of-return regulation on the grounds that it would provide greater incentives for cost efficiency, be simpler to operate, and be less vulnerable to capture. It was also meant to wither away when competition arrived in markets where it was feasible. However, the scope, complexity, and tightness of RPI − *X* regulation have so far increased over time in Britain.

The chapter is structured as follows. In section 6.1 we discuss the origins and characteristics of RPI − *X* regulation. In section 6.2 we consider the scope and structure of the price caps. Regulators must decide which prices are to be regulated, how average price should be defined, whether there should be any subsidiary restrictions on relative prices, the extent of cost passthrough, how to regulate quality and investment, and the length of regulatory lag. The *X* factors determine the minimum rate of decline of real prices over time and the way they are set is described in section 6.3. Regulators take account of factors such as the cost of capital, the asset

---

1. Manchester Airport, which is in local authority ownership, has also been subject to RPI − *X* regulation since 1987; see MMC (1987).

base, expected productivity improvements, growth of demand, and the use of yardstick information. In section 6.4 we assess the performance and prospects of RPI − X regulation.[2]

6.1 The Origins and Nature of RPI − X Regulation

6.1.1 The Origins of RPI − X Regulation

The first use of a price cap in Britain was for the dominant firm that supplied contraceptive sheaths. The Monopolies and Mergers Commission (MMC 1982) recommended that the rate of increase in the firm's average price should be limited to the rate of increase of a cost index less 1.5%, that the Office of Fair Trading (OFT) should monitor its implementation, and that it should review the control after five years. The cost index was not firm specific. It had fixed weights and included as components the index of average earnings in manufacturing, a general retail prices index, and the wholesale price of rubber. The previous regulatory system specified a maximum rate of return on capital for the firm and the MMC's reasons for abandoning this are instructive. First, since the firm produced many other products whose prices were unregulated, arbitrary allocations of costs and assets to the regulated sector had to be made. Second, measurement of the rate of return was difficult because of different accounting treatments of capital and depreciation. Third, it was argued that rate-of-return regulation weakened the incentives for cost efficiency.

Although there are many recognizable features of RPI − X in the 1982 MMC report, the catalyst for the development of RPI − X regulation as applied to utilities was the Littlechild Report (1983) on the regulation of BT's profitability after privatization.[3] Littlechild argued (p. 6) that "the primary purpose of regulation is to protect the consumer" and that competitive entry, where feasible, was to be preferred to regulation. In the event, as we discuss in section 7.4.2, Littlechild's assumptions about competition in telecommunications were not realized when BT was privatized

2. For surveys of price cap regulation, see Acton and Vogelsang (1989), Cave (1991), Rees and Vickers (1992), Liston (1993), and the symposium in the Rand Journal (1989), especially Beesley and Littlechild.
3. Littlechild has played a prominent role in the development of British regulatory policy and practice. In addition to his 1983 report on BT, he wrote a report on the regulation of the water industry (Littlechild 1986), was a member of the MMC when it recommended new price controls for Manchester Airport in 1987 and when it investigated British Gas's pricing in the contract market in 1988, and is the first Director General of Electricity Supply.

in 1984, and RPI — *X* regulation has been more complex than was originally intended.

Littlechild listed five criteria on which regulatory regimes were to be
assessed:

1. protection against monopoly,
2. encouragement of efficiency and innovation,
3. minimization of the burden of regulation,
4. promotion of competition,
5. proceeds from privatization and prospects for the firm.

Five regulatory schemes were compared by Littlechild. These were (1) no
explicit regulation, (2) a maximum rate-of-return regime, (3) an output-
related profits levy scheme,[4] (4) a profit ceiling, and (5) the RPI — *X* system, which limits the average rate of growth of regulated prices to the rate
of growth of the Retail Prices Index (RPI) less *X*%. The RPI is the primary
index of consumer prices in Britain. Option 1 was dropped from consideration for obvious reasons. This left three schemes that regulated profits
and one, RPI — *X*, that constrained prices. Littlechild argued (p. 34) that
regulation of profits was undesirable:

Rate of return control, whatever the variant, suffers from two major defects. First,
it is burdensome and costly to operate, reduces the incentive to efficiency and
innovation, and distorts the pattern of investment. Second, it covers the whole
business, or a large part of it, and it does not focus explicitly on the particular
services where monopoly power and public concern are greatest.

Instead Littlechild recommended RPI — *X*, which he called the "local
tariff reduction scheme" because he assumed it would apply only to local
telephone services and that there would be competition in other services.
In terms of the five criteria RPI — *X* scored well according to Littlechild.
It would protect against monopoly by focusing precisely on the services of
monopoly concern. The fact that it was based on capping prices rather
than profits would give the firm an incentive to achieve productive efficiency and would promote innovation because any cost reductions would
be kept by the firm. The burden of regulation would be low because it only
required the calculation of simple price indexes, there was no need to
measure the asset base or rates of return, cost allocation between competitive and monopolistic parts of the firm was unnecessary, and future movements of costs and demand did not have to be forecast. Because regulation

---

4. For a discussion of the problems of an output-related profits levy, see Glaister (1987).

would be relatively simple, there was less danger of regulatory capture than with profit regulation. On the promotion of competition RPI $-$ X also scored well. While it would reduce the incentive for entry into local telephone markets, the RPI $-$ X scheme would not affect the incentive to enter the long-distance market where competitive entry was more likely. Finally, Littlechild asserted that RPI $-$ X would give the firm good prospects and thus privatization proceeds would be high.[5]

The apparent success of the RPI $-$ X scheme for BT has led to similar schemes being applied in Britain to the gas industry in 1986, airports in 1987, water in 1989–90, and electricity in 1990. There has also been considerable interest abroad in the use of price caps (see section 7.3 for more details on its application in the telecommunications industry in the United States).

6.1.2 Characteristics

A firm subject to RPI $-$ X has to ensure that a weighted average of price increases in one year does not exceed the percentage increase in the Retail Prices Index less X. The Retail Prices Index is used rather than an industry-specific cost index because it cannot be manipulated by the regulated firm, and it gives consumers clear and predictable signals about prices. In the water industry the system is called RPI $+$ K. Real prices are scheduled to increase, but otherwise it operates in a similar way to RPI $-$ X. The X factor can vary from year to year but is exogenous to the firm between price reviews, and the number of years between price reviews—the regulatory lag—is fixed. The price cap applies to an average of prices if the firm sells multiple products, and the firm is usually allowed some freedom to alter relative prices within the overall constraint. Some costs might be passed through to consumers within the period of regulatory lag, such as the costs of purchasing gas or electricity from producers.[6] The firm might also be subject to some monitoring of its investment and input purchases and to regulation of its quality standards. We will discuss the characteristics of RPI $-$ X under the headings of institutions, cost passthrough, relative prices, regulatory lag, investment incentives, quality of service and

---

5. Littlechild's proceeds criterion is only relevant when the initial X was set at privatization. When the time comes to *reset* X, the regulator will have to consider the interests of the firm's shareholders. Beesley and Littlechild (1989) argue that because of this the regulator has fewer degrees of freedom in resetting X than in the original setting.
6. In the case of the water industry the cost passthrough provisions are more complex; see section 6.2.4.

setting *X* factors, and will sometimes compare the properties of RPI − *X* with those of versions of rate-of-return regulation.

6.1.3 Institutions

The institutional and legal framework established when BT was privatized in 1984 formed the model for the other utilities. The important features are the legislation, the licenses, and the regulators. The 1984 Telecommunications Act provides the legal framework. Under the Act the Secretary of State for Trade and Industry (now called the "President of the Board of Trade") grants licenses to BT and other firms. He thus determines policy on *entry*. The Act gives license-holders general duties. Specific details of the regulation of BT's *conduct*, for example, the details of price control, are contained in its license. The industry regulator, the Office of Telecommunications (Oftel), was set up and is headed by the Director General of Telecommunications (DGT). He has the duty to monitor and enforce license conditions. The DGT also advises the Secretary of State on licensing policy. License conditions can be changed by the DGT if the firm agrees. In the event of disagreement the DGT can refer the matter to the Monopolies and Mergers Commission (MMC), which can decide on appropriate license changes. The MMC thus acts as a regulator of last resort over conduct issues. Much of the power of the industry regulators stems from their ability to threaten referral to the MMC. Typically firms have preferred to avoid the uncertainties of an MMC review. The possibility of going to the MMC does, however, give the firms some protection against the possibility of overzealous regulation and BG referred itself to the MMC in 1992 (see chapter 8). Some regulatory duties are shared with the traditional competition policy authorities. The Director General of Fair Trading (DGFT) has joint powers with the DGT to make competition references to the MMC under the Fair Trading Act 1973 and the Competition Act 1980.[7] But references about telecommunications mergers can only be made by the DGFT.

This framework allows the Secretary of State, the DGT, and the MMC considerable discretion, since their duties are only laid down in general terms. If the DGT's role was simply to check that license conditions were

---

7. The situation in the water and electricity cases is similar, since the DGFT has concurrent powers with the industry regulators over competition references. But in the gas case the industry regulator, Ofgas, has had no powers relating to competition in the market for larger customers. The 1993 MMC reports on gas, however, did recommend that Ofgas's powers be extended to give it full regulatory responsibility, jointly with the DFGT, for this market.

satisfied, then it would be very limited. Regulation would be light and inexpensive, as envisaged in Littlechild (1983). In practice the DGT's ability to change the license, for example, when reviewing the X factor, gives him a much more active role. The DGT's criteria for making such changes are not defined in the legislation, and he is not required to give detailed reasons for his decisions. The vaguely defined duties of the DGT mean that his decisions are unlikely to be struck down by the courts, and the British experience of RPI $- X$ displays a noticeable absence of legalism. The effectiveness of the regulatory regime instead depends in part on the individual that heads the industry regulatory body.

6.1.4   Cost Passthrough

In section 2.3 we characterized pure price cap regulation as not allowing any cost passthrough, whereas rate-of-return regulation allows for complete passthrough of all costs. In practice RPI $- X$ schemes often have some degree of cost passthrough within the period before the next price review. If all costs could be passed through, then the regulatory scheme would be effectively the same as a cost-plus contract, so passthrough is confined to those costs that are thought to be outside the control of the firm and that are observable. As discussed in section 2.3 the degree of passthrough should depend on the degree of risk aversion of the firm and on the extent of cost uncertainty, at least in the model where the firm makes its effort decision before the realization of the exogenous cost parameter is known and so bears some risk. Only when the firm is risk neutral should there be no passthrough in this model. Cost passthrough is designed to protect the firm against upward movements in costs that it cannot control, and to give consumers the benefit of downward movements in costs before the next review. Consumers bear the risk of cost changes within the period of regulatory lag when there is passthrough.

Costs that can be passed through tend to be particularly variable and to form a relatively large part of the firm's total costs, as the model in section 2.3 would suggest. For example, BG can pass through an index of its gas purchase costs and in the electricity industry the costs of generation, transmission, and distribution, which account for about 95% of all costs, are passed through to consumers in the price cap for supply. The regulator has two main alternatives to allowing cost passthrough. A higher price cap could be set to compensate the firm for the risk of greater profit volatility (but note that this does not allow consumers to benefit from unexpectedly low costs), or the regulatory lag could be reduced.

6.1.5   Relative Prices

The regulator needs to decide how much freedom the firm can have over relative prices. Firms that face RPI − X can usually rebalance their prices to some extent. We gave some reasons why allowing such price flexibility might be desirable in section 3.3.2. Granting the firm flexibility increases its profits, and if the price cap can be designed so that consumers are no worse off (in aggregate), then social welfare definitely increases. Flexibility also allows the firm to alter relative prices when costs change, and to unwind any cross-subsidies inherited from the time of public ownership. Littlechild (1983) argued that regulating a basket of services rather than each individual price allows new types of tariff to be introduced without having to revise the license.

The two main ways of defining price indexes that have been used in Britain for multiproduct firms were described in chapter 3. Average revenue regulation can only be applied when products are commensurable, while tariff basket regulation works whether products are commensurable or not. We noted in the framework analyzed in section 3.3.2 that when the initial prices are nondiscriminatory, average revenue regulation that allows price discrimination will reduce consumer welfare, have an effect on overall welfare that is ambiguous, and lead to inefficient relative price structures. On the other hand, tariff basket regulation raises consumer surplus and welfare and can induce efficient relative prices (at least if the price cap lasts forever).

In practice the freedom to rebalance is not complete. Regulators generally have duties to prevent undue discrimination in pricing, and some forms of tariff rebalancing could be forbidden by this. Even when rebalancing is desirable because the tariff structures inherited from the days of public ownership involve inefficient cross-subsidization, there are often constraints on the speed of rebalancing for distributional reasons. These often take the form of subsidiary caps on the rate of change of fixed charges in two-part tariffs. We saw in section 4.3.3 that average price regulation can cause distortions if the firm faces competition in a market that is subject to the overall cap. Complete freedom in pricing may encourage anticompetitive behavior by the firm, and regulators have to monitor pricing carefully. A typical form of rebalancing is to raise prices for small users and to lower those for larger customers. This can sometimes be justified by reference to the unwinding of historical cross-subsidies, but might also be predatory since it is the markets for larger users that are usually subject to some competition.

6.1.6 Regulatory Lag

In section 3.5.1 we discussed the trade-offs involved in setting the regulatory lag. A long lag provides good incentives for productive efficiency but might adversely affect allocative efficiency. A pure version of a price cap would have an infinite lag, whereas rate-of-return regulation has frequent reviews of prices. Regulatory lag is perhaps the key feature that differentiates $RPI - X$ from rate-of-return regulation. In practice price caps cannot last forever because regulators have limited ability to commit themselves, and because changes in the firm's operating environment could give it excessive rents or drive it to bankruptcy. Similarly reviews are not instantaneous under rate-of-return regulation because of the direct costs of conducting reviews. As a rough characterization, under rate-of-return regulation reviews are frequent, and the regulatory lag is endogenous because either side can request a review, whereas under price caps the lag is relatively long, and the date of the next review is fixed in advance. The difference is one of degree rather than kind.

6.1.7 Investment Incentives

A major concern of price regulation is the provision of investment incentives, as we discussed in section 3.6. Averch and Johnson (1962) showed that if the firm is allowed to earn a rate of return that exceeds the cost of capital, then it has an incentive to choose a capital–labor ratio that is too high for the output level produced. But recent analysis has focused on the opposite problem of underinvestment, which arises because of the limited commitment powers of regulators. If the firm's capital is sunk, then there is a dynamic consistency problem that is especially acute if there is a limited number of production periods or if capital depreciates slowly. For instance, maximization of the regulator's objective once capital is sunk may require that prices only cover future avoidable costs. If the firm anticipates this ex post incentive for the regulator to cut prices, then it will not invest in the first place, and there will be a holdup problem. Commitment to future prices, if feasible, would be desirable ex ante. However, if the firm and regulator interact repeatedly, relatively efficient investment decisions can be encouraged.

In the British $RPI - X$ system industry regulators have discretion over license amendments—subject to agreement by the firm and appeal to the MMC—and the judicial constraints are unclear and largely untested. For instance, the criteria to be used in price reviews are not specified in the legislation. This means that there is a danger of opportunistic behavior by regulators. Firms also face the possibility that the regulatory framework itself might change. The Secretary of State might change licensing policy to allow new entry, as has happened in telecommunications. A Labour Government might impose tighter regulatory policies (the share prices of privatized utilities rose sharply when the Conservatives unexpectedly were reelected in April 1992). However, there are some features of the RPI − X system in Britain that act to protect firms from opportunism. The industry regulators have duties to ensure that firms are able to finance their operations, and in the case of the water industry the regulator must ensure that the firms earn reasonable returns on their capital (see section 10.3.2). Another protection for the firms is the option of appeal to the MMC if they do not agree to proposed license changes.

6.1.8   Quality of Service

An obvious problem with a price cap is that by itself it does nothing to encourage the provision of quality. On the contrary, under RPI − X the firm has an incentive to underinvest in quality for the given price level. Denote consumer surplus by $V(P, s)$, where s stands for quality of service and P is the capped price.[8] As in part I, let the welfare function be $V(P, s) + \alpha \pi(P, s)$, where $0 \leq \alpha \leq 1$ and $\pi(P, s)$ is the reduced-form profit function. Quality of service affects the demand for the product and increases costs even if the quantity sold is constant. The profit-maximizing firm chooses s to satisfy $\partial \pi / \partial s = 0$. An increase in s raises demand, and as long as price exceeds marginal cost, this increases profit. The firm balances this effect against the direct costs of quality improvement. But at the level of s chosen by the firm, the marginal social value of an increase in s is positive:

$$\frac{\partial V}{\partial s} + \alpha \frac{\partial \pi}{\partial s} = \frac{\partial V}{\partial s} > 0.$$

Thus if s were higher, welfare would increase. The problem is that the firm ignores the effect its quality decision has on *total* consumer surplus, $\partial V / \partial s$, and is interested only in the effect on demand at the margin. Thus there is a strong case, as Littlechild (1983) acknowledged, for regulation of quality levels under RPI − X.[9] Under rate-of-return regulation, however, there

---

8. This argument is based on Spence (1975).

9. Setting quality levels that take full account of the trade-offs requires estimation of consumers' marginal valuations, as well as of the costs of improvement. Consumers can be asked how much they are willing to pay for a given improvement, or how much they would need as compensation for a given reduction in quality. The water companies have been asked by the Director General of Water Services to conduct research into preferences for quality. Direct surveys are unfortunately prone to bias (Cave 1993).

can be good incentives for quality provision, at least if we believe in the Averch-Johnson effect, since quality can be raised as a result of the incentive to increase the capital intensity of production (Spence 1975).

6.1.9 Setting X Factors

The original hope about the RPI $-$ X scheme had been that it would set productivity incentives, but initial X factors were set to achieve several additional objectives. The government wanted to earn satisfactory proceeds from selling the firms and needed to ensure cooperation of incumbent management teams in the privatization process. After privatization a procedure for *resetting* X factors has had to be established. Regulators do not generally give detailed reasons for their decisions at review time, but some information about their procedures can be gleaned from the discussion papers that they issue before making their decisions (see section 6.3 and chapters 7 to 10 for more details).

When X factors and other license conditions relating to pricing are reviewed, regulators take into account the value of existing assets, the cost of capital, expected rates of growth of productivity and demand, and the progress of competition. One of the arguments for RPI $-$ X given by Littlechild (1983) had been that the regulatory burden was light because RPI $-$ X did *not* require the measurement of capital or rates of return. But inevitably regulators, who are concerned about allocative efficiency, have had to consider such factors at review time. Of course rate-of-return regulation also focuses on the capital base and on the allowed rate of return, so in this respect RPI $-$ X does not differ that much. Beesley and Littlechild (1989, 461), however, argue that

RPI $-$ X is more forward-looking than rate-of-return. The latter tends to be based on historic costs and demands, with adjustments for the future limited to (at most) an adjustment for inflation or the extrapolation of historic trends. In contrast, RPI $-$ X embodies forecasts of what productivity improvements can be achieved and what future demands will be and is set on the basis of predicted future cash flows.

We will see in section 6.3 how forward-looking information is used when price caps are reviewed.

6.2 Scope and Structure of Price Caps

In this section we describe in more detail the price caps used in Britain. We consider which products are regulated, the forms of the price indexes, restrictions on price discrimination and on the movement of particular prices, cost passthrough provisions, the regulation of both quality and investment, and regulatory lag. We discuss the levels of X in section 6.3. Table 6.1 summarizes the key information about RPI − X regulation in Britain.

6.2.1 Scope of the Controls

The first two lines in table 6.1 show the main products in each industry that come under RPI − X regulation. These are generally services where competition is weak or nonexistent, such as retail supply of electricity to smaller consumers and all water and sewerage charges. The set of regulated products does, however, include items where there is some competition, such as long-distance telephone calls. There has been a tendency to expand over time the set of regulated products. This is most apparent in the regulation of BT, where international calls, leased lines, and connection charges have entered the basket of regulated services. About 70% of BT's business (measured by revenue) is now covered by price cap regulation compared to about 50% in 1984. In the case of BG the nontariff or contract market (i.e., the market for larger industrial and commercial customers) was initially unregulated, and prices were individually negotiated. But following an MMC report in 1988, BG has been required to set prices according to published schedules against which it is not allowed to discount, although the level of the schedules has not been regulated.

The water industry and the electricity distribution and supply industry have regional structures, so price control is more disaggregated than in the simpler cases of BT and BG, which have been nationally and vertically integrated. Although the regional structures in water and electricity allow the use of yardstick competition, there are no explicit yardstick formulas in the price controls. Nevertheless comparative information was used in the initial price setting for water, and it will be used in the 1994 price review, although the way it will be incorporated is unclear. The vertical restructuring of the electricity supply industry means that price controls apply to the National Grid Company, which operates transmission, and to the separate distribution and supply businesses of the regional electricity companies (RECs), but prices of the competing generators were not regulated (see chapter 9).

6.2.2 Definitions of Price Indexes

The third line of table 6.1 shows the definitions of price indexes used. The tariff basket method applies to BT and, partially, to the water companies.

Table 6.1   RPI $-$ X regulation

	British Telecom	British Gas	British Airports Authority
Regulated	Inland calls International calls (since 1991) Line rentals Leased lines	Supply to small users	Airport charges at southeast airports
Unregulated	Apparatus supply Mobile services VANS	Supply to larger users (but price schedules must be published)	All other services (retail, parking, etc)
Price index	Tariff basket	Average revenue per therm	Average revenue per passenger
X (or K) values[a]	$X = 3$ (1984–89) $X = 4.5$ (1989–91) $X = 6.25$ (1991–93) $X = 7.5$ (1993–97)	$X = 2$ (1987–92) $X = 5$ (1992–94) $X = 4$ (1994–97)	$X = 1$ (1987–92) $X = 8, 8, 4, 1, 1$ (1992–97)
Price structure[b]	RPI $+$ 2 for rentals RPI $+$ 0 for all other prices RPI $+$ 0 on median user's bill	$X = 0$ cap on fixed charge for $<$ 5K therms	Same cap applies to Heathrow and Gatwick individually
Cost passthrough		All gas supply costs (1987–92) GPI $-$ 1 (1992–) energy efficiency factor	75% of extra security costs (1987–92) 95% of extra security costs (1992–)
Quality regulation	Fixed compensation for delays in repairs and connections Contractual liability	Compensation scheme	—
Regulatory lag[c]	Initially 5 years Now 4 years Next review 1997	5 years Next review 1997	5 years Next review 1998 MMC involved

a. WSCs denotes "water and sewerage companies," and WOCs denotes "water-only companies."
b. In addition there are some provisions against cross-subsidy and undue price discrimination.
c. The date given for the next review is the date by which the next review must be completed and is thus the date from which the new price controls apply.

Water supply companies	Electricity transmission (NGC)	Electricity distribution (RECs)	Electricity supply
Water and sewerage charges Trade effluent Infrastructure charge	All transmission	All distribution	REC customers additional cap for franchise customers (<1 MW)
All other activities (but Ofwat monitors diversification)	—	—	—
Tariff basket (modifed)	Average revenue per KWh	Average revenue per KWh	Average revenue per KWh
K varies by firm Over time average is RPI + 5.4 (WSCs), + 11.4 (WOCs) RPI + 0 for infrastructure charges	$X = 0$ (1990–93) $X = 3$ (1993–97)	Each REC has its X Range is from RPI + 0 to RPI + 2.5	$X = 0$ (1990–94) $X = 2$ (1994–98)
—	—	—	—
Cost of new environmental and quality regulations	—	—	Costs of power purchase, transmission, and distribution, fossil fuel levy
EC and UK standards for drinking water and bathing beaches Levels of service monitored Compensation scheme	—	—	Fixed penalties for performance failures (capacity element in pool price promotes supply security)
10 years (2000) 5 years at Ofwat's or firm's request Next review 1995	Initially 3 years Now 4 years Next review 1997	5 years Next review 1995	4 years Next review 1998

It requires that the weighted average of percentage price increases not exceed the rate of growth of RPI less X percent. The weight for each price increase is defined as the share in total revenue in the previous period (year) accounted for by that product or service. This is exactly equivalent to constraint (3.26), allowing for the X factor. The outputs of BT and the water companies are not commensurable (e.g., water supplied and sewage treatment, or local phone calls and long-distance calls), so methods based on aggregate output are not feasible.

Average revenue regulation (sometimes called the *revenue yield* approach) applies to the gas, airports, and electricity industries, where there are "natural" units of output (therms, passengers, and kilowatt hours). It operates as follows: the firm proposes a price change, and predicts total output and revenue given the new prices. Predicted average revenue can grow by at most RPI $- X$. Since the calculation of the current period's average revenue requires forecasts of demand in each market and of the change in the RPI, the firm has an incentive to act strategically in its forecasting, so a correction factor is included to claw back any gains or losses from forecasting errors.

6.2.3 Price Structure

Although each firm has some freedom to rebalance prices, there are some limits on its ability to do so. The fifth line of table 6.1 summarizes the restrictions on price structure. BT has to limit increases in single-line rental charges to RPI + 2, and multiple-line rentals to RPI + 5. Since 1993 it has had to restrict increases in any other price to RPI + 0, while satisfying the overall constraint of RPI − 7.5, and leased lines have a separate price cap of RPI + 0. BG faces a subsidiary cap of RPI + 0 on standing charges for those who consume less than 5,000 therms a year. There appear to be two reasons for restricting the rate of rebalancing. First, increases in line rentals and standing charges might adversely affect income distribution. The second reason, which applies to the BT case, is that one of the items in the tariff basket is long-distance calls where BT faces competition from Mercury and others. If it were allowed to rebalance without constraint, then it might cut prices in the long-distance market and recoup the revenue through higher charges to its captive domestic customers, while still satisfying the overall price control (see section 4.3.3 above).

Regulators have duties to prevent undue discrimination or preference being shown to customers. The legislation that paved the way for privatization gives regulators some discretion over how this is to be interpreted, but it appears that it was intended that prices should be roughly proportionate to attributable costs. Note that such uniform markups are unlikely to be consistent with the markups for Ramsey prices, which are determined by demand elasticities. In many industries prices, rather than price-cost margins, are uniform across the country. BG has maintained uniform pricing for tariff customers. Other examples are BT's connection charge (see section 7.5.4) and the nationwide system of postal prices. Moves to break up industries and encourage competition are, however, likely to increase the degree of "geographical de-averaging."

6.2.4   Cost Passthrough

In all of the industries subject to RPI − X regulation after BT, there are cost passthrough provisions. From 1987 to 1992 BG was allowed to pass through in full to its captive tariff customers the average cost of purchasing gas. Full passthrough does not provide much incentive to purchase efficiently, and since 1992 the cost passthrough regime has changed to allow the change in an *index* of gas prices, known as the Gas Price Index (GPI) less 1% to be passed through. In addition expenditure that reduces demand by improving energy efficiency E can be recovered by raising prices. In the gas case the degree of passthrough was reduced in the first price review, but in the review of BAA's prices for its southeast airports the proportion of additional security costs that could be recovered within the regulatory period was raised from 75% to 95%. This easing of the cost passthrough provisions was partly to compensate for the tough X factor that BAA was given (see CAA 1991, 31). In electricity supply each REC can pass through in full transmission and distribution charges, electricity purchase costs, and the fossil fuel levy in its overall cap. These account for 95% of REC supply costs. Because an REC can affect its electricity purchase costs, there is a license condition that requires the REC to purchase economically. Until 31 March 1993 there was also a supplementary price control that protected smaller customers against price changes. For customers with peak demands below 1 MW, the RECs could only pass through the fossil fuel levy. The RECs were largely protected against adverse movements in electricity purchase costs—the most volatile component of their costs—by contracts with the generators (see chapter 9 for more details).

The passthrough provisions for the water industry are more complex than those for gas, airports, and electricity supply, where the costs that can be passed through are mainly or exclusively operating costs. If statutory environmental or quality standards change in ways that were not anticipated at the previous review, then a firm can apply for cost passthrough. Since many of the costs associated with improving quality standards are *capital* costs, a simple formula as in gas or electricity will not work. The procedure for most companies is that the regulator calculates the net present value of the incremental costs up to the next review time, and new K factors, which determine the rate of increase of real charges, are set so that the present value of additional revenue equals the present value of the incremental costs. Financial and accounting criteria are used to ensure that the firm's financial position until the next price review is reasonable. One extreme version of the process would be to allow revenue to increase by enough in each year to match exactly the extra capital expenditure, but this could cause dramatic swings in prices; in practice the regulator allows only partial recovery of extra capital costs up to the next review. Thus the degree of passthrough in the water industry is determined on a case-by-case basis. Two companies have agreed with the industry regulator that a simpler method will apply to them, based on changing revenue to cover extra operating costs and extra capital costs (depreciation plus a rate of return on incremental capital), and this simpler procedure is likely to become more widely used.

6.2.5 Quality Regulation

Both theory and the evidence of BT's quality problems in the early years after privatization indicate that a price cap must be supplemented by quality regulation. Littlechild stated in his report on telecommunications (1983, 35) that "it would seem sensible to ensure that quality of service did not deteriorate as a result of the tariff reduction scheme." Rovizzi and Thompson (1992) outline four alternative mechanisms for regulating quality. First, the firm could be required simply to publish measures of quality. Second, a measure of quality could be included explicitly in the price cap. Third, customer compensation schemes could be set up. These work only if quality failures can be easily verified. Finally, minimum quality standards could be specified and backed by explicit legal sanctions (including fines or revocation of the license) or by implicit threats to revise the price cap. The Competition and Service (Utilities) Act 1992 reinforced the industry regulators' role in quality regulation. It gave them powers to set overall standards of service and to set up compensation schemes. The latter are now in place for all four utilities, and information about standards of performance is now published. The option of formally including quality measures in the price caps has not been adopted because of the difficulty of finding good summary measures of quality and because it does not compensate directly those who suffer from poor quality.

In the water industry there is strict statutory regulation of drinking water quality and of effluent discharges. Overall standards are set by the EC and by the UK government. Compliance with the standards is monitored by separate regulators (the Drinking Water Inspectorate and the National Rivers Authority mainly). The economic regulator Ofwat has a role in monitoring levels of service such as water pressure (see section 10.3.2). The regulator takes account of quality performance and objectives when setting price caps, and comparative information is potentially very useful here.

6.2.6   Investment Regulation

Investment issues have been especially prevalent in the water and airports industries, but regulators of other industries informally monitor capital expenditure. One example of informal monitoring is the concern expressed by Ofgas about the decline in BG's investment in the period before the MMC reports were issued in 1993. In the water industry firms are required, as part of the process of setting K factors, to give Ofwat details of their investment plans and the objectives that they are designed to achieve (e.g., compliance with a statutory quality standard or provision of new capacity to meet demand growth). These are audited, and planned investment expenditures play a crucial role in K setting process (see section 10.4.2). Each year Ofwat monitors capital expenditure and the achievement of objectives relative to plans. This is partly to ensure that the investment program is on track. But Ofwat has also taken the opportunity to use the information it gains from this monitoring exercise to ask the industry to withhold voluntarily some of its allowed price increases because of the decline in construction costs relative to initial expectations. In 1992 this process was formalized, and seventeen water companies had their K factors reduced through the cost passthrough mechanism.

The Civil Aviation Authority (1991) took account of investment issues when resetting the X factors for BAA's southeast airports. The MMC, which made recommendations to the CAA, had suggested that the X factor might be made contingent on work starting on a fifth terminal at Heathrow, but the CAA rejected this. The investment would mostly occur in the five-year period after the next price review in 1997. It will be interesting to see how investment in the terminal is accounted for in the X factor then—in its original proposal the CAA had suggested a regime of RPI $-$ 8 for each of the years from 1992–97 followed by RPI $+$ 7 in the following five-year period.

6.2.7   Regulatory Lag

As can been seen in table 6.1, lags of five years are common. For the water industry the lag is ten years, but either side can ask for a review after five years, as Ofwat has done for all water companies. BT's initial lag was five years, but this was shortened to four at the first review.

Although the formal lags are quite long there is scope for the regulators to intervene within the fixed period, thus shortening the effective lag. When the duopoly policy in telecommunications was reviewed, the opportunity was taken to include international calls in the basket of regulated services, even though this was only two years into the four-year regulatory period. As mentioned in the previous section, Ofwat has sought voluntary reductions in price increases and has used the cost passthrough mechanism to claw back some benefit to consumers from construction prices that were lower than expected. The 1993 MMC reports on the gas industry recommended reducing BG's X factor from 5 to 4. Such intervention goes against the spirit of RPI $-$ X regulation, which is to commit to a price cap for a fixed period. But effective lags might be longer than the formal lags if regulators do not claw back all cost savings at a price review, and X factors are set so that the firm earns returns that gradually fall to reasonable levels by the end of the regulatory period (see section 6.3.2).

6.3   Setting X and K Factors

In setting the level of a price cap the regulator has a number of duties and objectives. The firm must be able to finance its operations, which requires that attention is paid to projected accounting and financial information— the cap must not be so tight that the firm is driven to bankruptcy or is unable to finance its investment. The regulator seeks to provide incentives for productive efficiency and to obtain allocative efficiency. Reducing excess profits might also be an objective. In addition the impact of the level of the price cap on competition has to be considered.

Setting the caps is thus not easy. Factors that enter the process are (1) the cost of capital, (2) the value of the existing assets (the asset base), (3) the future investment program, (4) expected future changes in productivity, (5) estimates of demand growth, and perhaps (6) the effect of X on actual and potential competitors. We will discuss in some detail the estimation of the cost of capital and the methods used to value existing assets, before describing the process of financial modeling used in setting caps.

6.3.1 Cost of Capital and the Asset Base

At first sight it might seem strange to emphasize the role of the cost of capital and the asset base when one of the objectives of the RPI − X system is to escape the well-known inefficiencies of rate-of-return regulation. But each regulator has the duty to ensure the firm can finance its operations, and it is clear that regulators pay close attention to these issues when setting X and K factors. Littlechild (1986, 30) acknowledges that "rate of return considerations are necessarily implicit in setting and resetting X." Shareholders will be unwilling to invest in sunk assets if they expect to earn rates of return that are below the cost of capital, while allocative efficiency and the extraction of rents require that the rate of return equals the cost of capital. It is important to estimate both the cost of capital, which is the return that could be earned elsewhere on assets of equivalent risk, and the asset base on which this return is earned. In part I we discussed the regulatory problem when there is asymmetric information, and noted that the regulator's ability to measure total costs plays an important part in regulatory schemes. In practice, while operating costs are generally observable from published accounts, capital costs have to be imputed because sunk assets are typically owned by the regulated firm rather than rented or leased. To do this, it is necessary to define an asset base and to estimate a cost of capital. This procedure does not provide information on the shape of the cost function but does give an estimate of the total cost of production. This cost estimate is an essential input for the determination of the price cap if allocative efficiency and rent extraction are to be promoted. In this section we concentrate on the problems of measuring the cost of capital and the asset base. We discuss their role in setting X in section 6.3.2.

In principle it is the cost of capital of the firm's *regulated* business that is of interest. This cost cannot be observed directly and must be inferred from the available financial data. One problem is that the regulated activities are only one part of the firm's business, and the available data are on the market value of the firm as a whole. Assumptions have to be made about the effect of the unregulated activities on the cost of capital. Another problem is that stock market data are useful in determining the cost of *equity* capital, but the regulator is interested in the cost of capital to the firm from whatever source, and so account must be taken of the cost of *debt*. A final problem is that the cost of capital depends on the risk characteristics of the project to be financed, but most methods of estimating the cost of capital assume that the project has the same characteristics as the firm as a whole.

Two main methods are used to estimate the cost of equity capital.[10] One method uses the capital asset pricing model (CAPM). In this model the cost of equity capital is given by the risk-free rate plus the firm's risk premium. The risk-free rate is usually measured by the return on government securities such as Treasury Bills or indexed-linked long-term bonds. The firm's risk premium is the product of its "beta" factor and the "market risk premium." The beta factor is the covariance of the firm's rate of return with the return on a well-diversified portfolio, usually the stock market as a whole, divided by the variance of the return on the diversified portfolio. If it is assumed that the future will resemble the past, this is in principle straightforward to estimate because it is the slope of the regression line of the firm's return against the market return. The market risk premium is the premium that investors require to hold the market portfolio rather than a risk-free asset. Investors should not require compensation for bearing risks that are specific to particular firms because in a well-diversified portfolio specific risks are uncorrelated with each other. But the risk associated with the stock market as a whole is undiversifiable, and investors require a risk premium—the market risk premium—to hold a well-diversified portfolio of equities. The beta factor of a share is a measure of its contribution to the risk of bearing the portfolio as a whole. If the stock market return increases by one percentage point then the firm's return will increase by beta percent on average.

There is room for considerable debate about each of the terms in the CAPM equation. The real risk-free rate is usually estimated to be about 3–4%, and there is some debate about the market risk premium, especially whether it should be estimated as an arithmetic average or a geometric average of past values. In Britain figures in the range 7–9% have often been quoted, based on arithmetic averages. Beta factors can be estimated using different data sets. Oftel (1992b) reports a value for BT's beta of 0.74, below that of BG (then 0.8) and above the average for the water industry

---

10. For more details, see Ofwat (1991a), Water Services Association and Water Companies Association (1991), and Grout (1992).

of 0.6. BT (1992) argued that the use of data including the stock market crash of 1987 biased its beta downward and that a figure in the range 0.85–0.9 should be used. The MMC (1993c, 193) quoted values for BG's beta of between 0.81 and 0.86. A further point to note is that regulators have tended to look at pretax rates of return, but investors are interested in posttax rates of return and there is no simple formula for getting from a pretax rate to a posttax rate because shareholders have differing marginal tax rates.

An alternative method of estimating the cost of equity capital is the dividend growth model (DGM). If dividend growth is constant, then the price of a share is the initial dividend divided by the difference between the cost of equity and the rate of dividend growth. The DGM reverses this equation. The cost of equity is defined to be the dividend yield (the dividend divided by the share price) plus the growth rate. The dividend yield is observable, but an assumption must be made about the growth rate. The need to assume that dividend growth is constant and to choose a value for this growth rate means that there is much arbitrariness with this method, and it is often used as a (questionable) check on CAPM-based results rather than to produce the main estimate of the cost of equity.

There are two methods of getting to the figure for the overall cost of capital once a figure for the cost of equity is derived. One way is to adjust the *equity* beta for the firm's gearing or leverage in order to derive an *asset* beta. A debt beta can be determined in a similar way to an equity beta, and the asset beta is then the weighted average of the equity beta and the debt beta, with weights equal to the shares of equity and debt in total firm value. The asset beta can then be used in place of the equity beta in the standard CAPM formula. Asset betas are of independent interest,[11] but they have not been widely used to determine the cost of capital, partly because of tax complications.

The alternative method of deriving the cost of capital figure is to combine the cost of equity with an estimated cost of debt in a weighted-average cost of capital equation, with the weights again given by the relative shares of equity and debt. This is the cost of capital for the firm as a whole. Ofwat (1991a) considered evidence from both CAPM and the DGM and concluded that the cost of equity capital is 5–7% and that the cost of debt is 3–5%, yielding a weighted-average cost of capital

---

11. Ofwat (1991a) calculates an average asset beta for the water industry of 0.48, above the average of 0.2 for U.S. water utilities, indicating that the latter face significantly lower risks.

of 5–6%.[12] At privatization K factors for the water and sewerage companies had been set on the basis of a cost of capital of 7%. The water industry replied to Ofwat's consultation paper with a suggestion, based on CAPM, that the overall cost of capital is 9.5%. The CAPM has also been used to estimate the cost of capital for BG's transportation business. BG estimated that the required return for new investment was 10.8%, while Ofgas argued that it was in the range 5.7–8.4%. The MMC in 1993 concluded that the required return for BG was in the range 6.5–7.5%.

Modeling the risk of regulatory tightening is an important problem when considering the cost of capital. The correct way to model this risk is probably to see it as a factor that lowers expected future cash flows, thus reducing expected profitability without altering the cost of capital per se. This is because regulatory risk is specific to the firm and should be diversifiable. But regulators are not likely to agree to this way of modeling the risk—if they did they would be admitting that there is a possibility of future expropriation. An alternative way to take account of the risk would be to adjust the cost of capital figure derived from the conventional CAPM or DGM. Grout (1992) argues for such an adjustment. Unfortunately, there are no simple ways of estimating how large an adjustment is appropriate.

If shareholders and debt-holders are to be willing to finance new investment, they must expect together to earn the cost of capital. This is assured if the price for the output from the new assets is set so that the present value of the cash flows attributable to the new assets is equal to the present value of future capital expenditure. While it is clear theoretically what should happen for new investment, the more difficult problem is to set prices for the outputs produced with the *existing* assets. This turns out to be equivalent to the problem of determining the "value" of the firm's capital. If the existing assets were transferable to other activities without cost, then the conceptual problem of determining their value would be simple. The existing assets would have to earn the cost of capital and should be valued at replacement cost, which in a well-functioning secondhand capital goods market is equal to the resale value of the assets. If this was not the case, the assets would be costlessly transferred to other activities, and no firm would want to replace them. At the other extreme is the case where all existing assets are sunk so that the opportunity cost of using them in their present activity is zero. Then, as we discussed in section 3.6,

---

12. Figures for rates of return and the cost of capital are in real terms unless otherwise stated.

a regulator whose objective is to maximize short-run welfare would want to ensure that prices are set to cover future avoidable costs only, since the capital is already sunk. This implies an asset valuation of zero. There are great problems with both of these solutions. Most of the assets of the utilities are sunk, and market values were lower than replacement costs at privatization and have remained lower since then. Valuation at replacement cost at review time would generate large price increases and windfall gains for shareholders at the expense of consumers. On the other hand, attributing a zero value to the existing assets would make the windfall gains go in the opposite direction, and so shareholders would be reluctant to finance future sunk investments for the reasons discussed in section 3.6.

In the long run the existing assets will usually depreciate and be replaced by new assets earning at least the cost of capital. This means that at some future date all assets will have been created since privatization; since new assets earn the cost of capital, asset value will then equal replacement cost (if expectations are realized). Over time we should expect, other things being equal, to observe accounting rates of return earned by utilities that rise toward the cost of capital. An important point to note is that this will entail rising prices over time, unless technical progress substantially cuts the cost of replacing and operating the assets, or the cost of capital falls, or there is slack that can be eliminated.

In the meantime the regulator needs to determine a valuation of the existing assets that is positive but below replacement cost. We discuss in the next section how this valuation can be used to set X factors. The issue of the valuation of existing assets has been addressed in the water and gas industries. In the water case at privatization the valuation of the existing assets was called the *indicative value*. This is discussed in more detail in section 10.4.2. The valuation was calculated on the basis that the existing owners should neither gain nor lose from the change in regime. Calculation of the indicative value required estimation of the cash flows that the existing assets would have generated *if the regulatory regime had not changed*. The discounted value of these cash flows is defined as the indicative value (IV).

A simple version of the IV is as follows: the hypothetical cash flows are defined as $zK_{t-1} + D_t$, where z is the accounting rate of return on existing assets chosen by the regulator (see sections 10.3.1 and 10.4.2), K_{t-1} is the replacement cost value of assets at the end of period $t − 1$ and D_t is the depreciation of these assets in current cost terms during period t. Denoting the market discount factor by $\delta = 1/(1 + r)$, where r is the cost of capital, the present value of these hypothetical cash flows is

$$\text{IV} = \Sigma_{t=1}^{T} \delta^t(zK_{t-1} + D_t).$$

T is the date at which the initial replacement cost value of asset K_0 has depreciated completely, unless the assets have an infinite lifetime. We can show (after some manipulation) that

$$\text{IV} = \frac{z}{r} K_0 + \frac{(r - z)}{r} \Sigma_{t=1}^{T} \delta^t D_t. \tag{6.1}$$

If there is no depreciation, then $\text{IV} = zK_0/r$. The IV equals the replacement cost of the assets in place at the end of period 0, K_0, if and only if the accounting rate of return is equal to the market cost of capital. For $z < r$, it can be shown that $\text{IV} < K_0$.

This complicated procedure was necessary because assets that were in the public sector had no observable market value before privatization. There were also some private firms, the statutory water companies, that were brought into the new regulatory regime but in many cases were either not quoted on the Stock Exchange or subsidiaries of larger firms without separate share prices.

When resetting K values for the water industry, Ofwat has the advantage of some data on market values that were not available before privatization. Ofwat (1992a) suggests using these to derive new values of the existing assets. There can be problems of circularity when using actual market values, since these will depend on the market's expectations about the regulator's valuation of the asset bases. If the stock market expects higher values to be attributed to the assets in place at the next review, then the market values will be higher. Ofwat (1993c) therefore has announced that it will use the initial market values established at privatization together with the sum of capital expenditure less depreciation up to the next review date in resetting the K factors.

In its 1992 submission to Ofgas on the rate of return for its transportation assets, British Gas (1992) proposed that these assets should be valued at their market price, which they calculated at 62% of replacement cost. It suggested that the proposed cost of capital for new investment of 10.8% could be converted into a projected figure for the rate of return on existing assets by multiplying 10.8% by 0.62, the "market-to-assets" ratio (MAR). Ofgas and the MMC argued about the values of the cost of capital and the MAR but accepted the methodology (see section 8.4.4). It appears, however, that there is a bias in this process. The aim is to find the accounting rate of return on existing assets that ensures that market value is at the level determined by the regulator. We can use equation (6.1) to find the appropriate accounting rate of return. The value of the existing assets is fixed by the regulator at some current or updated market value. Set the left-hand side of (6.1) equal to this market value (MV). The accounting rate of return z is now the unknown in (6.1). Solving for z gives

$$z = r \left[\frac{MV - \Sigma \delta^t D_t}{K_0 - \Sigma \delta^t D_t} \right]. \tag{6.2}$$

If there is no depreciation, then z should equal the cost of capital times the MAR, MV/K_0, as British Gas proposed and the MMC accepted. But in general when depreciation is positive and MAR < 1, the method proposed by British Gas will give an upward bias to the accounting rate of return, since the MAR exceeds the term multiplying r in (6.2). The extent of this bias depends on the rate of depreciation of the existing assets and the cost of capital. Estimating the accounting rate of return in (6.2) is more difficult than simply multiplying the cost of capital by the MAR, since it requires information on future depreciation schedules. The difficulties, however, should not be overemphasized. All that is required are information on the current cost value of the base period assets, the projected lives of these assets, and forecasts of changes in the relative price of capital goods.

The problem caused by this bias is probably not as important as the primary problem of determining the asset base. There is no obvious way to determine a valuation of existing assets when market values are below replacement costs. Using market values makes some sense because shareholders need to be convinced that they will not be expropriated at review time. But this runs the risk of circularity, and the use of market value is not feasible for firms about to be privatized or that are subsidiaries and not separately quoted. To avoid circularity, some base period market value has to be chosen and some form of indexation adopted. As we will see later, capital valuation is a crucial input into setting prices, as it is with rate-of-return regulation, but there is a heavy burden on the regulator and there are few operational principles.

6.3.2 Financial Modeling

In this section we describe how regulators use forward-looking financial modeling to determine X factors. Detailed calculations are not in the public domain; some information about procedures is contained in Beesley and Littlechild (1989), MMC (1990a), CAA (1991), Cave (1991), and

Ofwat (1991a). Financial models are used to project both accounting statements, such as profit-and-loss accounts and balance sheets, and the cash flows a firm will generate. To make projections, the regulator needs to make specific assumptions about productivity improvements, demand changes, and capital expenditures and general assumptions about macroeconomic factors such as future interest rates and real wage growth. We will discuss the firm-specific assumptions below, but first we will see how financial modeling is used to choose an X factor.

The X factor is derived in an iterative procedure. An initial guess at X is put into the model, which then projects accounting statements and cash flows. If these are unacceptable to the regulator, a new X factor is chosen. There seem to be two main ways of determining acceptability and thus finally choosing X factors. One is to focus exclusively on the cash flows and to ignore the accounting statements. The cash flow (pretax) in any period is defined as revenue less operating costs and capital expenditure, and this does not depend on any arbitrary accounting conventions about classification of costs as current or capital, nor does it depend on depreciation. Different X factors are put into the model, generating alternative cash flow streams. The chosen X factor is then the one that generates cash flows whose present value at the cost of capital is equal to the value of the existing assets (which is the capital base fixed by the regulator). This implicitly ensures that new investment earns the cost of capital because the present value of the positive cash flows attributable to new investment less the present value of the future capital expenditure will be zero. This procedure lies behind the original setting of K factors for water and will be the basis of resetting Ks. Since the firm will be in business for longer than the period of regulatory lag, assumptions are required about demand growth, operating costs, and investment that go beyond the regulatory period. Assumptions about *future* levels of X are also necessary. In section 6.2.6 we mentioned that the CAA had in mind a regime of RPI + 7 in the second regulatory period when it proposed RPI − 8 for the first five-year period. Future Ks were assumed for the water industry when the initial Ks were set. But unless the regulator has a good idea about future levels of the caps, this process will not uniquely determine the current cap. A tough initial price cap followed by an easy one can produce the same present value of cash flows as an intermediate cap for both periods.

The cash flow procedure has some attractions, but its operation requires a large number of assumptions and does not generate a unique price cap. It is also close in spirit to rate-of-return regulation if the valuation of existing assets effectively ensures that all past efficiency gains are clawed back at the price review. While its focus on long-run rates of return makes it an attractive approach for the regulation of industries with large investment requirements, it might be less suitable for industries with scope for efficiency gains. When the first *K* factors for the water industry were set, more attention was paid to accounting ratios than to cash flows, but Ofwat wants to make greater use of cash flows at the next review.

Regulators of other industries appear to have focused exclusively on accounting ratios, including debt-equity ratios, interest cover (the ratio of pretax profits to interest payments), dividend cover, return on capital employed, earnings per share, dividends per share, operating profits, and net cash flow. Ofwat is *required* to ensure that the levels and trends of these are "appropriate" when resetting *K* factors at cost passthrough applications. Accounting rates of return depend on conventions about depreciation schedules, and on whether capital is valued at historic cost or current cost. There are few principles to guide the regulator in looking at these accounting ratios. Judgment must be exercised to determine whether particular values are appropriate. Interest cover and the debt-equity ratio are of concern to prospective lenders, so the regulator must ensure that the projected ratios are such that they do not jeopardize potential lending. Return on the replacement cost value of capital is also an important factor for regulators. In its price reviews in 1988 and 1992 Oftel took some account of BT's rates of return in both historic cost- and current cost-accounting (CCA) terms. Ofgas decided in the 1991 tariff market review that appropriate CCA rates of return for British Gas were in the range 5–7%, and the MMC (1993a) suggested that CCA returns on existing assets should be in the range 4–4.5%, where this figure was based on adjusting the cost of capital for the market-to-asset ratio as explained in section 6.3.1. Similarly the CAA (1991) looked for CCA rates of return of about 7% for BAA.

In telecommunications, gas, and electricity *X* factors are constant throughout the regulatory period, and it appears that regulators generally prefer to have constant factors. Movement to new price levels is thus gradual and smooth. For BAA and most water companies, however, the *X* or *K* factors are not constant. This is presumably because of the large investment programs in these two industries. Allowing the *X* or *K* factors to be "profiled" in this way increases the regulator's degrees of freedom in generating accounting ratios that are acceptable.

Oftel (1992a) considered the timing of the elimination of excess returns and concluded that the firm should gradually share with consumers any cost savings that exceed those expected at the last review, with the X factor set so that accounting rates of return fall to reasonable levels by the time of the *next* review. It argues that greater sharing will reduce the incentive for cost reduction which RPI $- X$ is designed to promote. The Oftel procedure effectively lengthens the regulatory lag.

The accounting approach to price cap setting can be combined with the cash flow approach. In particular firms would be given some indication about future levels of the cap and about the regulator's valuation of existing assets, as has happened in both the water and airports industries. This can help to ease the problem of regulatory risk, although regulators are careful to say that they are not binding their successors by telling firms what future levels of the cap are assumed.

Whichever method of setting the caps is used, it will rely on assumptions about productivity improvements, demand growth, and capital expenditure, since these help to determine the cash flows and accounting statements, and the effect on entry will need to be assessed. The problem of information asymmetry is likely to be acute. In estimating productivity improvements, the regulator will ideally look for a figure for total factor productivity growth. Sources of such estimates might be detailed examination of the firm's costs in the past, comparative data if the industry is regionalized, comparisons with other industries, and general economywide productivity trends. Similar sources might be used to estimate demand growth for the firm. Information on capital expenditure is likely to be more firm specific than that on productivity and demand growth and so might require detailed auditing by the regulator. There is very little published information on the assumptions that are used by regulators. There are also complications caused by the fact that competitive entry is more likely the higher the price cap, and the regulator has to consider whether the short-run loss to consumers from a high price cap is balanced by the long-run gain from increased entry (although we argued in section 4.2.2 that the effects of price caps on entry are too uncertain to justify this method of entry promotion). It is clear that X factors are not set simply on the basis of expected efficiency gains.

6.4 Assessment

RPI $- X$ has some desirable properties both in theory and in practice. It provides incentives for cost efficiency, although these become weaker as the review date approaches, and the absence of legalism in the British regulatory system allows regulators to be forward-looking. But it has not been a panacea. Its coverage and complexity has increased, and it has had to be supplemented by controls on quality. The prospect of regulatory discretion may reduce the incentive to invest and raise the cost of capital, and the operation of RPI − X depends on the individuals who are the industry regulators. Price caps have generally become tighter in industries where there have been reviews, and some regulators have made increasing use of implicit regulation. Rather than simply checking that license conditions are satisfied regulators have actively influenced firms' decisions on the level and structure of prices and on quality and investment.

What are the prospects for RPI − X? In industries where greater competition is feasible and desirable, the role of price regulation will depend critically on the evolution of competition. Competitive forces are likely to play an increasing role in telecommunications and in retail supply in both the gas and electricity industries. If this competition is effective, then price caps for final consumption in these markets could eventually be dropped, fulfilling the hopes of Littlechild (1983). But parts of each industry will remain naturally monopolistic for the foreseeable future, and prices will still have to be regulated. One area of increasing regulatory focus will be the terms of access to the naturally monopolistic networks for rival firms (see chapter 5). However, if competition takes time to arrive and to be effective, then regulation of final product prices will remain an important feature of these industries for many years. In the following chapters we discuss the process of regulatory reform in telecommunications, gas, electricity, and water and the role RPI − X regulation has played in each industry.

Telecommunications

Telecommunications was the first network utility industry in Britain to be privatized.[1] Policy decisions about the appropriate competitive and regulatory framework for a private utility therefore first arose in the industry, and a pattern was set that has been followed to varying degrees with gas, airports, water, electricity supply, and rail. Elsewhere in the world, notably in the United States, Japan, and several countries within the EC, governments have been rethinking their approach to the industry, and many countries have embarked on programs of privatization and/or liberalization. Within Britain the industry has the longest and richest history of regulation, and controversy over policy toward the industry shows no sign of abating.

We begin our review of the telecommunications industry in Britain by outlining the technology of the industry, its chief economic characteristics, and the structure of the industry in Britain today. Market failures— mainly natural monopoly cost conditions in parts of the industry and a history of actual monopoly over nearly all of the industry—provide the rationale for policy intervention, and in section 7.2 we set out some of the broad policy options. These are grouped under the headings of structure, entry conditions, pricing, and investment and quality, but the interrelationships between those issues will also be clear. Recent policy toward the industry in the United States is briefly discussed in section 7.3, and the policy choices made in Britain before and after the privatization of BT in 1984 are described in section 7.4 and 7.5. Finally, in section 7.6 there is an assessment of policy to date.

The 1980s began with BT, then part of the Post Office, having a complete monopoly over network operation, all services conveyed over the network, and the supply of virtually all apparatus connected to the network. Mobile telephony barely existed, BT's quality of service was mixed, and waiting times for new phone lines were long. Initially some steps were taken toward liberalization, but after deciding to privatize BT the government chose to limit the degree of entry into the industry, notably by its Mercury/BT "duopoly policy." With privatization the Office of Telecommunications (Oftel) was established to regulate the industry, and RPI $- X$

---

1. Parts of this chapter draw from Armstrong and Vickers (1992).

price control was applied to BT's regulated activities. We describe how Oftel has acted in a reasonably procompetitive manner within the limits set by government, and how RPI − X regulation, contrary to initial aspirations, has had to become tighter and farther-reaching over time and has been supplemented by a considerable amount of additional implicit regulation. In 1990, as earlier limitations on competition expired, policy toward entry in the industry was reviewed, and a more liberal regime is now in place. At present, however, BT remains dominant throughout many areas in the industry.

7.1   The Telecommunications Industry and Its Economic Characteristics

Since Bell's invention of the telephone in 1876, the telecommunications industry has grown to be of tremendous size and complexity. Customers now use a telecommunications network for many purposes other than basic voice telephony, each of which places different demands on the network, and a network operator must ensure that all of these different kinds of message are correctly and efficiently transmitted between the various senders and receivers. In recent years the switching and transmission technology used in the industry has converged toward those used in the computing and broadcasting industries, and a full account of telecommunications should include the links between the three industries.

7.1.1   Elements of Telecommunications Technology

In thinking about the economics of the industry it is useful, though not always easy, to distinguish between (1) the public network and its operation, (2) the apparatus attached to the network, and (3) the services provided over the network.[2] A telecommunications network connects users by a combination of exchanges and transmission links. Networks typically are configured hierarchically, with users connected to local exchanges (using a "local loop"), which in turn are linked by trunk or long-distance lines to trunk exchanges, and ultimately to the international network. This is efficient given the trade-offs that exist between exchanges and transmission. For instance, suppose that there are two towns. Then two possible network configurations would be (1) to have each house in the two towns being connected to a single central exchange (located some-

---

2. We will not discuss the upstream industry that supplies the equipment (exchanges, cables, etc.) that comprises the public network.

where between the towns) or (2) to have each house connected to a local exchange (one in each town), and these two exchanges then being connected by a single high-capacity line. Since there are scale economies (at least up to some threshold level) in building lines of high capacity between two points, configuration 2 typically is the more efficient network. (These scale economies are derived not just from the technology but also from the need to acquire land rights.)

In a modern network, however, this hierarchy is quite complex. In BT's network, for instance, every residential customer is connected to a local exchange (often via a "remote concentrator"), every local exchange is connected to at least two main exchanges (so-called digital main switching units, or DMSUs), and every DMSU is connected to every other DMSU. Therefore between any two customers not in the same local area there are always at least four possible routes depending on which of the two or more DMSUs at each end the route uses; see figure 7.1 for a schematic picture of a network with four DMSUs and eight local exchanges. (Of course, since all DMSUs are mutually connected, there are many possible routes that use more than one inter-DMSU line.) This flexibility is extremely useful for ensuring that the network is reliable. For instance, if one

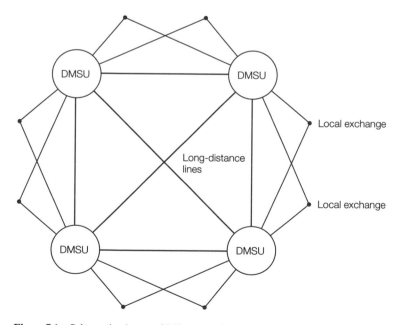

Figure 7.1   Schematic picture of BT's network

of these four routes is full, then the call can be rerouted along an alternative route, and if a DMSU breaks down, all calls in that area will still be able to get through.

Telecommunications technology is changing fast, the new technology for transmission being fiber optics and modern exchanges being electronic and programmable rather than electromagnetic. In Britain almost all major exchanges are now connected by fiber-optic cable, although it is still rare for the final local loop to be fiber-optic rather than copper wire. The advent of fiber optics has meant a dramatic reduction in the cost—especially the long-run marginal cost—of making long-distance calls. Moreover, once a fiber-optic cable has been laid, the cost of expanding its capacity is more or less independent of the length of the cable, this cost being the increased need for the technology at each end of the cable that concentrates the signals to be carried along the cable (i.e., the increased use of multiplexers). The advantage of using fiber-optic cable in the local loop is that it has a far greater carrying capacity than the older copper wires and is able to carry sufficient information to convey, for instance, high-quality TV signals. However, if a customer requires only the simple voice telephony service, then copper wire has ample carrying capacity.

Modern electronic exchanges are becoming increasingly sophisticated and are able to perform such tasks as recording the origin and destination of all calls (which is needed for itemized billing) and automatically finding the most efficient route for a particular call. In addition a modern exchange can enable the same long-distance cable to be used both for switched (i.e., channels paid for by the minute) and leased (i.e., dedicated channels leased by the month) capacity, so that the physical distinction between switched and leased circuits vanishes. However, the cost of exchanges together with the software that is needed to operate the exchanges is not falling nearly as fast as transmission technology, and the result is that transmission links are becoming cheaper relative to exchanges. This process is likely to result in the network having fewer major exchanges than was the case in the past. Moreover BT has argued that technological change has resulted in switching costs being more dependent on the number of lines connected to an exchange rather than on the number of actual calls routed through the exchange (i.e., that switching costs have become more access related than usage related).

Although radio technology is used in the traditional fixed-link network —for instance, in satellite transmission—the distinctive feature of mobile networks is that the *final* local link from users to the local exchange is a radio link. Both wire and radio methods of transmission are increasingly able to transmit digital rather than analog signals, which means that convergence with computing technology is becoming ever more important. One example of this is the growing market for electronic mail, which enables computers connected to a telecommunications network to send digital messages to each other. Moreover, as fiber-optic and satellite communication become more prevalent, there potentially is increasing convergence with parts of the broadcasting industry. For instance, any household with the capability to receive satellite TV signals also could potentially use the satellite to transmit and receive telecommunications signals.

In addition to traditional telephones, the apparatus attached to the public network by users now includes mobile phones, radiopagers, answering machines, telex and fax machines, TV sets, and computers. Moreover many private automatic branch exchanges (PABXs) with their associated private networks are attached to the public network. The services provided over the network are the basic voice telephony service together with the various "value-added" network and data services (VANS). The latter include such services as e-mail, directory inquiries, the transmission of fax messages, recorded messages, on-line data services, and, potentially, TV services.

7.1.2 Economic Characteristics

For the purposes of policy analysis the important economic features of the industry include its multiproduct nature, the nonstorability of its output, together with time-varying and stochastic demands, sunk costs and capacity constraints, the existence of externalities between users, elements of natural monopoly in some parts of the industry, and the complex vertical structure of the industry. The last three factors deserve particular discussion because externalities and natural monopoly are the market failures that provide the main rationale for policy intervention, and vertical issues affect the ease with which regulation is carried out.

The telecommunications industry supplies a great number of different products and services, ranging from the supply of telephones to the supply of large private exchanges, from the supply of telephone calls to various locations at various times of the day to the leasing of dedicated private lines by the month.[3] Telecommunications users are a very disparate group —business users largely wish to make calls only in office hours, some users

---

3. The current list of prices for the services offered by BT fills a hundred-page book.

wish only to transport data, and so on—and so there is much opportunity for various kinds of price discrimination, including nonlinear pricing. With the possible exception of certain services such as fax and data transmission, the basic services offered by a network operator are nonstorable.

A positive network externality between users arises because existing subscribers benefit when new subscribers join. This may have policy implications for pricing structure, possibly justifying a subsidy to rental charges to encourage new users to join the network, and it is fundamental for policy on interconnection between rival networks, for without interconnection a small network would be severely disadvantaged relative to a large one. The possible wider social benefits of having a telecommunications network—for example, provision to sparsely populated areas and the ability to obtain emergency services—are another kind of positive externality in a broad sense. In addition many telecommunications services are subject to capacity constraints, and so negative externalities arise from network congestion (i.e., the inability of some users to make calls due to other users filling the capacity on links and exchanges). The likelihood that a given call is made successfully is an important aspect of the quality of service. These points, together with the above-mentioned systematic variation of demand over time, make the use of peak-load pricing schemes prevalent and desirable for many services (see section 3.1.2). The fact that so much of a modern telecommunications network is electronic, and therefore reliable and energy efficient, means that the cost of operating a network of a given size and configuration does not increase greatly with the actual use made of the network—short-run variable costs are small.

There is no strong reason to expect significant natural monopoly in the supply or manufacture of apparatus or in the supply of services over a network, but aspects of network operation and construction may be naturally monopolistic to a degree.[4] At the most local level there would be wasteful duplication if houses had telephone wires from several suppliers, or if a local area had competing exchanges.[5] But, if additional wiring is

---

4. The empirical evidence on natural monopoly in network operation is mixed. For instance, Evans and Heckman (1983) and Hunt and Lynk (1991) find evidence to support the hypothesis that prior to divestiture, the Bell network in the United States was not a natural monopoly, whereas Röller (1990) reaches the opposite conclusion. At a less aggregated level, Shin and Ying (1992) argue that the regional networks in the United States are not naturally monopolistic.

5. However, in New Zealand the privatized telephone company, New Zealand Telecom, now faces competition at the local level from Clear Communications Inc., a company that is laying down a competing local network in most of the country's major cities.

occurring anyway—laying fiber-optic cable to supply cable TV, for example—then it might be efficient to allow these cable TV companies also to provide a competing local telecommunications service. Mobile telephony is another and growing source of local competition which, since local cables need not be laid, does not entail any wasteful duplication. Also large users could find it privately cost-effective to bypass the local network altogether and connect directly to the long-distance network. (Such local bypass has become prevalent in recent years in the United States.) However, it is reasonable to expect that most fixed-link network operations will remain naturally monopolistic at the local level, at least in the short term.[6] Of course the fact that there is a monopoly operator in each local area does not imply that there need be a single nationwide monopolist of local services.

Traffic on trunk and international lines is much heavier, and this means that once economies of scale in building capacity are exhausted, competition along such routes is more likely to be efficient. This suggests that there is little reason to expect severe natural monopoly conditions in trunk and international networks, and this conclusion is reinforced if rivalry provides a competitive stimulus both for cost reduction and the introduction of new products and services over time.

There are several dimensions of vertical relationships in the industry. To make use of the network at all, a user must possess the relevant apparatus to connect to the network, and so the industry that manufactures and supplies apparatus can be regarded as vertically related to network operation. (Even within this sector there is a vertical aspect since manufacturers and suppliers of apparatus are not always integrated; see section 7.5.2.) Within network operation the main vertical aspect is that between local, long-distance, and international operations. To complete a long-distance call, a customer must utilize links and exchanges within two local areas (at the origin and at the destination of the call) in addition to a long-distance line and one or more trunk exchange (see figure 7.1), and to make an international call local, long-distance and international components typically will be needed. Therefore local network operation could be regarded as an essential input for the "production" of longer-distance calls as well as being a final product in its own right. International telephone calls have an extra dimension of complexity, since, to complete such calls,

---

6. For a discussion of how local telephony in the United States is becoming more competitive, see Baumol and Sidak (1994).

the telephone networks of two (or more) countries need to interconnect. The interconnection arrangements of the second country typically will lie outside the authority of the domestic regulatory body, and so there will be a need for international agreements between the various regulatory bodies. Also, since a mobile telephone call will usually involve the use of a fixed-link network as well as mobile transmitters and receivers, fixed-link network operation is an essential input for mobile network operators. Finally, network operation as a whole is clearly a necessary input for those who supply *services*—including basic voice telephony—over the network.

As we have said, telecommunications technology is changing rapidly, and it is hard to predict exactly how the network will evolve in the years ahead. For example, the future balance between radio and cable links at the most local level is very uncertain, as is the future extent of fiber-optic cable in the network and hence the extent of future integration between telecommunications and the broadcasting and data services sectors. The influence of competition and regulatory policies upon incentives for dynamic efficiency and innovativeness is of particular importance in the telecommunications industry.

7.1.3 The Industry in Britain[7]

What is naturally monopolistic in the cost sense and what is actually monopolized need not coincide. Until 1981 British Telecom (BT) enjoyed a statutory monopoly on all aspects of network operation and almost all aspects of apparatus supply, and BT still dominates virtually all aspects of fixed-link network operation and basic voice telephony in Britain. In addition BT holds strong positions in mobile telephony, apparatus supply, and the supply of VANS. Because of this market power, the industry is overseen by the Office of Telecommunications (Oftel), the regulatory body that monitors and enforces operators' license conditions and acts as advisor to the government on licensing matters and the regulatory environment generally.

Telecommunications is a growth industry, with BT's call volumes increasing by 5% to 10% per year in the past decade (although this has slowed down dramatically in the 1990s due to the recession and increased competition), while VANS and mobile services have been growing even

---

7. The data contained in this section have been taken from the BT Share Prospectus, July 1993, Oftel's Annual Report for 1992 and BT's Annual Report for the year ending 31 March 1993.

faster. About 90% of British households in 1991 had a telephone, compared to 42% in 1972. At the time of writing, the only nationwide fixed-link competitor to BT is Mercury, a subsidiary of the international telecommunications company Cable and Wireless. Indeed, from the time of privatization until 1991, BT and Mercury enjoyed a protected duopoly, and further entry into fixed-link public network operation was banned. Mercury has concentrated on providing a long-distance network, and except for its larger customers, it has not laid cable for the local loop directly into homes and businesses. (However, within the City of London Mercury has a very extensive local network.) Therefore, except in the relatively rare event that both customers involved in a call are connected directly to its network, calls making use of Mercury's network must use BT's local, and possibly trunk, lines for either the local pickup or delivery (or both) of its calls, and for this service it pays to BT interconnection charges. In the 1993 financial year BT estimates that it had market share of 87% in the U.K. business market for calls and exchange lines (compared with 94% two years previously), 76% of the international market (compared with 85% two years previously), and 97% of the residential market for calls and exchange lines (compared with virtually 100% two years previously). Mercury supplies the vast majority of the remainder in these markets.

Following the duopoly review (see section 7.5.5), more than sixty new operators have applied for licenses to compete in some form with BT and Mercury. Among these are British Rail, British Waterways (in association with the U.S. trunk operator Sprint), the National Grid Company of England and Wales (whose telecommunications subsidiary is called Energis), and AT&T. Also, following the review, cable television companies are now permitted independently to offer a local telephone service; at present this sector is very small but growing fast. (At the end of 1991 about 300,000 homes had been connected with cable TV, although only a fraction of these also used the cable company's telecommunications service.)

By contrast to fixed-link telephony, the mobile sector has been characterized by almost symmetric duopolistic competition between Cellnet, in which BT has a majority stake, and Vodafone. The latter company has succeeded in gaining slightly over half the market, which at the end of 1992 served a total of about 1.4 million customers. (This market was virtually nonexistent until the early 1980s.) By any measure, mobile network operation has been very profitable. Until recently mobile network

Table 7.1 Performance of British Telecom

	1981	1982	1983	1984	1985
Turnover (£m)	4,554	5,708	6,377	6,830	7,585
Operating profit (£m)	753	1,007	905	1,531	1,856
Return on capital employed (%)[a]	9.4	11.9	9.7	16.7	18.3
Return on sales (%)	16.5	17.6	14.2	22.4	24.5
Employees (1,000s)	247	252	249	245	238
Investment as percentage of turnover (%)[b]	29	25	24	22	24

Source: BT Annual Reports. Financial years end on 31 March.
a. Capital employed is defined as total assets less current liabilities.
b. Investment is defined as the purchase of tangible fixed assets.

operation for voice services was also limited to just two firms, but several new entrants were licensed in 1991. These entrants (called Personal Communications Networks, or PCNs) use digital rather than analog technology. After a merger there are now two PCN operators, one of which—Mercury One-2-One, jointly owned by Cable and Wireless and US West (a "Baby Bell")—was launched in 1993.

Apparatus supply has become much more competitive over the past decade: whereas BT had a statutory monopoly in the supply of telephones before 1981, in 1991 it supplied about 53% of all telephones sold in that year. Over the same period its supply of private branch exchanges fell from 83% to 38%. The VANS sector has also been quite competitive.

In the year ending March 1993 BT's revenue (not including subsidiaries such as Cellnet) was £13.2 billion, which was divided in the following manner: inland calls 38%, exchange line rentals 17%, international calls 14%, apparatus supply 8%, and other sales and services (leased lines, VANS, telexes, etc., as well as interconnection payments from Mercury) 23%. The company employed around 170,000 people (compared with 210,000 the previous year) and made an operating profit before interest and tax of £2.0 billion, which is 15.8% of total turnover and represents a return on capital employed of 14.6% on a historic cost basis. Table 7.1 gives information on BT's sales, profits, employment, and investment over the past decade. Oftel (1992a, 8–10) reports a breakdown by service of BT's financial results, on the basis of a form of fully allocated historic costs. According to these figures BT faces a substantial deficit on the provision of access (connections and line rentals) but earns high rates of return on calls, especially long-distance and international calls.

1986	1987	1988	1989	1990	1991	1992	1993
8,317	9,339	10,185	11,071	12,315	13,154	13,337	13,242
2,118	2,349	2,609	2,807	3,210	3,531	3,415	1,972
19.3	21.2	22.1	21.8	22.5	22.4	21.0	14.6
25.5	25.2	25.6	25.5	26.0	26.8	25.5	18.5
234	236	236	243	248	227	210	170
24	22	23	26	25	22	19	16

7.2 Policy Questions

This section aims to offer a general perspective on policy issues for regulating a modern telecommunications industry. Discussion is organized under the four broad headings of structure, entry, pricing, and quality. In subsequent sections we describe how policies have been chosen in the United States and Britain.

7.2.1 Structure

The fundamental policy issue concerning structure is whether naturally monopolistic activities such as local fixed-link network operation (in the present state of technology) should be vertically separated from potentially more competitive activities such as long-distance network operation. There is the further issue of whether fixed-link network operation as a whole should be separated from the supply of services (both basic voice telephony and VANS) over the network, the supply and manufacture of apparatus, and the provision of mobile services.

As discussed in chapter 5, vertical separation has the advantage that it removes the incentive for the firm in the natural monopoly activity (e.g., local telecommunications)—firm M—to behave anticompetitively toward a particular set of firms in the potentially competitive activity (e.g., the long-distance market). In addition it makes the task of regulating the natural monopoly activity more straightforward. For instance, regardless of whether or not there is vertical separation, whenever there is competition in the long-distance market, there will be a need for the regulation of the terms of access to the monopolized input. This access regulation necessarily will be done only imperfectly and will need partially to rely on information obtained from firm *M*. The advantage of vertical separation is that whatever regulatory scheme is imposed, there need be no systematic bias toward one long-distance operator over another. If, on the other hand, firm *M* also operates in the more competitive activity, then the regulator will have constantly to monitor the possibility that *M*'s competitive business is being granted more favorable terms of access than its rivals. Moreover it should be borne in mind that there are a variety of nonprice means the integrated firm can use to disadvantage its rivals in the more competitive sector. In the telecommunications context these include manipulating the *quality* of access (so that rivals' customers experience connections that are less clear or more congested than the incumbent firm's) and requiring different ease of access for its rivals' customers from its own (e.g., by forcing these customers to dial a lengthy access code or to have more complex billing arrangements). But vertical separation can damage cost efficiency if there are significant economies of scope between the activities concerned, and if these economies of scope cannot be obtained by means of contractual relations between two separate firms.[8]

Another aspect of structure is regional. For example, if local and long-distance network operation has been separated, there is the possibility of having separate local network operators, each a monopolist in its own region. This enhances the effectiveness of regulation of local telecommunications by facilitating cost comparisons and forms of yardstick competition.

7.2.2   Entry

As discussed in chapter 4, a policy of free entry is appropriate for most industries because of the benefits of competition in terms of low prices and incentives for cost reduction and innovation. The issue is less straightforward in parts of the telecommunications industry because of (1) elements of natural monopoly, (2) the presence in almost all countries of a dominant and integrated incumbent firm, and (3) the incumbent firm being regulated.

---

8. There is a second argument for separating mobile and fixed-link network operation. Since mobile telephony is probably the most important source of competition for the local fixed-link networks, it seems plausible that this local competition will be less vigorous if both technologies are under common than separate ownership. This is therefore a kind of horizontal separation.

As regards point 1, we have seen that arguments are sometimes advanced for restricting entry. First, when there are economies of scale there is a trade-off between the benefits to consumers of more competition and higher costs as more firms enter. In particular a policy of free entry might, in some circumstances, lead to excessive entry from the point of view of overall efficiency.

Turning to point 2, and assuming that a degree of entry is desirable, the presence of a dominant and integrated incumbent telecommunications firm raises the issue of entry deterrence. As mentioned in section 4.2, the presence of switching costs for consumers provides a source of incumbency advantage. Switching costs—in the economic rather than the engineering sense—are prevalent in the telecommunications industry, and a regulator keen to encourage competition should find ways to reduce these costs as much as possible. There is a switching cost when a consumer is required to change a telephone number if a different network operator is chosen. (This involves a substantial cost, since a user must notify possible callers of the new number.) The regulator can eliminate this cost by ensuring that there is full "number portability" so that telephone numbers are not the private property of the incumbent network operator. A second source of switching costs is the possible inconvenience of using one operator's network rather than another's. If, for instance, a customer of one company can use a competitor's long-distance line simply by prefixing a two-digit code, then there is no need to go to the trouble of obtaining contractual relations with a second firm. (This policy of "equal access" is discussed further in section 7.5.1.)

Unless the monitoring of anticompetitive behavior and incumbency advantages is very effective, it may also be desirable to *help* new entrants into network operation while they build their sunk cost networks to develop an effective competitive challenge to a dominant incumbent (see section 4.2.2). If the incumbent is vertically integrated, one way of doing this is to set favorable terms of interconnection to the incumbent's network. Another way to assist entrants is to allow them to enter selectively in the more profitable markets (e.g., in urban areas or high-usage customers) while placing universal service and other obligations only upon the incumbent (i.e., to allow entrants to cream-skim). A third way to assist entry might be to protect recent entrants from further entry while they establish themselves and recoup the sunk costs of building their networks. However, such a policy will also benefit the incumbent operator, and usually to a much greater extent. Moreover it is likely that the greater threat to an entrant comes not from further entry but from the dominant incumbent firm. If there is a policy of actively helping entrants, the regulator must monitor constantly the possibility that this help does not go too far, and that inefficient as well as efficient entrants are not put in place. As we will see shortly, the question of how to promote entry in the face of a dominant incumbent firm has been a very controversial topic in British telecommunications policy.

As for point 3, it is clear that price regulation of the incumbent firm can act to inhibit entry (see section 4.3.3). The fact that the incumbent firm is required to offer a low price for some service will probably mean that entrants will also be forced to offer lower prices than they otherwise would, and this can deter or inhibit entry. Therefore there may be a trade-off between the short-term benefit to consumers resulting from low regulated prices and the long-term benefit to consumers of a more competitive industry. In addition placing a ceiling only on the incumbent firm's *average* price can have a distorting effect on entry conditions. Since a low price in the more competitive market (e.g., long-distance calls) allows the incumbent to charge a higher price in the captive market (local network operation), there is a danger that the incumbent has an incentive to match its rivals' prices very aggressively. This again can discourage efficient entry.

Second, there is the possibility of cream-skimming when regulation requires the operator to pursue a policy of cross-subsidy. For instance, if the incumbent's access charge to customers is required to be set below cost (measured in an appropriate way), and if the other network services are potentially very competitive, then a successful policy of free entry might mean the firm becoming unprofitable overall unless entrants are required to contribute toward the loss-making activity of providing access. Another common regulatory policy is to require that rental and connection charges be geographically uniform, even though the cost of network provision typically is far higher in rural than urban areas. Such a policy can induce entry in the more profitable urban sector, again leaving the incumbent firm unable to cover its costs. However, in any such cases the regulator should consider either changing the pricing policy or finding some other means to fund the cross-subsidy before resorting to a ban on entry.

7.2.3 Pricing

Since, in the medium term at least, competition cannot be relied upon to contain market power in many parts of the telecommunications industry, the control of pricing is central to regulatory policy. Pricing policies fall naturally into two groups: those involving prices to users for final consumption of telecommunications services, and those involving the price of interconnection for rival operators to the incumbent's network.

Desirable pricing structures for a multiproduct monopoly were discussed in section 3.1.[9] Broadly speaking, when prices need to cover some fixed costs, then prices (if uniform) typically need to exceed marginal costs. The welfare-maximizing prices that yield enough revenue to cover total costs, Ramsey prices, involve the price/marginal cost markup for each service being inversely related to the elasticity of demand and related to cross-elasticities of demand.[10] Empirical evidence from the United States suggests that demand for access to the network and for local calls is rather inelastic, whereas demand for longer-distance calls is more elastic. Evidence in the United Kingdom seems to indicate that demand for all services is fairly inelastic (see Beesley 1981, Annex). Culham (1987) estimates Ramsey pricing for Britain under various assumptions about costs, own-price elasticities, and the importance of network externality effects—because of difficulties of estimation he ignores cross-elasticities in his calculations—and concludes that the rental charge should be much higher and longer-distance calls much cheaper than usually is the case.

However, for the reasons discussed in section 3.1, Ramsey prices are rarely implemented in practice. Indeed pricing policy often does not take account of basic cost differences in serving one group of customers from another, let alone the demand elasticity factors that are involved in Ramsey pricing. For example,

1. because of the greater dispersion, it is more expensive to provide the infrastructure for local service provision in rural than urban areas, and this cost difference is rarely reflected in charges;

2. elements of scale economies mean that it is cheaper to serve traffic on the busier trunk routes, and while some routes do have a lower charge than others, this is to a lesser extent than cost differences would warrant;

3. charges for calls, in Britain at least, vary on the basis of *distance* rather than, say, on the number of exchanges a call involves. Thus, for example, all calls within London are charged at the local call rate, a rate that does not reflect costs;

---

9. Pricing policy for the telecommunications industry, especially in the U.S. context, is thoroughly examined in Mitchell and Vogelsang (1991).
10. The Ramsey formulas also need to be modified in the presence of network externalities; see Mitchell and Vogelsang (1991, sec. 4.4).

4. it may be that calls themselves are overpriced compared to fixed charges, given the structure of network costs, in which case fixed charges should be increased and usage charges reduced. (BT has consistently argued that this is the case in Britain.)

As mentioned in the previous section, policy-induced cross-subsidy can result in inefficient entry in those markets that generate supernormal profits. However, even without this undesirable effect on entry, the regulator should consider whether such pricing policies really do benefit consumers in aggregate. Unless there are particular overriding factors, prices should reflect costs, and if it costs more to connect a rural than an urban customer to a network then—at least on economic efficiency grounds— the connection charge should be higher in rural areas. Of course there may well be distributional concerns or some notion of fairness that prevents the regulator from moving toward de-averaged prices, but it is not clear why the telecommunications industry and some of the other utility industries should receive special treatment in this respect.

Perhaps more so than the other utilities, telecommunications metering technology provides great scope for quite sophisticated nonlinear tariff schedules, whose use may be desirable. For instance, a tariff with quantity discounts provides a more efficient way to keep as many people on the network as possible (something that is desirable because of network externalities), at the same time serving the larger customers fairly efficiently, than does a simple two-part tariff. However, as with other forms of price discrimination, the regulator should monitor the possibility that such tariffs provide the incumbent firm with a profitable way to distort competition (e.g., in the market for large customers).

Turning now to policy toward the pricing of interconnection in the industry, it is clear that this question is bound up with policy toward entry. If it is thought desirable to assist entrants, then one obvious way to do this is to offer advantageous terms of interconnection to the dominant firm's network. For a discussion of the relationship between the optimal access price and the incumbent's marginal cost of providing access, see section 5.2.

7.2.4 Quality
Since consumers gain from high quality as well as low prices for the offered services, price control should be supplemented by quality control. Without such control the regulated firm has an incentive to reduce its standard of service. Some aspects of the quality of telecommunications

services relate to current expenditures—for example, the speed of installations and repairs, the responsiveness of directory enquiries, and the maintenance of public call boxes. Others depend on capital investment—for example, having adequate capacity to avoid congestion, and modern switching and transmission technology for new services and more reliable network operation. Policy options for promoting quality range from the explicit incorporation of quality indexes into the price control formula (so that by offering a high-quality service the operator will have a more generous price cap), liability for damages, and standard financial penalties for poor quality to less formal methods such as warning the firm that low quality now will be reflected in lower prices at the next price review (see section 6.1.8 and 6.2.5).

In this section we have discussed telecommunications policy options in four important areas—structure, entry, pricing, and quality. The interrelationships between those topics, for example, between vertical relationships and the ease of entry, and between pricing policy and the ease of entry will have been evident. We now examine how policymakers in the United States and Britain have chosen from these options.

7.3 Regulatory Reform in the United States

No discussion of telecommunications policy can be complete without some mention of the dramatic developments in the United States in the early 1980s.[11] For decades AT&T was the dominant integrated telecommunications firm in the United States, with a more or less complete monopoly over apparatus manufacture and supply (through its subsidiary Western Electric), and network operation both at the local and especially the long-distance level. For much of this time the industry regulator, the Federal Communications Commission (FCC), acted in a way that inhibited entry into the industry. However, after a long legal battle, a rival operator MCI was granted permission to build and operate a microwave link between Chicago and St. Louis in 1972, and a slow but steady growth of competition occurred subsequently in network operation with the result that AT&T faced a degree of competition along most large city-pair routes.

---

11. For the historical background see Brock (1981), and for a collection of articles on the breakup of AT&T, see Evans (1983). For recents surveys, see Noll and Owen (1989), Phillips (1991), and Baumol and Sidak (1994).

It was, inter alia, AT&T's allegedly anticompetitive behavior toward its rivals that induced the Department of Justice to bring its antitrust case against the firm in 1974. This case, which was settled in 1982, culminated in the Modification of Final Judgment (MFJ) requiring the breakup of AT&T on 1 January 1984. This was a notable piece of structure regulation and the main results of the Judgment were as follows:

1. Seven Regional Bell Operating Companies (RBOCs) were created and received the local network assets of the formerly integrated AT&T company. Each of these companies is of roughly equivalent size to BT.

2. The United States was partitioned into 192 Local Access Transport Areas (LATAs), and the services within each LATA are provided by a Local Exchange Carrier (LEC), an LEC being one of the RBOCs, GTE, or one of a number of smaller local companies. The RBOCs were (largely) banned from providing lines between different LATAs within their region (the interLATA service—in effect the long-distance service), leaving these routes to be provided by the new AT&T company together with its long-distance rivals (together termed the Interexchange Carriers, or IXCs).

3. Except in a few states, the IXCs were banned from offering most services within any LATA (intraLATA services).

4. AT&T was allowed to keep its apparatus manufacturing arm, Western Electric, and the RBOCs were banned from engaging in apparatus manufacture.

5. The RBOCs were banned from entering the VANS and entertainment markets within their own regions.

The reason why the RBOCs were banned from long-distance services, apparatus supply and VANS was because they were perceived to have bottleneck facilities that would invite discrimination against rivals if they were permitted to operate in these more competitive markets. In recent years the RBOCs have mounted a campaign to be allowed to enter both the interLATA and VANS markets within their regions.

Regulation of interstate services, which involve the IXCs, is done by the FCC, whereas all intrastate services, which involve both the IXCs and the LECs, are managed by the various state regulators. The IXCs pay access charges to the LECs for local transportation of their calls, and all IXCs have "equal access" in the sense that almost all users can subscribe to a default IXC of their choice, or alternatively they can use any other carrier by dialing a relatively short five-digit code. This means that there is little systematic difference in the ease with which a customer can connect with one long-distance operator over another. Since 1989 AT&T (but not the other IXCs) has been subject to price cap regulation of its major services, whereas the LECs' final product prices generally have been governed by rate-of-return regulation. The form of the price cap adopted for AT&T leaves comparatively little scope for "rebalancing," or changes in relative prices. There are three separate caps—for residential and small business services, for toll-free 800 services, and for services to large business—and within each of these caps no price for any service can change in real terms by more than 5% in a year. Since 1989 the required overall reduction in average real prices was at least 3% per year for each of the three baskets (i.e., in terms of $RPI - X$, X was set at 3).

Since 1991 the terms of the IXCs access to the major LECs' local networks have also been subject to a price cap. The method of pricing access by LECs is almost invariably to charge a uniform per-minute price for incoming and outgoing calls, this price being designed to cover a fixed fraction of the LECs' costs. Recently, however, proposals have been made by LECs to start offering nonlinear charging schemes for access.

While AT&T is clearly the major provider of long-distance services, it is by no means completely dominant, and its rivals by 1989 had gained a market share of about 30% in the interstate market for switched services and private lines.[12] Moreover the FCC currently operates a regime of almost completely free entry to the interLATA market (with the notable exception of the RBOCs).

7.4 Framework of Competition and Regulation at Privatization

This section describes the competitive and regulatory framework established in Britain at the time of BT's privatization in 1984. An appendix to this chapter lists some of the main events in British telecommunications policy over the past decade.

7.4.1 Background to Privatization

The privatization of BT was not on the policy agenda at the beginning of the 1980s. Rather, the focus was on tighter financial control of the firm, and some steps toward liberalization were taken.[13] The 1981 British Telecommunications Act split BT from the Post Office, abolished BT's legal

---

12. See Mitchell and Vogelsang (1991, table 2.1).
13. See Foster (1992, ch. 4).

monopoly over network operation and the supply of network services, most apparatus supply, and VANS, but did not allow so-called simple resale.[14] As a result of the ending of BT's legal monopoly over network operation, Mercury (a subsidiary of the recently privatized UK telecommunications company Cable and Wireless), the first potential competitor to BT, was licensed to operate a nationwide fixed-link telecommunications network. The ending of BT's monopoly on the supply of telephones meant that, instead of being required to rent a telephone from BT, a customer had the option of buying a telephone either from BT or from one of a number of independent suppliers. Overall these measures did little to threaten seriously BT's dominance throughout the industry, but the 1981 Act nevertheless took the important first steps toward competition.

Tighter financial controls over the nationalized industries, which were largely the result of macroeconomic monetary policy commitments at the time, were preventing BT from investing in network modernization to the extent that was efficient on microeconomic grounds. An attempt to overcome this problem of underinvestment by allowing BT to borrow from private capital markets (via "Buzby bonds") did not get off the ground, partly because of the legal difficulty of distinguishing such borrowings from public sector borrowings. Instead privatization—the sale of equity rather than debt—was the favored solution (see Department of Industry 1982). Henceforth BT could borrow without increasing the so-called public sector borrowing requirement (PSBR). Moreover, since privatization proceeds are treated curiously in the national accounts as negative public expenditure, privatization had the advantage of reducing the PSBR yet further. The macroeconomic commitments of the government, then, had an important influence on privatization policy toward BT, even though the principal effect of that policy is microeconomic rather than macroeconomic.

7.4.2 Framework at Privatization

Having resolved to privatize BT, the government had to choose between the policy options discussed in section 7.2. The main question concerning structure policy was whether BT should be broken up—for example,

---

14. Resale is a kind of wholesaling activity in telecommunications services. Resellers lease lines from BT or Mercury by the month, say, and sell services by the minute after either adding value (e.g., supplying data to subscribers) or not (so-called simple resale). The Beesley Report (1981) had recommended that *all* forms of resale of leased capacity be permitted, not just value-added services.

whether its local network services, long-distance services, and apparatus supply businesses should be separated—in order to reduce the potential for anticompetitive behavior. One possible model that could have been followed was that recently implemented in the United States. In the event, however, the British government decided to privatize BT intact as an integrated and dominant firm. A important reason for this decision was the desire to privatize BT rapidly, and BT's management was strongly opposed to a breakup. However, there were *some* structural constraints placed on BT. It was required to keep separate accounts for network operation, apparatus supply, supply of VANS, and both mobile network operation and any future apparatus manufacturing business were required to be placed in separate subsidiaries. BT was also forbidden from carrying TV services on its public network, though it was permitted to own stakes in cable TV companies. These safeguards were put in place to check the possibility of unfair cross-subsidy between these various activities.

Having decided against any radical structural remedies, it was necessary to determine policy toward entry in the industry. In November 1983, a year before privatization, the government announced its "duopoly policy"—that for the next seven years only BT and Mercury would be licensed to operate a nationwide network with fixed links.[15] This duopoly policy also prevented cable TV companies from providing telecommunications services except as agents of one of the duopolists. The government's prohibition on unrestricted resale that has already been mentioned was extended until at least 1989. This collection of policies severely limited competition in the main telecommunications service for the rest of the decade. Its stated rationale was to protect the infant Mercury and induce it to enter, and to give BT time to adjust to the prospect of further competition. (The duopoly policy, like the policy of keeping BT intact, was also in the interests of BT and its management, whose cooperation was important for the achieving the government's objective of a speedy privatization.) The terms on which rivals to BT—at that time just Mercury in the fixed-link sector—could interconnect with BT's networks were only rather vaguely described in BT's license at its privatization. In the first instance BT and any rival should attempt to reach a mutually satisfactory agreement without the involvement of Oftel, but if this turned out not to be possible, the DGT had the power to fix the interconnection terms (with BT or the rival operator having the right of appeal to the MMC).

---

15. The duopoly policy statement is reproduced in DTI (1990, app. 1).

As we will see, interconnection has continued to be a major issue after privatization.

At around the time of BT's privatization the technology for mobile telephony was being developed and the government had also to decide on policy toward this industry. Partly because of the scarcity of available frequencies, a duopoly policy was adopted here also, and two companies were licensed as network operators, Cellnet (with BT as majority share-holder) and Vodafone. However, unlike the situation of fixed-link tele-phony, these two firms started from a symmetric position (initially neither had any customers), and subsequent competition has been reasonably effective.[16]

As for price regulation, the government was anxious to avoid the per-ceived problems of U.S. rate-of-return regulation in terms of cost ineffi-ciency, regulatory burden, and vulnerability to capture (see chapter 6 for more details). The Littlechild Report (1983) recommended RPI − X price cap regulation, thus starting a pattern that would be followed by the other utilities. The government accepted this advice, and its chosen basket of regulated services included switched inland calls (except from public call boxes) and line rentals. In fact Littlechild had suggested that only local calls and exchange line rentals be included and that long-distance services be left unregulated with competition from Mercury and others being left to bring down prices there. However, in his report he also suggested a more liberal policy toward competition than the government's adopted duopoly policy (see Littlechild 1983, 38).

The price control formula was to run for the five years until July 1989 and X was set at 3. The form of the price cap was of the "tariff basket" type, where the average percentage price increase of BT's regulated products (where the weights in the index are given by the previous year's revenue shares for the various products) must be no greater than RPI − 3. This price control formula is probably simpler than those of the other utility industries in the sense that it has no cost passthrough component. Except for an undertaking that line rentals would not increase by more than RPI + 2 in any year, BT had wide discretion to vary relative prices within the regulated basket. However, BT was not permitted to discrimi-nate in its charges for calls along similar routes, nor was it permitted to

---

16. The mobile sector had a form of structure regulation whereby the two mobile network operators were prohibited from retailing air time except via subsidiaries. The result has been very vigorous competition and low profits amongst the retailers; see Geroski et al. (1989).

vary rental or connection charges according to the cost of serving any given user. International call charges, the charges for leasing private lines, connection charges, the charges for VANS and apparatus manufacture and supply, were not regulated.

Save for a general duty on the regulator to promote the interests of consumers and producers will respect to the price, quality, and variety of services, quality was not explicitly regulated at the time of privatization.

7.4.3 The Institutional Framework at Privatization

The policy decisions taken by the government appeared in the 1984 Telecommunications Act, in BT's License to operate its network granted by the Secretary of State for Trade and Industry under the Act, and in parliamentary statements such as the duopoly policy statement. The Act also established the Director General of Telecommunications, the first DGT being Bryan Carsberg (now Sir Bryan), as head of the Office for Telecommunications (Oftel), the main regulatory body for the industry. Future regulatory policy would be shaped by Oftel as well as the DTI. The DGT is required to ensure that all reasonable demands for telecommunications services are met and that their provision can be financed, and he has other duties including the promotion of competition. The DGT is responsible for enforcing license conditions (including price control), and he may make orders that require compliance which, if ignored, could result in liability for damages to third parties. In the unlikely event that BT persists in noncompliance with an order, its license may be revoked by the Secretary of State. The power to license new entrants lies with the Secretary of State, though some decisions may be delegated to the DGT or exercised subject to his advice. The DGT can change license conditions either by agreement with the licensee or by making a successful reference to the Monopolies and Mergers Commission. (In either case, however, there must be public consultation before licence conditions may be changed.) Thus in effect there are three regulatory bodies—the DTI, Oftel and the MMC—and this pattern has been adopted in other utility industries.

The regulatory authority of Oftel goes beyond the powers and duties in the Act because it has always the threat of a reference to the MMC to seek regulatory change. The result is a kind of *implicit* regulation—almost regulation by bargaining between Oftel and BT—and this style of regulation stands in marked contrast to the rather legalistic style of regulation in the United States.

7.5   Development of Competition and Regulation

In the years up to 1991, when the duopoly policy for BT and Mercury was abandoned, the DTI itself was in the background as far as regulation was concerned, and Oftel held center stage. We will discuss regulatory developments since privatization under the following headings, which became important roughly in chronological order: the initial interconnection agreement between BT and Mercury, apparatus manufacture and supply, service quality, the level and structure of retail prices, the duopoly review of entry conditions, and interconnection in the present and potentially more competitive environment.

7.5.1   The 1985 Interconnection Determination

The effectiveness of Mercury's competitive challenge to BT, as well as that of any subsequent entrant, depended crucially on the terms of interconnection to BT's network. No one would be able to use Mercury's long-distance links without using BT's local links at either end unless Mercury itself were to build a substantial nationwide local network. This would be grossly inefficient and unattractive to Mercury given the natural monopoly conditions in local network operations (except in the case of the very large telecoms users). Even if Mercury *were* to succeed in having many of its customers directly connected to its network, so that these customers did not need access to BT's local lines to get to Mercury's network, in most cases these customers would be calling a BT customer, in which case BT's lines would be needed for delivery of the call. In effect, therefore, BT had a monopoly on a necessary input for Mercury's operation, and any chance of effective competition required that the price and quality of this input be suitably controlled.

The policy dilemma was that if BT was forced (e.g., because of constraints on the level of its rental charges) to cover the fixed costs of local network provision and operation and public service obligations partly out of call charges (i.e., if BT has an "access deficit"), and if Mercury had access to BT's local network at marginal usage cost, then this could over time lead to inefficient cream-skimming with the result that BT would be unable to cover these fixed costs. On the other hand, in the face of BT's overwhelming dominance at the time of privatization, competition was bound to be very limited at least initially, and in danger of being stifled altogether.

BT and Mercury were not able to agree interconnection terms after BT's privatization, and Oftel was called in to determine Mercury's interconnect charges. Oftel made its ruling in October 1985, thus allowing Mercury finally to enter the switched voice telephony market in 1986, four years after its license was granted. Condition 13 of BT's License entitles BT to charges that cover the fully allocated costs of providing interconnection, including relevant overheads and a reasonable rate of return on the relevant assets. In its ruling Oftel required that Mercury pay for all the direct costs of providing interconnection (labor, laying cable, altering exchanges, etc.) and that Mercury should pay a per-minute charge for its use of BT's local networks, this charge depending on the time of day and how far into BT's networks Mercury picked up and delivered its calls.[17] In the (unlikely) event that Mercury's annual interconnection payments became greater than 7% of BT's annual revenue for national calls, these interconnection payments would be increased. Unless either side wished to change the arrangement, these interconnection charges would automatically adjust over time according to an RPI − 3 formula.

The DGT stated that these interconnect charges were designed to contribute to the costs, including a proportion of the required capacity expansion and a reasonable profit, of using BT's network, but the exact method by which these interconnection terms were arrived at was not made public. Certainly the relationship between these charges and the marginal or average cost of providing interconnection, for instance, is not clear. Recently, however, the DGT has stated that the 1985 ruling was designed to exempt Mercury from any contribution to BT's alleged access deficit (at least until the 7% level had been reached), and so Mercury was granted advantageous interconnection terms in the interests of helping it get started (see DTI 1991, 70). In other words, generous interconnection terms were used as a means of assisting entry in the face of BT's incumbency advantage.

Unlike later policy in the United States, BT was not required in the determination to provide full "equal access" to Mercury's customers. To use Mercury's long-distance network, users had to become customers of Mercury, and unless they had very large demands for telephone services, they would not be connected directly to its network but instead would use BT's local lines. To gain access to Mercury's network, a user needed to

---

17. For instance, Mercury would have to pay BT 6 pence per minute for BT to deliver a Mercury call using a "short national" segment at peak time.

purchase a "blue button" telephone that had stored in it the lengthy access code necessary for this, and at the time this special telephone was markedly more expensive than a standard telephone. Therefore, as well as going to the trouble of changing from BT to Mercury, the user had also to invest in a new telephone, and this combined switching cost will have deterred many potential Mercury subscribers. One variant of equal access would have been for *all* users to be required to key in a short access code—one for each of BT and Mercury, depending on which network is to be used— for each long-distance call they make, a system that would not have any bias for one operator over the other (but which would lengthen dialing generally a little).[18]

At the time the 1985 determination was viewed as being broadly favorable to Mercury. In the subsequent years, however, there were complaints from Mercury concerning the scope, speed, and quality of the interconnection provided by BT (see Beesley and Laidlaw 1989, 27). Since the determination Mercury has not made great inroads into BT's share of the switched long-distance market, and interconnect arrangements between the two operators were amended as a result of further determinations in 1988 and 1989 as well as by mutual agreement. The 1991 duopoly review and the likelihood of further entry into the industry has again brought the contentious issue of interconnection to the center of policy debate (see section 7.5.6). In 1992 the two firms could not agree on a further revision to the original 1985 determination, and they asked Oftel to undertake a full review of the agreement.[19]

7.5.2 Apparatus Manufacture and Supply

BT's apparatus supply business ranges from supplying telephones and answering machines to supplying private automatic branch exchanges

---

18. Hull, which for historical reasons has an independent local telephone company, has this form of equal access to both the BT and Mercury national networks, and Mercury has achieved a market share there of about a half, compared with a national share of less than 10%; see DTI (1990, para. 9.1). For a fuller discussion of equal access, see DTI (1991, app. 3).

19. The final outcome of the review was not known at the time of writing (December 1993). The two mobile operators also need to obtain interconnection agreements with BT, both to use BT's long-distance cables and to deliver calls made on a mobile phone to a fixed-link phone. Such agreements have been much less problematic. However, because BT is a majority shareholder in Cellnet, there is the danger that it has an incentive to offer that company more favorable interconnection terms than Vodafone. Oftel monitors the two interconnection agreements and the implicit threat that it will take steps should an asymmetry become apparant has prevented this from being a problem.

(PABXs), the exchanges used in private networks. At the time of privatization BT dominated the supply of most types of customer apparatus—large PABXs, which it chose not to supply, being the main exception—but did not itself engage significantly in their manufacture.[20] Concern already existed that BT's dominance in network operation would give it unfair advantages over its rivals in apparatus supply, and such worries were exacerbated when BT proposed to acquire a majority stake in Mitel, the Canadian PABX manufacturer, in 1985. The bid was referred to the MMC by the Office of Fair Trading on competition grounds.

BT and Mitel argued that the merger would lead to synergies both between manufacturing and network operation, and between manufacturing and apparatus supply. The concerns for possible adverse effects on competition were (1) that BT's apparatus supply arm would unfairly favor Mitel's products over those of other apparatus manufacturers, and (2) that independent apparatus suppliers, for whom Mitel had been a major source, would be discriminated against by Mitel, with a consequent reduction of competition in apparatus supply.

The MMC (1986a) adopted a compromise.[21] They recommended that the merger be permitted subject to conditions limiting, inter alia, cross-subsidy and the purchase by BT of Mitel apparatus for use or supply in the United Kingdom before 1990. The Secretary of State allowed the merger subject to weaker conditions. It was questionable whether the conditions could both safeguard effective competition and allow the claimed synergy gains. In any event Mitel's subsequent performance as a BT subsidiary was poor, and in 1992 BT sold its stake in the company at a substantial loss compared with its original investment. Since its privatization, BT's market share in all areas of apparatus supply has gradually been eroded, and policy toward this aspect of the telecommunications industry has become less controversial.[22]

7.5.3 Quality of Service
Quality of service was particularly prominent among the public's concerns over BT's privatization, and there was the worry that a change in the

---

20. See Oftel's 1992 Annual Report, tables 10.1 and 10.2.
21. See Gist and Meadowcroft (1986).
22. The main area of controversy in recent years was an investigation by Oftel in 1991 that concluded that there was an unfair cross-subsidy from BT's main network business to its apparatus supply business (Oftel 1991). The DGT required BT to produce a five-year plan, to be agreed with him, showing how the apparatus supply business will be restored to profit.

priorities of management from public service to the pursuit of profit could lead to a decline in quality. As a private company BT's quality of service initially was not explicitly regulated, and it became the subject of widespread public criticism, especially in 1987 (when there was also an engineers' strike and a severe storm that disrupted some services).[23] BT's position was not helped by the fact that it had stopped publishing its service quality indicators after privatization. Oftel intervened to improve quality and information about quality. It found that while dimensions of quality such as repair and installation delays and the proportion of call boxes working had not worsened as much as some claimed, BT's quality was not as good as might have been expected given technological advance. The DGT concluded that BT should resume publication of its quality of service statistics on a six-monthly basis and should face financial penalties in some form for poor quality, as would firms in more competitive markets.

As discussed in chapter 6, in addition to informal pressures, the broad alternatives were the formal incorporation of some quality variables into the price control formula, and a mixture of fixed penalties and contractual liability for poor performance. The latter approach was adopted for matters such as repair and installation delays, with standard compensation terms for residential users and larger compensation to businesses depending on the damage caused. It would be impractical for BT to offer compensation for individual failed calls, but this and other aspects of network modernization have been encouraged by moral suasion backed up by the implicit threat of referral to the MMC or harsher price reviews in the future. The quality of BT's service to consumers has improved considerably in recent years.[24]

The 1992 Competition and Service (Utilities) Act—part of John Major's "Citizen's Charter" initiative—amended the 1984 Telecommunications Act and gave the DGT new statutory powers regarding BT's quality of service, and in particular the authority to set performance standards and

---

23. Partly in response to that criticism, BT did not increase the prices of regulated services in 1987, though it was entitled to an average increase of 1.3% under the RPI − 3 formula. The criticism of BT's consumer service is mirrored by Mercury's complaints about the quality of its interconnection to BT's network.

24. For instance, table 6 in Oftel's 1992 Annual Report reports that the percentage of national calls that fail has fallen from 4.3% in 1987 to 0.3% in 1992 and that the percentage of faults that are repaired within two working days has increased from 74% to about 98% over the same period.

compensation terms for public telephone operators (see Rovizzi and Thompson 1992).

7.5.4 Pricing

Apart from the issue of interconnection charges discussed above, there have been several important episodes of regulatory concern about pricing —the rebalancing of local and long-distance call charges in 1985 and 1986, the first price review in 1988, the controversy over the balance between exchange line rentals and call charges in the 1990 duopoly review, and, most recently, the 1992 price review. Average prices for regulated services were required to fall annually in real terms by 3% until 1989, then by 4.5% until 1991, then by 6.25%, and finally by 7.5% from 1993 onward. As well as this steady tightening of the price cap, the scope of regulation has broadened to include leased lines, connection charges and international call charges, leased lines being regulated by a separate cap, and international calls being included in the principal tariff basket. Within the overall $RPI - X$ constraint, BT was free initially to rebalance its relative prices subject to a ceiling on the real increases in domestic (but not business) rental charges of 2% per annum. However, regulatory control over price structures has also been increasing over time. Table 7.2 shows real price movements of some of BT's regulated services since privatization.

Perhaps the most striking aspect of table 7.2 is the massive drop in the price of peak-time long-distance calls relative to other services. BT chose not to increase rental charges by as much as was permitted in the three years from 1986, something that is perhaps curious given its recent insistence on being freed to increase these further, but even so these charges have not fallen in real terms despite real average charges having fallen by more than 40%. Recently BT has sharply reduced call charges for the weekend period.

Rebalancing of Call Charges   The issue of rebalancing became prominent in 1985 when BT made its first price changes as a private company. Some rebalancing was justified because large cross-subsidies from highly priced long-distance calls to cheap local calls and rental charges resulted from the pricing structure inherited from the public sector era. Moreover technological advances such as fiber-optic cable and digital exchanges had amplified these cross-subsidies. In addition to this cost-based motivation, however, BT was keen to rebalance quickly because it feared competition from Mercury. Since Mercury's strategy was primarily aimed at business

Table 7.2   Changes in selected real BT prices (%)

	1984–84	1985–86	1986–87	1987–88
X in RPI $-$ X formula	3.0	3.0	3.0	3.0
Actual overall change	−3.1	−3.3	−2.8	−4.0
Residential line rental	+1.9	+1.4	+1.2	−4.0
Local calls				
Peak	+1.6	−0.5	+16.0	−4.0
Cheap	+1.6	−0.5	−5.9	−4.0
National "b" calls				
Peak	−18.2	−12.3	−18.0	−4.0
Cheap	+1.6	−0.5	−8.5	−4.0

Source: Calculations based on Oftel Annual Report for 1992, table 5.2
a. Quantity discounts introduced and international calls regulated in 1991–92.
b. In the 1992–93 BT was not required to decrease its average price by as much as 6.25%
because of forecasting errors in revenue for the previous year. The precise reduction
required is currently under discussion between BT and Oftel.

users, who make a high proportion of peak-time long-distance calls, there
was an additional incentive for BT to choose to reduce charges in this area
in particular.[25]

However, such rebalancing was problematic in two respects. First, it
tended to favor large users (especially of peak-time long-distance services)
over smaller users. Many residential customers, especially those on lower
incomes, soon discovered that an overall constraint of RPI − 3 was entirely consistent with their bills rising in real terms. Second, BT's rebalancing involved price cuts in the areas where competition was stronger
and increases where its market power was most entrenched. (We saw in
section 4.3.3 how average price regulation produced these incentives.) If
pushed too far, "rebalancing" could undermine liberalization, even in its
limited duopoly policy form. Oftel investigated (Oftel 1986) and concluded
that rebalancing up to 1986 was justified by relative costs but that there
was no need for further rebalancing between local and long-distance call
charges. Since then there has been no move of great significance between
these two services. Nevertheless, it seems possible that Mercury would
have made greater inroads into the long-distance market had BT not been
allowed to rebalance in this way, for instance, by regulating long-distance
and local services with separate caps.

25. Ideally BT would have liked to reduce its prices only on those routes that faced competition from Mercury, but provisions against such price discrimination in BT's License prohibited such behavior.

1988–89	1989–90	1990–91	1991–92[a]	1992–93[b]	Cumulative change
3.0	4.5	4.5	6.25	6.25	45.3
−4.4	−4.4	−4.1	−6.5	−2.4	−43.0
−4.4	+1.6	+1.6	+1.9	+2.0	+4.6
−4.4	−7.7	−13.2	−2.2	−3.8	−17.8
−4.4	−4.2	+0.2	−1.1	−3.8	−19.6
−4.4	−7.7	−18.2	−5.5	−3.8	−64.6
−4.4	−7.7	−2.5	−0.8	−3.8	−26.8

The 1988 Price Review   The 1988 price review (see Oftel 1988) determined the regime of price control for BT for the period after July 1989 until the subsequent review period. The main conclusions, which were agreed with BT (thus avoiding an MMC reference), were that there should be

1. a tightening of X in the main cap from 3 to 4.5, with BT not to raise its regulated prices before August 1989,

2. an increase in the scope of control to include connection charges and operator-assisted calls,

3. a continuation of the separate RPI + 2 cap on domestic rental charges, and its extension to include business line rentals and connection charges,

4. a requirement that BT introduce a "low user" scheme,

5. a four-year duration of the new regime, so that the regime would last until 1993.

Additionally prices for BT's previously unregulated domestic leased circuits were brought under a separate cap of RPI − 0.

The low-user scheme that Oftel asked BT to introduce involved giving customers the option of half-price rental charges together with 30 units of free calls per quarter (worth about £1.50 in 1993) but requiring that calls in excess of the 30 unit limit be charged at a much more expensive rate than the standard charge per unit (about 20p instead of 5p per unit in 1993), before charges fell back to the standard rate after 150 units. (Certain types of line were excluded from this scheme, including multi-line users

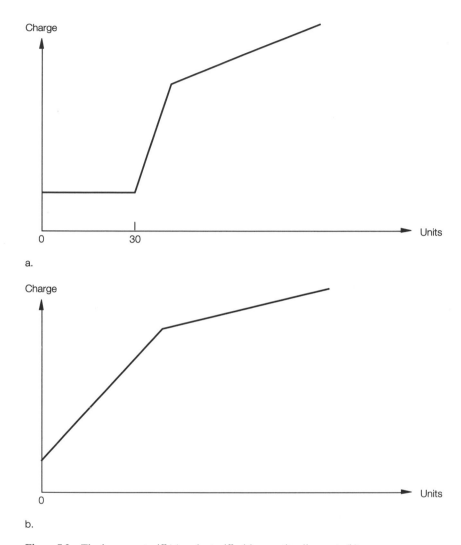

Figure 7.2   The low-user tariff (a) and a tariff with quantity discounts (b)

and lines used for burglar alarms, etc.) Oftel (1992a, para. 136) indicates that 1.5 to 2 million customers benefit from this low-user scheme (which was strengthened in the 1992 review). The scheme encourages network membership and so has advantages on network externality grounds, in a way that is targeted on users who might otherwise not join. It also promotes social objectives. However, it seems unlikely that the resulting tariff is the best possible. Figure 7.2a shows schematically the tariff obtained by taking the minimum of the low-user scheme and BT's standard two-part tariff, which in combination is the overall tariff BT offers to its customers (if we ignore the quantity discounts granted to large users). We argued in section 2.1.4 that a good nonlinear tariff would probably offer quantity discounts in some form, so a superior low-user scheme perhaps might look like figure 7.2b, where low users were given the option of choosing a two-part tariff with a low fixed charge and higher usage charges.[26]

BT's rate of return in current cost terms, which is not public information, was a key determinant of the tightening of X to 4.5.[27] The DGT has since stated that X was set "at a level which gives BT an expectation of covering the cost of capital employed for the services under control, and takes account of the risk for BT while providing demanding targets for improvements in customer service and increased efficiency."[28] The role of rate-of-return considerations for regulatory reviews under RPI $-$ X regulation was discussed in chapter 6.

Pricing Changes Resulting from the Duopoly Review   The duopoly review, though primarily concerned with liberalization, contained important changes to BT's price cap regime, and it is convenient to describe these now. An important point is that these changes occurred midway between two regulatory reviews and so to some extent went against the spirit of price cap regulation which is to give the firm a *commitment* to a pricing regime for a fixed number of years. This regulatory lag gives the

---

26. However, the analysis in section 2.1.4 ignored the possibility of network externalities among users, and in some circumstances this might affect the outcome.
27. When investigating whether BT's rebalancing in 1985 and 1986 was justified, Oftel (1986) also analyzed the appropriate rate of return for BT to see whether the company was making excessive profits. The DGT estimated that the acceptable historic cost rate of return fell in the range of 17.5% to 19%, whereas the actual rate of return was about 20% overall, and he concluded that no action need be taken until the 1988 review.
28. See BT Share Prospectus, November 1991, p. 26. See also Oftel (1992b).

firm an incentive to cut its costs by allowing it to keep any extra profits that result from increased efficiency for the duration of the period.

The duopoly review White Paper (Department of Trade and Industry 1991) announced agreement between the DGT and BT that X in the main cap should increase from 4.5 to 6.25 and that international switched services should be included in the main tariff basket, with an immediate 10% reduction in international call charges (to be counted toward the overall RPI − 6.25 reduction).[29] In addition international private circuits were brought under the RPI − 0 cap on domestic private circuits that was introduced in the 1988 review. As a result of these changes, regulated services now account for about 70% of BT's turnover, compared with 50% in 1989.[30]

Second, the DGT indicated willingness to accept greater tariff flexibility subject to some conditions. Thus BT is now able to offer tariffs with quantity discounts together with optional tariff schemes, for instance, low call charges combined with a high rental charge, provided that they are reasonable in relation to costs and not unduly discriminatory.[31] We saw in section 2.1 above that such optional tariffs can be Pareto improving if the regulated firm has no competitors and the good is sold for final consumption. However, as we discussed in section 4.3, the effect of offering these quantity discounts needs to be monitored, since they can otherwise provide BT with a means of selective price cutting in the market for large users, where its main competitive threat from Mercury and the new entrants exists. Thus the duopoly review document (DTI 1991, para. 6.17) states that any quantity discounts offered by BT should satisfy the following: they must apply to a reasonably broad category of customers, they must eventually make the revenues obtained from different classes of customers be proportional to the incremental costs of serving these customers, and they must not amount to predatory pricing. It remains to be seen exactly how it is these principles will be put into practice.

Third, on rebalancing, the DGT decided against relaxing the contentious RPI + 2 cap on exchange line rentals and connection charges for

---

29. The cost of providing international services is falling relatively quickly, and the figure of 6.25 was derived by keeping constant the estimated stream of BT's profits under the RPI − 4.5 regime after including international services.

30. Oftel (1992a, 9).

31. BT's price list for January 1993 states that all domestic users will receive a discount of 5% on all calls made in excess of £75 (excluding VAT), this discount rising the more calls are made. In addition for a £4 monthly fee a user can obtain a 10% discount on all calls. Thus BT is now offering optional two-part tariffs.

residential and single-line business users but agreed to an increase to RPI + 5 for multi-line businesses. Being thus constrained in rebalancing between call and rental charges, BT argued that liberalization without a requirement for competitors to make adequate payments toward its access deficit would lead to unfair and inefficient cream-skimming. We will discuss this issue, which is the crux of recent disputes between BT, its actual and potential rivals, and Oftel, in section 7.5.6.

The 1992 Price Review   The 1992 price review (see Oftel 1992c) determined the regime of price control that will hold for the period from July 1993 until July 1997. Its main conclusions, which again were agreed with BT (thus avoiding an MMC reference), were that there should be

1. a further tightening of X in the main price cap from 6.25 to 7.5,

2. a reduction in the standard connection charge from £152.75 to £99,

3. a continuation of the RPI + 2 cap on domestic and single-line business exchange line rentals,

4. a requirement that no other individual prices should increase by more than RPI + 0 in any year,

5. a stipulation that any quantity discounts offered by BT will *not* count when assessing BT's compliance with the RPI − 7.5 price cap (i.e., that such discounts will fall outside the tariff basket),

6. an extension of the low-user scheme introduced in the 1988 review to cover roughly that quarter of BT's customers who use the network least.

This new regime constitutes a yet further strengthening of regulation compared to the outcome of the 1988 price review and the duopoly review. The DGT has stated (Oftel Annual Report for 1992, para. 1.11) that under this new regime BT should be able to earn between 16.5% and 18.5% on capital employed by the end of 1997 (on an historic cost basis), which is broadly in line with Oftel's estimate of BT's cost of capital.

The standard connection charge applies to any connections that require fewer than 100 hours of labor. Since 100 hours of labor would cost BT well in excess of £99, there is ample scope for it incurring losses in connecting at least some customers (especially those in rural areas). If it is the case that by charging £99 BT is required to subsidize connections even in typical urban areas, this could inhibit the scale of entry of the cable TV companies into local telecommunications. The fact that any quantity discounts offered by BT will not count toward the calculation of BT's average price index reduces the incentive for BT to use quantity discounts as a means of predatory pricing against its present and future rivals.

This section has described the history of the regulation of BT's prices since privatization. We have seen that the basic principle of price cap regulation has been retained in each of the regulatory reviews, but that the cap has been tightened and extended in scope over time. BT's profits during this period were probably at a rather high level initially but have gradually fallen as a result of tighter regulation together with the slow reduction in its market share.

7.5.5 The Duopoly Review of Entry Conditions

Some measures of liberalization occurred in the year or so before the review of the fixed-link duopoly policy.[32] The government's commitment not to allow simple resale expired in 1989, and domestic, but not international, simple resale was permitted. Also the various somewhat arcane restrictions on connecting private networks were lifted. The duopoly policy in the mobile area also expired in 1989. In that year, following the advice of Oftel, the government announced its intention to license Telepoint and Personal Communications Network (PCN) operators to compete with Cellnet and Vodafone.[33]

The main duopoly review began in November 1990 when the government's commitment not to license fixed-link network operators to compete with BT and Mercury expired, and the result was the White Paper *Competition and Choice: Telecommunications Policy for the 1990s* (Department of Trade and Industry 1991). Its central conclusion was that the duopoly policy should be ended and that any application for a new license to offer domestic telecommunications services should be considered "on its merits," although the duopoly policy in respect of international calls was to be retained for the "short term."

International services present special problems because they require arrangements with overseas operators. When someone in Britain makes an overseas call, the British operator must pay the overseas operator to

32. For an analysis of policy and policy options toward entry in the British telecommunications industry, see Beesley and Laidlaw (1989).

33. Telepoint is a portable technology whereby users can make, but not receive, calls provided that they are within range of a suitable base station. To date it has not been commercially successful, and none of the original licensees now offers the service. PCNs use a more sophisticated version of the traditional cellular technology with smaller cells, higher frequencies, and the ability to carry digital signals. There are two PCN operators of which one, Mercury one-2-one, launched its service in 1993.

deliver the call (another kind of interconnection agreement). These payments are arrived at by bilateral negotiation. The vast majority of overseas operators are monopoly operators within their respective countries, and in such cases there is the danger that they could play off the competing British firms to force up these interconnection payments, and prices in Britain as a result. Because of this Oftel in 1987 determined that BT and Mercury should normally be required to make common interconnection payments (and to receive the same payments for delivering overseas calls) in order to preserve a strong negotiating position. (This arrangement is termed *parallel accounting*.) Such a policy might be more difficult to implement if there were more international operators. For the time being, instead of ending the duopoly policy in this market, the government decided to pursue international competition by allowing the simple resale of international leased lines, provided that the overseas country also operates a similar regime.

The duopoly review resulted in cable TV companies being allowed to use their cable networks to offer a telecommunications service in their own right, and not necessarily acting with either BT or Mercury, but national public telecommunications operators not being permitted to carry TV services on their telecommunications networks for a decade (although they can compete as before for local cable franchises through subsidiaries).[34] Clearly this measure will deny BT and Mercury many economies of scope in supplying TV services along the same lines as telephone services. The fear was that no cable TV company could possibly compete with BT if BT was allowed to supply TV, and hence that a policy of laissez-faire might eliminate these cable companies and with them an important and much needed source of competition to BT in local telecommunications. In other words, this prohibition on BT's entry into the entertainment market was introduced to assist entry into the local telecommunications market (see section 4.2.2). The telecommunications sector of the cable TV market is at present growing very fast (albeit from a small base) and may prove to be a significant rival to BT in the medium term. Since cable TV companies will only lay cable in the local area and

---

34. In fact in 1993 BT announced that it wished to offer a video-on-demand service to be launched in 1994 in which customers could dial a number and then immediately receive the film of their choice along their telephone lines. BT argued that this was not a television service because no two customers received the same signal simultaneously. Oftel has indicated it is not against video-on-demand provided that BT makes its network available to any independent company that wishes to offer a similar service. If successful, such a service would be damaging both to video rental chains and to cable TV companies.

will not construct trunk networks, interconnection arrangements with trunk operators will play an important role in ensuring the viability of the service.

In addition the duopoly review permitted mobile operators to provide fixed-link services, and the use of the assets of public sector network industries such as British Rail for telecommunications was encouraged. Also it was proposed that the allocation of telephone numbers be administered by Oftel rather than BT and that a user's number should be "portable" from one telephone company to another (provided that the user's address remained unchanged). This is important because otherwise BT's customers would incur a large cost in switching to a rival operator arising from the inconvenience of changing number. In a similar vein, the DGT also stated that equal access should be introduced "as soon as possible" (see section 7.5.1).

As a result of the review the DTI has received well over sixty applications for new network licenses, although some of these have not yet been granted. A number of these were applications for optical fiber-based networks utilizing the land rights held by other utilities. These include the U.S. long-distance operator Sprint in association with British Waterways, British Rail, the National Grid Company of England and Wales, and the Scottish Hydro Electric Company (see Wigglesworth and Barnes 1992). More recently AT&T has announced its intention to enter the British market. At the end of 1993 there is no significant fixed-link entrant yet offering a service (although Energis, the telecommunications subsidiary of the National Grid Company, claims that it will launch a trunk service with wide coverage in mid-1994). Partly this is due to the length of time it takes to obtain a license and to construct a large-scale network, but partly it is due to the continuing uncertainty surrounding the future arrangements for interconnection between rival operators, and we now turn to this issue.

7.5.6   Interconnection in the Competitive Environment

The most controversial issue arising from the duopoly review has been the question of the charges for the interconnection of potential new entrants, as well as Mercury, to BT's network, and the relationship between these charges and BT's retail tariffs. This issue falls into two parts: How should interconnection payments be regulated, and what should be the level of interconnection payments?

Regulating Interconnection Terms   The framework that was put in place when Mercury was BT's only rival was relatively cumbersome, involving as it did months of negotiation between the two parties which, if this was unsuccessful, was followed by a determination from Oftel that also took several months. Such a system is not practical or desirable when there are several rivals each settling terms to interconnect with BT (as well as between themselves).

In June 1993 Oftel published a consultative document concerned with the future regulation of interconnection in the more competitive environment (Oftel 1993). One obvious solution to the problem of dealing with many entrants is for BT and Oftel to publish agreed terms for standard interconnect services, at least for wide classes of entrant. For instance, BT and Oftel could agree to a charge per minute for BT delivering a call that connects to its network at a given depth into the network at a given time of day, and this charge would be available to all rivals within a broad class. However, Oftel seems to be against this method since "standard charges, agreed in advance with the regulator, could lead to unnecessary rigidities and inflexibilities in the fast moving U.K. telecommunications market" (Oftel 1993, para. 13). While this is certainly a disadvantage, it can be partially overcome by fixing standard charges that any rival can use if desired but leaving rivals with the opportunity to negotiate mutually preferable terms with BT if such terms were possible (i.e., to have a regime of "optional tariffs" for interconnection as described in section 3.3.2). This system would have the twin advantages that (1) if the two parties do decide to negotiate better terms then, while this is in progress, the rival can still offer a service by interconnecting using the standard terms (in contrast to the original 1985 scenario in which, while Mercury and BT were in disagreement, Mercury could offer no service), and (2) there would be no need to go to Oftel and use its limited resources for a lengthy and unpredictable determination.

If some form of standard charge regime is put into place, the questions remain as to what should be the level, the structure, and the mechanism for changing the charges over time. The desirable level of the charges is discussed below. The desirable structure of charges is made more complicated by the fact that BT's retail tariff is not cost related in many respects (see section 7.2), even if we ignore the problem of the access deficit. For instance, since its retail tariff for calls is distance dependent rather than being dependent in addition on the number of switches involved in a call, does this mean that interconnection charges should follow the same pattern? If such charges were also to be distance related, then there would be imperfect incentives for efficient network construction in that a rival "might not wish to interconnect with BT at the closest point to the customer if it faced a similar charge connecting at a central and remote point" (Oftel 1993, para. 53). On the other hand, if charges were more cost related, then "this would create anomalies between retail tariffs and network charges, and put pressure on retail tariffs to be de-averaged" (para. 52). If Oftel is indeed determined to keep BT's retail tariff in its present form that bears little relation to costs, this will inevitably cause problems when it comes to choosing interconnection charges.

As for the question of how charges should move over time, all the arguments we have described for the superiority of price cap over rate-of-return regulation in retail tariffs apply equally to interconnect charges, and so an RPI − X formula for yearly reductions seems natural, especially given that retail tariffs also move in the same way. However, Oftel has indicated that it does not wish to do this before the end of the present review period in 1997 (para. 40).

Finally, Oftel proposes that a form of accounting separation be applied to BT's "retail" and "network" arms, to be termed BT-Retail and BT-Network, respectively.[35] BT-Network would sell wholesale network services to all retailers (including BT-Retail) at some nondiscriminatory and regulated set of charges, and BT-Retail would sell on these services to final customers. These two organizations would prepare separate accounts. Of course a prohibition on cross-subsidy between the two organizations will be essential; otherwise, the accounting separation has no purpose. One simple way to do this would be to forbid BT-Retail from setting retail prices that are below the corresponding charge from BT-Network (or possibly to forbid prices less than some given markup over BT-Network's charges). At the time of writing, the outcome of the consultation process is not yet known, and it is unclear exactly how the future regime will operate.

The Access Deficit   BT claims that it incurs a large loss in providing local network services to users, in particular in providing the final link into a user's home and the facilities dedicated to the user in the local exchange, and that it must fund this access deficit from the profits it makes on calls.

---

35. This policy is to be contrasted with the more radical suggestion from the MMC to separate structurally the retail and network arms of the present British Gas; see chapter 8.

Moreover the constraints on increases in the rental and connection charges described above forbid BT from rebalancing its tariff to eliminate this cross-subsidy, or at least to eliminate the cross-subsidy within a suitable period of time.

Because of this entrenched cross-subsidy, if rivals in the long-distance market were granted interconnection at charges equal to the average cost (let alone the marginal cost) of providing interconnection, then competition in the long-distance market could drive prices there down toward average cost and BT would no longer make sufficient profits from calls to fund the access deficit. BT argues that because it has to contribute to the access deficit, so too should its rivals, and that therefore interconnection payments should include an access deficit contribution in addition to the usual conveyance charge. This argument is related to the *efficient component pricing rule* proposed by Baumol and described in section 5.2.2 above. This rule proposes that interconnection payments should be equal to the direct cost of providing interconnection plus the opportunity cost incurred by BT in terms of lost profits when a rival operator carries a call. If each long-distance call supplied by rivals would otherwise be supplied by BT (i.e., if competition results in a one-for-one displacement of calls), then the opportunity cost to BT of carrying the rival's call is the profit it forgoes in not providing the long-distance call itself, and this opportunity cost should be added to the direct cost when setting interconnection charges. If interconnect charges did not contain an opportunity cost contribution, then as well as removing the profits that provide the source of funding for the access deficit, entrants who are less efficient than BT in providing long-distance services would be profitable.[36]

As it stands, this argument has some force. There are, however, at least two reasons why we might not wish to take it at face value. First, the calculation of the "access deficit" is very sensitive to the precise accounting conventions used. Because the costs that may be unambiguously attributed to one service rather than another amount to only 20% of total costs (Oftel 1993, para. 56), a way must be found to allocate the remaining 80% of joint and common costs in order to arrive at a figure for the "profitability" of a particular service. This will necessarily be somewhat ad hoc. For

---

36. It is possible to argue that Mercury was already paying something toward the access deficit under the original 1985 interconnect determination by the time of the duopoly review. Its interconnection payments initially were said to reflect costs and were indexed on an RPI − 3 basis. Real transmission costs have fallen by substantially more that 3% a year since 1985, however, and so payments must have exceeded costs by 1991.

instance, at present BT compiles accounts that group revenues and costs under the headings of access, local calls, long-distance calls, international calls, leased lines, among others. (These accounts—known as the *Financial Results by Service*—are prepared for Oftel and are published for the years 1989–91 in Oftel 1992a.) In 1991 the residential access service, for instance, had a turnover of £1,368 million and operating costs of £1,896 according to these figures, and so the access deficit in that year could then be simply defined as the difference of these numbers. However, it is not obvious that "access" is a service in the same sense that a local call is. Equally one might think that exchange lines are provided purely so that customers can make calls. BT's cost allocation methodology requires that "access" be defined as a service with turnover given by the line rental charge together with an annualized connection charge, and with a cost given by the cost of providing the local line into a customer's home and the cost of the dedicated facilities in the local exchange, together with the allocated joint and common costs. This is controversial insofar as the local line into a customer's home and the dedicated local facilities are both necessary inputs in the making of any call, and in this regard it might seem reasonable to allocate some of these costs to other services. If this were so, then the costs for the "access" service would be correspondingly reduced, as would the "access deficit." In other words, there is the danger that too many costs are being loaded onto the provision of the access service according to BT's methodology.

If there were indeed a pressing access deficit, it seems curious that BT did not take advantage even of its limited freedom to rebalance in the period 1986–88 (see table 7.3). Moreover, as discussed in section 7.5.4, the form of rebalancing proposed by BT will lower prices in competitive markets and increase prices in captive markets. Giving BT a complete freedom over relative prices could well act to deter entry because of the incentives that average price regulation gives BT to price aggressively in competitive markets.

The second reason why access deficit contributions might not be desirable, or at least might be waived initially, is because of the possible need to assist entry. Because of BT's advantages as the dominant integrated firm, it might be desirable to assist entry, and one natural way to to do this is to provide generous interconnection terms while entrants recoup the fixed costs of network construction.[37]

---

37. However, see DTI (1991, 73) for the DGT's remarks on the "danger that the assistance of new entrants can be carried too far."

If the access deficit is a real problem, in the sense that a continuation of the prohibition on rebalancing in the present more competitive environment would make BT unprofitable or at least result in substantial inefficient entry, then there are several alternative remedies, including the following:

1. Setting the per-minute interconnection charges at a sufficiently high level to finance the access deficit.

2. Requiring rivals to make a lump-sum payment toward BT's access deficit, and setting the per-minute interconnection charges closer to marginal costs of providing interconnection.

3. Financing unprofitable public service obligations (including the deficit) by direct public subsidy to BT.

4. Placing public service obligations (e.g., a requirement to serve all reasonable demand or to attain a certain level of geographical coverage) on rivals.

5. Allowing BT the freedom to rebalance in order to eliminate the deficit.

Moreover it is not just a matter of interconnection prices: the extent and quality of interconnection are important too, and this was a continuing problem after the original interconnection ruling in 1985. For instance, the ease with which a user can connect with a rival company may be vital. If, say, a form of equal access were indeed to be introduced, then much of BT's incumbent advantage in the long-distance market might be removed.

In the event the DGT decided against allowing a relaxation of the rebalancing constraint on rental and connection charges, and this policy has been continued in the new price regime which lasts until 1997 (indeed in the 1992 review the regime for connection charges was tightened further). However, in the White Paper the DGT acknowledged BT's concerns and proposed (para 7.22) that "BT should receive a contribution to its deficit on exchange lines through the interconnection agreement" with rival operators, namely that the access deficit might pose a problem and that option (1) should be used. In fact these access deficit contributions (which are defined in Condition 13.5A.4 in BT's License) are closely related to the profit that BT forgoes if a rival operator carries a call and so can be regarded as the opportunity cost element of Baumol's efficient component pricing rule.

As mentioned in section 7.5.1, in the 1985 interconnection agreement Mercury did not have to make an explicit access deficit contribution, but in the White Paper the DGT suggested that Mercury should pay a contribution for increases in its business (though it could receive a discount because of its limited public service obligations) and that new entrants should pay from the start. However, after vigorous protests from the nascent telecommunications operators following the publication of the White Paper, and the possibility that further entry simply would not occur under these terms, the DGT drew back from the idea of full access deficit contributions being required from all rival operators from the start and proposed instead that the access deficit charge should in certain circumstances be waived until either BT's "market" share had fallen below 85% or equal access had been introduced, and that such entrants should be required only to pay BT's direct cost of carrying their calls.[38] In effect the DGT took the view that the access deficit poses no serious problem to BT's profitability until competition becomes sufficiently strong and that waiving access deficit contributions was a legitimate means with which to encourage entry into the industry (see Oftel's 1991 Annual Report, paras. 1.8–1.13).

The conditions under which the DGT might waive the access deficit contribution from a given entrant, either wholly or in part, are set out in the postduopoly review version of condition 13 of BT's License and include considerations about the breadth of competition provided by the entrant, its economies of scale, BT's economies of scale, and the availability of number portability. At the time of writing, it is not clear how these principles will be interpreted in practice, and at present any entrant faces significant uncertainty about whether it will have to pay access deficit contributions, a factor of considerable importance for the future profitability of entrants that can only act to inhibit further entry into the market. It is therefore vital for Oftel to put in place a policy toward interconnection that will be stable for the next few years in order for new entrants to make considered judgments about whether and to what extent to enter the market.[39]

---

38. The definition of the "market" has so far remained quite vague. It could mean the entire nationwide long-distance market, as competitors would like, or something much narrower, as BT would like.

39. The conditions under which a mobile operator can be granted an access deficit contribution waiver is quite different from that for fixed-link operators. To get a waiver, a mobile operator merely needs to demonstrate that it offers a substantially different service to that of BT. This accords with section 5.2.2 which argued that for services that are almost independent, BT's opportunity cost is small if a rival carries a call.

Oftel's approach is a compromise. In simplified form, and assuming that there is indeed a significant access deficit, the dilemma is essentially as follows. Regulatory policies are such that the incumbent makes a loss (the access deficit) in a more or less captive market (the provision of local telephone services). There is the prospect of more competition in the market for long-distance services. If the telecommunications industry were contestable, with BT being vulnerable to hit-and-run entry, then there would be the immediate problem that BT could no longer finance the access deficit by supernormal profits on calls: another means of finance would have to be found. Higher rental and connection charges (option 5 above) are a natural answer, except that factors such as network externalities and possibly distributional considerations might make it desirable to have *some* degree of access deficit. That being so, and if a public subsidy is ruled out, then a cross-subsidy from long-distance retail charges is the only solution. A guiding principle for such a cross-subsidy is that competitive distortions in the market for long-distance services should be minimized, and under the stated assumptions (which include contestability) this principle is implemented by the efficient component pricing rule which incorporates a form of access deficit contribution.

In reality the industry of course does not remotely resemble a contestable market, and the cream-skimming problem is not an immediate one. On the contrary, as Mercury's own experience indicates, BT's dominance is not in jeopardy in the short term, and it is bolstered by substantial incumbency advantages. Moreover, since interconnection charges are a large component of an entrant's costs, actual entry could be severely inhibited if access deficit contributions were required from the start. In the longer term, however, and especially if competition does indeed develop effectively, then the access deficit must be diminished and/or financed differently.

7.6 Assessment

Before the 1981 British Telecommunications Act, BT, which then was still part of the Post Office, had a more or less complete monopoly of all aspects of network operation, apparatus supply, and the supply of services over the network. In the areas of apparatus supply and VANS, this picture has changed dramatically over the past decade. The new mobile services have also benefited from vigorous competition. In the primary business of fixed-link voice telephony, however, BT's dominance remains firmly established. This mixed picture is partly due to the fact that economic characteristics vary across sectors, for example, in the degree of natural monopoly, but it is also related to differing policy approaches.

The 1981 Act began partial liberalization of the industry. Shortly afterward the government decided to privatize BT, and major policy decisions had to be taken concerning structure, entry conditions, pricing and quality, and investment. The main structural decision was to privatize BT intact, rather than breaking it up vertically (or regionally) along the lines of AT&T. While this avoided delay in privatization and will have preserved any economies of scope in the supply of services, it has required regulation to be more detailed and complex subsequently. Although the forced restructuring of private firms is not without precedent, as the cases of AT&T, the British beer industry, and (if the MMC recommendation had been followed) British Gas illustrate, it is unlikely that BT will be broken up. The time for restructuring was before privatization, as occurred (though not to the fullest extent) in the electricity supply industry. After privatization, issues of breach of faith with shareholders and policy credibility more generally make restructuring more difficult. A quasi-structural measure short of divestiture has recently been proposed; it would require BT to publish separate accounts for its retail and network businesses, thus facilitating better information flows and a stronger check against cross-subsidy and anticompetitive behavior. It is not yet clear how effective accounting separation will be in these respects.

The BT/Mercury duopoly policy announced in 1983 was the key decision on entry conditions. Its stated rationale was to induce Mercury to enter and to give both firms time to adjust to the more competitive environment envisaged for the future. As with policy on structure, pressure from BT management and the urge to privatize speedily were also important factors. In our view the duopoly policy has been detrimental to development of competition, and its main beneficiary has been BT itself. Oftel made the important 1985 ruling on the terms of interconnection between the BT and Mercury networks, and it has monitored competition in areas such as apparatus supply and mobile networks. At the end of the 1980s, as previous commitments to restrict competition expired, further liberalization occurred in areas such as mobile services, private networks, and resale. However, no major review of entry conditions in fixed-link telephony could occur until the seven-year duopoly policy expired at the end of 1990. The relatively procompetitive thrust of recent policy that was decided in the duopoly review is a welcome development that stands in contrast to the decisions that were taken at the time of BT's privatization. The ensuing controversy over interconnection terms and tariff rebalancing illustrates the point that regulation is often needed as a complement, rather than a substitute, to competition.

The centerpiece of conduct regulation since privatization has been the control of pricing. Contrary to original hopes for "regulation with a light rein," it has proved necessary to strengthen it in several respects over time. The level of X in the main cap has been tightened successively from 3 to 7.5, and the scope of regulation has increased so that 70% of BT's business now is subject to price control rather than the 50% that was controlled at privatization. Oftel has been proactive in this tightening of regulation, albeit within the constraints set by the earlier decisions made by government. The 1988 price review, the duopoly review, and the 1992 price review successively tightened and broadened price control, and virtually all aspects of network operation are now regulated. After a difficult start, improvements in quality have been one of the successes of regulation.

Against the background of a history of vertically integrated nationwide monopoly, progress toward a more competitive and better regulated telecommunications industry in Britain was made during the 1980s. In important respects, however, it was a decade of lost opportunities. The deliberate restrictions on competition contained in the duopoly policy, together with insufficient attention paid to overcoming BT's incumbency advantages, acted to preserve the essentially monopolistic character of the old system in the core area of network operation. Neither did the duopoly policy enhance the prospects for competition in the longer term. A new and more liberal policy on competition in telecommunications is now in place. Procompetitive regulatory policy will be needed to see it through.

Postscript

In December 1993 Oftel published a new Mercury/BT interconnection determination. This gives Mercury a full waiver of access deficit contributions on the first 10% of market share (this position being reviewed annually). Mercury was unhappy with some aspects of the determination, and it is currently involved in a legal dispute with BT and Oftel. In March 1994 Oftel published a statement on future policy toward interconnection. Proposed are three stages for policy. First, the new Mercury/BT determination will be used as a basis for determinations involving the new entrants in the short term. Second, for 1994–95 BT will be required to offer a standard price list for interconnect services. Finally, for the regime from 1995 onward Oftel plans to undertake further consultation about the long-term issues, including the use of access deficit contributions and incremental costs as a basis for charges. Therefore policy in this area is still far from settled.

Appendix: Some Important Events in British Telecommunications Policy

1981   Beesley Report recommends liberalization of the resale of leased circuits (including simple resale).

British Telecommunications Act splits BT from the Post Office and begins liberalization (without simple resale).

1982   White Paper announces the government's intention to privatize BT.

Mercury is licensed as a national network operator in competition with BT.

1983   Littlechild Report on price regulation for BT recommends $RPI - X$ price control.

BT/Mercury duopoly policy announced.

1984   Telecommunications Act establishes new regulatory framework, Oftel, and $RPI - 3$ price control on inland calls.

BT is privatized: 50.2% of its shares are sold.

1985   Oftel rules on the terms of interconnection between Mercury's and BT's networks.

BT's first price changes after privatization involve major rebalancing of call charges.

BT's bid for Mitel is referred to the MMC and cleared subject to conditions in 1986.

1986   Mercury launches its switched service.

BT continues with rebalancing of call charges.

1987   BT's quality of service comes under criticism.

1988   BT accepts contractual liability for some aspects of poor service and standard compensation terms are set.

Review of BT's price controls raises X to 4.5 and extends the scope of regulation.

1989   The use of private networks is liberalized and BT's charges for leased lines are capped at $RPI - 0$.

More mobile operators (Telepoint, PCNs) are licensed.

1991   White Paper ends the duopoly policy.

Price control is extended to international calls, with X being correspondingly increased to 6.25.

Controversy over interconnection terms with new entrants.

Government sells second tranche of BT's shares.

1992   Several new fixed-link operators are licensed.

Review of BT's price controls raises X from 6.25 to 7.5.

BT sells Mitel.

Bryan Carsberg retires as DGT to be replaced by Bill Wigglesworth as acting DGT.

1993   Final tranche of BT's shares is sold.

Donald Cruickshank becomes new DGT.

BT announces alliance with MCI, the U.S. trunk operator.

8

Gas

The gas industry presents an excellent case study of the problem of regulating and restructuring a dominant, vertically integrated firm. Transportation of natural gas has natural monopoly characteristics, but production and supply to larger customers (and probably to smaller customers) are potentially competitive. When British Gas (BG) was privatized, the government chose not to restructure the business. BG remained the incumbent monopolist for transportation and supply and was also the only U.K. purchaser of gas from the producers. It faced a price cap in the market for smaller customers while in the market for larger customers there was initially no explicit regulation, other than the general provisions of U.K. and EC competition policy. In this market the government relied on competition with other fuels and on existing liberalizing legislation which *allowed* competing suppliers access to BG's pipeline network. Such competition, however, was not actively promoted.

It is not surprising that competition in gas supply was initially slow to arrive, and its emergence has required positive action by the regulatory authorities. Shortly after privatization BG's pricing policy in the market for larger customers was criticized in a Monopolies and Mergers Commission report (MMC 1988), and various remedies were proposed that focused on regulating its *conduct*. A further investigation by the Office of Fair Trading (OFT) in 1991 suggested that the regulation of conduct had not achieved the objective of enhancing competition and proposed that the *structure* of the industry should be changed. In particular it recommended that transportation (and storage) should be run as a separate subsidiary of BG and that BG's de jure monopoly over smaller users should be abolished, or at least reduced. At about the same time the price cap in the market for smaller customers was tightened significantly. Competition in the market for larger customers has grown rapidly since the OFT report, but disagreement between the industry regulator and BG about the future of regulation and competition led to the referral of BG and the gas industry as a whole to the MMC in 1992. The MMC recommended in 1993 that BG should separate its transportation business from its supply business and divest itself of the latter, that the monopoly franchise over smaller users should be progressively eliminated, and that the price cap should be relaxed partly in compensation.

The chapter is organized as follows. In section 8.1 we analyze the economic characteristics of the gas industry. Section 8.2 considers the policy questions that relate to the industry. The framework of competition and regulation before and at privatization are described in 8.3, and in section 8.4 we consider how this framework has developed.

8.1 The Gas Industry and Its Economic Characteristics

8.1.1 Economic Characteristics

The supply side of the gas market is characterized by the successive vertical stages of production, transmission, distribution, and supply. Natural gas must first be extracted or produced. In Britain this is performed mainly by oil companies operating on the United Kingdom Continental Shelf (UKCS).[1] Production is not naturally monopolistic. The marginal cost of extracted gas can be expected to rise over time because the most accessible fields are exploited first. Once extracted, the gas is transmitted to the beachhead. It then enters the national and regional high-pressure transmission networks and the regional distribution pipelines, where pressure is reduced.

Both transmission and distribution have natural monopoly characteristics in any region. Pipeline costs are sunk, and it would be inefficient to have competing networks, although some limited bypass of the network might be efficient for new customers. A retail supplier of gas has to purchase it from the producers, move it through the transmission and distribution networks and sell it to final customers.[2] In addition the supplier usually needs access to storage facilities to help to meet peak demands. If access to the transportation network can be obtained from the pipeline company, then there can be many competing suppliers. Having access to the transportation network means that the supply of gas to final customers is potentially highly competitive. Sunk costs in supply are small. The main assets are working capital and contracts with producers and customers that can be resold on exit. If there are many competing suppliers, an exiting firm can sell its contracts at prices close to replacement costs. In addition, when there are many suppliers, tacit collusion in the product market will be more difficult to sustain. Since gas is a relatively homogeneous commodity, price competition in supply is likely to be

---

1. Most extracted gas comes from the North Sea, but there is also some production in the Irish Sea (BG has a large field in Morecambe Bay).
2. Suppliers are sometimes called "traders" or "shippers."

strong. Suppliers can, however, offer differentiated contracts to customers with variations in the degree of passthrough and in the extent of seasonal pricing.

The demand for gas is seasonal and stochastic, with demand on very cold days being up to five times higher than on summer days. Thus any gas supplier needs mechanisms for coping with such demand variability. One mechanism is to vary the amount of gas taken from producers. A second option is to use temporary storage facilities. BG uses the Rough field as a seasonal store. This is a nearly depleted field that is filled during the summer months and run down during the winter peak. Its maximum outflow is 10% of peak-day demand. Emergency supplies come from gas stored in salt cavities in Humberside and from liquefied natural gas holders. Daily demand peaks are covered by local gas holders and line-packing (increasing the pressure in the transmission pipes during periods of low demand in order to store gas in the transmission system). A third way to manage peak loads is to offer contracts to customers who are prepared to have their supplies interrupted on days of peak demand in return for a lower unit price. Such "interruptible" customers are typically industrial customers who use gas for space heating and have alternative sources of fuel. Peak-load pricing is an option for reducing the need for expensive storage facilities, but its feasibility depends on metering technology. For the majority of households, pricing according to the time of day or week is not currently desirable because of the expense of the meters required.

Gas faces some competition from alternative fuels, including oil, liquefied petroleum gas, electricity, and coal. Cross-elasticities of demand are low in the short run in markets where consumers have made sunk investments such as central heating systems, although they tend to be higher for customers, typically industrial firms, who can quickly and cheaply switch to alternative fuels. Long-run elasticities are higher, but the evidence presented by the Department of Energy (1989) does not suggest that interfuel competition at the aggregate level is strong.

8.1.2 The Industry in Britain

In March 1992 thirty-six companies produced gas from the UKCS. Twelve of these controlled 90% of production, and the three largest producers were BG with a share of 18.7%, BP with 14.9%, and Shell/Exxon with 21.6% (Ofgas, 1993, 9). BG has the largest share of reserves. Prices paid by BG for gas bought from its Exploration and Production unit are negotiated at arm's length. BG's contracts with producers operating on the UKCS are long term, usually for twenty-five years. In terms of the analysis in section 5.1.1, the possibility of opportunistic behavior by BG, which used to be the only purchaser of gas from the UKCS, means that long term contracts have been necessary to encourage investment in gas fields. The recent growth of competition in the market for gas will reduce this holdup problem and might allow for shorter contracts or even a spot market in gas. Prices under BG's contracts are related to exogenous indexes. Those with Old Southern Basin producers were signed before the oil price shocks of the 1970s, and purchase prices in these contracts are typically related to the economywide Producer Price Index. When the privatization of BG was being prepared, some commentators expressed concern that the Old Southern Basin contracts provided an average cost of purchasing gas that was below the marginal cost of new fields. Since competitors would only have access to the latter, the prospects for entry were poor. This argument is not as strong now as in 1985 because (1) the Old Southern Basin contracts form a declining share of BG's supplies— down from 43% in 1986–87 to 31% in 1990–91—and (2) there was a sharp decline in oil prices in 1986 and general weakness since then, which reduced marginal gas purchase costs relative to average costs.[3] Later contracts have related gas prices to the prices of competing fuels such as heavy fuel oil, gas oil, crude oil, electricity and the general index of retail prices for fuel and light (MMC 1988, 22).

BG is the only firm with a transmission and distribution network covering most of Britain (but not Northern Ireland).[4] BG is also the dominant gas supplier. In 1992 it had 18.4 million customers who consumed less than 25,000 therms.[5] All such customers face a regulated tariff, and most are domestic households. Average annual domestic consumption is between 640 and 670 therms depending on the weather. About 70% of BG's supplies by volume go to the tariff market. Real tariff prices fell by 16% between 1986–87 and 1992. Since August 1992 those who consume between 2,500 and 25,000 therms a year have been allowed to purchase from competitors, and 13% of those in this range have done so. In the nontariff market (also called the "contract market"), where usage exceeds 25,000

3. The average price paid per therm by British Gas (including the gas levy) was 17.9 pence in 1986–87 and 18.7 pence in 1992 (MMC 1993c, table 3.5). In real terms purchase prices fell by about 25%.
4. Kinetica, which is owned by PowerGen and Conoco, has built a pipeline to service a power station in Humberside, and there are some very small localized distribution systems supplying liquefied petroleum gas (Ofgas 1992b).
5. One therm is equivalent to 29.31 kilowatt hours.

therms, BG has faced growing competition since 1990. In 1992 the total volume of sales in the nontariff market was about 7 billion therms (MMC 1993c, 65). BG supplied 5.8 billion therms, of which 2.5 billion were consumed by "firm" customers (those whom BG guarantees not to interrupt) and 3.3 billion were used by interruptible customers (including 0.25 billion by electricity generators). BG's nontariff prices fell by over 30% in real terms from 1986–87 to 1992. Competitors supplied 1.2 billion therms to firm customers (32% of the total firm market above 25,000 therms) but did not offer interruptible contracts. There were twenty-eight competitors in retail supply, including oil and gas producers, all but one of the regional electricity companies, and independents.

The share of gas in final energy consumption in the United Kingdom (measured by volume) in 1991 was 33%. Excluding transport use the share was 48.1% (MMC 1993c, table 2.2). Total sales of natural gas have grown slowly in recent years because of mild winters, the recession, and the slump in house building. The average rate of growth in the volume of natural gas consumed from 1987 to 1991 was about 1% (Department of Trade and Industry 1992, table 42). This was in line with average growth of final energy consumption of 0.94%, so the market share of natural gas remained constant during this period. Recently, however, a boost to the demand for gas has come from the new electricity generation market. Since the privatization of the electricity supply industry in 1990 and 1991, the development of combined cycle gas turbine technology, and the relaxation in 1991 of an EC restriction on the use of gas in power stations, there has been a move to build new generating plants that burn gas. This issue will be examined in more detail in section 9.4, but the key point to note here is that the potential demand for gas from this source is very large and could have a considerable effect on gas prices generally and the rate of depletion of gas reserves. While total gas consumption was the same in 1992 as in 1991, the demand for gas from generators rose by 98% (Department of Trade and Industry 1993a, table 42). BG expected total U.K. gas sales to increase from 20 billion to 30 billion therms a year between 1991 and 1998, of which 7.5 billion will be for electricity generation (MMC 1993c, 86).

In the financial year 1992 BG had total turnover of £10.5 billion, of which £8.1 billion came from U.K. gas transmission, distribution, and supply. In this section of its business it made current cost operating profits before exceptional charges and taxation of £1 billion and had tangible fixed assets of £18.5 billion measured in current cost terms, which represented a current cost rate of return of 5.4%. There were 79,000 employees in Britain.

8.2 Policy Questions

The main policy questions can be divided into those concerned with the *structure* of the industry and those concerned with the regulation of *conduct*, although there is inevitably some overlap between the two. In the first category there are questions about the vertical, regional, and horizontal structure of the industry. The main issues in conduct regulation concern the level and structure of prices, including transportation prices.

The first question for policymakers is whether there should be vertical integration between the different stages of the production and supply chain. The possibilities range from complete integration of all four stages to complete separation. The main question is whether ownership of the transportation business should be separated from the gas supply business. Under this option gas suppliers would rent the use of the transportation firm's pipelines and storage facilities, and the transportation firm would not be allowed to be a retail supplier. Vertical separation might be necessary to prevent an integrated firm from gaining special advantage in the supply market. A further benefit of vertical separation is that it reduces the regulator's information disadvantage when setting access prices because a separate transportation firm would have its own accounts, and perhaps its own share price. Among the costs of separation are the one-off costs of reorganization and the possible loss of economies of scope of an integrated firm. Since separation entails that transactions through the vertical chain are at transparent prices, decisions on entry and investment will be made on the basis of predicted future prices, and if these are not socially efficient there could be inappropriate decisions (Green and Newbery 1993b). The separation question will be examined further in section 8.4.

If transportation is vertically separated from supply, then in principle there will be a level playing field for suppliers, at least as far as access terms are concerned. There remains the horizontal problem, however, that the supplier previously owned by the transportation firm might be dominant, and in particular might control the bulk of gas production either through ownership of production facilities or through long-term contracts with independent producers. The dominant supplier might act strategically in its gas-purchasing policy to foreclose entry, and some restrictions on its contracting behavior might be required to facilitate competition. One option is to force the dominant supplier to sell some of its contracted gas. More radical options, such as setting up a daily spot market in gas, might also be considered, although as in electricity such a spot market would probably need to be supplemented by contracts and would depend on metering technology.

A further question for policy on vertical structure is whether the transportation firm should itself be separated into a national transmission company with one or more separate companies operating regional transmission and local distribution. Regionalization would increase the ability of the regulator to use yardstick competition and of capital markets to compare performance. If the distribution companies were allowed to supply gas, as well as distribute it, then rival suppliers might be discriminated against in access terms, so there might be a case for banning distribution companies, as well as the transmission company, from supplying gas. A regional split would entail greater transactions costs and breakup costs than the simpler option of keeping an integrated transportation firm.

The policy questions relating to horizontal structure are relatively simple. Gas production is relatively competitive because the minimum efficient scale of gas rigs is not large relative to the size of the market. Unlike production, the transmission and distribution stage of the supply chain are naturally monopolistic, and there is a case against allowing horizontal competition in transportation. There might be an argument for allowing new entrants to build new pipelines serving new customers, but general direct competition in transportation is likely to be uneconomic unless technologies change or demand grows rapidly. The final horizontal issue concerns the extent to which supply should be competitive. It is a business with few sunk costs, and supply to larger customers is certainly not naturally monopolistic. But the feasibility of competition for smaller customers is unclear because of the relatively high metering and marketing costs in this segment of the market, and policy issues include whether and how fast the market should be liberalized and whether the supply business of the dominant firm should be horizontally split.

In the regulation of *conduct*, regulators need to consider which markets should have price regulation. Typically the market for smaller users will have to be regulated unless competition is strong. The regulator needs to decide what the level of any cap on prices should be. The extent of cost passthrough must also be determined. The volatility of gas purchase prices at the beachhead, and their importance in determining final selling prices, imply a prima facie case for allowing some passthrough of gas costs. If there is vertical separation, then the cost of transportation would be out of the control of the supplying firm, and there might be a case for allowing passthrough of transportation prices. But one reason not to allow transportation prices to be passed through between price reviews is that they are likely to be stable and predictable, unlike gas purchase costs. Natural gas is an expensive product to transport long distances and to distribute to rural areas, and there is significant seasonal variation in the demands of smaller customers. A question for policy is whether there is sufficient price differentiation that reflects the relative costs of serving different regions and markets with different seasonal demands. Competition can itself induce more cost-reflective pricing. Another issue is whether rebalancing between the fixed charge and the usage charge should be allowed. A final question related to a market regulated by a price cap concerns the trade-off between the quality of service (e.g., on obtaining a supply, meter reading, continuity of supply, and emergency service) and price.

In the market for larger customers the questions about pricing are bound up with the degree of direct competition in this market. If there is a dominant firm, should its price level be regulated? One consideration here is that if the price level is set too low, then competitive entry might be discouraged. Should the dominant firm's price structure be regulated? If the firm is allowed to price discriminate, then entry might be foreclosed.

A final question concerns the terms of access to the pipeline network. If there is complete vertical separation of transportation from supply, then the transportation firm needs to be able to cover its costs if the government is not able or willing to subsidize it. The setting of access charges is especially difficult if there is little or no vertical separation.

8.3 Framework of Competition and Regulation at Privatization

8.3.1 Background to Privatization

The history of the gas industry before the privatization of BG in 1986 has been described by Vickers and Yarrow (1988, 245–54) and by the Monopolies and Mergers Commission (MMC 1988), and the discussion here will be brief. The early industry was highly fragmented with 1,046 companies under private or municipal control at the time of nationalization in 1948. Gas was produced mainly by burning coal, and this was a localized activity because the costs of long-distance transmission and distribution were excessive. The 1948 Gas Act amalgamated these companies into twelve Area Boards, and the Gas Council was created. The Gas Council acted as a channel of communication with the government and raised finance for the Area Boards.

Three technological developments in the 1950s and 1960s facilitated the restructuring of the industry. First, the rise in the price of coal stimulated the development of technologies for producing gas from light petroleum distillates. Second, liquefied natural gas began to be imported, mainly from Algeria, and was distributed via a high-pressure pipeline. Third, and most important, the discovery of substantial gas reserves under the North Sea in 1965 led to a massive program of conversion of all appliances to use natural gas and to the construction of a national high-pressure transmission system to convey gas to the Area Boards.

The creation of the national transmission network led to further centralization of the industry. The Gas Council was renamed the British Gas Corporation (BGC) under the Gas Act of 1972 and took over the operations of the twelve Area Boards. The BGC had a monopoly over the sale of gas and also was granted monopsony powers for gas extracted from the United Kingdom's sector of the North Sea. These technological changes transformed the industry from one of local and regional production and distribution to a centralized purchaser and distributor of North Sea gas.

The first steps toward liberalization of the gas supply market were made in the 1982 Oil and Gas (Enterprise) Act. In the same year Secretary of State for Energy Nigel Lawson announced that market forces would be given a greater role in the allocation of resources in the energy sector, and the 1982 Act was part of this philosophy. It allowed for access to the existing pipeline network by competing gas suppliers.[6] The Act effectively excluded the domestic market from potential competitors by stating that consent to supply customers who were already within twenty-five yards of an existing main would not be granted unless the annual demand was for at least 25,000 therms. The legislation was completely ineffective—by the time of the 1988 MMC report on the nontariff market, the only agreement in existence was one that was negotiated before the 1982 Act (and was renegotiated after the 1986 Act). It was not until 1990 that the first new competitive gas flowed through British Gas's pipes.

The 1982 Act separated BGC's oil exploration and production assets from the main business. These were privatized in 1984. It also abolished the de jure monopsony of BGC over the purchase of North Sea gas, but the de facto monopsony remained because of the requirement to land all gas from the United Kingdom's sector of the North Sea in the United Kingdom and the absence of any alternative buyers (McGowan et al. 1990, 8).

---

6. Access to the network is also called "common carriage."

8.3.2   Framework at Privatization

The Gas Act 1986   The Gas Act of 1986 paved the way for the privatization of BG. It established the Office of Gas Supply (Ofgas), with a Director General of Gas Supply (DGGS) at its head,[7] and a separate Gas Consumers' Council. The Secretary of State and DGGS have the primary duty "to secure that persons authorised to supply gas ... satisfy ... all reasonable demands for gas and to secure that such persons are able to finance the provision of gas supply services." Subject to these primary duties they must protect the interests of consumers over price, continuity of supply, and the quality of gas supply services; promote efficiency and economy; protect the public from dangers; and "enable persons to compete effectively in the supply of gas through pipes at rates which, in relation to any premises, exceed 25,000 therms a year." BG was granted a franchise over the market for those with annual demand less than 25,000 therms, was required to offer these customers a fixed tariff and was ordered not to show any "undue preference" in setting the tariff. The tariff could include a standing charge and was allowed to be related to the customer's location and other factors, such as the load factor (the ratio between average demand and peak demand), that might be relevant. The absence of any requirement to promote competition in the tariff market was rectified by the Competition and Service (Utilities) Act 1992 which required the Secretary of State and the DGGS to secure effective competition "between persons whose business consists ... of the supply of gas" without the restriction to the market for more than 25,000 therms a year. Competition for consumers with annual demands in between 2,500 and 25,000 therms has been allowed since August 1992.

A public gas supplier is required to be authorized by the Secretary of State and has duties to develop and maintain an efficient, coordinated, and economical system of gas supply; to comply with any reasonable request for supply (except in the market for more than 25,000 therms a year); and to avoid any undue preference in the supply of gas. The authorization can be changed if the DGGS and the supplier agree on the terms. In cases where they cannot agree on terms, the DGGS can refer the gas supplier to the MMC which can determine whether any practice that acts against the public interest requires an amendment to the authorization.

---

7. The DGGS from 1986 to 1993 was Sir James McKinnon. He was replaced by Clare Spottiswoode in November 1993.

Under the 1986 Act the DGGS could only make a reference in relation to the tariff market, but this has been amended by the 1992 Act which empowers the DGGS to make references if any matter that relates to the "conveyance and storage of gas by any public gas supplier" appears to act against the public interest. The Secretary of State can also amend an authorization if a monopoly or merger situation exists under the terms of the 1973 Fair Trading Act or if there is an anticompetitive practice under the terms of the 1980 Competition Act.

The 1986 Act barred competing pipeline networks by precluding (except in very special circumstances) the Secretary of State from licensing a supplier for areas within twenty-five yards of existing gas mains. To encourage competition via BG's own pipelines the access provisions of the 1982 Act were extended. Any person may apply to the DGGS to secure a right to have gas conveyed by the pipelines of a public gas supplier, and the DGGS may specify the terms on which access is allowed if the two parties cannot agree themselves. These terms include prices for access and the terms on which backup gas is supplied. Prices for gas transportation should cover the appropriate proportion of the operating costs of the system, should cover depreciation, and should allow for a rate of return equivalent to that earned by BG on its system generally. This is similar to the clause in the Telecommunications Act 1984 which allows the DGT to determine the terms of interconnections. It was recognized that one of the reasons for the failure of competition to emerge after the 1982 Act was that competitors needed access to the public supplier's backup supplies. The 1986 Act established obligations on BG to provide backup supplies if required.

No restructuring of BG was proposed in the legislation for privatization. BG was to have a legal monopoly in the tariff market and an effective monopoly in the nontariff market, where it was not subject to any particular restraints on anticompetitive behavior. It also retained its de facto monopsony powers.[8]

The Authorization   The authorization (license to operate) issued to BG at the time of privatization in 1986 contains the details of the price control in

---

8. For an interesting discussion of the debate within the government about restructuring BG before privatization see Lawson (1992, ch. 19). Nigel Lawson, as Chancellor, and the Prime Minister, Margaret Thatcher, had wanted vertical and regional separation, but Peter Walker, the Energy Secretary at the time of privatization, believed that BG should be kept intact to enable it to compete around the world. Because of the political urgency to sell BG, Walker's view prevailed. Walker later became a director of BG.

the tariff market. From 1987 to 1992 there was a three-part formula: maximum allowed average revenue in the tariff market was equal to the average cost of purchasing gas, plus a nongas component that grew by the percentage change in the Retail Prices Index less an X factor of 2%, and a correction factor. The formula was known as an RPI $- X + Y$ cap, where the Y factor denotes the cost passthrough term. The original justification for full cost passthrough of gas costs was that gas was supplied to BG under existing long-term contracts that could not be changed. Such contracts allowed for variation in gas prices, and BG would bear substantial risks if it could not alter its own selling prices in response. The X factor was thus effectively a productivity discipline for nongas costs. Such costs included the costs of operating and maintaining the transmission and distribution systems and the storage facilities, and the costs of trading gas (e.g., marketing and metering costs). In 1993 the proportion of the final selling price in the tariff market driven by gas costs was 42%, with transportation and storage accounting for 40%, trading costs 16%, and a small profit margin accounting for the remainder (MMC 1993c, table 4.12, based on BG figures). Because BG, like most network utilities, set a two-part tariff for domestic customers, revenue from the standing charge was included in the calculation of average revenue.[9] The authorization, however, contained a further cap that prevented BG from raising the standing charge in real terms. The motivation behind this was presumably protection of smaller and poorer domestic households because standing charges, like lump-sum taxes, can be regressive.[10]

Several points can be made about the price control formula that applied to BG from 1987 to 1992. First, it constrained average revenue so, as discussed in section 3.3.2, the firm had an incentive to choose relative prices that were not close to Ramsey prices. Second, the formula allowed the average cost of all BG's gas purchases, including those that were destined for the nontariff market, to be passed through to tariff consumers. Yarrow (1991) argues that BG's pricing behavior in the nontariff market could have an effect on the price in the tariff market. Since the regulated

---

9. Since 1990 BG has set simple multiple-part tariffs with quantity discounts. The thresholds for quantity reductions are at 5,000 therm intervals, so for almost all domestic customers the tariff is still effectively two part. The tapering of tariffs reduced the incentive some large tariff customers had to waste gas in order to qualify as contract customers and thus obtain lower prices.

10. See Feldstein (1972a, b) for theoretical analyses of the distributional effects of two-part tariffs in a public utility pricing context.

price equals a constant plus the average cost of gas, an increase in sales to the nontariff market will raise average cost and thus the regulated price if the marginal cost of gas exceeds the average cost. This suggests that there is clear potential for distortion—for example, this type of incentive might lead to underpricing in the nontariff market in order to expand demand in that market and hence raise the permitted price in the tariff market. Such underpricing is good for nontariff consumers in the short run but might act to deter entry of competitors. Third, the fact that there was complete passthrough of gas purchase costs acted to blunt the incentives for BG to purchase efficiently. Fourth, Price (1989) argues that storage costs in the transmission system (e.g., gas holders and linepack) counted as nongas costs and so were subject to the $RPI - X$ cap, whereas the use of seasonal gas supplies to meet the winter peak counted as a gas cost that could be fully passed through. This asymmetry might lead to suboptimal investment in storage facilities and excessive use of seasonal gas supplies. Fifth, the level of X chosen appeared low. Bishop and Kay (1988) report that in the period 1983–88 the average annual increase in BG's total factor productivity was 6.2%, considerably above BG's X factor of 2%.

The authorization also contained conditions about accounting information, BG's pricing policy in the nontariff market, and access and storage terms. BG was required to keep the accounts of the gas supply business separate from those of the rest of its business. This was a very minimal requirement. There was no requirement to achieve accounting separation of the tariff and nontariff businesses, despite the fact that the former was subject to price regulation while the nontariff market was subject to no explicit regulation. Both parts of the business were included in the gas supply business as defined by the authorization. Similarly there was no requirement to separate the accounts of the natural monopoly elements, such as the transmission and distribution businesses, from those of the potentially competitive part of the business (i.e., the supply of gas). As Yarrow (1991) emphasizes, no attempt was made to ring-fence the naturally monopolistic parts of the industry. Finally, it might have been possible to require regional information in the accounts to facilitate yardstick competition in regional distribution, but again the authorization did not require this.

For the nontariff market BG was required to publish a schedule of the maximum price payable for gas and a general statement of its willingness to enter into negotiations for gas supplied, but it was not required to offer a nondiscriminatory tariff. It was required to prepare a statement setting out general information about the terms on which it was prepared to enter negotiations for the access to its pipelines and storage facilities and to give examples of prices.

Privatization   The light regulation imposed on BG at privatization was much criticized at the time. Indeed the later privatization of the electricity industry involved a radical restructuring, perhaps partly as a reaction to the weakness of the regulatory framework created for gas. The X factor of 2% in the price control formula was hardly challenging, for it required lower productivity gains than those BG had previously achieved while in public ownership. BG was privatized in December 1986 for £5.4 billion, and new debt of £2.5 billion was injected into the balance sheet. All the equity was sold, but the restriction to a maximum of 15% on the holding of any individual and the existence of a golden share held by the government meant that capital market competition, especially the threat of takeover, was constrained. BG was transferred to the private sector with its monopoly and monopsony powers intact, with effectively no regulation in the nontariff market, and with light regulation in the tariff market.

8.4   Development of Competition and Regulation

There have been four main developments since privatization. First, the price cap in the tariff market was reviewed, and the new formula started operating from April 1992. Second, soon after privatization BG's pricing policy in the nontariff market was referred to the MMC by the OFT. The nontariff market had been left unregulated at privatization (apart from the minor requirement in the authorization that maximum prices should be published), but it soon became clear that BG's discriminatory pricing policies in this market were hindering the development of competition. Third, in 1991 the OFT reviewed the growth of competition since the 1988 MMC report and recommended a degree of vertical separation of BG, as well as other policies designed to facilitate competition in the nontariff market. Fourth, arguments about the implementation of the OFT proposals led to the second referral of BG to the MMC in 1992 that resulted in more radical recommendations for structural reform.

8.4.1   Price Control in Tariff Market
The formula regulating BG's pricing in the tariff market was reviewed in 1990–91. Ofgas would have referred the matter to the MMC if BG had not accepted the new proposals and after BG relented the new formula

came into operation in April 1992. In 1990–91 the tariff market accounted for 65% of the volume of BG's gas sales, 80% of its sales revenue, and 80% of gas business profits (Ofgas Annual Report 1991, 10). Ofgas set four objectives for the review: to secure a fair price for consumers, to allow BG to earn a reasonable rate of return, to provide incentives to increased efficiency, and to minimize the burden of regulation. The reasons behind the new formula are contained in a series of papers on the new gas tariff formula published by Ofgas and in Dorken (1992).

The formula, which was intended to last until 1997, differed from the original in several ways. It can be summarized by

$$(RPI - 5) + (GPI - 1) + E.$$

The first major change to the formula was that the X factor for nongas costs was increased from 2% to 5%. This parallels the progressive tightening of the price cap that BG has faced. Second, the cost passthrough term, which previously allowed actual average gas costs to be passed through in full, has now been changed to allow for the passthrough of an *index* of gas costs, rather than actual gas costs. This index, known as the Gas Price Index (GPI), is based on the escalation clauses in BG's own contracts with producers and has fixed weights. The allowable gas cost in the cap is now the initial base period average cost of gas, adjusted for the increase in the GPI less a 1% efficiency factor. If BG can negotiate favorable deals for new gas or can renegotiate old contracts and can beat the index, it can keep the extra profits; under the previous formula a reduction in gas purchase costs was passed through to consumers. The third change is to allow for the inclusion of a term denoted the E factor relating to energy efficiency. This is to encourage BG to consider whether a given increment to gas demand is more efficiently satisfied by supply-side measures such as purchasing new gas supplies from producers or by demand-side measures which promote energy conservation, such as better insulation (Ofgas 1991a, 12). The E factor allows reasonable expenditures that act to reduce demand to be passed through to consumers. It remains to be seen how this factor will work in practice. Finally, at the same time as the price cap was introduced, Ofgas agreed with BG a list of key standards of service, and BG's authorization was amended. If BG fails to meet these standards, then Ofgas has indicated that it might seek a review of the tariff market formula. A new scheme in which customers who receive poor service are compensated was also agreed in principle.

In setting the new X factor of 5%, and the 1% factor that applies to the Gas Price Index, Ofgas estimated a reasonable rate of return for BG's tariff market. After considering an economic rate of return based on the capital asset pricing model (see section 6.3 for a discussion of this model) and the current cost rates of return of comparable companies, Ofgas concluded that current cost returns in the range 5–7% were appropriate. It was envisaged that BG would earn returns in this range if it successfully achieved the productivity target implicit in the X factor. The productivity target itself was based on (1) the observation that BG had achieved cost savings since privatization that were in excess of those assumed when the original X factor was chosen, (2) a detailed analysis of BG's costs, and (3) comparisons with other comparable industries such as the British electricity industry and foreign gas utilities. Inevitably the final estimate of reasonable productivity growth is a matter of judgment, but 5% seems quite high given the rate of technical progress in pipeline operations (which is low relative to that in telecommunications) and the slow rate of growth of demand for gas in the tariff market. This suggests that in setting X at 5%, Ofgas considered that the price level for the nongas business of transportation and storage was initially excessive in relation to reasonable costs. Indeed the MMC (1993a, 46) stated that Ofgas assumed "annual savings in non-gas costs of 2.4%" when setting the X factor of 5%.

The main structure of the formula remains as before. It is still based on average revenue per therm supplied to the tariff market, although Ofgas did consider changing to a tariff basket formula. It argued that the potential for relative price distortions arising from an average revenue formula was small because of the subsidiary price cap on the standing charge and because BG set the same tariff across the country. It was acknowledged that the position might have to be reviewed if BG moved to introduce a differentiated tariff. The subsidiary cap on the standing charge limiting it to grow by no more than the RPI remained as before for customers below a 5,000 therm a year threshold, but the restriction did not apply for tariff customers above this threshold.[11] Ofgas (1991c) argued that for domestic consumers existing standing charges did not recover the costs that they were supposed to relate to (e.g., meter reading, billing, and maintenance of service pipes), and the fact that this underrecovery was especially large for larger tariff customers explains the relaxation of the cap on the standing charge for them. The cap for smaller customers was justified by the argu-

---

11. Price (1991b) notes that since privatization BG has not increased the standing charge as much as the subsidiary cap allowed. This appears to have been a strategic policy to avoid adverse publicity.

ment that there was room for BG to reduce the relevant costs in real terms.

Ofgas (1991b) considered three arguments for preserving the pass-through of gas costs. First, BG has limited control over its gas costs because of its long-term contracts. Several points temper the force of this argument. The proportion of BG's supplies that comes from new gas will increase significantly in the late 1990s. Contracts are frequently renegotiated, and there is scope for trade-offs between price and other aspects of service. Finally, BG's wide portfolio of contracts allows it flexibility in choosing which gas to take. Second, since gas costs form over 40% of BG's cost of supplying the tariff market, volatility in energy prices will increase the risks that BG faces, and a higher rate of return may be justified if passthrough is not allowed. On average the price level will be higher than when cost passthrough is allowed. Ofgas could find no evidence that tariff consumers are prepared to pay a premium to avoid the risk of future energy price changes. Third, since BG faces competition in the nontariff market from other fuels and from independent gas suppliers, it has every incentive to buy gas efficiently to avoid erosion of its position in the nontariff market. This argument would of course be weakened if competition from other fuels and gas-to-gas competition were weak. The overall conclusion of the review is that cost passthrough is still warranted but that BG should be given an incentive to improve its purchasing costs; an incentive has been created because it is not actual costs that are passed through but an index of costs with fixed weights, albeit one based substantially on BG's own contracts.

The cost passthrough term in the formula is still based on average cost pricing, even though one based on the marginal cost of gas may be more in accord with allocative efficiency considerations. There are practical difficulties in making the passthrough term depend on marginal cost. If the marginal cost of gas at the beachhead exceeds average cost, as happened in the mid-1980s, then allowing passthrough of marginal costs will generate supernormal profits for BG. If the marginal cost of gas is below average cost, then average costs will not be covered and there will be problems over the viability of the firm. Thus the avoidance of any mention of marginal cost in the tariff market formula is perhaps understandable.

The potential for distortion under the old formula that Yarrow (1991) highlights appears to be diminished because of the use of the GPI rather than actual average costs, but the maintenance of separate regulation of gas and nongas costs means that there might still be an incentive to meet peak loads by expensive seasonal supplies rather than by the use of nongas costs such as storage facilities.

8.4.2   The 1988 Monopolies and Mergers Commission Report

There was no explicit regulation of the nontariff market in the immediate period after privatization. It was assumed that competition with other fuels and any gas-to-gas competition arising from the legislation permitting access would be sufficient to restrain abuse of BG's dominant position there. In any case BG's behavior was subject to the standard provisions of U.K. and EC competition law. However, no new entrants made use of the access provisions in the period 1982 to 1987. After a number of large customers complained about BG's pricing policies in the nontariff market in 1987, in particular the failure of gas prices to match the decline in oil prices, the OFT referred the supply of gas to the nontariff market to the MMC.

At the time of the MMC report (1987–88) BG had about 21,000 nontariff customers, and 38% of BG's gas by volume was sold to this sector, generating 26% of BG's gas revenues. Nontariff customers were almost exclusively industrial and commercial customers. Firm contracts that could not be interrupted during peak periods accounted for 51% of nontariff sales by volume and 63% by value. BG's shares of the total market for energy consumption in the industrial and commercial sectors were 35% and 38%, respectively, although it should be noted that many industrial and commercial firms were tariff customers.

The 1988 MMC report found that BG was practising extensive discrimination. BG's contracts with nontariff customers were confidential, and prices were individually negotiated. The MMC found that that this operated against the public interest in four ways. First, it imposed higher prices on those customers less well placed to use alternative fuels, and this distorted downstream competition. Second, BG was able selectively to undercut any competing suppliers because it related its nontariff prices to the prices of the alternative supplies of gas or gas substitutes available to the particular customer. The ability to do this might have deterred entry. Third, the lack of transparency in pricing meant that customers were uncertain about future gas costs, which increased the risks businesses faced. Finally, the refusal to supply interruptible gas to customers whose alternative fuels were gas oil, liquefied petroleum gas, or electricity imposed additional costs on those users.

Having identified these adverse effects, the MMC had to propose remedies. It argued that regulation of the *level* of prices was inappropriate for the nontariff sector because of the need for BG to react quickly to changing demand and supply conditions and because this might make new entry more difficult, and that "ultimately the only effective means of remedying the adverse effect of the present monopoly situation is direct competition in gas supply" (MMC 1988, 103). This indicated a change from previous U.K. energy policy which had emphasized competition from other fuels (McGowan et al. 1990). Three major proposals emanated from the MMC's desire to promote gas-to-gas competition; they concerned pricing, access terms, and the availability of gas for potential competitors in gas supply.

BG was required to publish price schedules for both firm and interruptible gas that might relate to factors such as volume, load factor, and degree of interruptibility but not the alternative fuels available to particular customers. It was not allowed to negotiate around this schedule and could not discriminate in pricing or supply to nontariff customers. One implication of this was that BG could not refuse to supply interruptible gas to those who requested it. The MMC believed that published price schedules would remedy the four problems it had identified. They would reduce price discrimination, which would mean that arbitrary cost disadvantages imposed on customers who were less able to switch to competing fuels would be removed. Competition from other potential gas suppliers would be encouraged by removing the ability of BG selectively to undercut competitors, and the transparency of BG's prices would help competitors. Greater transparency in prices would also reduce the uncertainty that customers faced. The ban on BG's refusal to supply interruptible gas to some customers would reduce costs for those firm customers who wanted an interruptible supply. It was recommended that the requirement to publish price schedules should apply for five years at least.

The second recommendation made by the MMC was designed to make the legislation about access to the network effective. In between the 1982 Act which first required BG to make its pipelines available and the MMC report in 1988 there had been ten new approaches made to BG, none of which had resulted in agreement. There was thus no effective gas-to-gas competition. The MMC proposed that BG publish more information about access terms so that potential competitors would have a clearer idea about the costs of transmission and distribution that they might incur. It also proposed that "Chinese walls" be set up between those in BG involved in access negotiations and those involved in gas purchasing and supply. The MMC was concerned that information about the identity of potential customers and the potential sources of gas would be of value to BG in deterring entry, although selective undercutting would anyway be banned by the requirement to price on a schedule.

The MMC's third recommendation related to the de facto monopsony that BG had over gas purchases. BG tended to contract for 100% of each new gas field, which meant that potential competitors had difficulties acquiring sufficient gas supplies. Gas producers relied on BG's sales in the tariff market for most of their own sales, and they were unwilling to jeopardize their relationship with BG by selling gas to others, or by acting as suppliers themselves. To remedy this, the MMC recommended that BG initially contract for no more than 90% of any new field and guarantee not to contract for the balance within two years of the date of the initial contract. This was the "90/10 rule."

The MMC report focused on remedying the adverse consequences of BG's conduct in the nontariff market. BG's pricing policy before 1988 had been highly discriminatory (see Kay 1991; Price 1991a), since it was able to identify the use each customer made of the gas and what its alternative fuel sources were, and could price accordingly. The requirement to price to a schedule did not entirely remove discrimination because BG was allowed to relate charges to volume and volume-related pricing is a classic form of second-degree price discrimination. One of the predictions of simple non-linear pricing models (see section 2.1.4) is that marginal price for the highest unit of consumption will be equal to marginal cost, and Price (1991b) presents some evidence that the introduction of price schedules in the nontariff market has led to marginal prices close to marginal cost. BG has chosen not to relate the schedules to location or load factor. Some 60% of nontariff customers benefited from the introduction of nondiscriminatory schedules, while 20% faced higher prices (MMC 1993c, 72).

The MMC chose not to tackle the monopoly problem in the nontariff market by control of price levels but instead to encourage competition. Provision of more information about access and the setting up of Chinese walls may be helpful in encouraging competition, but they do not address two of the central issues—what the terms of access to BG's pipeline network should be and whether BG should be vertically integrated. The Gas Act 1986 contains some guidance for the DGGS in setting access terms when the two sides cannot agree, and Ofgas interpreted this to require average cost pricing. The MMC was concerned that this would be considerably above the marginal cost of transportation and suggested that the

DGGS might recommend changes to the Gas Act to enable him to determine transportation charges that would facilitate effective competition.

The first access agreement was signed in February 1990 between BG and Quadrant (a joint venture between Esso and Shell) and by December 1992 there were thirty-two agreements. Underlying the early transportation prices has been a 4.5% rate of return which was decided by Ofgas when determining rates for another entrant, Agas. BG considered this to be a short-term expedient in order to facilitate the development of competition, and the dispute over the appropriate rate of return for transportation was one of the main factors behind the second referral to the MMC in 1992. Although Ofgas had some influence on the level of BG's third-party transportation charges, it did not control the internal charges that BG set for its own supply business. Access charges for competitors had exhibited geographical variation, but BG treated the cost of transporting its own gas as an overhead, which meant that customers further from beach heads were cross-subsidized by customers nearer to the beach heads. This might have deterred potential competitors from supplying more distant markets, and encouraged cream-skimming in markets close to the beachheads.

The MMC believed that contracts with both customers and producers acted as barriers to entry because of the difficulty competitors had identifying potential customers and gaining access to gas supplies.[12] The problem of the opacity of customer contracts was solved by the adoption of price schedules, and the 90/10 rule was designed to remedy the lack of gas for competitors. The rule operated from 1989 to 1991. Since it applied only to new fields, it would take time before competitors had access to significant quantities of gas.

8.4.3 The 1991 Office of Fair Trading Gas Review
In 1991 the OFT conducted a review of the progress of competition since the 1988 MMC report. A summary version of this review was published in October 1991. The OFT found that most of the gas contracted for by competitors was destined for electricity generation. The Department of Energy estimated that 37% of the 7.5 billion therms of new contracted gas for that period was for supply by companies other than BG (OFT 1991, 4). However, BG itself estimated that it contracted for only half of new gas

---

12. See Aghion and Bolton (1987) and Rasmusen et al. (1991) for theoretical analyses of the role of contracts as barriers to entry.

during this period (Brown 1991). Only 7% of total newly contracted gas was destined for supply by competitors to the traditional nontariff market (i.e., the nongeneration market). The OFT understood the intention of the MMC recommendations to be the encouragement of competition to supply the traditional nontariff market, and it concluded that the remedies introduced after the 1988 MMC report had been "ineffective in encouraging self-sustaining competition to BG" (OFT 1991, 24). The OFT identified a number of obstacles to the growth of competition, in particular the lack of available gas supplies for competitors, BG's tariff market monopoly, and its control of transportation and storage. As a result BG could cross-subsidize, discriminate against rival suppliers, and set interruptible prices that competitors could not match.

The main source of gas available to competitors before 1994 was that already contracted to BG. The OFT recommended that BG release some of its contracted gas, that swap contracts be converted to release arrangements, and that a new form of the 90/10 rule be introduced to allow competition to develop. It also suggested that the government should consider its policies on the import and export of gas. Gas exports have been permitted since 1986, and the government announced in 1992 the removal of all remaining restrictions on imports.

To encourage competition further, the OFT recommended that the tariff market threshold be reduced. Apart from the direct benefits to consumers free to choose their suppliers, and the reduction in the BG's dominance as a gas purchaser, this might give competitors an incentive to enter the interruptible market. Interruptible contracts were not directly profitable for BG. Since 1988–89 BG's average price for interruptibles has been below the average cost of purchasing gas (MMC 1993c, table 3.5). The reason for offering such contracts is that they reduce the need for expensive storage facilities and thus help BG to serve profitable firm customers with variable demands, including tariff customers. Reducing the tariff market threshold might induce competitors to enter simultaneously both the profitable tariff market and the interruptible market. The OFT also recommended that competitors be given nondiscriminatory access to BG's storage facilities.

A necessary condition for successful gas-to-gas competition is access to the transportation network on reasonable terms. BG cross-subsidized geographically when setting its own internal transportation charges. There was no requirement in the MMC's recommendation on access for BG to treat its own gas supply business on the same basis as its competitors. This was considered by the OFT to be the inevitable result of a situation where competitors relied on an incumbent for transportation. The remedies suggested by the OFT were the divestment of the transportation and storage system, or at least the creation of a separate subsidiary to operate the system on a nondiscriminatory basis at arm's length from the rest of BG, and regulation of transportation charges by Ofgas.

The OFT review focused on the structural remedies of release of gas, reduction of the monopoly threshold, and the creation of a separate transportation and storage subsidiary, but it also enhanced the regulation of conduct recommended by MMC (1988). It recommended that price schedules remain until competition had increased and that there be improved communication with Ofgas about intended changes to price schedules to avoid the problems that appeared in 1991 over the schedule for the generation market.[13] The OFT proposals were backed by the threat that if BG did not voluntarily agree to new undertakings, there would be another MMC reference.

BG agreed to a set of undertakings based on the OFT proposals in March 1992 after threatening to withdraw from the new tariff market formula agreement. It agreed to set up two separate business units. BG Transportation was to conduct transportation (from shore terminal to meter) and storage, and would operate at arm's length from BG Trading, which would own the contracts with producers and would supply gas. The OFT recommendation that BG sell some of its contracted gas to competitors was also agreed, and BG agreed to reduce its share of the traditional nontariff market (both firm and interruptible) to 40% (about 2.8 billion therms) by 1995. BG was to sell at least 500 million therms of gas in October 1992 to independent suppliers, and similar amounts in each year up to 1995. In the year 1995–96 it would be required to sell at least 250 million therms. In the event BG offered contracted gas for sale before October 1992 at a standard price per therm consisting of the weighted average cost of gas (BG's own purchase price) plus administration costs. Thirty-two bidders acquired gas in allocations of between 10 and 17.8 million therms. By December 1992 competitors had a 20% share of the

---

13. BG had set prices in its special contracts for generation that were apparently below the marginal production cost of gas (Ofgas Annual Report 1991, 29). This led to a surge in demand for generation—part of the reason for the "dash for gas"—and in early 1991 BG imposed a 35% price increase to ration available supplies. Although BG was free to set the level of its price schedules, Ofgas was concerned that it had done so in a discriminatory manner, since selected customers were told about the proposed price increase and advised that they could sign contracts at the previous prices. After the threat of legal action by Ofgas, BG announced a new interruptible schedule that halved the original price increase.

traditional nontariff market, a substantial increase on the 8.5% market share a year earlier.

The use of a market share target is an unusual measure in competition and regulatory policy. The only other examples appear to be the original limit on direct sales by the large electricity generators, and the limit on own-generation by the regional electricity companies. The rationale for it in the gas case is unclear. There is no guarantee that a reduced market share for BG will be accompanied by greater competition or lower prices (see Shaw 1992). The simplest and most profitable way for BG to reduce its share of the nontariff market is to increase prices, although the MMC (1993a) could find no evidence that price levels had generally been raised in the non-tariff market. Market share fixing by quotas or voluntary export restraints is a feature of some international trade policies, but analysis shows that it can facilitate collusion (Krishna 1989). There is also the danger that BG's published price schedules will act as "focal points" for tacit collusion with the new independent suppliers.

The OFT review concluded that the conduct regulation of the 1988 MMC report had not been sufficient to stimulate competition and that additional structural remedies were necessary. Although it argued that full divestment was the best option, it was willing to accept the creation of a separate transportation and storage subsidiary as a compromise.

8.4.4   The 1993 Monopolies and Mergers Commission Report

As part of its deal with the OFT in March 1992 BG agreed to regulation by Ofgas of its access charges. A key input in the determination of the level of access prices is the rate of return that investors require. BG (1992) submitted a paper to Ofgas on the rate of return for BG Transportation in July 1992. Using the CAPM they claimed that the rate of return required on new investment in the stand-alone transportation subsidiary would be 10.8% in real terms before tax. This would not be an appropriate rate of return for the existing assets, however, because, it was argued, the market value of these assets was only 62% of their replacement cost, and the market value had always been below replacement cost since privatization. If the existing assets earned the proposed rate of return on new assets, there would be a large increase in shareholder value at the expense of consumers (see section 6.3.1 for a discussion of this issue). BG suggested that the current cost rate of return for the 1992–93 contract year should be 6.7% (which is 0.62 times 10.8%).

Ofgas did not accept BG's proposal on the rate of return. It argued that transportation was a low-risk business and was only willing to allow the rate of 4.5%, which had been used since 1989 to fix transportation prices. Facing a tougher price cap in the tariff market, a forced reduction in its market share in the nontariff market, what it perceived as an uneconomic rate of return for transportation, and perhaps anticipating that Ofgas itself would make a reference, BG asked the President of the Board of Trade to refer its whole business to the MMC. Under the terms of the Fair Trading Act 1973 he asked the MMC to investigate two subjects, the supply of gas through pipes to both tariff and nontariff customers, and the transportation and storage of gas by public gas suppliers. Two parallel references by Ofgas under the Gas Act 1986 were into the transportation and storage of gas and the fixing of tariffs for the supply of gas. The Gas Act references were more limited in their scope, since Ofgas could only refer matters concerning the tariff market and transportation and storage and the MMC could only recommend changes to the authorization, but the reasoning underlying the two reports that the MMC published in 1993 is the same.

The MMC made four main recommendations: first, that BG should be required to divest its trading (i.e., supply) business by 31 March 1997, that before then BG should operate transportation as a separate subsidiary, and that there should be regulation of charges and conditions; second, that the monopoly threshold should be reduced to 1,500 therms from March 1997, and that complete abolition might be considered by 2000 or 2002; third, that transportation and storage should be subject to price regulation, with the rate of return on new investment in transportation and storage in the range 6.5–7.5%, and the return on existing assets in the range 4–4.5%; finally, that the tariff market price cap should be relaxed from RPI − 5 to RPI − 4 from 1994, that the formula should only apply to those below the 2,500 therms threshold, and that a further adjustment to the X factor should be considered to ensure that tariff customers bore some of the costs of divestment and restructuring. We will describe in more detail the reasons behind these recommendations before assessing the report.

The MMC first assessed the progress of competition in the nontariff market. The nontariff market is that for consumption over 25,000 therms,[14] and like the OFT, the MMC excluded gas supplied to power generators from consideration. It noted that competition had grown

---

14. Although competitors had been able to supply customers in the range 2,500 to 25,000 therms since August 1992, BG continued to set a tariff in this market segment, and prices were constrained by the tariff market price cap.

quickly since the 1988 MMC report and the 1991 OFT review. By May 1993 about 55% of the firm nontariff market was supplied by competitors, but there was no competition for interruptible contracts. Market shares held by competitors were highest in the high-load factor, medium-demand market, and lowest for large-volume markets. Suppliers were not keen to supply the largest users because they had limited gas supplies and did not want to depend on a few large customers. There was also some variation in the market shares held in different regions by competitors. The pattern of competition was related to the fact that BG's transportation charges for competitors reflected load factor and location, while its own price schedules in the nontariff market did not.

The growth of competition had been assisted by the means of (1) forcing BG to set price schedules, (2) requiring it to release gas to competitors, and (3) progressively reducing its market share, and may also have reflected a low rate of return underlying transportation charges. The MMC was concerned that competitors were vulnerable to increases in transportation charges. In 1992 the average selling price of competitors was about 31.7 pence per therm, of which the gas cost was 19.6 pence and the transportation price was 8.4 pence, leaving a small margin of about 3.6 pence to cover trading costs and profit (MMC 1993c, table 3.14). Competitors' prices were on average about 10% lower than BG's, but this advantage could be eliminated if BG changed the level or structure of its third-party transportation charges while not altering its own price schedules.

The MMC argued that the *introduction* of competition to date had required these artificial measures but that competition could only be *sustained* in the longer term if competitors had nondiscriminatory access to the transportation network and storage facilities. The MMC (1993a, 17) said that "the integrated nature of BG's business ... is unable to provide the necessary conditions for self-sustaining competition." Even if BG had separate subsidiaries for transportation and trading, as agreed in the undertakings to the OFT, the problems of conflict of interest would not be resolved. There had been delays in offering quotations and in reading meters, and both the structure and the level of transportation charges and BG's operational requirements for competitors affected their ability to compete. Ofgas (1992b, 13) had argued that without full separation there might be problems over access to the network for competitors in the event of capacity shortages, transportation pricing that disadvantage competitors, asset and cost allocation that favor the transportation side of BG, and the confidentiality of information. Regulation of such behavior would be costly and difficult given the asymmetries of information. Since the MMC believed that competition would not be self-sustaining without vertical separation and that competition in supply was desirable, it concluded that the situation acted against the public interest, and recommended divestment of BG's trading business in its reports under the Fair Trading Act. Within the terms of the narrower Gas Act references the MMC did not have the authority to recommend divestment, so instead its proposed remedy was that BG should establish separate units for trading, and transportation and storage, by the end of March 1994 at the latest.

Since divestment could not be immediate, interim measures were proposed. The recommendation was that the market share targets, the gas release scheme, and the requirement to set published price schedules, should all continue. The definition of the market used for the market share targets should be extended to include users between 2,500 and 25,000 terms, and BG's share limited to 55% of this market from December 1993 (the old target was 40% of the market above 25,000 therms). This implied that the volume of sales lost by BG would be the same as under the previous target. Sales for power generation were excluded from the definition. The MMC recognized that there was a danger that BG might have to raise its interruptible prices to meet the market share target[15] and that there could be some flexibility in the interpretation of market shares to take account of the special case of interruptibles, but on balance it believed that the target was a useful temporary measure. Similarly it decided that it would be premature to drop the requirement to set price schedules, but that once competition was self-sustaining they could be replaced by a requirement not to discriminate unduly. The MMC (1993a, 31) argued that the gas release scheme was "not an acceptable or necessary element for sustaining competition in the longer term" but that it should continue in the interim, and its extension beyond 1995–96 might need to be considered.

In its analysis of the tariff market, the MMC noted that the price cap had reduced real prices by 16% between 1986–87 and 1992 and that the quality of service was high. Competitors in the range 2,500 to 25,000 therms a year had already taken over 5% of this market in 1993 (MMC 1993c, table 3.15), but, as in the nontariff market, they were vulnerable to changes in the terms and conditions for access to BG's transportation network and storage facilities. In this market competitive selling prices

---

15. BG announced price increases for the interruptibles market of betwen 2.1% and 12.5% in October 1993.

averaged 36.5 pence per therm, with gas purchase costs of 19.9 pence, transportation costs of 11.5 pence and a margin of 5.1 pence for competitors' trading costs and profits. The MMC argued that the extension of the market share target to include this part of the tariff market should encourage competition and limit BG's dominance. It was also suggested that the scope of the price cap could be reduced to include only those below 2,500 therms a year, that BG should have an obligation to supply in the range 2,500 to 25,000 therms, and that it should set published price schedules in this range until there is effective competition.

The main structural question for the MMC in its analysis of the tariff market was whether BG's statutory monopoly should be reduced or abolished. Rival suppliers were keen to have access to this market, but user groups were generally satisfied with BG's performance on prices and quality. The MMC did not believe that BG's conduct in the tariff market was against the public interest, but it suggested that competition might lead to a more efficient allocation of resources by inducing prices that are more cost reflective, and also perhaps by lowering the overall price level. The three forms of cross-subsidy in the tariff market were from large customers to small customers, from customers close to beachheads or in urban areas to those remote from beachheads or in rural areas, and from those with low-peak demands to those with high-peak demands. Competition might force BG to unwind these cross-subsidies, and some users might be worse off. In particular BG calculated that prices for the 12 million customers consuming less than 700 therms a year would have to rise, and those taking less than 100 therms a year would see prices almost doubling if BG's prices were to reflect the higher costs of supplying very small customers. However, those in the range 1,500 to 2,500 therms could see price reductions of between 8% and 10%. The MMC felt that the benefits of competition would outweigh the cost, and it proposed the reduction of the threshold to 1,500 therms a year. Since it did not see competition as being effective until vertical separation occurred, the proposed date for the reduction was set at 1 April 1997.

Because of the complexities and uncertainties associated with allowing competition, the MMC was cautious about the complete abolition of the monopoly. It said (MMC 1993a, 28) that "no decision as to the timing of so significant a step as removal of the monopoly should be taken, except after the fullest consideration of the advantages and disadvantages of doing so." It expected to see abolition of the monopoly by 2000 or 2002 but did not make a formal recommendation to this effect. Difficulties over safety, security of supply, and social obligations were noted. If a competing trader should fail to put sufficient gas into the system while its customers continue to use gas, there would be a risk of an explosion as air enters the system. In the MMC's view legislative changes were necessary to deal with these issues.

In general the MMC was content to leave most of the details of the regulation of transportation and storage to Ofgas.[16] It favored RPI − X regulation, with an adjustment for differences between expected and actual throughput. It was satisfied with BG's proposed structure of transportation prices which had some differentiation between locations. It argued that there should be confidentiality of information and ring-fencing of the transportation and storage unit from the other parts of BG until divestment of BG Trading happened. In the Gas Act conclusions (MMC 1993b) it recommended changing BG's authorization accordingly.

The major recommendation on price regulation for transportation and storage was on the rate of return, the issue that had precipitated the references. As we have explained BG had argued for a CCA (current cost accounting) rate of return of 10.8% on new investment and a return on existing assets of 6.7%. Ofgas (1992c) estimated the cost of capital for new investment to be in the range from 5.7% to 8.4%. Although Ofgas agreed with BG that the return on new investment should be multiplied by the ratio of the market value to replacement cost to find the CCA return on existing assets, it argued that this ratio was in the range 0.48–0.61. Ofgas suggested that reasonable CCA rates of return for existing assets based on CAPM lay in the range 2.7–5.1%, well below BG's target of 6.7%. Ofgas also made comparisons with utilities in other countries and considered U.K. evidence on current cost returns. On the basis of the evidence of both the CAPM and rates of return earned by comparable companies Ofgas concluded that the rate of return on existing assets should be in the range 2.5–5%. After further research this range was revised to 2–4%. The MMC's range for the return on new investment was 6.5–7.5%. It stressed that judgment was required in assessing required rates of return. Apart from the CAPM evidence the MMC took account of CCA rates of return earned in other utilities in Britain, of the public sector required rates of return of 6% for nontrading activities and 8% for nationalized industries and of a survey of fund managers' views that showed that they looked for real rates of return on equities of between 6% and 8%. To convert the

---

16. For details of the Ofgas proposals, see Ofgas (1992a) and MMC (1993d, ch. 11).

6.5–7.5% range to a range of returns for existing assets, it used 0.6 as the ratio of market value to replacement cost, giving 4–4.5%. Since the original rate of return used to set transportation prices since 1989 was 4.5%, the effect of the MMC's recommendation should be that the average level of transportation prices will not increase, although this will depend on the proportion of divestment costs that is passed on to consumers.

The MMC argued that there should be no difference in the expected rates of return between the tariff market and transportation. It judged the price cap in the tariff market of RPI − 5 to be too tight to generate returns in the tariff market sufficient to attract new investment, partly because of the fall in market share above 2,500 therms. It recommended changing the X factor to 4% and applying the formula only to users of less than 2,500 therms a year. It did not accept BG's suggestion that there should be cost passthrough for transportation charges, and the structure of the formula remains as determined in 1991. Finally, it noted that the cost of vertical restructuring, estimated at £130 million a year over ten years, had to be paid for, and it suggested that Ofgas should pass on "an appropriate proportion of the costs of such restructuring to tariff users" (MMC 1993a, 52) and that Ofgas should take account of such costs in setting transportation and storage costs.

BG had criticized the regulatory system in general, and the MMC thought it appropriate to give its views. It argued that the system was fundamentally sound and that vertical separation would improve the information available to Ofgas and would help to improve its relationship with BG. It declined to make any comment on the way regulatory affairs are conducted, and recommended that the DGGS's powers should be extended to full regulatory responsibility, jointly with the DGFT, for the nontariff market.

The main objective of the MMC was to encourage self-sustaining competition, consistent with its position exhibited in the 1988 report. It proposed to ensure this by vertical separation, by reducing and possibly abolishing the monopoly threshold, and by tight control of BG's conduct in the interim through the continuation of the price schedules, the gas release scheme, and the market share target. It argued that the introduction of competition in the nontariff market had been of benefit to users. They had greater choice, lower prices, and BG had been encouraged to lower its costs. In its view the sine qua non for future effective competition was full vertical separation. Although this entailed costs—since a demand- and supply-balancing regime would have to be established, any scope

economies between trading and transportation would be lost, and transactions costs would be incurred—the MMC argued that these did not
offset the expected benefits of competition. The MMC (1993a, 42) quoted
BG's estimate that cost of creating separate subsidiaries would be £50
million a year for ten years and that the extra annual cost of divestment
would be £80 million, but stressed that these estimates were uncertain and
probably too high and that in an case they were small in relation to the
size of BG's gas supply business.

The MMC recommended that BG divest itself of trading, whereas the
OFT and Ofgas had expressed a preference for divesting transportation
and storage. The important difference is that the latter option ensures that
the naturally monopolistic business is ring-fenced from the potentially
competitive parts, which include exploration and production, appliance
trading and servicing, and the international business besides trading. The
MMC appears to have been influenced by BG's argument that its ability
to compete abroad would be lower if it did not have a large asset base at
home to maintain its credit rating. The precise allocation of existing assets
and businesses to the two parts of the business was left unclear by the
MMC. It suggested that appliance trading and servicing would fit most
appropriately with trading but that exploration and production and BG's
international business might gain from continued association with transportation and storage. The exploration and production unit would not be
allowed to supply customers directly, and its gas would have to be sold to
other traders if it remained with transportation and storage. But if the
MMC's worries about vertical integration are valid, then the suggestion
that exploration and production might remain with transportation and
storage is strange. There would be an incentive for BG Transportation
and Storage to favor the traders who purchased the exploration and production unit's gas, and detailed conduct regulation would be necessary to
prevent this. If neutrality is important, then the better option would be to
divest transportation and storage.

Other options for separation were also considered and rejected by the
MMC. The option of splitting BG Trading into separate regional companies, which was mentioned by Ofgas (1993), was not taken up because
of the extra costs involved and because the number of competitors was not
a problem. The Hammond et al. (1985) suggestion that BG be split along
the lines of the electricity supply industry into the national (and possibly
regional) transmission system, with integrated regional distribution and
supply companies, was also rejected because of cost and the difficulty of

ensuring nondiscriminatory access to the regional distribution networks. Similarly the MMC did not believe that the storage system should be split from transportation because BG's storage facilities are used to provide security of supply as well as to service seasonal peaks. It did argue that accounting separation of storage facilities might be desirable since competitors might want to set up their own storage facilities.

In view of the MMC's competitive objectives, its caution over the timetable for abolition of the monopoly threshold is surprising. The proposed timetable of partial reduction to 1,500 therms by 1997 and abolition, after further analysis, by 2000 or 2002 seems timid. Many competitors expected that after the reduction of the threshold to 2,500 therms in August 1992 the monopoly would be abolished much sooner. Of course introducing a competitive market for all customers is not simple. More sophisticated meters would be needed. It would require a new Gas Act and an appropriate licensing regime that would allow for concerns about safety, security of supply, and social obligations. There appear to be two further reasons why the MMC did not suggest a faster abolition of the monopoly threshold. First, the MMC stressed the necessity of having the conditions for self-sustaining competition in place (i.e., a neutral transportation and storage unit) before reducing the threshold. But since the MMC recommended that transportation and storage be operated as a separate subsidiary before divestment of BG Trading in 1997, it is not clear why the threshold should not be reduced earlier. Second, competition will induce cost-reflective pricing. While this is allocatively efficient, there might be severe political consequences if cross-subsidies are unwound quickly, leaving many smaller customers worse off. The political constraint within which the MMC operated was tightened by the government's announcement in the Budget of March 1993 that domestic fuel bills would be subjected to value-added tax from April 1994. BG had argued that 12 million smaller-tariff customers would lose from competition because BG did not recover the fixed costs of supplying them. Such calculations depend critically on the assumptions used to allocate shared costs to different customers, and it is therefore difficult to know what to make of this claim. The independent gas companies have claimed that competition would benefit all consumers, partly because BG's supply costs are too high, but this claim is also hard to substantiate.

The recommendation that tariff consumers should bear an appropriate proportion of the net costs of vertical separation is opaque. Net costs are not defined. Presumably the argument for this is that since it is consumers who will gain from the changes, they should pay. Smaller consumers, however, are likely to lose as cross-subsidies are unwound, and in any case under the proposed timetable full competition would not be allowed until 2000 at the earliest.

8.5 Assessment

The regulatory regime established for the gas industry at privatization was seriously inadequate, and regulatory reform has subsequently been necessary. In 1986 BG retained a de facto monopsony in gas purchasing, had a pipeline monopoly, was the statutory monopolist in the tariff market, and was in effect unregulated in the nontariff market. There was no explicit regulation of anticompetitive behavior. There had been legal liberalization that established competitors' rights to access, but because the terms of access were not regulated, this was completely ineffective, and no entry occurred as a result of liberalization alone. One lesson to be learned from the case of BG is that when an incumbent is vertically integrated and potential competitors must use its network, simply allowing access without regulating the terms of access is insufficient to promote competition. The initial price cap in the tariff market was generous, and it has since been tightened.

The 1988 MMC report recommended limited regulation of conduct. BG was banned from pricing selectively in the nontariff market, and the requirement to purchase no more than 90% of the gas of new fields sought to restrain its monopsony power. But on the key issue of access terms the MMC recommended simply that better information be provided, without requiring any explicit regulation of access terms.

Although competition grew quickly after the recommendations of the 1988 report were implemented, this was mainly in the new market for electricity generation. The OFT review in 1991 argued that the competition that did exist in the traditional nontariff market would not be self-sustaining because of the competitors' lack of gas supplies and BG's incentive as an integrated firm to give its own trading business preferential treatment. It wanted BG to divest its transportation and storage business but was prepared to accept the compromise of separate subsidiaries. The market share target for BG that arose from the OFT review is a crude way of promoting entry, since its main effect might simply be for BG to set higher prices, especially in the interruptibles market. Similarly the gas release program can only be a temporary measure to ensure that competitors can supply some gas.

The progress toward vertical separation has been slow. In its 1993 reports the MMC recognized that self-sustaining competition required complete separation of trading from transportation. Although we believe it might be preferable to divest transportation rather than trading, because this ensures proper ring-fencing of the naturally monopolistic activities, and that the introduction of competition into the tariff market could be quicker than the MMC proposed, we believe that the main thrust of the MMC's recommendations is appropriate.

In the event, however, the government did not accept the MMC's main recommendation that trading should be divested. Instead, it decided that BG should be allowed to retain ownership of both trading and transportation, while operating them as separate business units. But on the reduction of the tariff monopoly the government was more radical than the MMC recommended. The tariff monopoly for those using less than 2,500 therms will end in April 1996. All nondomestic users will be free to obtain competitive supplies from that date, and competition for domestic customers will be phased in over a two-year period. In the first year competitors will be limited to a market share of 5%, rising to 10% in the second year. The operation of these market share limits will be determined by the DGGS. Full competition for domestic gas supply will be allowed from April 1998, when domestic electricity supply is also scheduled to be opened up.

One lesson to be learned is that it is far better to achieve structural reforms to promote competition before an integrated monopolist is privatized. The very different approach that the government adopted when privatizing the electricity supply industry suggests that it did not take long to recognize the mistakes made in the case of British Gas. Another lesson is that regulatory attention to access terms is necessary for the development of competition.

9

Electricity

The government's plan to privatize the electricity supply industry (ESI) in England and Wales was announced early in 1988. The accompanying proposals for regulatory reform were radical by any standard, and contrasted sharply with the then recent privatization of British Gas as a vertically integrated nationwide monopolist. In brief they involved

1. vertical separation between generation and transmission,
2. horizontal breakup and liberalization of generation,
3. a regional structure for distribution and retail supply,
4. phased liberalization of retail supply.

Instead of being organized within an essentially administrative structure, bulk power is now traded in a kind of spot market.

Electricity technology requires extremely tight coordination between generation and transmission, but vertical separation was nevertheless chosen, with the aim of fostering competition in generation. The new structure came into being on 31 March 1990, after two years of intense activity to devise regulatory and contractual arrangements. Privatization of all but the nuclear parts of the industry followed (in Scotland and Northern Ireland as well as in England and Wales). It is too early to judge the overall success of this bold experiment, but major controversies have already arisen in the first four years since restructuring, for example, about whether conditions for effective and efficient competition in generation have been created, and the implications of electricity privatization and regulatory reform for the British coal industry.

The British ESI presents an extraordinarily rich case study in industrial organization and policy, not only because of the radicalism and importance of the reforms but also because of the diverse issues that their analysis requires. These include the theory of the firm ("markets versus hierarchy"), commodity price risk, contracts and hedging, repeated oligopolistic interaction, locational network pricing, environmental externalities, and social questions, in addition to all the regulatory issues familiar from industries like telecommunications and gas.

These issues arise sharply in the ESI because of the economic characteristics of the industry, which are discussed in section 9.1. The main policy options for organizing the industry are set out in section 9.2. Then the competitive, regulatory and contractual framework established at the time of privatization is described in section 9.3. Section 9.4 examines a selection of subsequent competitive and regulatory developments—the questionable effectiveness of competition in generation; the chain of contracts between fuel input suppliers, generators, regional electricity companies and customers; the pricing of transmission; and prospects for environmental regulation. A preliminary assessment and discussion of policy concludes the chapter.

9.1   The Electricity Supply Industry and Its Economic Characteristics

9.1.1   Economic Characteristics

Electricity is a product that is generally nonstorable.[1] Demand fluctuates by time of day and year, as the weather varies, and randomly. Supply is also subject to unpredictable outages. However, equilibrium between supply and demand must be maintained continuously and throughout the system. This combination of circumstances poses considerable problems for the organization of supply.

Electricity supply involves five vertically related stages of production:

1. supply of energy inputs,
2. generation,
3. transmission,
4. distribution,
5. supply to final customers.

The main energy inputs are fossil fuels (coal, gas, oil, and orimulsion[2]), nuclear fuels, and renewables (including water power for hydroelectricity).

All the main energy sources involve environmental costs of one kind or another. Quite apart from resource depletion issues, the burning of fossil fuels causes emissions of pollutants, notably carbon dioxide, sulphur dioxide, and oxides of nitrogen. In the United Kingdom the ESI is the main

---

1. This statement requires some qualification. Electric storage heaters use off-peak power to produce heat at other times. There is also a sense in which some hydroelectric power can be stored. The National Grid Company has a pumped storage business in the Welsh mountains. Water pumped uphill at night can produce hydroelectric power the following day, thereby effectively storing some night-time electricity. This is economically efficient, provided that the day/night electricity price ratio is high enough, despite the energy efficiency loss that the process involves.

2. Orimulsion is produced from bitumen.

producer of CO_2 and SO_2, and only the transport sector emits more NO_x. Concern about the greenhouse effect and acid rain requires that these emissions be controlled. Efficient pollution control involves a combination of capital investment to extract pollutants (e.g., desulphurization equipment and clean coal plant), substitution away from "dirtier" fuels (e.g., some kinds of coal) toward cleaner technologies (e.g., gas and non-fossil fuels), and perhaps lower electricity consumption (see section 9.4.4). However, reduced demand for British coal imposes social costs in terms of highly concentrated unemployment in mining areas.

The catastrophic environmental consequences of a nuclear accident such as Chernobyl are obvious. The risk of accident in a system like that in Britain or France (where most supply is nuclear) is much debated, as is the safety of nuclear fuel reprocessing and disposal of toxic wastes. Safety considerations also mean that nuclear stations have huge decommissioning costs.[3] Hydroelectric power avoids these environmental problems but may impose costs in terms of visual amenity and ecological damage.

In addition to fuel costs, electricity generation is capital intensive, and investment costs are sunk. Capital intensity varies between energy sources. Nuclear power involves the largest fixed capital costs and the longest lead times. Its proportionately low operating costs mean that it is efficient to run nuclear stations more or less continuously—they are "base load" plant. Gas, on the other hand, used to be the most expensive fuel source, but with the lowest ratio of fixed to variable costs. It was used primarily to serve demand peaks. In respect of fixed–variable cost ratios, coal was in between nuclear and gas, with coal stations being run except at times of low demand. The past tense is used here because environmental cost considerations and new combined cycle gas turbine (CCGT) technology have enhanced the efficiency of gas in relation to coal. Which is more efficient at the margin is a controversial question (see section 9.4.2).

An efficient system will typically contain a mix of plant types. The variability of demand, relative energy costs (including environmental costs), and the cost of capital are the prime determinants of the optimal mix. In view of changing circumstances, and the sunk costs and long lead times associated with power station construction, actual mix will generally differ from what is ex post optimal. A good system of investment incentives will encourage movement toward (the moving target of) the optimal mix.

---

3. See Yarrow (1988) for an analysis of the costs of nuclear power.

In the short run, electricity supply is constrained by the capacity limits of power stations. Supply security requires that total capacity exceed expected demand with a margin to allow for uncertainties. There are start-up costs whenever a station is switched on, and so it may be better to keep it running for a period when it is not producing rather than turning a station off and on again. In any case system security creates a need for some plant to be up and ready to supply (called "spinning reserve") to cope with sudden demand requirements. Thus a power station that is not currently producing electricity may still be supplying a valuable electricity call option.[4]

In the longer run, theory and evidence both indicate increasing returns at low levels of production and approximately constant returns otherwise. Very small generating units are inefficient, but reasonable estimates suggest that minimum efficient scale for fossil-fuel generation is around 400 megawatts (MW) capacity[5] (perhaps less for some CCGT plant). There are some economies from multiple-unit operation, and Joskow and Schmalensee (1983, 53) arrive at a rough estimate of 800 MW for minimum efficient plant scale. It is not clear whether any further economies exist at firm level. Minimum efficient scale for nuclear generation appears to be at least double that for fossil-fuel generation. To put these numbers into perspective, total capacity in England and Wales is about 60,000 MW.

Electricity is costly to transport, and therefore the pattern and sizes of plant that are most efficient depend on demand as well as supply considerations. This leads to the subject of transmission, and its close relation to generation. (The distinction between "transmission" and "distribution" is that the former is high voltage and national in scope, whereas the latter is regional and local. The national transmission grid is somewhat analogous to the motorway system in the road network, or trunk routes in telecommunications.) Transmission is capital intensive, and costs are sunk. It is a naturally monopolistic activity in the sense that duplication of cables between two locations would generally be inefficient, and systemwide network optimization is required.

Electricity is not "transmitted" in the sense that electricity sold by generator G to buyer B moves from G's location to B's location (it is like gas

---

4. The pumped storage stations described in footnote 1 are useful for this purpose because of their low startup costs.
5. See Joskow and Schmalensee (1983, ch. 5). A kilowatt (KW) = 1,000 watts, a megawatt (MW) = 1,000 KW, a gigawatt (GW) = 1,000 MW, and a terawatt (TW) = 1,000 GW.

and water in this respect). Rather, G supplies some power into the general system at one location (or "node") on the system, and B withdraws some power at another. There is no direct physical trade. Thus at any time there are suppliers into the system from generators at numerous nodes and withdrawals from it by consumers at a vast number of others. Power flows cannot be directed along particular paths in the transmission system. They are allocated by nature according to physical laws.[6]

It is essential that a balance between supply and demand be maintained continually throughout the system. Otherwise nonlocalized power outages (blackouts, etc.) happen. This paramount need for *electrical equilibrium* calls for extremely close minute-by-minute coordination between generation and transmission. This is a major reason why the two activities have typically been vertically integrated. If economies of scope between them were large enough, then generation and transmission might *jointly* have natural monopoly cost conditions, even though generation per se does not.[7] A central question for structural policy, then, is whether the gains from competition in generation outweigh the costs of any losses in coordination between generation and transmission. This partly depends on how well they can be coordinated in the event of deintegration.

In addition to the costs of constructing and maintaining transmission capacity, a major element of transmission cost is power loss. The rate of loss is an increasing (approximately quadratic) function of the net power flow along transmission lines. Since net flows are what matter for losses, power supplies at some nodes in the network will reduce, rather than increase, losses. In the simple two-node example in figure 9.1a in which the net flow is from north to south, incremental supply at N will add, perhaps considerably, to losses, whereas incremental supply at S will reduce them. Incremental demands affect losses similarly (but with opposite sign of course). Overall efficiency therefore requires that locational price differences take account of incremental losses. In the example just given, producers and consumers at N should face appropriately lower prices than those at S on efficiency grounds.

In the short run, transmission capacity limits may constrain power flows and hence the overall efficiency (and indeed capacity) of the system.

---

6. Electricity flows according to Kirchoff's laws, "essentially following the path of least resistance" (Hogan 1992, 215).

7. See Kaserman and Mayo (1991) and Kerkvliet (1991) for empirical evidence on economies of scope.

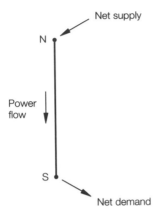

a. Two-node network

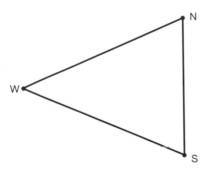

b. Three-node network

Figure 9.1 Simple transmission networks

Suppose that in the example northern generators are much more efficient than those in the south, despite losses. If north–south transmission capacity is limited, however, part of southern demand may have to be met by the inefficient southern generators. The degree of competition that they face from the north may be limited correspondingly.

In a more complex system—even one so simple as the example in figure 9.1b—supply/demand at node W might affect transmission capacity between N and S as well as losses. (Recall that power flows cannot be directed.) In general, then, the optimal price at any node depends not only on the marginal generating cost of electricity but also on the effect on systemwide losses of incremental supply/demand at that node, and the effect on transmission constraints as reflected in their shadow prices. On the theory of the spatial pricing of electricity, see Bohn et al. (1984) and Hogan (1992).

Regional distribution companies take power from points on the national transmission grid at high voltage levels and reduce voltages by transformers to levels appropriate for industrial and domestic usage (the latter being 240 volts in Britain). Distribution, like transmission, is characterized by capital intensity, sunk costs, and natural monopoly cost conditions in any given area: duplication of wires would be inefficient.

The retail supply of electricity to final consumers has generally been done by the distribution companies in their respective areas, though some large industrial customers were supplied directly from the transmission grid. However, although the distribution of electricity to a consumer in region A must be via the wires of the distribution company in region A, there is no economic reason why other aspects of retail supply must also be provided by that company. The acquisition of bulk power, marketing, billing, and so on, can, at least in principle, be carried out by generating companies, distribution companies in other regions, or independent retailers. As in the case of gas, given proper terms of third party access to transmission and distribution, retail supply is potentially competitive, not naturally monopolistic. Nevertheless, the smaller customers of regional distributional companies are effectively captive unless metering technology is sophisticated enough to allow competition. The expense of installing a meter is a significant switching cost in relation to the electricity needs of small users.

To summarize, the economic characteristics of electricity supply include nonstorability and demand variation; environmental and social costs associated with the main energy inputs; capital intensity and sunk costs throughout the industry; natural monopoly in the transportation activities of transmission and distribution, but not in generation or retail supply; and the need for very close vertical coordination, especially between generation and transmission.

9.1.2 The Industry in the UK[8]
The new industry structure will be described more fully in section 9.3.2. Briefly, in England and Wales there are now three large generators (National Power, PowerGen, and Nuclear Electric), a nationwide trans-

---

8. For more detail, see Department of Trade and Industry (1993a).

mission company (National Grid Company), and twelve Regional Electricity Companies for distribution and supply. A number of independent power producers are entering generation with CCGT plant, often in joint ventures with RECs, but REC ownership stakes must not exceed 15% of their requirements. There are also electricity imports via interconnectors with Scotland and France. The RECs compete with each other and with the generators to supply large customers, but each REC currently has a monopoly to supply smaller customers in its area. In Scotland there are two vertically integrated regional companies (Scottish Power and Hydro-Electric) and a nuclear generating company (Scottish Nuclear). In Northern Ireland there are rival generators, and Northern Ireland Electricity, which was privatized in 1993, carries out transmission, distribution, and supply.

In the United Kingdom in 1992, 304 terawatt hours (TWh) of electricity were supplied, net imports were 17 TWh, losses were 28 TWh, and consumption was 293 TWh. From 1988 to 1992, growth was 7%. The value of electricity supplied through the public distribution system was £17 billion. There are more than 25 million consumers.

Total capacity in March 1993 was 65 GW, of which the major generating companies had 61 GW. The estimated shares of fuel inputs in electricity generation in England and Wales (as distinct from the whole United Kingdom) in 1992–93 were coal 66%, nuclear 20%, oil and orimulsion 5%, gas 1%, and electricity imports from France and Scotland 8%.[9] In the next few years, however, gas is expected to displace coal to a substantial extent. British Coal has estimated that by 1997–98 the shares will be coal 38%, nuclear 21%, oil and orimulsion 4%, gas 29%, and electricity imports 8%.[10]

The rest of this chapter focuses on the industry in England and Wales. The performance of the main companies in the year to March 1993 was as follows: National Power made a pretax profit of £580 million on turnover of £4,348 million, and PowerGen made a pretax profit of £425 million on turnover of £3,188 million. Nuclear Electric had an operating profit of £661 on electricity sales of £1.4 billion. National Grid Company made a pretax profit of £350 million in current cost terms on turnover of £1,396 million. In total, the twelve RECs' revenue from distribution was £3,751 million (the range being £189–428 million with an average of £313 million)

9. House of Commons (1993, 26).
10. Derived from House of Commons (1993, table 6).

and their operating profit was £1,042 million in current cost terms (range £39–121 million, average £87 million). Their revenue from supply totaled £13,921 million (range £536–1,805 million, average £1,160 million), and they made small losses or profits in current cost terms.[11]

9.2 Policy Questions

In view of the economic characteristics of the industry, especially the need for very close coordination between generation and transmission, a policy of vertically integrated monopoly—administrative hierarchy rather than any attempt to have competitive markets—has some attractions. The integrated generation/transmission company would run those of its power stations that met demand at minimum cost at each point in time, account being taken of transmission constraints and losses. In the longer run, generation and transmission investment would be planned to give the optimal mix and capacity to meet prospective demand with reasonable security of supply. At least that is the theory.

But this scheme would allow no room for competition, and its associated incentives, in generation. A variation on the policy of vertically integrated monopoly is to maintain integration of the main generation/transmission company but to liberalize generation, at least partially. One form of liberalization is to require the integrated company to seek competitive bids from independent generators when expanding generation capacity, and to allow it to build its own capacity only if that is lower cost than the rival bids.[12] If the integrated firm favored own-generation uneconomically, it could be penalized, for example, by not being allowed to recover the extra cost in prices to consumers.

Another form of liberalization, which goes further by allowing independents access to distribution companies or even to customers, and hence combines liberalization of generation with some liberalization of wholesale or retail supply, is to permit third party access to the integrated firm's transmission network. As in other industries, access terms are crucial to the effectiveness of competition.

---

11. Offer (1992a, 6–7, and 1993c, 6–8).
12. The 1978 Public Utility Regulatory Policy Act (PURPA) in the United States requires electric utilities to buy power at prices reflecting avoided cost from independent suppliers with cogeneration equipment and some small suppliers using renewable energy sources. Some states have required utilities to use bidding systems for this purpose. See Joskow (1989).

Finally, and most radical, is the option of vertical separation between generation and transmission. This allows horizontal breakup, as well as liberalization, in generation, and is potentially the most competitive policy, though much depends on practical implementation. But electricity supply technology does not permit links between generation and transmission simply to be severed, because of the need for intimate operational coordination. There are also economic pressures for vertical linkages, by contract if not by co-ownership, but these could undermine a policy of vertical separation.

Various forms of competition between generators are conceivable with vertical separation. One possibility is contract competition—generators competing to supply the transmission grid under long-term contracts. This might offer generators and the grid reasonable insurance against risks, but it would tend to be unwieldy and inefficient ex post because events might well unfold in such a way that the generators contracted to supply at particular times were not the most efficient (though tradability of contracts might ease this problem). Quite apart from the usual complexities of contract specification and enforcement, the grid operator would have to be given considerable authority over generators to deal with short-run contingencies.

At the other extreme is the possibility of a spot market in electricity, and price competition half-hour by half-hour, say. This diminishes some of the problems of long-term contract competition, though the grid operator obviously still needs short-run authority, but has poor risk properties, especially since the economic characteristics of electricity make spot price volatility inevitable. However, a spot market can be combined with longer-term contracts for hedging these risks. This is essentially what the new system in England and Wales involves (see section 9.3.2). There are a number of commodities that are traded on spot markets and for which there are also markets for standardized longer-term contracts such as forward, futures, and option contracts. In principle the same could happen for wholesale electricity, and a few "electricity forward agreements" have been traded.

Vertical integration between transmission and distribution is common but not technologically or economically necessary. There is little reason to expect geographical economies of scope between distribution activities in different regions. Yardstick considerations make the option of regional separation attractive, and it also makes possible retail supply competition between regional companies. Simple vertical integration between transmission and distribution is incompatible with regional separation, however, because transmission is naturally monopolistic over large areas that contain several regions. But an alternative is joint ownership of the grid by regional distribution companies, and this is indeed the new system in Britain.

Simplest of all, perhaps, is the option of complete separation between transmission and distribution. (If the grid was in public ownership in an otherwise privatized regime, then vertical separation would be entailed by policy on ownership in any case.) Another major issue concerning the vertical structure of the regional distribution companies is whether, and if so to what extent, they are allowed to generate power for themselves. Options range from laissez-faire to a partial or total ban, with compulsory competitive tendering and/or regulatory audit of economic purchasing as additional alternatives.

Finally, on structural policy, the central question concerning retail supply is how far to liberalize. Should the distributors be granted monopoly rights to supply at least the smaller customers in their region, should there be limits on supply competition from generators or interregional competition, or is laissez-faire appropriate?

Turning to conduct regulation, the first question is about the scope of price control. Regulation of transmission, distribution, and supply to captive retail customers is necessary because of natural and de facto monopoly. But it is less clear whether generation and supply to larger customers are in need of regulation—much depends on whether liberalization and restructuring policies create conditions for effective competition. This question will be examined in section 9.4.1 in the light of British experience.

Second, there is the question of cost passthrough. This is difficult in electricity supply because the generation component of cost, which accounts for well over half of the total, tends to be volatile, at least if bulk power is traded in a spot market. Thus the trade-off between minimizing the risks faced by regulated supply companies (which they may seek to hedge themselves by entering longer-term relationships with generators) and maximizing their incentives to purchase power economically is particularly awkward. However, regulatory audit and/or competitive tendering requirements may ease the latter problem somewhat, and elements of yardstick competition can be introduced if regulated retail supply has a regional structure.

Third, there are several important aspects of pricing structure. The importance for efficiency of spatial price differences in transmission has already been mentioned. To the extent that metering permits, time-of-day or year pricing is highly desirable because by shifting some peak demand, it saves on high capital costs (see the discussion of peak-load pricing in chapter 3). The issue is whether price regulation will be of a form that creates good incentives with respect to pricing structure. Since electricity has a natural unit of measurement (kilowatt hours), average revenue regulation is relatively straightforward to apply. But marginal costs differ greatly by time of day/year, and average revenue regulation might create excessive incentives (relative to Ramsey pricing) to reduce peak demands. There is also the danger that regulation applied to an average or index of prices that includes partly competitive as well as monopoly services—for example, supply charges to both large and small customers—may distort competition (see section 4.3.3).

These are just a few of the monopoly regulation questions that arise in electricity supply. Nearly all the general issues discussed in more detail in chapter 6 on RPI − X regulation are relevant as well. In addition, of course, *environmental* regulation is important. Discussion of policy options in this regard—which include pollution standards, taxes, permits, and quotas—is deferred until section 9.4.4.

9.3 Framework of Competition, Regulation, and Contracts at Privatization

9.3.1 Background to Privatization

The history of the ESI in Britain prior to the 1980s is summarized in Vickers and Yarrow (1988, 282–85).[13] Before nationalization in 1947 there were several hundred local electricity suppliers, consisting of municipal undertakings and regulated private firms. As well as making the whole industry state owned, nationalization brought a very centralized structure, with a Central Electricity Authority being responsible for the generation and supply of bulk electricity and having control over fourteen regional Area Boards.

Subsequent reorganization in Scotland led to a system with two independent vertically integrated companies—the South of Scotland Electricity Board (SSEB) and the North of Scotland Hydro-Electric Board (NSHEB). Following some of the recommendations of the Herbert Com-

---

13. See further Green and Newbery's (1993a) analysis of the ESI under nationalization and privatization.

mittee, the 1957 Electricity Act gave more autonomy to the twelve Area Boards in England and Wales, and set up the Central Electricity Generating Board (CEGB) for generation and transmission. An Electricity Council was established as a policy forum for the industry, in place of the CEA, but no independent regulatory body was set up, and ministerial control continued. In sum, generation and transmission were vertically separated from distribution and supply, albeit within a coordinated overall structure. The CEGB supplied bulk power to the Area Boards on terms set out in the Bulk Supply Tariff (BST), an administrative pricing structure.

The industry was influenced by general policy toward nationalized industries in the 1960s and 1970s (see Vickers and Yarrow 1988, ch. 5). Marginal cost pricing principles were adopted (but see Slater and Yarrow's 1983 criticisms of their implementation when plant mix was suboptimal), and there were implicit subsidies to the protected British coal industry. As emphasis shifted to tighter financial limits in the late 1970s and 1980s, the industry had to generate large cash flows for the exchequer, and significant price increases happened shortly before privatization.

The Monopolies and Mergers Commission conducted efficiency audits of the industry (see MMC 1981). In addition to the implicit coal subsidy just mentioned, the MMC reported that the main problems related to investment, especially plant construction times and costs and investment appraisal, and that technical operating efficiency appeared to be reasonably good.

An important measure of regulatory reform before privatization was the 1983 Energy Act.[14] This removed the legal monopoly over generation previously enjoyed by the CEGB. Third-party access to transmission and distribution was opened up (but on vague terms), and the Area Boards were required to publish tariffs, reflecting their avoidable costs, at which they would buy from private generators. In the event, no significant competition came about, and the episode provides an object lesson of how liberalization per se does not necessarily create conditions for effective competition. First, there was no effective regulation of grid access terms (the parallel with gas is apt). Second, the CEGB changed the structure of the BST by increasing the fixed charges payable by Area Boards and reducing the cost per unit of bulk power supplied. Since the avoidable

---

14. Obviously the 1984–85 coal miners' strike in which the government defeated the National Union of Mineworkers was of great importance for the industry; see Vickers and Yarrow (1988, sec. 9.5).

costs of Area Boards depend on the latter element, the purchase prices offered to private suppliers had to come down correspondingly. This simple entry deterring move went unchecked. In short, there was inadequate regulation for competition. At the time of the 1987 election, policies to liberalize the market were limited in scope and had little practical effect.[15]

9.3.2 Restructuring, the Pool and Regulation[16]

The Conservative manifesto at the election affirmed the intention of privatizing the ESI, and in February 1988 the basic proposals for structural reform were announced in a White Paper *Privatising Electricity* (Department of Energy 1988). Major questions had to be settled in the following year or two, including the following:

1. How would generation and transmission coordinate their activities when vertically separated?

2. How would the parts of the industry be regulated?

3. What contracts (e.g., with British Coal) would be set up?

4. Would competition (e.g., in retail supply) be restricted or totally free?

We discuss structural policy and these questions in turn below, but first a brief overview of the institutional framework is called for.

Institutional Framework   The institutional structure for regulation in the ESI is broadly similar to that for other utility privatizations. The 1989 Electricity Act enabled privatization to take place and established the post of Director General of Electricity Supply and the Office of Electricity Regulation (Offer). The first DGES is Professor Stephen Littlechild, who played a central role in devising the RPI − X form of price control for BT. Regulatory powers are divided between the Director General, the Secretary of State,[17] and the MMC as in the other regulated utilities.

The Act gives the Secretary of State and the DGES general duties to see that all reasonable demands are met, to ensure that licensees can finance their authorized activities, and to promote competition in generation and supply. They have further duties to protect consumer interests, to promote

15. See Vickers and Yarrow (1988, 294).
16. For more details, see James Capel (1990) and CRI (1992a).
17. Initially the Secretary of State for Energy. Now, following absorption of the Department of Energy into the Department for Trade and Industry, the President of the Board of Trade.

efficiency and R&D, to ensure safety of operations, and to take account of environmental considerations. The details of regulation, described below, are contained in licenses granted under the Act, which are issued by the DGES under the authority of the Secretary of State. There are separate licenses for generation, nuclear generation, transmission, public electricity supply (including distribution and retail supply), and "second-tier supply" (i.e., competition in supply against regional companies).

Industry Structure The old and new structures of the industry in England and Wales are depicted in figure 9.2. The central element of restructuring was the division of the CEGB into four parts. A new National Grid Company (NGC) took over the transmission activities of the CEGB, and its generation activities were divided between three successor companies: National Power, PowerGen, and Nuclear Electric.

The initial plan was to privatize *all* CEGB's power stations, including nuclear stations, which were to belong to National Power. In this plan National Power would have had about two-thirds of the former CEGB's generating capacity, the remainder being PowerGen's. A major reason for this (otherwise very odd) asymmetric duopoly structure was to facilitate privatization of the nuclear stations by packaging them with a large amount of nonnuclear capacity. Nuclear power is unattractive to private investors because of enormous future costs of decommissioning and toxic waste disposal, liability risk, and significant regulatory risk regarding future environmental policy. Future cost liabilities are funded in the new regime by a requirement that the regional electricity suppliers must buy specified proportions of their power from nonfossil sources, which are virtually all nuclear. A fossil fuel levy, which is effectively a tax on electricity purchases that is paid to Nuclear Electric, funds this "nonfossil fuel obligation". (In addition VAT was put on electricity and other fuels in the 1993 budget.)

However, even when bundled with National Power's other generating plant (itself more than half of CEGB capacity), nuclear plant proved unsellable, as had been widely foreseen, and the government had to abandon its plan to privatize the industry in its entirety.[18] First, the aging Magnox stations were withdrawn, and in November 1989 all nuclear plant was withdrawn from privatization. A central plank in the rationale for the

---

18. This and other policy-making problems in the 1988–90 period are discussed in Vickers and Yarrow (1991b).

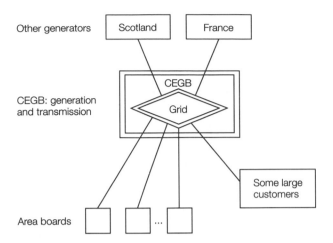

a. Old structure of the industry in England and Wales

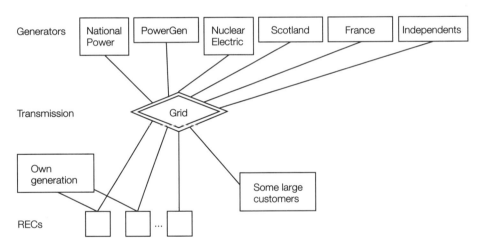

b. New structure of the industry in England and Wales

Figure 9.2   The old and new industry structures

National Power/Powergen duopoly of nonnuclear generation having collapsed, an opportunity existed for a more procompetitive industry structure. But this opportunity was not taken. Twenty months had elapsed since the privatization White Paper, and major aspects of coordination, contracts, and regulation were not settled. Further restructuring would also have lost managerial goodwill. Given the need to have the new structure in operation well before privatization, there was a danger of the sale not being possible before the next election, which might have been called (but was not) in 1991. Moreover the Electricity Act had already passed into law and additional legislation would have been needed. The government resisted calls for a more competitive structure, and stuck to the policy of privatizing National Power and PowerGen otherwise intact, with nuclear stations remaining with state-owned Nuclear Electric.

The transmission grid, having been vertically separated from generation, became vertically integrated with distribution. The twelve Regional Electricity Companies (RECs), the successors to the Area Boards, jointly own NGC. Structural reform therefore *moved*, rather than removed, vertical integration. The integration (via joint ownership) of transmission and distribution appears odd, especially in view of their history of separation. Again salability is a factor in explaining the decision—private investors are more likely to be willing to buy the grid if it is bundled with other assets. Some possible economic consequences of this measure of integration will be discussed below.

The Pool   The need for very close coordination between generation and transmission has already been stressed. Without integration, elaborate methods for coordination are required. It is evident that structural reform was announced in 1988 without detailed thought having been given to these issues. Ironically the danger arose that coordination via contracts would end up approximating the integrated structure that had been rejected. Eventually, however, the following system was devised.

A wholesale power pool, which is virtually a spot market for bulk power, was created. Generators are paid the *pool purchase price* (PPP) for electricity supplied into the pool, and RECs, retail suppliers and large users pay the *pool selling price* (PSP) for electricity taken from it. There is potentially a different pool purchase price for every half hour, and hence more than 17,500 annually (similarly for the pool selling price). The pool is operated by NGC.

Each morning, generators must submit bids specifying for each generating set its availability and the price at which power is offered for the following day. In effect, then, multiple-plant generators bid stepped supply *functions* into the pool (Green and Newbery 1992). The pool operator, NGC, ranks generating units by offer price and constructs a "merit order". (If bid prices reflected marginal costs and adjustment was made for transmission losses, this would be the efficient merit order.) Combining this with estimates of demand, the grid operator derives an estimated market-clearing price for each half-hour of the following day. This is called the *system marginal price* (SMP). If bids reflected marginal costs, SMP would be the operating cost per unit of the marginal plant in the merit order.

In addition to SMP, the pool purchase price includes a capacity payment. When the grid operator calculates SMPs a day ahead, there remains considerable uncertainty about both supply and demand. There is a risk that sudden outages of plant or surges in demand will cause an excess of demand over capacity and power failure as a result. An estimate is made of this *loss of load probability* (LOLP) for each half hour. The estimated cost to consumers of a loss of power is called the *value of lost load* (VOLL). This was set at £2 per kWh initially and is indexed. Incentives for generators to build capacity are strongly influenced by the capacity payments that they expect to receive in the future. If (declared) capacity is large in relation to demand, then LOLP will be small; on the other hand, if capacity margins are tight, LOLP could significantly increase prices. Thus the mechanism introduces an equilibrating tendency. But it is important to realize how sensitive investment incentives are to the level of VOLL, which is set by regulation not by market forces.

In sum, the price paid to generators who are called upon to supply electricity in a given half-hour is

PPP = SMP + LOLP(VOLL − SMP).

The second term in this expression is the capacity payment. A capacity payment, which depends on their bids, is also made to generators with declared available capacity that do not get called upon to generate.

The pool selling price exceeds the pool purchase price by an amount known as *uplift*:

PSP = PPP + uplift.

Uplift has several components. It includes the costs of, and hence creates incentives for, the provision of reserve and reactive power to stabilize the system. It also takes account of constraints in the system. Bottlenecks in the transmission system and dynamic constraints caused by the costs and lags of starting up generating stations mean that the (unconstrained) merit order used in the SMP calculation might not be feasible given these constraints. In particular some plants may become "constrained on"—they are run even though they bid more than SMP—and others may be "constrained off." For example, a plant on the side of a transmission bottleneck where there is excess demand has a good chance of being constrained on provided that its bid is not too much higher than SMP. This is an example of how transmission constraints can limit competition between generators. The behavior of pool prices over time is discussed in section 9.4.1.

Regulation Forms of RPI $-$ X price control apply separately to transmission, distribution, and REC supply charges. (Pool prices are unregulated except that the "value of lost load" part of the capacity payment is set administratively.) In all three cases there is a form of average revenue regulation—the cap applies to the average charge per kWh. Since neither this nor the inflation rate can be predicted with perfect accuracy for the period ahead, there are correction factors to adjust for forecasting mistakes ex post.

The X for transmission charges was initially set at zero. The cap applies to average revenue from "use of system" and "existing connection" charges, where average revenue is defined as total revenue divided by the average maximum annual demand over recent years adjusted for an "average cold spell." Use of system charges consist of (1) a system service charge and (2) infrastructure charges that vary by region. Charges for new connections to the grid are subject to rate-of-return regulation, as are charges for use of the French and Scottish interconnectors.

The controls on the distribution charges of the twelve RECs vary from RPI + 0 to RPI + 2.5 (as shown in table 9.1). As in the water industry, the financing of investment expenditure is a reason for allowing charges to increase relative to inflation. No yardstick element was incorporated into price controls for distribution, despite the regionalized structure of the industry (but yardstick information may be valuable at review times). The same is true of price controls for retail supply by the RECs—yardstick regulation (e.g., applied to power purchases) could have made supply margins very volatile.

Customers whose maximum demand is no more than 10 MW constitute the "right to tariff" market. They have the right to be supplied at published tariff rates. Larger customers negotiate contract terms. The supply price control for each REC has applied to its average supply revenue from

Table 9.1 RPI + X controls on distribution charges

REC	X
Eastern	0.25
East Midlands	1.25
London	0.00
Manweb	2.50
Midlands	1.15
Northern	1.55
Norweb	1.40
South Eastern	0.75
Southern	0.65
South Wales	2.50
South Western	2.25
Yorkshire	1.30

all its customers, whatever their size or location (but see below on the 1993 supply price review). It takes the form RPI $- X + Y$. The X term was set equal to zero for all RECs. The *cost passthrough* element Y is given by

$$Y = T + U + E + F$$

plus pool administration charges, where T and U relate to transmission and distribution charges, which are separately regulated, E relates to electricity purchase costs, and F relates to the fossil fuel levy. Together these items amount to about 95% of supply costs. In the year to 31 March 1992 the split was transmission 3.9%, distribution 23.8%, generation 58.3%, and fossil fuel levy 9.3% (Offer 1992a, 11). Thus the supply price control applies to the remaining 5% of costs. Passthrough of electricity purchase costs is subject to an economic purchasing obligation (condition 5) in the RECs' licences. Recall that the fossil fuel levy is a tax on electricity sales to compensate RECs for the obligation placed on them to buy quantities of power generated by nonfossil fuels. In effect it is a tax to subsidize unavoidable costs (of decommissioning, etc.) associated with nuclear power.

In addition to this RPI $- X + Y$ control, a subsidiary cap of RPI $+ F$ was put on supply charges to "franchise customers" (i.e., those with a maximum demand below 1 MW) for the period to 31 March 1993. Given the potential volatility of fuel prices, this might appear to impose considerable risk on the RECs, but this is not really the case. First, there is an escape clause in the event that unforeseen changes in circumstance cause losses. Second, the (mostly three-year) contracts given to the RECs at the time of vesting to a large extent determined their electricity purchase costs for the period in question.

The initial price controls for transmission, supply and distribution were set for three, four, and five years, respectively, from 31 March 1990, with a corresponding sequence of regulatory reviews, beginning with the 1992 transmission pricing review of NGC's price control for the period after 1 April 1993.

Contracts   The initial "vesting contracts" had two main purposes—to reduce risk and to provide interim protection for the British coal and nuclear industries. Risk sharing is an important motivation for vertical relationships between generators and retail suppliers of electricity. In the new regime the former sell into a potentially volatile spot market, and the latter buy from it. If generators and suppliers, respectively, have contracts with their fuel suppliers and customers that fix price terms, both are exposed to large risks from pool price volatility. Since high pool prices are good for generators but bad for retail suppliers, with the opposite being true of low pool prices, there is large scope for mutually beneficial risk sharing.

However, electricity cannot be traded directly between buyer and seller —each must trade with the general pool. Contractual arrangements must therefore be purely *financial*. For example, a contract might specify that a generator will pay a REC a sum proportional to the difference between the actual spot price and some agreed benchmark price for each half-hour of the year. If, for example, the benchmark price was £20 per MWh and if the contract notionally related to 1,000 MW of volume, then for a half-hour in which the actual spot price was £30 per MWh, the generator would pay £5,000 to the REC.

Such "contracts for differences" may be two-way, in which case the REC pays the generator if the spot price is below the benchmark price, or one-way, in which case no payments are made in that event. Two-way contracts for differences are like forward contracts. Financially it is as if the REC had agreed to buy a flow of 1,000 MW for the whole year at a fixed price of £20 per MWh. One-way contracts for difference are like options. The REC is protected against upward pool price movements but enjoys the benefit of downward movements. Since a power station is rather like an option contract in financial terms—it earns the difference between the spot price and marginal operating cost if it runs and zero otherwise—one-way contracts for differences may offer a good way of hedging for generators, especially if the benchmark price accords with their marginal costs. The lump-sum fee paid by the REC for such a contract would go toward the capital cost of the power station. Although these simple examples convey the basic principles of contracts for differences, in practice they are much more complex and sophisticated.

As with financial and commodity contracts generally, trade in electricity contracts could take a variety of forms ranging from bilateral negotiation between the parties to a transparent market with independent traders. In fact the initial contractual structure was determined by government. These "vesting contracts," together with associated restrictions on competition (see below) were designed in a way that protected British Coal. National Power and PowerGen contracted to buy 65–70 million tonnes annually from British Coal at prices considerably in excess of expected international coal prices for the period 31 March 1990 to 31 March 1993. An RPI − 5 formula applied to these coal prices, and they were also linked to the £/$ exchange rate. It has been estimated that the implicit subsidy to British Coal was close to £1 billion in 1990–91 and about half that amount in 1992–93.[19]

Corresponding contracts were established between the generators (National Power and PowerGen) and the RECs, and these were assigned to supplying the RECs' captive customers. The RECs had some other contracts with the generators that they could (and did) terminate after a year. In addition, as described above, the RECs have to buy given quantities of nonfossil (in effect nuclear) generated electricity, the extra cost of which is financed by the fossil fuel levy. This tax was set at about 11% of the final electricity price (reduced to 10% in 1992), and the proceeds, which mostly go to Nuclear Electric, have considerably exceeded £1 billion annually. In sum, the establishment of the spot market for bulk power was accompanied by a comprehensive set of medium-term vertical contracts which, among other things, entailed a large measure of protection (until 1993) for the British coal and nuclear industries.

Competition   The implicit subsidies in these arrangements, as well as the interests of participants in the industry, argued for limits on the extent of liberalization, at least for the duration of the contracts in question. The restrictions on own-generation by RECs have already been mentioned. In retail supply, transitional *franchise* monopolies were created. For the first four years of the new regime, the franchise covers consumers with peak demand less than 1 MW—they can be supplied only by their regional REC. Thus competition exists only for larger users, of whom there are

---

19. Offer's initial Review of Economic Purchasing, p. 9.

about 4,000 and who account for about 30% of the total market by volume. By early 1993 more than 40% of these users had chosen a supplier other than their REC. From April 1994 the franchise limit reduces to 100 kW, creating about 40,000 more noncaptive customers (around 50% of the market), and four years after that it is set to disappear altogether. Moreover, unless permitted by the DGES, National Power and PowerGen were not to have a combined market share in excess of 15% of sales in any REC's area until 1994, this limit to be relaxed to 25% for the following four years, and abolished from 1998.[20]

Privatization   Privatization of all but the nuclear electricity companies in England and Wales and in Scotland took place in the months following the establishment of the new industry structure. First, in December 1990 the twelve RECs in England and Wales, and hence the NGC which they jointly own, were sold, raising £8 billion for the exchequer. Second, in March 1991 the majority (60%) of the shares in National Power and PowerGen were sold, raising £2.2 billion. The other 40% remains state owned for the time being. Finally, Scottish Power and Scottish Hydro-Electric were privatized in June 1991 for £2.9 billion. In total therefore more than £13 billion was raised, making the ESI one of the largest two elements of the British privatization programme (the other being telecommunications).

9.4   Development of Competition and Regulation

The arguments that surrounded the restructuring and privatization of the ESI have not diminished since. Two issues have been especially controversial—the questionable effectiveness and efficiency of competition in electricity generation, and the emerging severe consequences for the British coal industry of incentives in the new system, which have led to a dramatic "dash for gas" (the RECs' part in this and their supply prices have been subject to review). In addition there has been a regulatory review of the structure and level of transmission pricing,[21] and developments in environmental regulation are of ever increasing importance for the industry. In this section we consider these four topics in turn.

---

20. In 1990, following requests from the generators, the DGES relaxed the direct sales limits in four regions. They have now been relaxed completely.
21. A review of price control for distribution will be concluded in the summer of 1994.

9.4.1 Competition in Generation

The unregulated asymmetric duopoly of nonnuclear generation enjoyed by National Power and PowerGen has been described above. On the face of it, such a concentrated industry structure appears likely to be seriously inefficient. Allocative inefficiency—large price-cost markups—could well result from the market power of the incumbent generators, and major distortions of productive efficiency—excessive entry, possible biases between fuel inputs, and so on—could follow. These inefficiencies might even be exacerbated by incentives in the regulatory system, for example, the ability of RECs to pass through their electricity purchase costs to customers. To assess the extent of these possible dangers, we will consider, first, some theoretical analysis of the generation oligopoly and, second, the empirical evidence on pool prices since privatization, which the regulator has repeatedly reviewed (Offer 1991, 1992b, 1993b).

Theoretical analysis of the concentrated generation oligopoly must take account of a number of important industry conditions:

1. capacity constraints,
2. the repeated nature of oligopolistic interaction with daily bidding,
3. entry of new competitors,
4. the existence of contracts with purchasers of electricity,
5. the threat of regulatory intervention.

The first two factors and the concentrated structure of the industry suggest that there may be large scope for the exercise of market power. This may or may not be checked adequately by the last three factors.

Consider the effect of capacity constraints. If they were absent, then under Bertrand price competition the pool price would be close to marginal cost. But with capacity constraints present, this is not the case. Calculation of equilibrium pricing by profit-seeking firms in capacity-constrained static oligopoly is a complex matter,[22] but it is simple to show that always bidding at marginal cost cannot be rational for participants in the British electricity spot market.[23] In 1990 the capacities of National

---

22. See Kreps and Scheinkman (1983). Equilibrium in pure strategies may fail to exist—an indeterminacy famously discussed by Edgeworth—in which case the analysis must consider mixed strategy equilibria. See von der Fehr and Harbord (1993) for an analysis of mixed strategy equilibria in a model of the British electricity supply industry.

23. Pool prices as a whole must cover not just marginal generation costs but also capacity costs, the costs of reserve power, and so on. The LOLP and uplift elements of the pool (selling) price relate to the latter.

Power, PowerGen, and Nuclear Electric were about 29.7 GW, 18.7 GW, and 8.8 GW, respectively (there have since been substantial plant disposals; see below). The cross-channel interconnector has a capacity of 2 GW, and the Scottish link has a capacity of 850 MW, though this is to increase to 1.6 GW by 1995. On a typical winter day demand peaks at about 48 GW with the night-time low around 28 GW (the amounts generated need to be somewhat larger to allow for losses.) In the summer the approximate range is 13–25 GW. Except in the summer therefore, even if PowerGen, Nuclear Electric and the interconnectors were producing at full capacity, National Power would be a residual monopolist with substantial market power. For a large part of the year it would certainly not find it optimal to bid at marginal cost: such bidding would be a strictly dominated strategy (not just nonequilibrium behavior). Note that this would rarely be the case in this simple static model if National Power's capacity had been divided between three companies and PowerGen's between two. Note also that the asymmetry between firm sizes exacerbates the problem.

This calculation is very simplistic, but it suffices to show that given the industrial structure chosen for generation at the time of privatization, the electricity pool could not be expected to operate for much of the time as a normal competitive market in which bids reflect marginal costs. This is a damaging criticism, not least because of the importance of marginal cost bidding for the efficiency of the system as a whole.

Green and Newbery (1992) have performed an analysis of the British electricity spot market using the approach of supply function equilibria (Klemperer and Meyer 1989). This approach seems natural because supply functions for the day ahead are effectively what the generators bid into the pool.[24] Calibrating the model to the circumstances of the industry, Green and Newbery find in their base case (demand elasticity of 0.25) that the symmetric duopoly equilibrium price is about 80% higher than the level implied by marginal cost bidding (£41 per MWh versus £23 per MWh). (With a symmetric five-firm equilibrium, on the other hand, the equilibrium price is much closer to marginal cost at about £27 per MWh.) Very large profits and welfare losses result.[25] Matters are yet worse in the

---

24. In addition to submitting price bids, generators make capacity declarations. Nondeclaration of capacity increases the capacity element in pool prices insofar as it increases the probability of lost load. Nondeclaration is formally equivalent to making an infinite price bid in respect of the capacity in question.
25. As noted above, transmission bottlenecks may further enhance the market power of some generating stations.

asymmetric case because the larger firm stands to gain relatively more from keeping price high and so submits a steeper price schedule. As a result there is productive inefficiency—industry costs are not minimized because the merit order is distorted—as well as allocative inefficiency.

Large profits attract entry, and Green and Newbery go on to consider the impact on prices of costs. In their base case, 8 GW of independent CCGT capacity is the equilibrium extent of entry in the simulation for 1994. Entry on this scale brings prices down substantially, but at great cost in terms of excess capacity. (By contrast, there is no entry in the simulation for the symmetric five-firm case.)

These calculations must be put in perspective. They are estimates of how firms in the industry would behave at static supply function equilibrium in the absence of contracts and if there were no threat of regulatory intervention. Variation of these assumptions would of course lead to different quantitative estimates, but the central points are robust: spot market competition per se will not lead to prices that are close to marginal cost, given the structure of the industry, and large inefficiencies—productive as well as allocative—may follow.[26]

Extending the analysis to incorporate dynamic interaction between generation opens the possibility of tacit collusion (which has played no part in the strictly noncooperative static analysis market power above). This is not the place for discussion of tacit collusion in dynamic games (see Tirole 1988, ch. 6), but the conditions could hardly be more favorable than with daily repeated bidding, inelastic demand, and capacity constraints.[27]

In fact, however, as we will describe below, pool prices have not been as high as these simple oligopoly models suggest. In large part that is because they do not take account of *contracts* between generators and RECs. To see how contracts affect the pricing incentives of a firm with market power, consider the situation of a pure monopolist with unit cost c facing inverse demand $P(Q)$ who has sold forward quantity X.[28] The first-order condi_____

26. Von der Fehr and Harbord (1993) question the applicability of Green and Newbery's supply function method on the grounds that the generators bid discrete step functions into the pool rather than smooth supply functions. They examine mixed strategy equilibria in a multiple-unit auction model of the industry and show that the same general conclusion holds—namely that pricing significantly above marginal cost is to be expected.

27. For an analysis of dynamic oligopoly with capacity constraints, see Brock and Scheinkman (1985).

28. See Anderson (1990) for a general survey, Allaz and Vila (1993) for a multi-period Cournot model with strategic behavior, and Powell (1993) for analysis related to the circumstances of the British electricity market.

tion for profit maximization implies a price-cost markup $(P - c)/P$ equal to $(1 - s)/\eta$, where η is the elasticity of demand and $s \equiv X/Q$ is the proportion of equilibrium output sold under contract. The monopolist's price and profit are strictly decreasing in X: selling more output forward under contract reduces residual monopoly power. A qualitatively similar effect holds when there is duopoly, in which case strategic behavior might also arise.

Given the choice, firms with market power may therefore limit their forward sales by contract so as not to undermine that market power. They may nevertheless choose to make some such sales in order to reduce their exposure to spot price volatility and/or if contract premia are sufficiently high. However, the generators were privatized with much of their output for the next few years effectively sold forward via contracts. In the period of given contracts immediately following privatization, one would expect contracts significantly to curb incentives to exercise market power. But as the vesting contracts expire, this may cease to be so. Helm and Powell (1992) associate the increase in pool prices in 1991–92 with the expiry of a portion of the vesting contracts, and sharp price rises also occurred after contracts expired on 31 March 1993 (see below). Incentives to enter new contracts henceforth are complex. Contract terms—for example, the size of the implicit insurance premium against spot price volatility—may be influenced by the possible effects of contracts on spot market interaction and on incentives for new entry as well as by risk-sharing considerations.

Whereas the threat of entry may not have much direct effect on spot market competition, it is likely to have a much stronger effect on competition for contracts, especially longer-term contracts, and hence indirectly on spot market competition in the future. Indeed, in principle, RECs have the alternative of signing long-term contracts with independent power producers (IPPs), subject to the availability of fuel inputs, sites, and grid connections. However, as in the Green-Newbery model, such entry may be excessive and inefficient from the social point of view.

The other important constraint upon the exercise of market power by the generators is the threat of regulatory intervention. Prices as high as those in the simulations by Green and Newbery, for example, would make the introduction of regulation very likely. This suggests that a form of limit pricing may be practiced, with the aim of deterring entry by the

regulator.[29] Regulatory intervention is not just a theoretical possibility:
the DGES accepted a recommendation by the House of Commons Select
Committee on Energy in 1992 that he should decide by 1995 whether to
refer the large generators (or the structure of the generation market) to the
MMC, and following Offer's 1993 review of pool prices he announced that
he would make the decision sooner rather than later (see below).

Although this discussion has abstracted from many aspects of competition in generation (including the provision of reserve and other ancillary
services), it has shown the importance of a number of interacting forces.
These can be summarized under the five headings mentioned at the beginning of this section:

1. The industry structure is one of concentrated, asymmetric, capacity-
constrained oligopoly. Demand is rather inelastic. In such a setting, short-
run spot market competition by itself will not produce prices that reflect
marginal costs. Reasonable estimates suggest markups of around 80%
over marginal cost if competition took that basic form. The asymmetry
between firms is likely to cause productive inefficiency too.

2. The repeated nature of interaction between firms, which bid daily into
the pool, is favorable to tacit collusion, which would create even higher
markups.

3. However, in the longer term such behavior would be likely to attract a
great deal of entry, leading to inefficient excess capacity. Thus one market
failure (unchecked market power) could lead to another.

4. But short-run spot market competition is heavily influenced by the
existence of contracts, which blunt the incentive to exercise power in the
spot market. The generators were privatized with contracts in place for the
initial years of the new system. As these expire, their incentives in the spot
market may alter. The terms on which the generators are willing to enter
new contracts may be influenced by this, and also by the threat of entry by
IPPs into the long-term contract market. Again, entry might not be socially efficient.

5. Finally, there is the threat of regulatory intervention, which might introduce an element of "limit pricing" into the calculations of generators.

---

29. Glazer and McMillan (1992) analyze limit pricing by a monopolist to forestall the imposition of regulation. If the regulator were thought to be more influenced by market shares
than by price levels in judging the adequacy of competition, then low pricing by the major
generators might not be a good way to deter regulatory intervention. Insofar as shares of
generating capacity were thought to be relevant, plant disposals by those generators might
be part of a strategy to satisfy the regulator that no intervention was needed.

Table 9.2 Behavior of average pool prices (p/kWh)

	1990–91	1991–92	1992–93	April–June 1993
SMP	1.74	1.95	2.26	2.61
Capacity payments	0.01	0.13	0.02	0.01
Uplift	0.09	0.16	0.14	0.27
PSP	1.84	2.24	2.42	2.89

Source: Offer (1993b, 8). Years are April to March.

Pool Price Evidence Table 9.2 summarizes movements in pool price components between April 1990 and June 1993. The pool selling price has steadily increased. Between 1990–91 and 1991–92 the 22% increase in PSP was caused partly by higher SMP and also by sharp rises in uplift and especially capacity payments. Capacity payments have since fallen back almost to zero following regulatory intervention (see below). From 1991–92 to 1992–93 SMP continued its upward trend, but the rate of increase of PSP moderated as uplift, as well as capacity payments, declined. But from April to June 1993 SMP and uplift again increased very sharply. The average PSP in that quarter was 62% higher than in the corresponding period three years before, an increase of 45% in real terms.

Offer first reviewed pool pricing late in 1991. In addition to questions about the general level and rate of increase of PSP and its components, there was concern about a large "spike" in pool prices (to 16 pence per kWh) for three half-hours on a sunny afternoon in September (subsequently exceeded by a 33-pence spike in December). Occasional pool price spikes reflecting tight capacity margins, and hence high LOLP, are to be expected, but not in September. In fact the spike then was due to high SMP caused by running expensive flexible plant to meet security standards.

The review found, perhaps not surprisingly in view of the discussion above, that the major generators were able to influence pool prices. One method of manipulation was to declare unavailable some plant that was later redeclared available. Since the LOLP calculation is based on declared capacity, this practice, which Offer concluded was an abuse of a dominant position, increased pool prices. Plant closures could also be used as a way of increasing pool prices via LOLP. To avoid manipulation of capacity availability, the DGES proposed the introduction of a license condition to prohibit monopolistic behavior in respect of capacity declarations and plant closures, including information provision and a system to give third parties rights to buy plant that the main generators want to close. There is now an independent assessor who monitors their plant closures with a view to preventing anticompetitive behavior.

The uplift element of prices, which includes the cost of transmission constraints, was also examined. The review found that generators might be manipulating some bids to profit from transmission constraints. For example, the grid will run some plant at National Power's Fawley site on the south coast even if its bid price significantly exceeds SMP. For most of 1991 that plant was bid in at a high price. A general report on "constrained-on" plant was issued by Offer the following year, and a general review was called for. In the meantime the generators agreed to submit cost-related bids for the plant in question.

Offer's pool price review of December 1992 revisited several of these issues. As to the general level of pool prices it concluded (p. 2) that

1. "National Power and PowerGen together have market power and exercised it in a significant way,"

2. "average avoidable costs of generation by National Power and PowerGen were greater than average Pool revenue," and hence that "it is difficult to object to an increase in bid prices over 1991/2 levels."

This combination of statements appears somewhat curious. Part of their reconciliation is that pool prices were artificially low in 1990–92 mainly because of the coal that the generators were contracted to take under the arrangements at vesting (pool prices were significantly below the prices projected by the government at the time of restructuring). The generators' income was protected, however, by their vesting contracts with RECs, and the DGES has since stated that pool revenues were about equal to avoidable costs if the coal premium recovered in those contracts is excluded from the calculation.

The existence of these contracts, most of which expired by March 1993, means that the initial years of the new system are not necessarily a reliable guide to the future. (In addition it should not be forgotten that the generators remained in public ownership for the first year.) Moreover a significant amount of new entrants' capacity is due to come on stream.

In the months after the contracts expired in March 1993, there were further sharp increases in pool prices. Following an investigation by Offer (1993b), the DGES announced that he would decide "sooner rather than later" whether to refer the generation sector to the MMC. Alternatives include the possible introduction of price controls and disposals of plant by the main generators. These have already been very significant. In the three years after March 1990, National Power disposed of more than 5 GW of plant, and PowerGen disposed of more than 1 GW. Their market shares of total output have declined correspondingly while those of independents and Nuclear Electric have risen. National Power and PowerGen have also made major labor force reductions (indicating that the nationalized CEGB was significantly overstaffed). The pool has reviewed its own workings and announced some reforms including demand-side bidding for large users (so that demand functions as well as supply functions can be bid into the pool) and system changes to reduce the probability of price spikes.

The future of competition in generation is uncertain. It depends upon complex interactions between the contract and spot markets, and may be heavily influenced by the actual and/or potential regulatory and competition policies. Given the industry structure chosen for privatization, the prospects appear somewhat bleak for an outcome that combines allocative efficiency—curbing the market power of the incumbent generators—and productive efficiency—efficient capacity levels, fuel mix, and merit order running. Both at the time and with the benefit of hindsight, the decision to create just a duopoly from the CEGB's nonnuclear generation assets, itself largely the result of the failed attempt to privatize nuclear power, appears to have been a large policy mistake.

9.4.2   Contracts and the Coal Crisis

One effect of the vesting contracts, and associated measures such as the supply franchises, was temporarily to suppress the operation of powerful market forces. As the expiration of these contracts approached, however, their strength began to show, and a rather different picture of the industry's future became apparent, including a sharply reduced position for British coal. This issue was brought to a head by British Coal's announcement in October 1992 that 31 of its 50 remaining deep mines would be closed, with the result that 30,000 mining jobs would be lost.[30] Political furor followed, and reviews of the proposed pit closures, and energy policy more generally, were carried out by the House of Commons Trade and Industry Committee and by the Department of Trade and Industry, which introduced a moratorium on closure of 21 of the threatened pits. At the

---

30. This would reduce the British coal industry's work force to 24,000. From 1910 to 1920 more than a million were employed, and there were more than half a million even in 1960. See Department of Trade and Industry (1993b, 24–25).

same time Offer was conducting a review of RECs' compliance with their license obligation to purchase power economically.

British Coal's announcement was based on the forecast that its sales to the ESI, its principal customer, would fall from 65 million tonnes in 1992–93 (the last year of the vesting contracts) to about 30 million tonnes per annum in the mid–1990s. The Select Committee Report (House of Commons 1993, 27–29) listed five reasons for the prospective contraction of British Coal's market:

1. coal imports,

2. other fuels, notably gas and nuclear,[31]

3. the new structure of the industry, including the nonnuclear generation duopoly and the (shrinking) supply franchises of the RECs,

4. environmental regulation,

5. currently high coal stocks.

Quite apart from considerations of social cost, the central economic question is whether such a decline in the market for British coal reflects true efficiency considerations, or whether market forces are distorted to the detriment of the industry.

On the question of British coal versus imported coal, the Select Committee concluded that British coal was more expensive (by about £5 per tonne) but that with productivity improvements it could be competitive at least for inland power stations within five years, given reasonable estimates of world coal prices and exchange rates. On the question of coal versus other fuels, there are several theoretically possible reasons why market forces might be distorted inefficiently against coal, including

1. subsidies to rival fuels, notably nuclear,

2. the private cost of coal to British Coal exceeding the social cost of its production,

3. larger markups, and less availability of contracts, for coal-produced electricity than for other fuels, perhaps associated with excessive entry by noncoal generators because of the industry structure in generation,

4. uneconomic purchasing of gas-produced electricity by RECs.

---

31. Heavy fuel oil and orimulsion are other sources of fossil fuel competition to coal. Hydro-electric power and other renewable energy sources are also of some importance. See Department of Trade and Industry (1993b, 47–48 and 54–55).

These possibilities will be discussed in turn below. Another possible source of distortion is that the discount rates used in investment appraisal by private electricity companies are higher than social discount rates because of regulatory risk. This could cause a bias, relative to social efficiency, toward less capital-intensive technologies. This point will be discussed in section 9.4.4 in relation to methods of pollution control, but it applies much more generally.

First, however, it is important to note that some major underlying forces had recently moved strongly against coal, especially relative to gas. A shift in market shares was to be expected on economic efficiency grounds—the issue is whether the decline in the market for coal, and in particular the dash for gas, were excessive. The forces operating against coal were the ending of the protection afforded by the 1990–93 contracts with the generators, the removal in 1991 of a European Community ban on using gas for electricity generation, the availability of gas, tighter environmental regulations,[32] and the much more efficient CCGT technology. There is consensus that gas is cheaper than coal for new power stations at current prices. But the relevant question is whether new gas stations produce electricity more cheaply than *existing* coal-fired stations, whose capital costs have been sunk.

Whether or not existing nuclear stations were economically justified investments in the first place, their capital costs have also been sunk costs, and future decommissioning costs cannot be avoided either. According to Nuclear Electric, although its average operating cost was 3.9 pence per kWh, the avoidable costs of existing Magnox and advanced gas-cooled reactor (AGR) power stations were in the range 1.2–1.5 pence per kWh in 1991–92, considerably below the cost of coal-fired electricity, but the Select Committee noted arguments that avoidable costs might be higher than this.[33] Early closure of the old Magnox reactors is a possibility, but it would involve high short-term reprocessing costs. The costs of the new pressurized water reactor (PWR) station at Sizewell B are mostly sunk, and it would now be inefficient to halt construction. In sum, subsidies to nuclear power go largely toward sunk capital costs and unavoidable

---

32. CCGT plant emits about half the CO_2 of coal-fired stations and little SO_2 (House of Commons 1993, 47). Coal-fired stations, on the other hand, need expensive FGD equipment to curb SO_2 emissions.

33. See Department of Trade and Industry (1993b, 49–53) and House of Commons (1993, 58–65).

decommissioning costs. Removing the subsidies would therefore do little to create a larger market for British coal.

Another source of nuclear competition comes from Electricité de France through the 2 GW cross-channel interconnector. The Select Committee argued for import restrictions unless reciprocal trading rights were granted, but these restrictions could be very costly to the U.K. economy and may well contravene EC law in any event.[34]

On unemployment the Select Committee concluded that "closure of the 31 pits would therefore have drastic consequences for jobs in particular areas of the country and much wider employment effects which would be offset only to a limited extent by new jobs in other energy industries."[35] As a result, and in addition to other distributional and social costs, it may be argued that the cost of coal production to the economy in terms of alternative output forgone may be lower than the private cost to British Coal. Such an argument must be treated with caution, for it can be made in relation to any part of the economy, but coal is notable for the localized intensity of job losses, which is likely to make the average duration of unemployment (and social costs generally) especially great.

National Power and PowerGen are the principal buyers of coal. The reasons why the concentrated industry structure in generation might lead to markups in their prices have been discussed above, where the evidence from Offer's pool price reviews was also summarized. The Select Committee expressed concern over this and the possible adverse implications for British Coal, and it recommended the introduction of some regulatory powers over the generators' pricing.[36]

However, perhaps the most controversial question of all concerned the dash for gas, in particular whether the RECs had complied with their license obligation to purchase power economically given the *prices* that they faced (whatever the underlying *costs*) when contracting for power from CCGT plant. In complying with the economic purchasing obligation, RECs can take account of "the future security, reliability and diversity" of sources of supply. There was concern that the ability of RECs to pass through to consumers their power purchase costs, including the prices paid to generators in which they themselves had equity stakes, may have provided little incentive for economic purchasing.

---

34. See House of Commons (1993, 70) and Department of Trade and Industry (1993b, 55–58).
35. House of Commons (1993, 86).
36. House of Commons (1993, 103).

The scale of the dash for gas has been remarkable. By late 1992 about 8.7 GW of CCGT plant was operational or under construction, compared with about 57 GW of total public capacity.[37] National Power and PowerGen have both made major investments in CCGT plant, and the RECs have interests in nine projects with a total capacity of 5.4 GW (Offer 1993a). The RECs' stakes come to 2.8 GW of this, which is about 35% of their own-generation limits.

The question of economic purchasing by RECs was the subject of a regulatory review by Offer in parallel with the Select Committee's deliberations. Offer's preliminary report, published in December 1992, said that the review had not so far suggested that RECs had breached the economic purchasing obligation in their supply licenses. The Select Committee noted criticisms of this preliminary report.[38] It concluded that prices for coal-produced electricity appeared to be in the middle of the range of prices in REC contracts for gas-produced electricity but that the comparison might be influenced by risk assessment.

In its final report Offer (1993a) reaffirmed its earlier preliminary finding that none of the RECs had violated its economic purchasing obligation, and that their stakes and contracts with IPPs were to facilitate competition in generation rather than to profit from cost passthrough to supply prices. The DGES also announced that the RECs' proposed coal-backed contracts with National Power and PowerGen for 1993–98 would not be considered a violation of the economic purchasing obligation (and would not count toward any yardstick element if one were introduced in the supply price review). Hence some protection financed by franchise customers can be given to British Coal for the period to 1998 when the franchise limits expire.[39]

The results of the supply price review for the RECs were announced by Offer in July 1993. From April 1994 the RPI − 0 cap will be tightened to RPI − 2, regulation will cease to apply to nonfranchise customers, and there are incentives to promote energy efficiency. No purchasing cost yardstick was introduced.

The conclusions of the government's review of energy policy were published in a White Paper in March (Department of Trade and Industry

---

37. See House of Commons (1993, 45).
38. See House of Commons (1993, 53–58).
39. See Helm (1993b), who argues that the DGES agreed to give cost passthrough to the coal contracts provided that the 1994 franchise reduction went ahead and that a further crisis for the remaining coal industry might happen in 1998.

1993b). The economic basis for the initial decision to close 31 pits was reaffirmed, as was a competitive market-based approach to energy policy, but political and regional difficulties with such a rapid closure program were recognized. A subsidy to enable British Coal to sell more to the generators was offered. As the Select Committee had recommended, this was linked to productivity and cost improvements which, it is hoped, will make British Coal internationally competitive in five years. The government stressed its intention to privatize British Coal as soon as possible, and British Coal will offer to the private sector any pits that it no longer wants to operate in the meantime. The government's review of the future of nuclear power was brought forward by a year, but no nuclear plant closures were accelerated. Increased regional aid was provided. The intention to set up an Energy Advisory Panel and to publish an annual Energy Report was announced.

The White Paper succeeded in winning parliamentary approval and a temporary stay of execution for about 12 pits, with some others being "mothballed" rather than closed, but it does little to increase the market for coal. The government has stressed that the prospects for coal in a competitive energy market, and with new environmental requirements, are limited. Subsequent statements by British Coal have indicated that closures are likely to continue.

The Coal Review did something in the short term for British coal, as distinct from coal in general, but despite the White Paper's remarks about stronger viability of British coal in the longer term, its main effect would seem to be slightly to ease a painful transition. The economic fundamentals do not favor coal in any event, but the market imperfections in the new electricity supply industry are not such as to inspire confidence that market signals are necessarily efficient.

9.4.3 Transmission Pricing

The spatial structure of electricity prices, which is largely shaped by the structure of transmission charges, is important for efficiency in several respects. In the short run it can influence the allocative efficiency of consumption decisions across the country, and in a purely price-based system it can have major effects upon merit order despatch and hence upon short-run productive efficiency. However, as was explained above, merit order despatch depends not only on the prices bid into the pool by generators but also on transmission constraints in the system—some plant may be "constrained on" because of these constraints, and other plant "constrained off." In the long run the spatial structure of prices has important effects on investment, and on generators' location decisions in particular. At present there is excess demand in the south and excess supply in the north. A primary objective of the system of transmission pricing should be to create incentives for efficient location decisions, and at the same there must be incentives for efficient capacity expansion by the National Grid Company.

The transmission charges established at the time of privatization had some zonal differentiation, but it was recognized from the outset that the charging structure did not provide adequate price signals to encourage an efficient pattern of investment. The transmission charges were subject to a review in 1992. As explained above, the transmission pricing structure distinguishes between connection charges for individual users and general use-of-system charges. Charges for new connections are regulated on a rate-of-return basis. A disputed question is whether these charges should obey the principle of "deep connection," according to which the cost implications of the connections elsewhere in the system, and not just their direct cost, should be reflected in charges. Economic efficiency requires that prices should indeed reflect overall costs.

Use-of-system charges, together with charges for existing connections, have been subject to RPI $-$ 0 price control applied to total revenues divided by a four-year average of maximum annual demand adjusted for an "average cold spell." Use-of-system charges consist of system service charges and infrastructure charges, which include some zonal differentiation. Suppliers (on the basis of their peak demands) and generators (on the basis of their capacity and output levels) pay about 75% and 25% of these charges, respectively.

In its 1992 review of the *level* of NGC's transmission charges, Offer increased X from zero to 3%. Thus from April 1993 NGC has faced RPI $-$ 3 price control on its average revenue. However, it is also important that the *structure* of transmission charges is regulated because there is little reason to expect that NGC's incentives are naturally in line with the public interest in this regard. Since NGC is jointly owned by the twelve RECs, there is a possible danger that it might distort its behavior in their favour, though there are measures to ensure arm's-length operation. But even assuming that NGC seeks to maximize its own profits, it is far from clear that it has good incentives for transmission pricing and investment.

In the north–south example of figure 9.1, for instance, it could be that incremental transmission costs would be higher for an additional power station at N than for one at S, while overall generation-plus-transmission costs favor N over S.[40] Then a profit-maximizing grid company subject to RPI $-$ X revenue regulation would want to discourage a new power station at N, despite its overall efficiency advantage, because the grid revenue implications are the same but grid costs are higher for new plant at N. Other regulatory mechanisms could also create problems. For example, an approach based on short-run marginal cost pricing would not encourage a profit-maximizing grid company to relieve transmission bottlenecks, which could be very profitable for it. More generally such a company would gain nothing from grid investment to promote the positive externality of more effective competition in generation.

Because of these and other problems, NGC is closely regulated. For example, it is required to facilitate competition in generation and supply and not to discriminate between users. The 1992 transmission pricing review by NGC was subject to close regulatory scrutiny. NGC (1992) proposed *investment cost related pricing* (ICRP) for use of system charges. In this approach use-of-system charges are based on the capital costs, together with associated operating and maintenance costs, of additional investment in grid capacity to meet peak transmission demands, and there is also a component to cover security and other network costs. The ICRP approach is based on NGC's own costs. It takes no account of the costs of transmission constraints or of losses in the system. Thus the ICRP approach does not incorporate the principles of optimal spatial pricing described in section 9.1.1. NGC rejected marginal cost-related approaches based on these principles as impractical and also rejected the principle of deep connection.

The ICRP method proposed by NGC was accepted by Offer.[41] Despite its failure to incorporate the principles of optimal spatial pricing, the method implies significantly wider zonal differentials. In the south (especially the southwest), charges to those taking power from the system are sharply increased, while charges paid by generators come down. In the north, charges move in the opposite direction, to the detriment of generators and the benefit of consumers. Thus stronger geographical incentives are given.

The overall assessment of these developments is mixed. The new charging structure is based on an approach that is not consistent with the

---

40. This example is discussed in Vickers and Yarrow (1991a, 217–18).

41. Following consultation on NGC's original proposals, some modifications were made concerning the treatment of spare capacity and the phasing of transition to the new system, but the basic principle of ICRP remained.

principles of economically efficient pricing, but it is generally a move toward a more efficient pricing structure, and some would argue that a faster
move would have been unacceptable on political or regional distributional grounds. It could also be argued that transmission charges are just
a part of the overall pattern of spatial price differentials, and that the pool
rules could be amended to take proper account of losses etc. More generally it is disappointing that the principles of economically efficient pricing
were not affirmed, at least as a medium-term objective. In the meantime
locational decisions will continue to suffer from distortions. From another
perspective, it is perhaps unsurprising that a privately owned semi-
independent grid company should focus on its own costs rather than those
of the electricity system as a whole. Even detailed regulation may be unable to overcome the misalignment of incentives (without creating other
distortions such as underinvestment because of regulatory risk). In the
light of these problems, it is not obvious that economic efficiency will have
been enhanced by the privatization of NGC.

9.4.4 Environmental Regulation

Although most of this chapter has been concerned with the control of
market power, it will have been evident that environmental regulation is
playing an increasingly important role in the electricity supply industry. In
particular, it is a key determinant of the economics of gas versus coal
(see section 9.4.2). Pollution from fossil fuel burning crosses international
boundaries—acid rain is a regional pollutant and the effects of carbon
emissions are global—and the United Kingdom is under international
obligations to reduce emissions. The Large Combustion Plants Directive
of the European Community requires SO_2 emissions from existing plant in
the United Kingdom to fall, relative to 1980 levels, by 20%, 40%, and 60%
by 1993, 1998, and 2003, respectively, and emissions of NO_x must fall by
30% by 1998. The United Kingdom is party to the United Nations Framework Convention on Climate Change, signed in 1992, which requires
emissions of greenhouse gases like CO_2 and methane to be reduced to
their 1990 levels by 2000. The European Commission is contemplating a
carbon tax.[42]

Demand side measures—energy efficiency schemes and taxes such as
the imposition of value added tax on domestic fuel and power announced

---

42. For further details, see Department of Trade and Industry (1993b, ch. 8) and House of
Commons (1993, 39–44).

in the 1993 budget—may go some way toward meeting these targets, but it is clear that the main contribution must come from less pollution per unit of electricity supplied. In the case of SO_2 emissions this can be done by a combination of (1) switching to fuels with lower sulphur content (coal with lower sulphur content, gas instead of coal, nonfossil instead of fossil fuel), and (2) capital investment (flue gas desulphurization (FGD) equipment, clean coal technology). Efficiency requires that a given level of pollution reduction be achieved at the lowest possible cost, or equivalently that the maximum reduction in pollution be achieved for a given level of abatement expenditure. It is important to ask whether regulation and incentives in the restructured ESI are likely to promote efficient pollution control.[43]

The broad methods of pollution control are *command and control*, where environmental regulators tell firms how to cut pollution, and incentive/market-based mechanisms, including taxes and charges, quotas, and tradable permits. The latter methods have the great advantage that the polluting firms themselves, which are likely to be considerably better informed than external regulators, have good incentives to find the most efficient combination of measures to achieve pollution reductions *provided* that they face appropriate price signals. In its environment White Paper (Department of Environment 1990) the government indicated its desire to move to more market-based approaches, but Helm (1991) argues that the system largely remains one of command and control.

Since privatization there has been a major shift from capital investment to fuel switching as the prime method of curbing SO_2 emissions. It had been planned to fit FGD equipment to 12 GW of coal-fired capacity, but this was reduced to 8 GW (to facilitate the sale of the generators according to Helm), and only 6 GW may be built in the event. Something like a quota system now operates, with National Power and PowerGen each having abatement targets. While this provides some incentives for intrafirm efficiency, the system is far from being market based.

Pollution charges or taxes would have superior efficiency incentives because they would lead to interfirm as well as intrafirm efficiency. Their quantitative effect is uncertain, however, and this is a disadvantage if the government's chief objective is to meet the quantitative reductions required by international obligations. The relative merits of price-based and quantitative methods are affected by uncertainty about the costs and benefits of pollution control more generally. Price-based methods are advan-

---

43. See Newbery (1990) for a detailed economic analysis of the acid rain problem. Newbery emphasizes the international nature of the problem, which we do not discuss here.

tageous if the marginal cost of abatement rises more steeply than the marginal benefit of abatement, but quantitative controls are superior in the opposite case (Weitzman 1974). Giving high priority to compliance with quantitative international obligations implies a steeply sloping marginal benefit of abatement for the government, and so the earlier point can be seen as an instance of this general principle.

Tradable pollution permits are a potentially attractive way of combining certainty of quantitative effect with incentives for both interfirm and intrafirm efficiency, but only if the permit market is competitive so that firms are price-takers there. Otherwise strategic behavior in the permit market can seriously distort incentives for efficiency (see Hahn 1984; Misiolek and Elder 1989; Newbery 1990). The nature of oligopolistic interaction in the final product market could be manipulated by behavior in the permit market, and it could also be a vehicle for strategic entry deterrence (an example of "input market predation" discussed in section 4.2.2). Unfortunately, the duopoly structure of coal-fired generation makes these dangers acute, because National Power and PowerGen would have great power in a market for SO_2 emission permits, for example. The standard efficiency argument for a market-based approach to pollution control does not apply in these circumstances.

Finally, the importance of the proviso that firms face appropriate price signals must be stressed. It is particularly significant in relation to the cost of capital because, as in the electricity supply industry generally, the choice of technique (e.g., whether to switch fuels or invest in FGD) is very sensitive to cost. Insofar as regulatory risk increases the private cost of capital, incentives in the privatized industry may be biased, relative to what is socially optimal, away from more capital-intensive techniques.

9.5   Assessment

The 1990 restructuring of the electricity supply industry in England and Wales is comparable to the 1984 breakup of AT&T in the United States in terms of the radicalism of regulatory reform. The economic characteristics of electricity supply create strong forces for vertical integration between generation and transmission. But instead of integrated organization there is now a quasi-spot market for bulk power, together with a comprehensive set of financial contracts between generators and suppliers (and some vertical integration between new "independent" generators and suppliers). There has been rapid entry into gas turbine generation, and the prospects for coal (especially British coal) have deteriorated sharply. Retail supply to large users has been liberalized, and a timetable has been set for full liberalization. As well as reform of monopoly regulation and competition policy for the industry, developments in environmental regulation are of growing importance.

Major criticisms of the CEGB in the old regime were that it had a bad record of controlling capital investment costs, that it built uneconomic nuclear power stations, and that it paid excessive prices for British coal. In terms of short-run operating efficiency, the CEGB's performance appears to have been reasonably good, except (as is now more apparent) for overstaffing. Can the new system, with the power pool at its center, achieve short-run operating efficiency despite the vertical separation of generation and transmission? Above all, are there efficient long-run investment incentives? On both counts, the new regime is open to question.

As for short-run efficiency, while the generators have good incentives to run plant efficiently and have reduced staff costs sharply, it is by no means clear that systemwide costs are minimized. The concentrated market structure in generation is not conducive to marginal cost bidding into the power pool by the main generators, with the consequence that merit order despatch could be distorted. Further distortions in merit order result from the way that losses are averaged instead of reflecting marginal costs, which can differ greatly across the system. In addition, without regulatory scrutiny, there could be strategic incentives for underdeclaration of available capacity in order to manipulate the "loss of load probability" element of the pool price. (Recall also that the related "value of lost load" element, which may become a key determinant of capacity investment incentives, is set by regulation and not by market forces.)

There are a number of potential investment incentive problems. First, the unregulated market power of the nonnuclear generation duopoly could attract inefficient entry. This could be exacerbated by the vertical integration and cost passthrough allowed to regional suppliers. It is a moot question whether the rapid building of gas plant is inefficient entry of this kind, or an efficient response to changing price signals (the regulator has not found evidence of uneconomic power purchasing by the regional suppliers). Second, factor prices—fuel costs and the cost of capital—might not accurately reflect true resource costs (i.e., the price signals might be wrong). Thus it is possible, for example, that the opportunity cost of British coal is lower than is reflected in the price of coal-produced electricity or that some regulatory risk premium is included in the rate of return used for private investment appraisal. If so, then the mix of generating plant and of environmental protection measures could be distorted. Third, the structure of grid pricing does not yet provide incentives for efficient location decisions. Fourth, it is unclear that there are good incentives for efficient investment in transmission capacity.

It is too soon to tell how important these potential problems will turn out to be. Restructuring and privatization occurred as recently as 1990–91, and since then the initial structure of vertical contractual arrangements determined by government has shaped market conduct to a considerable extent. Nevertheless, there are serious grounds for concern, which the experiences of the first few years of the new system do not dispel. The old problems of high coal prices and uneconomic nuclear power programmes may not recur, but the efficiency of short-run operation and of the mix, scale, and location of long-run investment may have been jeopardized.

Could these problems have been diminished, or are they an inevitable consequence of vertical separation? We share the view of many commentators that a far superior incentive structure would have been created by dividing the CEGB's nonnuclear generation capacity between several (e.g., five) successor companies rather than two. The government's initial desire to privatize the entire industry, including nuclear power (for which the economic case for privatization was highly questionable), is largely responsible for the duopoly structure. A less concentrated industry structure would have had the advantages of (1) stronger head-to-head competition, (2) a lower probability of regulatory intervention and so less regulatory risk, (3) reduced concern that entry might be inefficient, (4) less need to allow regional suppliers to integrate vertically into generation, and (5) providing a basis for more efficient environmental regulation. Structural remedies are not a panacea—much depends on accompanying conduct regulation—but the vertical separation of the British electricity supply industry would have had better prospects of success if accompanied by correspondingly radical horizontal separation. It can also be argued that vertical separation should have gone further and that the grid should be fully independent from the regional electricity companies (possibly still in public ownership).

In sum, the main aim of vertical separation is to create conditions for effective and undistorted competition in generation. The policy measures that accompanied vertical separation in the British electricity supply industry have not maximized the chances of achieving that aim.

Postscript

In February 1994 the Director General of Electricity Supply, having secured undertakings from National Power and PowerGen, decided not to refer them to the MMC. The first undertaking concerns industry structure: National Power and PowerGen have agreed to sell or dispose of 4,000 MW and 2,000 MW, respectively, of coal-fired or oil-fired generating plant. The second undertaking is a measure of conduct regulation: National Power and PowerGen have agreed to bid into the pool in such a way that for the next two years the average pool price does not exceed a cap, which has been calculated on the basis of their costs, that is about 7% lower than average price levels in 1993–94. A similar undertaking aplies to contract prices. Insufficient competition in generation has therefore led to the introduction of some price controls after all.

10

Of the four utility industries discussed in this book the water industry is the one where natural monopoly conditions are most prevalent. The scope for direct product market competition is limited and the main focus of this chapter is therefore on the regulation of conduct. The industry in Britain has a major investment program to meet statutory requirements for both drinking water quality and environmental quality, to make up for past underinvestment, and to meet demand growth. This means that water charges are scheduled to increase substantially in real terms, since technological improvement is very slow compared with that in, say, telecommunications.

The regulatory regime in the medium term inevitably focuses on the need to encourage necessary investment, but a number of other regulatory issues are also important. The existence of separate economic and environmental quality regulators means that there is a danger of inefficient outcomes, such as quality standards that do not properly reflect the cost trade-offs involved. The regional structure of the industry helps the economic regulator as yardstick competition can be used. It is in this industry that the regulator has been most worried about the potential for distortion caused by diversification. Finally, the fact that most domestic customers pay charges that are akin to lump-sum taxes, because their consumption is not measured, creates problems for pricing and also prompts the question of whether more metering is desirable.

In section 10.1 we discuss the economic characteristics of water supply and sewerage and the current structure of the industry in England and Wales. Section 10.2 describes the key questions about structure and conduct regulation. In section 10.3 we describe the background to privatization and the regulatory framework established then. Developments in regulation since privatization are discussed in section 10.4.

10.1   The Water Industry and Its Economic Characteristics

10.1.1   Economic Characteristics of Water Supply

Water is abstracted from underground sources and surface sources such as rivers and reservoirs, treated to remove natural and synthetic pollutants and distributed via a network of mains to the consumer. Used water is collected in sewers (known collectively as sewerage) and pumped to sewage treatment works. Sludge is removed and incinerated, dumped at sea, or used as fertilizer on farm land. Effluent, which is the liquid product of sewage treatment works, is treated before being discharged to rivers, estuaries, or the sea. Some raw sewage is not treated at all and is pumped directly into the sea. There are externalities at several stages of the water cycle. Rivers and lakes from which water is abstracted can be polluted by effluent from factories or sewage treatment works sited farther upstream. Underground water sources can be polluted by fertilizers or pesticides on agricultural land. These sources of pollution cause the costs of treating water to achieve acceptable quality to be higher than otherwise. The dumping of sewage sludge can cause harm to fish stocks and raw sewage that is pumped out to sea can lower the quality of nearby bathing beaches.

The demand for water is seasonal, reaching its peak in the summer when raw water availability is at its lowest level. Many customers in England and Wales, including about 95% of domestic households, have supplies which are not metered so their demand for water is not affected by the charges they pay (assuming income effects to be negligible). Charges for water and sewerage for these households are based on the ratable value of their properties (i.e., the assessed rental value of the property that was used as the charging base for local taxation until 1990) rather than on the amount of water consumed.[1] Those with meters are typically commercial and industrial customers and their demand for water is generally price inelastic. If a firm wants a bulk water supply of lower quality than that provided by the local company, say, for cooling a power station, then it can abstract untreated water directly from a river. The demand for sewerage services is complementary to the demand for water. Industrial plants produce different types of effluent, and treatment of this (known as trade effluent) is accordingly priced in relation to both strength and quantity. These customers have the option of partially treating effluent to reduce the costs of treatment by the sewerage firm.

Both the quality of the water and the standard of service that the supplier provides are important in determining demand. Drinking water quality has many dimensions. Consumers can easily judge whether water tastes or smells bad, and can see discoloration. But these observable aspects of quality might not be as important to consumers as those that

---

1. Most customers in new domestic properties are metered, although some companies charge them on a flat rate basis. Water companies are not allowed to use ratable values as a charging base after 31 March 2000.

affect health. Concentrations of metals, such as lead, and pesticides in drinking water cannot be checked by most households, and external regulation is necessary to ensure that the water is not harmful. Another aspect of quality is the level of service a firm provides. Customers want adequate water pressure, do not want to suffer flooding from sewers, and want leaks in the public system to be mended promptly.

On the cost side the industry is very capital intensive, and its fixed assets have very long lives. Many of the fixed assets have little or no alternative uses and so are largely sunk costs. Examples are reservoirs and the networks of water mains and sewers. Quality and environmental improvements typically require new processes and thus new capital equipment. Duplication of the fixed network of mains and sewers would generally be inefficient, although direct competition for some large customers might be desirable, especially if different qualities of water can be provided. Although general competition in water distribution is not desirable, there could be competition in the supply of water if there were a national grid (as in the cases of electricity and gas) or regional grids that could be used to distribute different firms' supplies, and sufficiently sophisticated metering technology.

The fact that water monopolies are local or regional means that there are some opportunities for indirect forms of competition. There can be competition between contiguous firms for the right to supply new houses and businesses that appear on the boundaries of the companies' supply areas, although this is likely to be minimal. If the water companies face similar operating risks, then a regulator can use yardstick competition to help determine prices, and the ability of the stock market to compare firms' performances is enhanced. The existence of a number of local natural monopolies means that there could be competition *for* the market via franchising.

10.1.2 The Current Structure of the Industry

There are ten companies in England and Wales that carry out both water supply and sewerage functions. They perform water abstraction, treatment, and distribution and provide sewerage and sewage treatment and disposal. The biggest water and sewerage company is Thames Water, which serves a population of 11.7 million in London and the Thames Valley. In the financial year 1991–92 its utility business had turnover of £750 million. There are also twenty-two companies that supply water but not sewerage services. The smallest of these water-only companies is

Cholderton in Hampshire which serves a population of 2,000 with a turn-over of about £100,000, and the next smallest is Hartlepools which serves 91,000, including many industrial customers, with a turnover of about £5 million. In 1992–93 the industry in England and Wales had an aggregate turnover of £5.1 billion, current cost operating profits of £1.47 billion, and capital expenditure of £3 billion (Ofwat 1993b). The replacement cost value of assets was £143 billion, but the combined market value (including debt) was about £15 billion. The total investment program for the period 1989–90 to 1994–95 is £17.9 billion in 1991–92 prices, and by the end of this period average charges will have risen by 25% in real terms. Compliance with quality and environmental regulations accounts for £4.8 billion of this program, and this, together with the associated increase in operating costs, will cause about two-thirds of the real price increase. Improved standards of service will cause just over 10% of the real price increase from 1989–90 to 1994–95, and growth in demand accounts for the remainder. When price limits were initially set in 1989 and 1990, planned total expenditure on investment in the five-year period after 1995 was expected to be £12 billion, with real prices increasing by about 20% over the period, but the investment program is still being determined. The final total is likely to be significantly higher.

In Scotland the water industry is owned and run by twelve regional and island councils. The industry has a capital expenditure program of about £5 billion over the period 1993–2008, of which about half is to improve water quality and half is for infrastructure maintenance and replacement. The government is keen to involve private capital in the industry, perhaps with some franchising, but outright privatization has been rejected at least until the next election. See McMaster and Sawkins (1993) for a discussion of the franchising options for Scottish water. In this chapter we will focus on the situation in England and Wales.

10.2   Policy Questions

In this section we discuss the various policy issues that arise generally in water regulation. In the following sections we discuss the policies that were chosen for the industry in England and Wales.

10.2.1   Vertical Structure

There are several feasible vertical structures for the industry. One option is to have integrated firms that supply water and collect and treat sewage. Alternatively the water and sewerage businesses could be separated. It is possible to separate water treatment and supply from distribution. Similarly sewerage services can be split into sewerage, which is essentially a pipeline business, and sewage treatment and disposal.

An important benefit of vertical separation in the water industry would be the improvement in the quality of the regulator's information. With integration some costs such as management, billing, and meter reading would be shared between the water and sewerage businesses. A firm that was relatively efficient in one business but of below average efficiency in the other might be tempted to allocate shared costs to the more efficient business. This might reduce the danger of the regulator discovering that the other business is inefficient. The costs of vertical separation include the loss of any economies of scope, and the possible loss of some internalization of externalities. The efficiency reason for integration between the water and sewerage functions arises because the businesses are mainly pipeline operations. Opportunities for economies of scope exist because experience gained in maintaining and servicing water mains will also be of use for sewers. Integration could also promote internalization of some externalities. If a sewage treatment plant is located upstream from a water treatment works, then the costs of water treatment will generally increase as more effluent reaches the river. If one firm owns both plants, this particular externality is internalized. Note, however, that the effluent might affect parties other than the water treatment works and joint ownership of the two plants will not alleviate these third-party externalities. There is thus a strong case for external regulation of effluent discharges, and if this regulation is strong enough, this argument for joint ownership is weakened. But the case for vertical separation is not proved. While there are benefits to separation, these should be balanced against the loss of scope economies and the costs of restructuring.

Vertical separation might, however, increase the scope for franchising. It would be possible to franchise out the operations of water supply, sewerage, and sewage treatment and disposal separately. In France, where franchising is widely used in the water industry, there are two types of franchise. Some municipalities grant short-term operating franchises, for up to ten years, and retain ownership of the infrastructure assets. This eases the problem of the transfer of assets when the franchise is reallocated. There are also longer-term franchises in which the franchisee may own some of the assets. These can last for twenty-five years or more, giving the firm an incentive to invest in the infrastructure, at least during the early years.

10.2.2 Horizontal Competition

There are three opportunities for horizontal competition in the water industry. First, if there were a national grid or regional grids, water suppliers could compete for customers via access to the pipeline network. To be feasible, this would need strict and continual monitoring of the quality of the water each company supplies to the grid.

The second opportunity for horizontal competition is at the boundaries of the designated regions, for example, to service new sites. The greater the number of firms the more likely is such competition. There is likely to be a direct trade-off between increasing the number of firms to generate increased competition at the boundaries and the loss of scale economies for each firm as the size of its area falls. But competition at the boundaries is likely to be minimal.

A third possible source of horizontal competition is direct competition for larger customers. Such competition might conceivably be economic despite duplication of pipelines, especially if the competing firm offers a different quality of water supply (or sewage treatment, if feasible). Product differentiation can overturn the typical result in homogeneous-goods models that entry will be excessive. A question for policymakers is to what extent such direct competition should be allowed or promoted.

10.2.3 Yardstick Competition

The local or regional basis of the water and sewerage industry provides the opportunity for both the regulator and the capital markets to use comparative information. In section 3.4 we presented a simple model of yardstick competition. The precise way that yardstick information is used in price regulation needs to be determined. An important question for policy is how many firms are necessary or desirable to conduct yardstick competition. Policymakers have to consider whether mergers that might generate scale and scope economies are undesirable because they reduce the number of independent comparators.

10.2.4 Price Control

Whatever the structure of the industry there is a need for regulation of prices in the monopolistic parts of each firm's business. Regulators must balance a series of objectives when setting price controls. Firms must be given the incentive to improve productive efficiency. They must also be encouraged to make necessary investments without being given an incentive to overinvest. Two issues that are particularly important, and about which regulators need to decide, are the cost of capital for new investment and the measurement of the capital base. In addition, since much new investment is driven by externally imposed environmental and quality regulations, there is a need to specify a mechanism that will allow firms to pass through reasonable incremental costs resulting from changes in these regulations in between general price reviews.

10.2.5 Quality Regulation

In section 6.1 we saw that firms subject to price caps typically will not have correct incentives to maintain quality. Ideally the price level for water should be increased to pay for improved water quality only if consumers are willing to pay for such improvements, and pollution externalities should be corrected until the marginal benefit of reducing pollution equals the marginal cost. If the quality and environmental regulators are separate from the economic regulator there is the potential for inefficiency. This is a special case of the problem of common agency, where one agent, here the firm, has several principals (regulators).[2] A theoretical analysis of the regulation of a monopoly by separate environmental and economic regulators is presented by Baron (1985). The equilibrium in his asymmetric information model when the two regulators do not cooperate, and the environmental regulator moves first, generates excessive pollution abatement and thus too high a consumer price, while the firm makes excess profits that are greater than those earned when regulators cooperate.

A simple model that captures the problems involved with separate regulation is instructive. This is based on Baron's model, but we assume complete information. The model applies to both quality regulation and the setting of pollution standards, although for simplicity we will use the quality interpretation. Suppose that at the first stage the *quality* regulator chooses the required standard s to maximize its objective function $U(s) - \omega cs$, where $U(s)$ is the consumer's direct utility, c is the cost of providing a unit of s, cs is the total cost of quality provision, and ω represents the weight the quality regulator attaches to the cost of achieving the standard. Assume that $U(s)$ is increasing and concave in s. At the second stage the *economic* regulator chooses the price p to maximize consumer surplus $U(s) - p$, subject to the firm breaking even, $p \geq cs$. It is optimal to set $p = cs$. Demand being inelastic, the socially optimal value of s is characterized by $U'(s^*) = c$. In equilibrium, however, the quality regulator sets s at

---

2. See Bernheim and Whinston (1986) for a general analysis of the common agency problem with hidden action and Stole (1991) for an analysis with hidden information.

the level given by $U'(s) = \omega c$. This exceeds s^* if $\omega < 1$, which means that the quality regulator takes insufficient account of the cost of quality enhancement. Overprovision of quality arises because of the difference in the objective functions of the regulators. In the water industry those who set standards for quality and the environment do not necessarily consider the effects on prices, and it is clear that there is no reason to expect the actual quality-price combination to be the optimal one. A question for policymakers is thus how to regulate pricing, investment, quality, and pollution simultaneously.

10.2.6   Methods of Pollution Control
A further question that is specific to environmental regulation concerns the methods of pollution control. Many of the extra costs of improving water quality arise because of third-party polluters such as farmers and industrial firms. On the "polluter pays" principle they should be charged for the extra treatment costs that their pollution generates. Determining liability is impossible when the pollution does not come from identifiable sources, such as when nitrates and pesticides from many different farms enter water sources, and in these cases (known as cases of non-point-source pollution) a second-best solution would be to tax the products whose supply causes the pollution.

When the source of pollution is known, there are two main options for its control: quantitative restrictions that specify for each pollution point the maximum amount of effluent, and market-based methods such as tradable permits and effluent charges. A well-known problem with simple quantitative restrictions is that marginal costs of reducing pollution will not usually be equalized across firms. Market-based methods can sometimes ensure equalization of marginal costs. One of the conditions for successful use of such methods is that it is the total quantity of pollution that matters rather than the location of its sources. An example where this might hold is the case of greenhouse gases. This condition does not generally hold in the water industry. Pollution in rivers, estuaries, and, to some extent, bathing beaches is localized. If a taxation system were used, tax rates would need to vary geographically because of differing initial pollution levels of the rivers and beaches. If a system of tradable permits were used, then trading would have to be restricted. Dischargers into a particular river should only be able to trade permits with the other dischargers into that river. There would then be few potential traders and permit markets would be thin, creating incentives for strategic behavior that might be inefficient (section 9.4.4).

10.2.7 Diversification

One question for policymakers is to what extent diversification away from the core businesses of water supply and sewerage services should be allowed. Running new businesses might take up excessive amounts of management time, and diversification might increase the cost of capital (if it is into riskier businesses and so raises the beta factor of the firm) and might allow scope for inefficient transfer pricing. Braeutigam and Panzar (1989) illustrate some of the problems that can be associated with the diversification of a regulated monopolist into a competitive market. In particular they argue that under rate-of-return regulation the firm has "incentives to misreport cost allocations, choose an inefficient technology (in some cases), undertake cost-reducing innovation in an inefficient way, underproduce in the noncore market, price below marginal cost in a competitive market which happens to be included in the set of core markets regulated by an aggregate rate-of-return constraint, and view diversification decisions inefficiently" (p. 390). In principle these undesirable features vanish under price cap regulation as long as the regulator has complete information. However, as discussed in section 6.1, the differences between rate-of-return and price cap regulation are smaller in practice than in theory, so the potential problems highlighted by Braeutigam and Panzar are still of concern. Regulators need to decide what restrictions on diversification and what remedies for its effects are necessary.

10.2.8 Metering

The general lack of meters for domestic households is an unusual feature of the British water industry. Since these consumers face a zero marginal price for water, they will consume until they are satiated, except insofar as environmental concerns curb use. If installing and servicing meters were costless, then there would be inefficient overconsumption where meters were not installed. Since meters are costly, however, there needs to be cost-benefit analysis for metering and its alternatives. Households that are metered will reduce their consumption. Their total water bill will be different with a metered tariff, so consumer surplus will change with metering. Large families that live in low-valued properties and thus pay relatively low charges under the current property value-based system are likely to suffer a loss of surplus when metered, whereas sole occupants of high-valued properties might gain. There would thus be distributional effects of compulsory metering as well as the effect on aggregate consumer surplus. For a water supply firm the benefits of installing meters include the reduction in operating costs as consumption decreases, the avoidance of extra capital costs because new reservoirs and other infrastructure investments can be canceled or postponed, and the avoidance of the costs of reducing leakage from the networks of pipes.[3] Total revenue earned by the firm might also change. Revenue will definitely be lower if aggregate consumer surplus is higher with meters, but otherwise it could either rise or fall. In addition the costs of metering will have to be borne by customers, the firm, or even the taxpayer if government transfers are feasible. Metering costs include the one-off costs of installation (which can be very large, especially for properties with multiple occupants) and the costs of reading and maintaining meters. Metering should be introduced only if the present value of benefits less costs is positive, and if this holds, the optimal time to install meters needs to be determined. Future improvements in metering technology might strengthen the case for delayed introduction. For more details on the economics of metering, see Warford (1966) and OECD (1987). The regulator will need to consider whether firms and customers have incentives to make efficient metering decisions, and what level and shape the tariffs for metered consumption should have.

10.3 Framework of Competition and Regulation

10.3.1 Background to Privatization
Ten water authorities were created by the 1973 Water Act. Kinnersley (1988, chs. 5–9) describes the foundation and performance of the water authorities. The principle underlying this reorganization was known as "integrated river-basin management." The catchment area of each river was included within a single authority's boundaries. The authorities had water regulatory functions in addition to their commercial functions of water supply and sewerage (see Vickers and Yarrow 1988, ch. 11). These regulatory functions included the planning and control of water resources, control of river quality and drinking water quality, and other services such as flood protection and land and highway drainage. The reorganization was designed to achieve the benefits of economies of scale and scope, but the combination of the regulatory and commercial functions in the same organizations meant that the authorities were both "poachers" (polluters of rivers via effluent discharges) and "gamekeepers" (regulators of river quality), and thus their objectives could conflict.

---

3. It is estimated that on average about 22% of water put into the supply network fails to reach the consumer because of leakage. The variation in leakage rates across companies is significant, with a range of 6% to 36% (Ofwat Annual Report 1992).

During the 1980s the water authorities were subject to three external disciplines relating to investment, borrowing, and operating costs. A useful description of these disciplines is contained in the MMC report (1986b) on Southern Water Authority and the water-only companies in its area. On investment they faced a two-part financial target, the first of which specified that new investment should earn the Treasury's required rate of return (5% for most of the 1980s), while the second specified "a low but increasing return on the current value of existing assets" (p. 7). Thus it was acknowledged that existing rates of return were low and had to be higher for new investment. This principle was continued when the price controls for the privatized authorities were set in 1989. Borrowing was controlled by an external financing limit. Any investment above this limit had to be financed out of retained earnings. Finally, there was a "performance aim" that specified a target figure for operating costs. Progressive tightening of the investment and borrowing constraints throughout the 1980s meant that more investment had to be financed by internally generated funds and real water charges increased. Even so there is a widespread perception that there was underinvestment during this period.

The statutory water companies (now the water-only companies) continued to supply water after the 1973 Act. They supply water to about one-quarter of the population of England and Wales but do not have sewerage functions. When the ten water authorities were privatized in 1989 there were twenty-nine privately owned water-only companies, and since then their number has been reduced to twenty-one by mergers. Until 1989 they were subject to a very different regulatory regime from that of the publicly owned water authorities. Dividends, transfers to reserves, and accumulated reserves were controlled (for more on these controls, see MMC 1986b, paras. 5.15–5.23). This was effectively a form of rate-of-return regulation in which any reductions or increases in costs were passed through to consumers.

The first steps toward the privatization of the water authorities were taken by the publication of a White Paper (Department of the Environment 1986) and a report by Stephen Littlechild on the economic regulation of privatized water authorities (Littlechild 1986). The White Paper suggested that the ten water authorities should be privatized in their existing form, including both commercial and regulatory functions, and with no separation of water supply from sewerage services. A system of price regulation was favored over direct controls on profits, the need for quality standards was acknowledged, and the option to use franchising was rejected because competition for the market would be very infrequent and because of the standard problem of underinvestment by the franchisee.

Littlechild was asked by the Department of the Environment to examine the applicability of RPI $-$ X price regulation. He was to assume that the authorities would be privatized in their existing form. He concluded that regulation would need to be permanent and had to cover quality as well as price. The existence of ten authorities would enhance the scope for competition by enabling capital markets to compare different authorities, and the operation of the takeover mechanism could force companies to be efficient. The regulator would also be able to make comparisons between the authorities' quality and price performances. A price cap rather than rate-of-return regulation was preferred because of its simplicity and because it preserves efficiency incentives. Since the regulatory system would need to be permanent, there would be a need for periodic revisions of the price cap in order to prevent prices deviating from costs for long periods. Littlechild recommended that revisions of the X factor should be based on an industry yardstick to ensure that no authority could influence its own revised X factor. He also suggested that there should be a single X factor for each authority rather than separate ones for water and for sewerage, and that there were virtues of simplicity in having a uniform value of X across all authorities.[4]

The White Paper suggested that the existing structure of the authorities would be maintained after privatization. In 1987, however, the Department of the Environment decided to abandon the principle of integrated river basin management and to set up the National Rivers Authority (NRA).[5] This is a public body responsible for the control of water pollution and the general management of water resources, including the licensing of abstractions. It has also taken over responsibility for land drainage, flood defense, and fisheries. The government has announced that it intends to incorporate the NRA and Her Majesty's Inspectorate of Pollution into a new Environment Agency. The separation of the environmental and quality functions from the water supply and sewerage businesses countered a major criticism of the original privatization proposals, which was that if the responsibility for prosecuting a firm for breaches of statutory

---

4. A uniform X was proposed on the assumption that capital structures could be adjusted and that the statutory water companies would not be included in the same regulatory framework as the authorities.
5. See Richardson et al. (1992) for an interesting analysis of the dynamics of policy toward the water industry.

standards was vested in another part of the same firm, then there would be large conflicts of interest.

10.3.2   Framework at Privatization

The Water Act 1989, the Water Industry Act 1991, and the Water Resources Act 1991   The framework of current regulation for the water industry was formalized by the 1989 Water Act and by the licenses issued to each firm (known as an "undertaker") under the Act. The 1989 Water Act has been succeeded by the 1991 Water Industry Act (which concerns economic regulation) and the 1991 Water Resources Act (which concerns the NRA). The 1989 Water Act provided for the setting up of the Office of Water Services (Ofwat) headed by a Director General (DGWS) following the models of Oftel and Ofgas. The first Director General is Ian Byatt who was formerly the Deputy Chief Economic Advisor to the Treasury. His primary duty is to secure that the functions of water and sewerage undertakers are properly carried out and "to secure that companies are ... able (in particular by securing reasonable returns on their capital) to finance the proper carrying out of [their] functions." This reference to reasonable returns on capital in the legislation is unique to the water industry and underlines the importance attached to investment, but neither "reasonable returns" nor "capital" is defined. Subject to this duty he also has secondary duties (1) to ensure that the interests of all actual and potential customers are protected with respect to prices, (2) to ensure that the interests of customers and potential customers in rural areas are protected and that there is no undue preference or undue discrimination in the fixing of prices, (3) to promote efficiency and economy, and (4) to facilitate competition. The DGWS has the right to make "inset appointments" that allow competition at the boundaries of water undertakers' areas. He can modify license conditions and can refer his proposed changes to the MMC if the undertaker does not agree to them.

The President of the Board of Trade has the duty to refer any proposed merger between water enterprises to the MMC provided that the values of the assets of the acquiring company and the company being taken over each exceed £30 million. When considering such a reference the MMC has the duty to "have regard to the desirability of giving effect to the principle that the number of water enterprises which are under independent control should not be reduced so as to prejudice the Director's ability ... to make comparisons between ... water enterprises." Thus the potential value of yardstick competition is enshrined in the legislation. Three merger references to the MMC were made around the time of privatization under the Act, and these will be discussed in section 10.4.1.

Undertakers will not be permitted to base any charge on the rateable value of a property after 31 March 2000, so by that date a new charging base will need to be determined. The metering issue will be discussed again in section 10.4.5. The statutory water companies were brought into the regulatory regime set up by the 1989 Water Act. The 1989 Water Act also contained provisions for the lifting of dividend controls for these companies. One of the key advantages claimed in the Littlechild Report for privatizing the water authorities was that the capital markets could encourage productive efficiency because inefficient companies would be disciplined by the takeover threat. This conflicts with the need to maintain a sufficiently large number of firms to enable the regulator to do yardstick competition, since the most likely acquirer is another water company. The nine English water authorities were privatized with a 15% limit on individual shareholdings until the end of 1994 and the restrictions on ownership of Dwr Cymru (formerly Welsh Water) are even stricter, so the idea of an active market for corporate control was downgraded.

Apart from the creation of the NRA there was no radical restructuring of the industry at privatization. In particular water and sewerage services were not separated, and franchising was rejected at an early stage. Competition at the boundaries was, however, allowed. No provision for common carriage was made in the Act, because in the absence of a national water transmission grid water is a local or regional business.[6]

The Licenses   The details of the regulation of the conduct of water undertakers are to be found in the licenses (known officially as the Instruments of Appointment). The main conditions relate to charges and to the pass-through of exogenous cost changes. Charges are controlled by a price cap of RPI + K. The charges for five services are included in the price cap. These are measured and unmeasured water, measured and unmeasured sewerage, and trade effluent. The price cap is a modified version of the tariff basket. A useful description of the formula and its operation is given in Centre for the Study of Regulated Industries (1991). Each company was given a specific K profile for ten years. Tables 10.1 and 10.2 show the K factors for the first five years that were set in 1989 and 1990.

---

6. Some companies have established regional grids as security against localized water shortages.

Table 10.1 *K* factors for water and sewerage companies

Company	K factor in year				
	1990–91	1991–92	1992–93	1993–94	1994–95
Anglian	5.5	5.5	5.5	5.5	5.5
Dwr Cymru	6.5	6.5	6.5	6.5	6.5
North West	5.0	5.0	5.0	5.0	5.0
Northumbrian	7.0	7.0	7.0	7.0	7.0
Severn Trent	5.5	5.5	5.5	5.5	5.5
South West	6.5	6.5	6.5	6.5	6.5
Southern	5.5	5.5	5.5	3.5	3.5
Thames	4.5	4.5	4.5	4.5	4.5
Wessex	4.5	4.5	4.5	4.5	4.5
Yorkshire	3.0	3.0	3.0	3.0	3.0

Note: These are the factors determined in 1989. Some figures have since been revised through interim determinations.

In the first full year of the new regulatory regime (1990–91) the average K for the water and sewerage companies was 5.35 (with a range of 3 to 7), while the average for the water-only companies was 11.4 (with a range of 3 to 25). Six undertakers had a constant K for all years until 1999–2000, while all other undertakers have lower K values in later years, reflecting the need for more internal finance in the early years because of the early investment peak. Under the terms of the licenses a review of price limits must be held after ten years, but either the undertaker or the DGWS can request a review after five years. The DGWS announced in July 1991 that he would conduct a review of all K factors after five years. The process of setting the original Ks and of resetting in 1994 will be discussed in section 10.4.2.

One of the risks that investors face is that environmental and quality standards might be tightened in a way not allowed for when the Ks were most recently set. This is covered in the licenses by allowing "Interim Determinations," a kind of cost passthrough. This mechanism seeks to ensure that cost changes that are genuinely exogenous and outside management control do not alter the wealth of shareholders. Thus the present value (at a cost of capital to be determined by the DGWS) of the incremental costs that will be incurred up until the next periodic review date is determined. If this present value exceeds a threshold proportion of base-period revenue, then the mechanism proceeds; otherwise, the process is delayed until the next year (if a new application is made) or until the next periodic review. If the threshold is passed, the original K values in the

Table 10.2 K factors for the water-only companies

Company	K factor in year				
	1990–91	1991–92	1992–93	1993–94	1994–95
Bournemouth	18.5	18.5	15.0	0.0	0.0
Bristol	5.0	5.0	4.0	4.0	2.0
Cambridge	12.0	10.0	8.0	0.0	0.0
Chester	4.5	4.5	4.5	1.0	1.0
Cholderton	6.0	6.0	6.0	6.0	6.0
Colne Valley	10.0	10.0	10.0	7.5	7.5
East Anglian	19.0	13.0	13.0	13.0	3.0
East Surrey	16.0	16.0	2.0	2.0	2.0
East Worcester	25.0	11.0	11.0	11.0	−1.0
Eastbourne	20.0	20.0	2.5	2.5	2.5
Essex	5.0	5.0	5.0	5.0	5.0
Folkestone	18.0	8.0	8.0	8.0	8.0
Hartlepools	3.5	3.5	3.5	3.5	3.5
Lee Valley	7.5	7.5	7.5	7.5	7.5
Mid-Kent	9.0	9.0	2.5	2.5	2.5
Mid-Southern	11.5	11.5	4.0	4.0	4.0
Mid-Sussex	16.0	16.0	16.0	0.0	0.0
Newcastle	8.0	8.0	8.0	2.0	2.0
North Surrey	8.5	8.5	8.5	8.5	8.5
Portsmouth	5.5	5.5	5.5	5.5	5.5
Rickmansworth	9.5	9.5	2.0	2.0	2.0
South Staffordshire	5.0	5.0	5.0	5.0	5.0
Sunderland	7.5	7.5	7.5	5.0	5.0
Sutton	12.5	10.5	8.5	8.5	3.5
Tendring Hundred	22.5	22.5	13.0	13.0	2.5
West Hampshire	7.5	7.5	7.5	7.5	5.5
West Kent	20.0	20.0	4.0	4.0	−1.5
Wrexham	15.0	15.0	0.0	0.0	0.0
York	3.0	3.0	3.0	3.0	3.0

Note: These were the K factors set in 1990. Some water only companies have since merged.

years until the next periodic review are adjusted until the present value of the extra revenue earned equals the present value of the incremental costs. In general there will be a large number of different profiles of K values that achieve this (one simple way to do this is to allow full recovery of increased expenditures in the years in which they occur), and the DGWS is required to look at various financial and accounting ratios to help determine which of the K profiles is acceptable. The use of financial and accounting criteria in determining the appropriate K profile after a cost passthrough application, however, would tend to push K factors up in the early years. The cost passthrough mechanism was meant to be forward-looking and long term, but the requirement to meet the financial and accounting criteria increases the role of short-term factors. Two companies agreed on license changes with Ofwat in 1993 that limit the types of cost that can be considered for passthrough, and at the same time the DGWS announced that he would simplify their cost passthrough procedures. Extra operating expenditure and capital costs (depreciation and a return on capital) would be identified annually, and revenues would be adjusted to cover these additional costs. This avoids the use of the financial and accounting criteria that apply in the present value-based procedure.

There are further license conditions on the prohibition of undue discrimination and undue preference, the provision of accounting information to the regulator, and the determination of quality of service information and targets. The DGWS monitors performance relative to agreed standards on aspects of quality of service such as pressure of mains water, hose pipe restrictions, flooding incidents from sewers, and speed of response to billing enquiries. He has indicated that he will consider asking the Secretary to State for the Environment to impose enforceable standards if performance relative to expectations is poor.

Undertakers are allowed to charge one-off fees, known as *infrastructure charges*, when new properties join the water or sewerage networks (in addition to the charge for the cost of connection). These charges are supposed to help the undertaker recover some of the additional costs it incurs by taking on an extra customer relating to the need for new capacity. They can be seen as a very imperfect substitute for long-run marginal cost pricing in an industry where metering is not widespread. Infrastructure charges were fixed at the time of privatization and were subject to a separate price cap of RPI + 0. The DGWS has expressed concern about both the average level of infrastructure charges and the variation across firms, and has announced his intention to require the phasing in of uniform charges of £200 for each service for all companies (Ofwat 1993c). This is below the current charge for most companies.

Environmental and Quality Regulation   The companies face tough environmental and quality regulation in addition to Ofwat's economic regulation. The European Community has issued directives on Drinking Water Quality, Bathing Beaches, and Urban Waste Water Treatment. The Drinking Water Directive requires that companies supply wholesome water (as measured by 57 parameters) and companies must achieve compliance with this directive by 1995. Progress on compliance with the directive is monitored by the Drinking Water Inspectorate (part of the Department of the Environment), which also monitors the few quality regulations set by the UK government that are stricter than the EC's regulations. Similarly the Bathing Beaches Directive, which affects eight of the water and sewerage companies, must be achieved by December 1995. The companies also have to achieve compliance with earlier pollution legislation that relates particularly to sewage treatment works that have failed to comply with their discharge consents or are at risk of failing to do so. The NRA is responsible for the interpretation and implementation of the legislation, and its duty under the 1991 Water Resources Act is "to such an extent as it considers desirable ... to promote the conservation and enhancement of the natural beauty and amenity of inland and coastal waters." There is no duty to balance the benefits of improvements in environmental quality against the costs.

The pollution control system is based on nontransferable quantitative restrictions. The NRA issues "consents" that specify the amount and strength of the effluent that each polluter (industrial plant or sewage treatment works) is allowed to discharge to rivers, estuaries and coastal waters.

10.4 Developments in Competition and Regulation

Since the privatization of the water and sewerage companies in 1989 there have been five salient issues. First, there have been a number of proposed mergers between water-only companies, three of which were referred to the MMC, which has had to trade off the possible synergy benefits of merger against the loss of comparators for yardstick competition. Second, the DGWS announced in July 1991 that he would be reviewing all price caps after five years and at the same time issued a consultation paper on the cost of capital. He has also encouraged firms to withhold price increases that were allowed under the original K settlement, and many companies have had their K factors reduced by the DGWS under the Interim Determination procedure to reflect lower than expected construction prices. Third, there has been some tightening of environmental and quality regulations, which has led to cost passthrough applications. Fourth, Ofwat has expressed worries about the diversification activities of the water and sewerage companies and has agreed amendments to the licences with the industry. Fifth, Ofwat has promoted a debate on the role of metering.

10.4.1 Yardstick Competition

The regional structure of the industry gives the regulator the opportunity to make comparisons between firms in setting prices and quality standards. We discussed the role of yardstick competition in section 3.4. In this section we discuss the methods used to implement yardstick competition in the initial K setting process, the prospects for using yardsticks at the periodic review, and the use of the legislation that tries to preserve the DGWS's ability to make comparisons by restricting mergers.

As part of the original K setting process a comparative efficiency review was undertaken by the Department of the Environment. This took into account the influence of various factors in the companies' operating environments that might explain differing operating costs. For a detailed description of the factors used, see MMC (1990a, 125). The factors were combined into an "explanatory factor index." It was assumed that there was a linear relationship between unit costs and the explanatory factor index, and regression analysis was used to estimate the coefficients of this line. The process can be thought of as a simple version of the procedure that Shleifer (1985) recommends for cases where there are observable differences in operating environments. He suggests that the regulator run a cross-sectional regression of unit costs on the observable factors that influence costs and that the regulated price allowed for any individual firm should be the cost level predicted by the regression for that firm's factors. As a result of the efficiency review firms were placed in four efficiency bands, and the banding determined the assumed reduction in operating costs. In addition it was assumed that a benchmark saving of 1% per annum was achievable by all firms "to cover the spur to efficiency associated with privatization and technological change in the future" (MMC 1990a, 125). The MMC did not reveal the exact process by which the bandings and baseline efficiency target were derived. The way the assumed reduction in operating costs fed into the calculation of K factors will be mentioned in the next section.

There are problems with this procedure. First, the regression sought to explain only operating costs; in practice there are difficulties in measuring total operating costs, since firms had some discretion over the classification of expenditure as current or capital. Second, even if operating costs can be correctly measured, in the long-run capital expenditure can usually substitute for operating expenditure; the original study did not take this into account. Third, the efficiency review compared measures of unit costs across companies; in the water industry there are problems in defining the output measure that acts as the denominator of unit costs. Not all the water put into the distribution system from treatment works is used by consumers because of leakages, and because most domestic customers do not have meters, measuring leakage is difficult. Measures of sewage volume are also troublesome because sewage varies in type and strength. Fourth, the residual between the actual unit cost and the predicted unit cost was treated as the measure of inefficiency (see Price 1992); this is not necessarily correct, since there could be genuine random differences caused by explanatory factors that are too difficult to measure (e.g., climatic difference). In any case all econometric estimates are subject to some degree of estimation error (which is likely to be larger the smaller the number of observations and the less variation there is in the explanatory factor).

Ofwat is currently discussing the yardstick methodology to be used for the next price review with the industry. It commissioned a report by KPMG Peat Marwick McLintock (1990) to consider various options. It seems likely that the basic econometric approach used in the initial K setting will be improved by constructing better data on costs, output measures, and explanatory factors. More sophisticated statistical techniques might be used to avoid the interpretation of the difference between actual and predicted costs as inefficiency alone. Econometric modeling is likely to be supplemented by techniques such as data envelopment analysis, which tries to show whether inputs are being used efficiently, and by the cross-sectional analysis of simple accounting ratios, which act as performance indicators. The difficulty of implementing yardstick competition is clear from this discussion, and the burden on the industry of information provision and on the regulator of information processing will be heavy. Nevertheless, yardstick competition is likely to play an increasingly valuable role once the large investment program, which at present is the main determinant of price changes, has stabilized.

The potential value of yardstick competition was recognized in the 1989 Water Act. The Secretary of State for Trade and Industry has the duty to refer all significant mergers to the MMC. In the summer of 1990 the MMC reported on three cases. The first and most important case was that of the Three Valleys merger (MMC 1990a) which involved three water-only companies to the northwest of London (Lee Valley, Colne Valley, and Rickmansworth) serving a population of about 2.3 million. These three companies shared an important water treatment works and had cooperated on this since 1970. Lee Valley was owned by the French company

CGE. The MMC found that the merger was against the public interest on the grounds that it would reduce the number of independent comparators that the DGWS would have, but that it could be allowed if the claimed gains from the merger were passed back to consumers in the form of lower prices. The merger was allowed on the basis that efficiency savings of 10% would be passed through to consumers after five years. In the Mid-Kent Water case (MCC 1990b) the MMC upheld the principle of maintaining the number of independent comparators by recommending that CGE should not have board representation at Mid-Kent Water (in which it had a minority shareholding of 29%) and should have no involvement with management. The Secretary of State for Trade and Industry then ordered CGE to reduce its stake to at most 19.5%. In this case there were few apparent synergy gains from the merger, unlike in the Three Valleys case. In the third case (MMC 1990c) Southern Water was allowed to maintain its minority shareholding in the Mid-Sussex Water Company because the company was already controlled by the French firm SAUR.[7] Other mergers in the northeast and southeast that were in place before the legislation took effect have not been affected, although the DGWS has agreed to integration of management in return for reductions in price limits. East Worcester Water Company was taken over by Severn Trent in 1993, and the K factor for the combined company was reduced (see table 10.3). East Worcester was small enough not to attract an automatic reference to the MMC. Ofwat welcomed the merger because of the benefits to consumers but was concerned lest it set a precedent for the takeover of other smaller companies.

Thus the MMC has taken seriously the value of maintaining the number of independent comparators to enable the DGWS to conduct yardstick competition and is only willing to reduce the number of comparators if there are substantial benefits from economies of scale and scope and if these benefits are shared with consumers. There are several reasons for preserving the number of firms. First, in section 3.4 we showed that the higher the correlation between firms' costs, the more likely it is that the benefits from separate operation outweigh the loss of possible scale and scope economies. Second, econometric analysis needs a large number of comparators to maintain degrees of freedom and to maintain the power of tests of the estimated coefficients. Third, as stressed by the DGWS in his evidence to the MMC inquiry on the Three Valleys case, losing data

---

7. Southern Water subsequently sold its stake in Mid-Sussex.

Table 10.3 Interim determinations for 1993–94 and 1994–95

| Company | Reductions in price limits | |
	1993–94	1994–95
Anglian	0.0	0.5
Cambridge	0.8	
Dwr Cymru	3.2	1.5
East Worcester	2.3	
Mid-Kent	0.5	
North Surrey	2.0	
North West	0.8	1.0
Northumbrian	2.0	
Severn Trent[a]	1.9	
South East	2.0	
South West[b]	0.5	0.5
Tendring Hundred	2.0	
Thames	1.0	0.4
Three Valleys	0.5	
Wessex	1.0	
Wrexham	11.2	
Yorkshire	0.7	1.1

Source: Ofwat Annual Report 1992, table 11.
Note: Price limits are defined as K plus any deferral of K from previous years that is available for use.
a. Severn Trent took over East Worcester in March 1993, and K factors for the combined company were changed to 4.55 in 1993–94 and 5.36 in 1994–95.
b. South West's K factor was raised to 11.5 for each year between 1992–93 and 1994–95 in its interim determination in 1991. The result of the interim determination in 1992 shown in this table was to reduce the K factors in 1993–94 and 1994–95 to 11.0.

points is important not just for econometric reasons but also because the effectiveness of efficiency frontier modeling depends crucially on the number of observations. Fourth, it is possible that the firms will collude against a regulator who is trying to operate yardstick competition and that such collusion might be more difficult the greater the number of firms. Whether these outweigh the benefits of synergy gains from merger can only be answered on a case-by-case basis.

10.4.2 Price Regulation

The water industry will need permanent price regulation, and in setting price limits, policymakers have to take account of the fact that the firms are required to undertake large investment programs. In this section we first discuss the general method of setting Ks at privatization and then consider the prospects for the periodic review due to take place in 1994–95 and the extent of Ofwat intervention in pricing since 1989.

The process of setting the K factors for the ten water and sewerage companies and the (then) twenty-nine water-only companies is described in the MMC report (1990a) on the Three Valleys merger and in Ofwat's cost of capital consultation paper (1991a; see also Cowan 1992). The K factors determine the rate of increase of real prices. As discussed in section 6.3, an important part of price setting in the water industry was the determination of both the cost of capital and the value of the existing asset base so that the Secretary of State could fulfill his duty of enabling the companies to earn reasonable returns on their capital. In the water industry investment issues were paramount because of the requirements to raise water quality, improve the water environment, replace depreciated capital, and provide for future demand growth. Since the scope for productivity improvement was low relative to, say, telecommunications, K setting was more concerned with the need to pay for investment than with providing incentives for productivity gains.

The Department of the Environment estimated on a CAPM basis that the cost of capital for new investment was 7% for the water and sewerage companies, rising to 8–8.5% for the water-only companies. The more difficult problem was to value the existing assets, as discussed in section 6.3. The water and sewerage companies were earning rates of return on the replacement cost of assets of about 2%, well below the estimated marginal cost of capital of 7%. Valuing the existing assets for K setting purposes at replacement cost would have caused a very large jump in prices and would have benefited existing owners at the expense of consumers. The existing owners were the government in the case of the water and sewerage companies and private shareholders in the case of the water-only companies.

In the end it was decided to value the existing assets by implementing the principle that the existing owners should neither lose nor gain from the change in regime (section 6.3). This meant projecting the cash flows that the firms might have been expected to earn on the existing assets if the previous regulatory regime had continued. Thus for the water authorities it was assumed that the existing assets would have earned the low rate of return on the replacement cost of the existing assets that the Treasury specified, as it did for all nationalized industries, until they were fully depreciated. These hypothetical cash flows were then discounted by the cost of capital to generate the initial value of assets, known as the indicative value. This was below the replacement value of the assets because the Treasury's accounting rate of return was below the cost of capital. If capital did not depreciate at all, the indicative value would be the initial replacement cost value of assets times the ratio of the accounting rate of return to the cost of capital. The indicative value is an important concept in what follows.

The next step involved projecting future operating costs and capital expenditure and working out the present value of this cash stream. Projected operating costs were adjusted for the efficiency factors derived from the yardstick competition exercise discussed in the previous section. The K factors were then set in order to ensure that the net present value of each firm's future cash flows was equal to the indicative value. Since there are many ways of profiling a revenue stream to ensure the same present value, additional criteria were needed to determine what the actual price increases in each year could be. One important consideration here relates to the investment holdup problem discussed in section 3.6. If prospective investors were promised that they would receive their returns but only after all the investment had been sunk, then there would be severe credibility problems, especially since regulators and governments cannot bind their successors. In the water case this meant that much of the increase in charges that was necessary to pay for the investment programme was front loaded. The practical way in which this was done was to ensure that various financial and accounting ratios, called *key indicators*, would be satisfied year by year. Because of the peak of investment this had the implication that prices would rise in real terms before the quality and environmental improvements had come through. In an effort to alleviate some of the burden of rising real water charges before privatization, the government gave the water and sewerage companies (but not the water-only companies) a "green dowry," which involved the writing-off of some debt (in effect converting it into equity) and the injection of just over £1 billion cash into their balance sheets. This served to relax the financial constraints and to lower K factors.

Although the process of determining the cost of capital for new investment and an initial asset base underlay the initial K setting process, the main determinant of the Ks appeared to be the financial and accounting criteria. Ofwat has made it clear that it regards the assumptions underlying the initial K factors as unduly generous, and hard bargaining at the periodic review in 1994–95 can be expected. It has issued consultation papers on the cost of capital (1991a) and on the valuation of capital (1992a) and has revealed a tough negotiating stance in these. Ofwat suggested that a weighted average real cost of capital was in the range 5% to 6% allowing for corporate taxation. This is considerably lower than the figure of 7% for the pretax real cost of capital used by the Department of the Environment in the initial determination. Ofwat also suggests that the key financial indicators can be relaxed. The Water Services and Water Companies Association (1991) have issued a detailed response to the Ofwat paper in which they argue for a cost of capital of 9.5% and for no relaxation of the key indicators. Ofwat (1993c) confirms that it intends to use the 5–6% figure for new investment.

The assessment of the value of the capital stock, which is an essential part of the primary duty of the DGWS, will be even more difficult than assessing the cost of capital, given the arbitrary nature of the original calculations. One option is to update the initial market values of the water and sewerage companies and adjust them for the levels of debt and for net capital expenditure in the period since the K factors were first set. An alternative would be to take a measure of current market value. But such valuation has the defect of being highly variable, and there is also a circularity involved, since current market valuations will depend on expectations about the regulator's valuations of capital. A third possible valuation measure would update the original indicative values. Since the initial market values at privatization were considerably below the indicative values and the adjusted indicative values would be almost certainly be above the adjusted market values proposed by Ofwat, it is not surprising that the industry seeks to measure the capital base on an indicative value basis (see Water Services Association and Water Companies Association 1993). Whichever method of valuation is used, the market values of the companies should gradually rise toward replacement cost values as the original assets are replaced by new assets earning the market cost of capital. Ofwat (1993c) has announced that it will value existing capital by taking the average stock market values of equity over the first 200 trading days after privatization, and adding a debt value and net capital expenditure in current cost terms since privatization.

The new price controls after the 1994 review will be set for ten years, with the option of either side seeking a review after five years again. The DGWS has announced that he takes a medium-term view of price caps. Since the initial price determination he has intervened actively in pricing decisions. For both 1992–93 and 1993–94 he sought and obtained price increases from most companies which were below those allowed in the original K settlement (see table 10.3 for details). The reason for such action was that the recession in Britain had driven down construction prices to a level 15% below that assumed in 1989. This cost clawback is allowed under the terms of the Interim Adjustment mechanism. There has also been one case in which K factors were increased. South West Water faced increased costs of over £300m in the years from 1992–93 to 1994–95, and its K factor in those years was raised from 6.5 to 11.5. The increased costs resulted from the tightening of environmental controls, which particularly affected South West. The Ks for 1993–94 and 1994–95 were subsequently reduced to 11.0. Although cost reductions, which are clearly due to factors outside the firms' control, are a reasonable basis to seek moderations of allowed price increases, there is the danger that the regulator could take too short term a view of pricing and profitability, and the incentive benefits of a price cap with a relatively long lag between formal reviews might diminish. This danger is, however, reduced if the criteria for cost clawback are clearly specified, and Ofwat has started to simplify both the criteria and methodology for Interim Determinations with license amendments, as we mentioned in section 10.3.2.

10.4.3 Environmental and Quality Regulation

Since privatization, some of the environmental and quality regulations have been tightened. The program for achieving compliance with the Bathing Beaches Directive was accelerated, and in 1990 the Urban Waste Water Treatment Directive was adopted. This required the phasing-out, by 1998, of the dumping of sewage sludge at sea, and additional facilities will be needed at sewage treatment works that discharge into the sea and estuaries. The NRA has tightened consents for discharges from sewage treatment works and the Drinking Water Inspectorate has required improvements at water treatment works where the inflowing waters had pesticide contamination.

The problem of multiple regulators with different objectives was discussed earlier and the possibility was mooted that quality and environmental standards will be set too high because of differing objectives between regulators. Byatt (1991) argues that new environmental and quality obligations should be properly costed and should not simply be imposed without consultation of those who have to pay for them. The investment program for the period 1989–90 to 1994–95, which in 1991–92 prices was originally expected to total £16.4 billion, has increased by 9.4% mainly because of the increased standards (Ofwat 1992b). In this five-year period average bills will have risen by 25% in real terms simply to finance the existing programs. Ofwat (1993a) considers two alternative scenarios for the course of average real charges, depending on the tightness of future environmental regulation. For five years *after* 1994–95 average real charges could rise by 19% if existing obligations are to be met and by 28% if potential obligations are added. There could also be further increases of 4% and 9% in the two cases, respectively, in the following five-year period.[8] These figures exclude the impact of possible improvements in levels of service such as water pressure and flooding from sewers, which by themselves could raise real prices by 14% in the first five years and 6% in the second five years. Whether the associated improvements in the environment and water quality are worth such a price is a key question for all the regulators, and Ofwat's focus on the potential costs of new standards is to be welcomed, although the question of how to measure the benefits remains. Decisions about the adoption, interpretation, and implementation of new obligations are for the Secretaries of State, but the DGWS has argued strongly for the cost (and hence price) implications of proposals to be taken into account. The Secretaries of State for the Environment and Wales responded to Ofwat's analysis in October 1993 by stating that there was no need for U.K. standards to be stricter than EC standards, that there should be full assessment of the benefits and costs of new standards, and that only those new standards that are already likely to be adopted should be included in the K setting process.

Whatever the level of standards, economic efficiency requires that firms minimize the costs of reaching them. There are three points here. First, there might be standard Averch-Johnson overinvestment effects if the reasonable returns that the DGWS is obliged to give the firms exceed the cost of capital. Second, the asymmetry of information between regulator and firms means that firms may have an incentive to overstate future costs in order to generate higher price increases now. They can then claim that the reason that actual costs are below what was anticipated is greater productive efficiency. This means that the expenditure plans require careful monitoring and certification and adds to the expense and complexity of regulation. Third, in ensuring that pollution reduction is efficient, some types of market mechanism should be investigated. The existing system is one of command and control (see Helm 1991), which prescribes not just the pollution standards but also how they should be met.

Since 1991 the NRA has set charges for discharge consents that specify maximum levels of pollution for each treatment works. Charges are based

---

8. These figures update those in an earlier study, Ofwat (1992b), which suggested that real prices in the first five-year period could rise by between 24% and 38%, with rises in the period from 2000–01 to 2004–05 of between 26% and 35%.

on the volume and strength of the effluent and the nature of the receiving waters, but their level is limited to the amount necessary to recover the NRA's administrative costs (NRA 1993). This is not a pollution tax in the conventional sense, which would require changes to primary legislation. In section 9.4.4 we discussed the relative merits of price-based and quantitative methods of pollution control. In the water context the government's international obligations are specified in quantitative terms, and it is possible that the marginal benefit of abatement is steeper than the marginal cost of abatement, indicating that quantitative controls should be used in preference to pollution taxes. Sometimes a combination of the two types of instrument is preferable to using just one. Helm (1993a) argues that the existing system of consents should remain in place to ensure that no risks are taken with the environment but that pollution should also be taxed. If the marginal cost of abatement is low, then the firm might reduce pollution below the level allowed by the consent in order to reduce tax payments. On the other hand, if abatement costs are high, the tax will have no effect. A permit system might also be considered, but this has the disadvantage that trading would have to be restricted by location to avoid excessive pollution in some regions, and trading would probably be thin or nonexistent.[9]

10.4.4 Diversification

Ofwat has been concerned about the possible adverse effects that diversification could have on the core businesses of water supply and sewerage services. In section 10.2 we discussed the conclusion of Braeutigam and Panzar (1989), whose model suggested that if there is pure price cap regulation, then diversification would not be distortionary. This result depends on the regulator having full information; this is clearly not the case in practice. In the water industry the regulator has an explicit duty to ensure that firms earn reasonable returns, so the price control is not a pure price cap. Such concerns should apply equally to the other utility industries considered in this book, and it appears that the reason why Ofwat particularly has taken up this issue is sensitivity over the rapid increase in real water charges. There are at least three practical reasons why diversification should worry a regulator. First, if a business owned by the group but not part of the core (regulated) business fails, then this could jeopardize

---

9. In the first six years of the tradable permits scheme used on the Fox River in Wisconsin, there was only one trade (Hahn 1989).

the ability of the firm to raise capital for the core business. Second, diversification makes estimation of the cost of capital more difficult by adding noise to rates of return and share prices. Third, there is the potential for cross-subsidization with services provided by the noncore business to the core business being overpriced.

To cope with some of these problems, Ofwat and the industry have agreed on license amendments giving the directors of the core business the duty to ensure that they have adequate financial and managerial resources to run the core business, and that they certify that this remains true after a diversification. The Competition and Service (Utilities) Act 1992 gave the DGWS a duty to ensure that transactions between unregulated subsidiaries and the regulated business are at arm's length and license amendments prohibiting cross-subsidization have been made. Implementing such a prohibition will require rules for cost allocation that will be difficult to determine given the asymmetry of information.

10.4.5 Metering

The metering issue is not unique to the water industry. The ability to run a spot electricity or gas market depends on all customers having sophisticated meters that can measure consumption frequently (half-hourly in the case of electricity). It is, however, in the water industry that the issue is most acute because only a tiny minority of domestic customers currently have meters and because the legislation requires the industry to find an alternative charging base to ratable values after 31 March 2000. Ofwat has consulted widely on metering. There are several questions that can be asked. Is a general program of metering desirable? If it is desirable, what should the tariff structures look like? What are the consequences of customers having the option of buying meters themselves? If there are still some households without meter, what is the most appropriate charging base?

Ofwat (1991b) considered all these questions. If meter installation and running costs were zero, then universal metering would be efficient. In practice the costs of metering are high. The Water Services Association (1990) reported that although 95% of properties could be metered at a cost of not more than £200, the cost of metering the remaining properties could be £1,000 per property. Metering trials that finished in 1993 produced evidence that the annual running costs of a metering system were just over £19 and that installation costs were typically in the range £165–200. Demand fell by between 2% and 21%, with an average of about 11%, although the extent of the reduction in demand will have depended on the particular tariff structures and levels used in the trials. Ofwat's view is that a rapid program of general metering would be uneconomic but that there was a good economic case for *selective* compulsory metering. Customers whose supplies might be metered include those in regions where supplies are short, those who have scope to economize on water use, and those for whom meter installation is simple.

On tariff structure, Ofwat preferred a two-part tariff for metered customers that had a relatively high marginal price in order to maximize the benefits from metering. The water industry had argued that since up to 80% of the costs of supplying water are fixed, standing charges should be relatively high. Ofwat argued that the relevant distinction is not between fixed and variable costs but between those that in the long run are related to the volume of water supplied and those that are related to the number of customers. This implies a high marginal price because many short-run fixed costs, such as the costs of building and running a new reservoir, are related to volume of water rather than numbers of customers. Seasonal pricing would also be desirable.

At present customers have the right to opt for a meter as long as they pay for the costs of installation. Ofwat is keen to improve customer awareness of this option in order to increase the number of meters installed voluntarily. Unfortunately, the customer's decision will not necessarily be efficient. We saw in section 4.2.2 that when there is competition private metering decisions can be inefficient. The argument in the water case does not depend on competition but on the fact that customers' bills, when not metered, are based on ratable values and thus bear little relationship to their consumption. A customer will choose to install a meter if the reduction in the *bill* exceeds the loss of direct utility as consumption falls plus the cost of installing the meter. Social efficiency requires that the reduction in the *costs* of supplying water as demand falls exceed the utility lost plus the metering cost (assuming that the regulator gives consumer surplus and profits equal weight). The customer will thus make an efficient decision to be metered if the reduction in the firm's costs equals the reduction in the customer's bill, and since the firm's profits will not be affected by such an efficient metering decision, there will, other things being equal, be a Pareto improvement. This holds if the metered tariff reflects marginal costs, but when this condition does not hold, there can be inefficiencies. Customers with high bills under the ratable value system but low consumption might have excessive incentives to choose a meter. Suppose that a customer has perfectly inelastic demand for water and chooses a meter. This decision must be inefficient because the meter does not affect the demand for water, but the installation and running costs of the meter have to be borne. Either profits are reduced or, if the firm is allowed to rebalance its tariffs to recover its lost revenue, other customers are worse off. Similarly some customers with low bills under ratable values but high and elastic consumption might not choose to be metered, though it would be efficient to meter them.

The costs of meter installation and operation mean that it is very unlikely that all water companies will choose to meter all customers. Only one water and sewerage company, Anglian, has announced that it intends to meter the majority of customers. Companies that do not want to meter will have to choose an alternative charging base. Water charges will remain quasi-taxes, and the fairness and efficiency of schemes will vary. Rajah and Smith (1993) and Pearson, Rajah, and Smith (1993) consider the distributional effects and administrative costs of different charging schemes. A flat rate license fee per household would have few administrative costs but would be marginally more regressive than the current ratable value system. Charges could also be based on household characteristics, such as the number of household members, house type, or the valuations used for the council tax (the latest system of local authority finance in Britain). These would incur greater administrative costs than a license fee and would be more regressive than current charges, but the effect would be very small. They would probably be seen by customers as more equitable than license fees. The scheme based on the number of household members has the advantage that it comes closest to ensuring that voluntary metering decisions are efficient. The choice of charging base is up to the companies, but some guidance from Ofwat can be expected.

10.5 Assessment

The new regulatory regime is in some respects superior to the one that existed until 1989. Price regulation and the setting and monitoring of environmental and quality targets are more open than under the previous regime. It is possible that the privatization of the investment program has brought forward the dates of achievement of the overall environmental and quality goals, since the government might not have financed the program in full if the water and sewerage companies had remained in public ownership, especially given the deterioration of the public finances during the recession of the early 1990s.

There is, however, little scope for increased product market competition, and the regulation of the water industry is inevitably detailed and expensive. Price levels are controlled, progress on investment plans is carefully monitored, and diversification is constrained. Prices in the short term have to increase over time. The fact that the investment program is now being undertaken by the private sector means that private sector rates of return must be earned. If private sector rate of returns exceed those of the public sector because of regulatory risk, prices in the long run might be higher than if the investment had been carried out in the public sector. The existence of separate environmental and economic regulators with different objectives and agendas is potentially inefficient. It remains to be seen whether a workable system of yardstick competition can be established. The burden on the economic regulator is clearly very great and will continue to be so for the foreseeable future.

11

Conclusions

The last five chapters of this book have described and analyzed the transformation of the utility industries in Britain from being state-owned monopolists a decade ago to firms with new owners, new regulatory institutions, new industry structures, new competitors, and new methods of controlling their behavior. Though these policies may be new, at least in postwar Britain, they address an old[1] and fundamental question of how to limit and control monopoly power in a way that promotes economic efficiency. Various economic, political, and technological developments are causing governments worldwide to reassess this question in the circumstances of their own industries, and it is therefore important to ask what lessons may be drawn from the experience in Britain, which, along with the United States, has perhaps been the leading exponent of regulatory reform in recent years.

In terms of form, the new regulatory frameworks in Britain have so far survived reasonably well. The system of independent and explicit economic regulation established for BT in 1984, and the $RPI - X$ method of price control in particular, have served and continue to serve as models for other industries. In substance, however, there has been considerable change. Regulation that was intended to be "with a light rein" has had to be supplemented and tightened repeatedly. Effective competition has not developed as initially hoped, and competition policies for the utility industries have had to be strengthened along with regulatory policy.

In this final chapter we summarize the conclusions and lessons that we draw from the recent British experience of regulatory reform under the headings of structure, liberalization, price and quality regulation, institutions and future challenges.

11.1 Structure

In all aspects—vertical, horizontal, and regional—British policy toward industries that contain natural monopoly elements has increasingly favored measures of structural reform. Three benchmark cases of vertical

---

1. Part 1 of Foster (1992) gives an interesting account of the historical development of the regulation of natural monopoly in Britain.

organization were described in the introductory chapter: (1) vertically integrated monopoly, (2) vertical integration with liberalization, and (3) vertical separation. The publicly owned British utilities were in form (1) at the start of the 1980s. In telecommunications BT was privatized in 1984 in a limited version of form 2, but there has been more liberalization over time, and there are now proposals for accounting separation. British Gas was privatized in 1986 notionally in form 2 but effectively in form 1, and subsequent developments, culminating in the 1993 MMC reports, have been toward form 3. The electricity supply industry was privatized in 1990–91 in form 3 as far as generation and transmission are concerned, but the new system has other elements of vertical integration, for example, between transmission and distribution (albeit at arm's length) and to some extent between distribution and generation. Vertical separation—between infrastructure and service operation—is also in prospect for British Rail. Thus vertical structure policy has moved over time toward separation both within industries (as in gas) and in the sense that later privatization proposals (electricity, rail), unlike the earlier ones, embraced structural reform.[2] The same is true of regional structure—compare telecommunications and gas (1984–86) with water, electricity distribution and supply, and railways (1989–94). Horizontal restructuring to promote head-to-head competition has so far only occurred in electricity generation (but to a seriously inadequate extent).

The main economic, as distinct from political,[3] disadvantage of structural reform is the loss of economies of scope. In particular contractual or market-based schemes have to be devised to replace internal coordination. It is ironic that this is probably more difficult for electricity and rail than for telecommunications and gas. The chief potential benefits of structural reform are that it facilitates more effective competition and regulation. It appears very difficult to combine vertical integration with a "level playing

2. Vertical separation was ordered in the beer supply industry too, following action by the competition authorities (see MMC 1989).

3. Interesting evidence on the relationship between privatization and policy toward structure comes from Sir Alan Walters. On the question of breaking up BT along the lines of AT&T he writes: "As Mrs Thatcher's former adviser, I can testify that all the relevant ministers, including the Prime Minister, were very keen on such a breakup. But we were eventually convinced that, because of the need to allocate liabilities and assets and prepare separate accounts, such a move would take two, perhaps three years to implement. With the need to search for a new political and economic 'window of opportunity,' this would have delayed privatization even longer" (Walters 1988, 66–67).

field" in competitive activities—the Monopolies and Mergers Commission (1993a, 17) saw an "inherent conflict of interest" between the two in the case of gas. Regional separation allows yardstick competition (and perhaps some direct competition in input or output markets). And the ring-fencing of natural monopoly improves information for regulation.

These conflicting considerations mean that there can be no universal prescription for structural policy. However, the difficulties that have been experienced with conduct regulation in the vertically integrated gas and telecommunications industries in Britain support the case for separation, and they are part of the reason why structural reform has been favored in other industries more recently. In our view British Gas should have certainly have been restructured vertically before privatization, and the government should have accepted the restructing recommended by the MMC, even though the company was sold to investors vertically intact. In telecommunications it remains to be seen whether effective and undistorted competition can prosper in the more liberal regime without full vertical separation.

The main criticism of structural reform in the electricity supply industry is that it did not go far enough to create conditions for effective and undistorted competition in generation in return for the more difficult coordination between generation and transmission. The limited nature of the horizontal breakup of the CEGB's generating assets was unnecessary, especially once nuclear stations had been withdrawn from privatization. Though the National Grid Company is kept out of generation (except for its pumped storage business), the regional distribution and supply companies are allowed to integrate vertically (up to limits), and they are joint owners of the grid. In our view a totally independent grid company would have been better. If a more competitive structure had been chosen for generation, there would have been less incentive for possibly excessive entry by independents into the generation market. As things stand, it is arguable whether the additional competitive pressure that they bring in generation promotes efficiency overall. Regional separation in electricity and water allows various forms of performance comparison, and although yardstick competition has not (yet) been implemented explicitly, the net benefits in terms of greater information flows are likely to be positive.

It remains to be seen how well vertical separation will work in the railway industry. As in electricity, a key issue is whether enough benefits of effective competition can be realized to outweigh additional costs of coordination in a deintegrated regime, for example, in relation to quality control. The complex economic characteristics of rail services, and especially the difficulties of contract specification and enforcement, suggest that efficient and competitive franchising will be difficult to achieve. Vertical separation could also be adopted for postal services, for example, between local delivery and collection, on one hand, and sorting and trunking, on the other. The relatively low level of sunk costs is favorable for competitive prospects, but again there are difficulties of contracting for end-to-end quality control, and there is the political constraint—in the short term at least—of nationwide uniform pricing.

11.2   Liberalization

Liberalization is obviously necessary to achieve the benefits of competition, but experience has underlined that it is far from sufficient. Effective competition requires more than legal liberalization—procompetitive regulatory policy is needed as well. Over the past decade in Britain, both legal liberalization and procompetitive regulatory policy have grown. In telecommunications the duopoly policy was ended in 1991, in gas the monopoly threshold has come down from 25,000 to 2,500 therms and will be abolished, and the monopoly supply franchises in electricity are being phased out over time. Regulation of access terms has become more explicit, competition policy sanctions have been applied in the industrial market for gas, there are moves toward equal access in telecommunications, and informal procompetitive regulation has been evident, for example, by Oftel in the apparatus market.

Substantial incumbent advantages have persisted in many activities, especially those related to vertically integrated networks, where the extent of competitive entry has been limited so far. Thus BT continues to dominate network operation, and in gas it has taken the blunt instruments of the market share quotas and the gas release scheme to curb British Gas. In other activities, including telecommunications apparatus supply and VANS, and in electricity generation and retail supply (counting geographical cross-entry) there has been a considerable amount of entry (indeed excess entry into electricity generation in the opinion of some).

In the utility industries, especially if the dominant incumbent has not been restructured, it is a formidable task to regulate in such a way that there are neither ineffective entry threats nor incentives for inefficient entry. The first of these dangers was prevalent in the 1980s in the British utility industries, and on balance it is still the greater problem. In some areas, however, the picture is becoming more mixed.

11.3 Price and Quality Regulation

RPI − X price cap regulation as developed in Britain differs from traditional rate-of-return regulation in important respects, but the economic (as distinct from institutional) differences—regarding cost passthrough, regulatory lag, and so on—are ones of degree rather than of a fundamental nature. RPI − X regulation has not evolved in accordance with Littlechild's original vision of clear incentives, a light regulatory burden, and rapidly emerging competition. The scope, toughness, and detail of price regulation have all increased, and it has been supplemented by new measures of quality regulation. Given the weakness of competition and regulation policy when privatizations occurred, these changes were necessary. In addition informal regulation of pricing, quality, and even investment has taken place between the formal price reviews. The regulatory burden, as interpreted by the regulators themselves, has been considerable. A captured regulator might have chosen to carry a lighter burden.

The framework of price control has proved to be broad and flexible enough to accommodate substantial variations in method, and the longer lag than typical in rate-of-return regulation appears to have beneficial incentive properties. Important questions for the future of RPI − X price regulation include the following. First, can it successfully incorporate yardstick competition? Regional separation allows regulatory incentives to be improved by using comparative information, but regulators have found this difficult to incorporate explicitly. It is unclear how (or whether) such information will be used in regulatory reviews where it is available. Second, how will practices of cost of capital estimation, and especially of rate base measurement, develop? Allowing new investment to earn a higher rate of return than existing assets will tend to put upward pressure on prices as old assets are replaced and the value of the rate base rises toward the replacement cost value. Only if there is either significant slack to be eliminated or technological progress will this upward pressure on prices be alleviated. Third, can price regulation be made consistent with conditions for effective and undistorted competition? The structure of final product prices is one aspect of this question, but most important perhaps is the question of how to regulate the price and other terms of network access.

11.4   Institutions

A notable feature of the new regulatory institutions in Britain is the discretion and independence enjoyed by the industry regulators. It is now quite clear that their role goes far beyond monitoring and enforcing license conditions and that the ability to seek license changes, either by agreement with the licensee or by making a successful reference to the MMC, is a source of considerable influence. This is most apparent at times of regulatory price reviews but is important much more generally. For example, BT's price structure and service quality were subject to implicit regulation by Oftel not long after privatization despite the absence of explicit powers at the time, and the electricity generators may have been influenced by Offer even though they were formally unregulated. The regulator's ability to seek license changes can give rise to a kind of "regulation by negotiation," which is conditioned by the possibility of a referral to the MMC. Ultimately there could be judicial review by the courts—of both regulators' and MMC decisions—but the legislation specifies regulatory duties with a generality that would appear to make challenge difficult. Prospective judicial interpretation of statutory requirements upon regulators to ensure that firms can finance their regulated activities might, however, turn out to be important for investment incentives.

Is regulatory discretion desirable? To date we believe that it has been beneficial overall. Most of the shortcomings in regulatory arrangements that we have discussed resulted from government decisions—the gas industry being the clearest, but not the only, case in point. The proactive use of regulatory discretion to strengthen competition and regulation can be seen in large part as an attempt to remedy some of the deficiencies in the initial regulatory frameworks. Moreover regulatory discretion has been exercised without the need for cumbersome legalistic procedures, and there has been little evidence of regulatory capture, so far at least. Independent regulation, together with privatization, has limited the ability of ministers and politicians to intervene in the industries concerned. Comparison with the era of nationalization suggests that this more arm's-length relationship between government and industry is a good thing—indeed it is an important part of the case for privatization—and on general grounds explicit interventions are preferable to hidden ones.

It is an open question whether regulatory discretion will be beneficial in the longer term. There is the danger of regulatory capture, on the one hand, and of excessive exercise of discretion leading to large regulatory risk, on the other. In both respects, however, the general competition authorities (at national and potentially also at EC level) offer a degree of protection against these dangers (unless they succumb to them also).

For the time being, rather than changing the structure of regulation, we would give attention to reforming conduct, for example, increasing the openness of regulatory decision making and of corporate reporting. Confidentiality may limit the amount of commercial data that can be published about competitive activities, but this point does not apply to regulatory reasoning and principles (e.g., about the cost of capital, or the determination of network access terms) or to naturally monopolistic activities. Much more transparency now exists than under nationalization, but the process can and should go further. Just as asymmetric information about industry conditions hampers the effective regulation of firms, asymmetric information about the process of regulation itself is also undesirable. Better information would enhance clarity and predictability, would lead to better public debate and scrutiny, and would minimize the danger of regulatory capture.

11.5 Future Challenges

Although technological developments have reduced the scope of natural monopoly in industries such as telecommunications, the need for regulation of firms with market power will not wither away in the foreseeable future. Unfortunately, it is overoptimistic to view regulation as a stopgap until sufficient competition arrives. It is obviously impossible to predict what will be the most important regulatory issues the years ahead, but we will conclude by highlighting two challenging problems.

The first is the question mentioned in the introductory chapter in relation to the AT&T case, which has been a major concern in the British utility industries: Can effective regulation of an integrated monopolist coexist with conditions for effective and undistorted competition in industries that contain both naturally monopolistic and potentially competitive activities? In the face of incumbent advantages inherited from previously monopolistic regimes, it can be hard to establish conditions for effective competition even when restructuring has occurred, but the difficulties are greater still when the dominant firm remains vertically integrated. In particular there is the vexing question of access pricing, which has yet to find a robust answer.

The second is the question of whether the regulatory system can provide a stable incentive structure that is conducive to efficient long-term *investment* by regulated firms. The future costs of failing to overcome the problem of regulatory risk could be very great. As well as large productive inefficiencies from underinvestment, there could be serious allocative inefficiency because of high prices needed to meet the regulatory risk premium in the cost of capital. Rate-of-return regulation as traditionally practiced in the United States and state-owned enterprise can both give rise to excessive investment incentives, among other problems, but it may be that the opposite danger of underinvestment is a problem for regulatory reform in a newly privatized regime, where the functions of investment and price control are separated.

Although the first decade since BT's privatization has seen a necessary increase in both competition and regulation in the utility industries, it is to be hoped that effective competition can develop in the next ten years in such a way that regulation and its associated shortcomings can diminish. The optimistic scenario is that effective and undistorted competition will emerge in those activities that are not naturally monopolistic, and can then be deregulated, and that the future regulation of remaining natural monopoly elements will create credible long-term incentive structures. A necessary (but not sufficient) condition for this is that the natural monopoly elements are separated either structurally or by very effective conduct regulation. The pessimistic scenario, however, is one of ineffective or distorted competition, and a need for increasing regulation of investment as well as prices and quality of service. At present the prospects are mixed.

References

Acton, J. P., and I. Vogelsang. 1989. Symposium on price cap regulation: Introduction. *Rand Journal of Economics* 20:369–72.

Aghion, P., and P. Bolton. 1987. Entry prevention through contracts with customers. *American Economic Review* 77:388–401.

Akerlof, G. 1970. The market for "lemons": Qualitative uncertainty and the market mechanism. *Quarterly Journal of Economics* 84:488–500.

Allaz, B., and J.-L. Vila. 1993. Cournot competition, forward markets and efficiency. *Journal of Economic Theory* 59:1–16.

Allen, F. 1984. Reputation and product quality. *Rand Journal of Economics* 15:311–27.

Anderson, R. W. 1990. Futures trading for imperfect cash markets: A survey. In L. Phlips, ed., *Commodity Futures and Financial Markets*, Amsterdam: Kluwer.

Armstrong, C. M. 1993a. Regulating a multiproduct firm with unknown costs. Economic Theory discussion paper no. 184. Cambridge.

Armstrong, C. M. 1993b. Multiproduct nonlinear pricing. Economic Theory discussion paper no. 185. Cambridge.

Armstrong, C. M., S. G. B. Cowan, and J. S. Vickers. 1992. Nonlinear pricing and price cap regulation. Institute of Economics and Statistics discussion paper no. 152. Oxford.

Armstrong, C. M., R. Rees, and J. S. Vickers. 1991. Optimal regulatory lag under price cap regulation. Mimeo. Institute of Economics and Statistics, Oxford.

Armstrong, C. M., and J. S. Vickers. 1991. Welfare effects of price discrimination by a regulated monopolist. *Rand Journal of Economics* 22:571–80.

Armstrong, C. M., and J. S. Vickers. 1992. Competition and regulation in telecommunications. Forthcoming in Bishop et al., eds.

Armstrong, C. M., and J. S. Vickers. 1993. Price discrimination, competition and regulation. *Journal of Industrial Economics* 41:335–59.

Auriol, E., and J.-J. Laffont. 1992. Regulation by duopoly. IDEI working paper no. 20. Toulouse.

Averch, H., and L. Johnson. 1962. Behavior of the firm under regulatory constraint. *American Economic Review* 52:1052–69.

Baron, D. P. 1985. Noncooperative regulation of a nonlocalized externality. *Rand Journal of Economics* 16:553–68.

Baron, D. P. 1989. Design of regulatory mechanisms and institutions. In Schmalensee and Willig, eds.

Baron, D. P., and D. Besanko. 1984. Regulation, asymmetric information, and auditing. *Rand Journal of Economics* 15:447–70.

Baron, D. P., and D. Besanko. 1987. Commitment and fairness in a dynamic regulatory relationship. *Review of Economic Studies* 52:413–36.

Baron, D. P., and R. B. Myerson. 1982. Regulating a monopolist with unknown costs. *Econometrica* 50:911–30.

Baumol, W. J. 1982. Contestable markets: An uprising in the theory of industrial structure. *American Economic Review* 72:1–15.

Baumol, W. J. 1983. Some subtle pricing issues in railroad regulation. *International Journal of Transport Economics* 10:341–55.

Baumol, W. J., and D. Bradford. 1970. Optimal departures from marginal cost pricing. *American Economic Review* 60:265–83.

Baumol, W. J., and A. K. Klevorick. 1970. Input choices and rate of return regulation: An overview of the discussion. *Bell Journal of Economics* 1:162–90.

Baumol, W. J., J. Panzar, and R. D. Willig. 1982. *Contestable Markets and the Theory of Industry Structure*. New York: Harcourt Brace Jovanovich.

Baumol, W. J., and J. G. Sidak. 1994. *Toward Competition in Local Telephony*. Cambridge: MIT Press.

Baumol, W. J., and R. D. Willig. 1986. Contestability: Developments since the book. *Oxford Economic Papers* (suppl.) 38:9–36.

Beesley, M. E. 1981. *Liberalisation of the Use of the British Telecommunications Network*. London: Department of Trade and Industry.

Beesley, M. E., and B. Laidlaw. 1989. *The Future of Telecommunications*. London: Institute of Economic Affairs.

Beesley, M. E., and S. C. Littlechild. 1989. The regulation of privatized monopolies in the United Kingdom. *Rand Journal of Economics* 20:454–72.

Berg, S. V., and J. Tschirhart. 1988. *Natural Monopoly Regulation*. Cambridge: Cambridge University Press.

Bernheim, B. D., and M. D. Whinston. 1986. Common agency. *Econometrica* 54:923–42.

Besanko, D., and D. Spulber. 1992. Sequential-equilibrium investment by regulated firms. *Rand Journal of Economics* 23:153–70.

Bishop, M., and J. A. Kay. 1988. *Does Privatization Work? Lessons from the UK*. London: London Business School.

Bishop, M., J. A. Kay, C. P. Mayer, and D. J. Thompson, eds. 1992. *Privatization and Regulation—The UK Experience*. Oxford: Oxford University Press, forthcoming.

Bohn, R. E., M. C. Caramanis, and F. C. Schweppe. 1984. Optimal pricing in electrical networks over space and time. *Rand Journal of Economics* 15:360–76.

Boiteux, M. 1956. Sur la gestion des monopoles publics astreints à l'equilibre budgétaire. *Econometrica* 24:22–40.

Bolton, P., and M. D. Whinston. 1991. The "foreclosure" effect of vertical mergers. *Journal of Institutional and Theoretical Economics* 147:207–26.

Bolton, P., and M. D. Whinston. 1993. Incomplete contracts, vertical integration, and supply constraints. *Review of Economic Studies* 60:121–48.

Bradley I., and C. Price. 1988. The economic regulation of private industries by price constraints. *Journal of Industrial Economics* 37:99–106.

Braeutigam, R. R., and J. C. Panzar. 1989. Diversification incentives under "price-based" and "cost-based" regulation. *Rand Journal of Economics* 20:373–91.

British Gas. 1992. *Submission to the Office of Gas Supply on the Rate of Return for Gas Transportation and Storage*. London: British Gas.

British Telecom. *Annual Reports*.

British Telecom. 1992. *Pricing for Choice*. London: British Telecom.

Brock, G. W. 1981. *The Telecommunications Industry: The Dynamics of Market Structure*. Cambridge: Harvard University Press.

Brock, W. 1983. Contestable markets and the theory of industry structure: A review article. *Journal of Political Economy* 91:1055–66.

Brock, W., and J. Scheinkman. 1985. Price setting supergames with capacity constraints. *Review of Economic Studies* 52:371–82.

Brown, C. 1991. *The Competitive Gas Market Takes Off*. London: British Gas.

Brown, S. J., and D. S. Sibley. 1986. *The Theory of Public Utility Pricing*. Cambridge: Cambridge University Press.

Byatt, I. C. R. 1991. Office of Water Services: Regulation of water and sewerage. In C. Veljanovski, ed., *Regulators and the Market*. London: Institute of Economic Affairs.

Caillaud, B. 1991. Regulation, competition and asymmetric information. *Journal of Economic Theory* 52:87–110

Capel, J. 1990. *The Electricity Supply Industry*. London: James Capel.

Cave, M. 1991. Recent developments in the regulation of former nationalised industries. Working paper no. 59, HM Treasury. London.

Cave, M. 1993. Utilities and their customers: Whose quality of service is it? Mimeo. Faculty of Social Sciences, Brunel University.

Centre for the Study of Regulated Industries. 1991. *The UK Water Industry: Charges for Water Services 1991/92*. London: Public Finance Foundation.

Centre for the Study of Regulated Industries. 1992a. *Regulated Industries: The UK Framework*. London: Public Finance Foundation.

Centre for the Study of Regulated Industries. 1992b. *Incentive Regulation*. London: Public Finance Foundation.

Civil Aviation Authority. 1991. *Economic Regulation of BAA South East Airports*, CAP 599, CAA. London.

Coase, R. 1937. The nature of the firm. *Economica* 4:386–405.

Cowan, S. G. B. 1992. Regulation of the water industry in England and Wales. Forthcoming in Bishop et al., eds.

Crew, M. A., and P. R. Kleindorfer. 1976. Peak load pricing with a diverse technology. *Bell Journal of Economics* 7:207–31.

Culham, P. G. 1987. *A Method for Determining the Optimal Balance of Prices for Telephone Services*. London: Oftel.

Dana, J. D. 1993. The organization and scope of agents. *Journal of Economic Theory* 59:288–310.

Demsetz, H. 1968. Why regulate utilities? *Journal of Law and Economics* 11:55–65.

Demski, J., and D. E. M. Sappington. 1984. Optimal incentive contracts with multiple agents. *Journal of Economic Theory* 33:152–71.

Department of Energy. 1988. *Privatising Electricity*. London: HMSO.

Department of Energy. 1989. The demand for energy. In Helm et al. eds.

Department of the Environment. 1986. *Privatisation of the Water Authorities in England and Wales*. Cmnd 9734. London: HMSO.

Department of the Environment. 1990. *This Common Inheritance.* Cm 1200. London: HMSO.

Department of Industry. 1982. *The Future of Telecommunications in Britain.* Cm 8610. London: HMSO.

Department of Trade and Industry. 1990. *Competition and Choice: Telecommunications Policy for the 1990s. A Consultative Document.* Cm 1303. London: HMSO.

Department of Trade and Industry. 1991. *Competition and Choice: Telecommunications Policy for the 1990s.* Cm 1461. London: HMSO.

Department of Trade and Industry. 1992. *Digest of United Kingdom Energy Statistics.* London: HMSO.

Department of Trade and Industry. 1993a. *Digest of United Kingdom Energy Statistics.* London: HMSO.

Department of Trade and Industry. 1993b. *The Prospects for Coal: Conclusions of the Government's Coal Review.* Cm 2235. London: HMSO.

Department of Transport. 1992. *New Opportunities for the Railways–The Privatisation of British Rail.* Cm 2012. London: HMSO.

Dixit, A. 1980. The role of investment in entry deterrence. *Economic Journal* 90:95–106.

Dorken, J. 1992. RPI − X: Then and now. In Centre for the Study of Regulated Industries (1992b).

Evans, D. S., ed. 1983. *Breaking up Bell.* Amsterdam: North-Holland.

Evans, D. S., and J. J. Heckman. 1983. Multiproduct cost function estimates and natural monopoly tests for the bell system. In Evans, ed.

Farrell, J., and C. Shapiro. 1990. Horizontal mergers—An equilibrium analysis. *American Economic Review* 80:107–26.

Faulhaber, G. R. 1975. Cross-subsidization: Pricing in public enterprises. *American Economic Review* 65:966–77.

von der Fehr, N.-H. M., and D. Harbord. 1993. Spot market competition in the UK electricity supply industry. *Economic Journal* 103:531–46.

Feldstein, M. S. 1972a. Distributional equity and the optimal structure of public prices. *American Economic Review* 62:32–36.

Feldstein, M. S. 1972b. Equity and efficiency in public pricing. *Quarterly Journal of Economics* 86:175–87.

Finsinger, J., and I. Vogelsang. 1982. Performance indices for public enterprises. In L. P. Jones, ed., *Public Enterprise in Less-Developed Countries.* Cambridge: Cambridge University Press.

Foster, C. D. 1992. *Privatization, Public Ownership and the Regulation of Natural Monopoly.* Oxford: Blackwell.

Freixas, X., R. Guesnerie, and J. Tirole. 1985. Planning under incomplete information and the ratchet effect. *Review of Economic Studies* 52:173–91.

Gasmi, F., M. Ivaldi, and J.-J. Laffont. 1992. Rent extraction and incentives for efficiency in recent regulatory proposals. Mimeo. Université de Toulouse.

Geroski, P., D. Thompson, and S. Toker. 1989. Vertical separation and price discrimination: Cellular phones in the UK. *Fiscal Studies* 10(4):83–103.

Gilbert, R. J. 1989. Mobility barriers and the value of incumbency. In Schmalensee and Willig, eds.

Gilbert, R. J., and D. M. Newbery. 1988. Regulation games. CEPR discussion paper no 267. London.

Gist, P., and S. A. Meadowcroft. 1986. Regulating for competition: The newly liberalized market for private branch exchanges. *Fiscal Studies* 7(3):41–66.

Glaister, S. 1987. Regulation through an output-related profits tax. *Journal of Industrial Economics* 35:281–96.

Glazer, A., and H. McMillan. 1992. Pricing by the firm under regulatory threat. *Quarterly Journal of Economics* 107:1089–99.

Goldberg, V. P. 1976. Regulation and administered contracts. *Bell Journal of Economics* 7:426–448.

Green, R. J., and D. M. Newbery. 1992. Competition in the British electricity spot market. *Journal of Political Economy* 100:929–53.

Green, R. J., and D. M. Newbery. 1993a. Regulation, public ownership and privatisation in the English electricity industry. Mimeo, Department of Applied Economics, Cambridge.

Green, R. J., and D. M. Newbery. 1993b. The regulation of the gas industry: Lessons from electricity. *Fiscal Studies* 14(2):35–52.

Greenwald, B. C. 1984. Rate base selection and the structure of regulation. *Rand Journal of Economics* 15:85–95.

Grossman, S., and O. Hart. 1986. The costs and benefits of ownership—A theory of vertical and lateral integration. *Journal of Political Economy* 94:691–719.

Grout, P. 1992. The cost of capital in regulated industries. Forthcoming in Bishop et al., eds.

Hagerman, J. 1990. Regulation by price adjustment. *Rand Journal of Economics* 21:72–82.

Hahn, R. W. 1984. Market power and transferable property rights. *Quarterly Journal of Economics* 99:753–65.

Hahn, R. W. 1989. Economic prescriptions for environmental problems: How the patient followed the doctor's orders. *Journal of Economic Perspectives* 3(2):95–114.

Hammond, E., D. Helm, and D. Thompson. 1985. British Gas: Options for privatisation. *Fiscal Studies* 6(4):1–20.

Hansen, R. G. 1988. Auctions with endogenous quantity. *Rand Journal of Economics* 19:44–58.

Hart, O. 1983. The market mechanism as an incentive scheme. *Bell Journal of Economics* 14:366–82.

Hart, O., and J. Moore. 1990. Property rights and the nature of the firm. *Journal of Political Economy* 98:1119–58.

Hart, O., and J. Tirole. 1990. Vertical integration and market foreclosure. *Brookings Papers. Microeconomics*: 205–86.

Helm, D. 1991. Privatization and environmental regulation in the water and electricity industries. *Royal Bank of Scotland Review* 172:30–37.

Helm, D. 1993a. Market mechanisms and the water environment: Are they practicable? In Centre for the Study of Regulated Industries, *Efficiency and Effectiveness in the Modern Water Business*. London: Public Finance Foundation.

Helm, D. 1993b. Regulating the transition to the competitive market. Paper presented to the London Business School seminar on energy regulation.

Helm, D., J. A. Kay, and D. Thompson, eds. 1989. *The Market for Energy*. Oxford: Clarendon Press.

Helm, D., and A. Powell. 1992. Pool prices, contracts and regulation in the British electricity supply industry. *Fiscal Studies* 13(1):89–105.

Henry, C. 1993. Public service and competition in the European Community approach to communications networks. *Oxford Review of Economic Policy* 9(1):45–66.

Hogan, W. 1992. Contract networks for electric power transmission. *Journal of Regulatory Economics* 4:211–42.

Holmstrom, B. 1982a. Managerial incentive problems—A dynamic perspective. In *Essays in Economics and Management in Honor of Lars Wahlbeck*. Helsinki: Swedish School of Economics.

Holmstrom, B. 1982b. Moral hazard in teams. *Bell Journal of Economics* 13:324–40.

Holmstrom, B., and P. Milgrom. 1987. Aggregation and linearity in the provision of intertemporal incentives. *Econometrica* 55:303–28.

Holmstrom, B., and P. Milgrom. 1991. Multitask principal-agent analyses: Incentive contracts, asset ownership, and job design. *Journal of Law, Economics and Organization* 7:24–52.

Holmstrom, B., and J. Tirole. 1989. The theory of the firm. In Schmalensee and Willig, eds.

House of Commons. 1993. *British Energy Policy and the Market for Coal*. Trade and Industry Committee, HC 237. London: HMSO.

Hunt, L. C., and E. L. Lynk. 1991. Industrial structure in US telecommunications: Some empirical evidence. *Applied Economics* 23:1655–64.

Joskow, P. L. 1987. Contract duration and relation-specific investments: The case of coal. *American Economic Review* 77:168–85.

Joskow, P. L. 1989. Regulatory failure, regulatory reform, and structural change in the electrical power industry. *Brookings Papers. Microeconomics*: 125–99.

Joskow, P. L., and R. Schmalensee. 1983. *Markets for Power*. Cambridge: MIT Press.

Joskow, P. L., and R. Schmalensee. 1986. Incentive regulation for electric utilities. *Yale Journal on Regulation* 4:1–49.

KPMG Peat Marwick McLintock. 1990. *Strategy for Comparative Efficiency Studies*. London: KPMG.

Kaserman, D. L., and J. W. Mayo. 1991. Determinants of vertical integration: An empirical test. *Journal of Industrial Economics* 34:483–502.

Kay, J. A. 1991. Vertical integration: The regulatory issues. In Centre for Business Strategy, ed., *Lectures on Regulation*. London: London Business School.

Kerkvliet, J. 1991. Efficiency and vertical integration: The case of mine-mouth electric generating plants. *Journal of Industrial Economics* 34:467–82.

Kinnersley, D. 1988. *Troubled Water*. London: Hilary Shipman.

Kleindorfer, P. R., and C. S. Fernando. 1993. Peak-load pricing and reliability under uncertainty. *Journal of Regulatory Economics* 5:5–23.

Klemperer, P. D. 1987. Markets with consumer switching costs. *Quarterly Journal of Economics* 102:375–94.

Klemperer, P. D., and M. Meyer. 1989. Supply function equilibria in oligopoly under uncertainty. *Econometrica* 57:1243–77.

Kreps, D., and J. Scheinkman. 1983. Quantity precommitment and Bertrand competition yield Cournot outcomes. *Bell Journal of Economics* 14:326–37.

Krishna, K. 1989. Trade restrictions as facilitating practices. *Journal of International Economics* 26:251–70.

Laffont, J.-J., and J. Tirole. 1986. Using cost information to regulate firms. *Journal of Political Economy* 94:614–41.

Laffont, J.-J., and J. Tirole. 1987. Auctioning incentive contracts. *Journal of Political Economy* 95:921–37.

Laffont, J.-J., and J. Tirole. 1988a. Repeated auctions of incentive contracts, investment, and bidding parity with an application to takeovers. *Rand Journal of Economics* 19:516–37.

Laffont, J.-J., and J. Tirole. 1988b. The dynamics of incentive contracts. *Econometrica* 56: 1153–75.

Laffont, J.-J., and J. Tirole. 1990a. The regulation of multiproduct firms. Parts I and II. *Journal of Public Economics* 43:1–66.

Laffont, J.-J., and J. Tirole. 1990b. Optimal bypass and cream skimming. *American Economic Review* 80:1042–61.

Laffont, J.-J., and J. Tirole. 1991. The politics of government decision-making: A theory of regulatory capture. *Quarterly Journal of Economics* 106:1089–1127.

Laffont, J.-J., and J. Tirole. 1992. Access pricing and competition. Mimeo. Université de Toulouse.

Laffont, J.-J., and J. Tirole. 1993. *A Theory of Incentives in Procurement and Regulation.* Cambridge: MIT Press.

Lawson, N. 1992. *The View from No. 11.* London: Bantam.

Leland, H. 1979. Quacks, lemons and licensing: A theory of minimum quality standards. *Journal of Political Economy* 87:1328–46.

Lewis, T. R., and D. E. M. Sappington. 1988. Regulating a monopolist with unknown demand. *American Economic Review* 78:986–98.

Liston, C. 1993. Price-cap versus rate-of-return regulation. *Journal of Regulatory Economics* 5:25–48.

Littlechild, S. C. 1983. *Regulation of British Telecommunications Profitability.* London: HMSO.

Littlechild, S. C. 1986. *Economic Regulation of Privatised Water Authorities.* London: HMSO.

Loeb, M., and W. A. Magat. 1979. A decentralized method of utility regulation. *Journal of Law and Economics* 22:399–404.

McAfee, R. P., and J. McMillan. 1987. Auctions and bidding. *Journal of Economic Literature* 25:699–738.

McGowan, F., G. MacKerron, and J. Surrey. 1990. *Regulation of the Privatised British Gas Industry.* Science Policy Research Unit, University of Sussex.

McMaster, R., and J. W. Sawkins. 1993. The water industry in Scotland—Is franchising viable? *Fiscal Studies* 14(4):1–13.

Mankiw, N. G., and M. D. Whinston. 1986. Free entry and social inefficiency. *Rand Journal of Economics* 17:48–58.

Milgrom, P., and J. Roberts. 1982. Predation, reputation and entry deterrence. *Journal of Economic Theory* 27:280–312.

Milgrom, P., and J. Roberts. 1992. *Economics, Organization and Management.* Englewood Cliffs, NJ: Prentice-Hall.

Misiolek, W., and H. Elder. 1989. Exclusionary manipulation of markets for pollution rights. *Journal of Environmental Economics and Management* 16:156–66.

Mitchell, B. M., and I. Vogelsang. 1991. *Telecommunications Pricing: Theory and Practice.* Cambridge: Cambridge University Press.

Monopolies and Mergers Commission. 1981. *Central Electricity Generating Board.* HC 315. London: HMSO.

Monopolies and Mergers Commission. 1982. *Contraceptive Sheaths.* Cmnd 8689. London: HMSO.

Monopolies and Mergers Commission. 1986a. *British Telecommunications PLC and Mitel Corporation—A Report on the Proposed Merger.* Cmnd 9715. London: HMSO.

Monopolies and Mergers Commission. 1986b. *Southern Water Authority, The Eastbourne Waterworks Company, Folkestone and District Water Company, The Mid Kent Water Company, Mid-Sussex Water Company, Portsmouth Water Company and West Kent Water Company.* Cmnd 9765. London: HMSO.

Monopolies and Mergers Commission. 1987. *Manchester Airport plc.* Report MMC 1. London: Civil Aviation Authority.

Monopolies and Mergers Commission. 1988. *Gas.* Cm 500. London: HMSO.

Monopolies and Mergers Commission. 1989. *The Supply of Beer.* Cm 651. London: HMSO.

Monopolies and Mergers Commission. 1990a. *General Utilities plc. The Colne Valley Water Company and Rickmansworth Water Company.* Cm 1029. London: IIMSO.

Monopolies and Mergers Commission. 1990b. *General Utilities plc and the Mid Kent Water Company.* Cm 1125. London: HMSO.

Monopolies and Mergers Commission. 1990c. *Southern Water plc and Mid-Sussex Water Company.* Cm 1126. London: HMSO.

Monopolies and Mergers Commission. 1993a. *Gas, Volume 1 of Reports under the Fair Trading Act 1973.* Cm 2314. London: HMSO.

Monopolies and Mergers Commission. 1993b. *British Gas plc, Volume 1 of Reports under the Gas Act 1986,* Cm 2315. London: HMSO.

Monopolies and Mergers Commission. 1993c. *Gas and British Gas plc, Volume 2 of Reports under the Gas and Fair Trading Acts.* Cm 2316. London: HMSO.

Monopolies and Mergers Commission. 1993d. *Gas and British Gas plc, Volume 3 of Reports under the Gas and Fair Trading Acts,* Cm 2317. London: HMSO.

Mookherjee, D. 1984. Optimal incentive schemes with many agents. *Review of Economic Studies* 51:433–46.

Nalebuff, B., and J. E. Stiglitz. 1983. Prizes and incentives: Towards a general theory of compensation and competition. *Bell Journal of Economics* 14:21–43.

National Grid Company. 1992. *Transmission Use of Charges Review.* NGC.

National Rivers Authority. 1993. *Charging for Discharging*. Bristol: NRA.

Neven, D. J., and J. S. Vickers. 1992. Public policy towards industrial restructuring: Some issues raised by the internal market programme. In K. Cool, D. J. Neven, and I. Walter, eds., *European Industrial Restructuring in the 1990s*. London: Macmillan.

Newbery, D. M. 1990. Acid rain. *Economic Policy* 11:297–346.

Newbery, D. M., and J. E. Stiglitz. 1981. *The Theory of Commodity Price Stabilization: A Study in the Economics of Risk*. Oxford: Oxford University Press.

Noll, R. G., and B. M. Owen. 1989. The anti-competitive uses of regulation: *US* v. *AT&T*. In J. E. Kwoka and L. J. White, eds., *The Antitrust Revolution*. New York: Harper Collins.

Offer. *Annual Reports*. London: HMSO.

Offer. 1991. *Report on Pool Price Inquiry*. Birmingham: Offer.

Offer. 1992a. *The Supply Price Control Review*. Birmingham: Offer.

Offer. 1992b. *Review of Pool Prices*. Birmingham: Offer.

Offer. 1993a. *Review of Economic Purchasing*. Birmingham: Offer.

Offer. 1993b. *Pool Price Statement*. Birmingham: Offer.

Offer. 1993c. *Electricity Distribution: Price Control, Reliability and Customer Service*. Birmingham: Offer.

Office of Fair Trading. 1991. *The Gas Review*. London: OFT.

Ofgas. *Annual Reports*. London: HMSO.

Ofgas. 1991a. *New Gas Tariff Formula: The Environment and Energy Efficiency*. London: Ofgas.

Ofgas. 1991b. *New Gas Tariff Formula: Economic Aspects*. London: Ofgas.

Ofgas. 1991c. *New Gas Tariff Formula: Tariff Structures*. London: Ofgas.

Ofgas. 1992a. *Gas Transportation and Storage*. London: Ofgas.

Ofgas. 1992b. *Separation of British Gas' Transportation and Storage Business*. London: Ofgas.

Ofgas. 1992c. *Estimating the Rate of Return for Gas Transportation*. London: Ofgas.

Ofgas. 1993. *The Gas Industry in Britain: Future Structures*. London: Ofgas.

Oftel. *Annual Reports*. London: HMSO.

Oftel. 1986. *The Review of British Telecom's Tariff Changes*. London: Oftel.

Oftel. 1988. *The Control of British Telecom's Prices*. London: Oftel.

Oftel. 1991. *BT's Apparatus Supply Business*. London: Oftel.

Oftel. 1992a. *The Regulation of BT's Prices*. London: Oftel.

Oftel. 1992b. *BT's Cost of Capital*. London: Oftel.

Oftel. 1992c. *Future Controls on British Telecom's Prices*. London: Oftel.

Oftel. 1993. *Interconnection and Accounting Separation*. London: Oftel.

Ofwat. *Annual Reports*. London: HMSO.

Ofwat. 1991a. *The Cost of Capital: A Consultative Paper*. Birmingham: Ofwat.

Ofwat. 1991b. *Paying for Water*. Birmingham: Ofwat.

Ofwat. 1992a. *Assessing Capital Values at the Periodic Review*. Birmingham: Ofwat.

Ofwat. 1992b. *The Cost of Quality*. Birmingham: Ofwat.

Ofwat. 1993a. *Paying for Quality: The Political Perspective.* Birmingham: Ofwat.

Ofwat. 1993b. *1992–93 Report on Capital Investment and Financial Performance of the Water Companies in England and Wales.* Birmingham: Ofwat.

Ofwat. 1993c. *Setting Price Limits for Water and Sewerage Services, The Framework and Approach to the 1994 Periodic Review.* Birmingham: Ofwat.

Oi, W. Y. 1971. A Disneyland dilemma: Two-part tariffs for a Mickey Mouse monopoly. *Quarterly Journal of Economics* 85:77–96.

Ordover, J. A., and J. Panzar. 1980. On the nonexistence of Pareto superior outlay schedules. *Bell Journal of Economics* 11:351–54.

Ordover, J. A., and G. Saloner. 1989. Predation, monopolization and antitrust. In Schmalensee and Willig, eds.

Ordover, J. A., G. Saloner, and S. C. Salop. 1990. Equilibrium vertical foreclosure. *American Economic Review* 80:127–42.

Organisation for Economic Cooperation and Development. 1987. *Pricing of Water Services.* Paris: OECD.

Organisation for Economic Cooperation and Development. 1992. *Regulatory Reform, Privatisation and Competition Policy.* Paris: OECD.

Palfrey, T. 1985. Uncertainty resolution, private information aggregation and the Cournot competitive limit. *Review of Economic Studies* 52:69–83.

Panzar, J. 1989. Technological determinants of firm and industry structure. In Schmalensee and Willig, eds.

Pearson, M., N. Rajah, and S. Smith. 1993. *The Distributional Effects of Different Methods of Charging Households for Water Services.* Report prepared for the Office of Water Services. Birmingham: Ofwat.

Peltzman, S. 1976. Towards a more general theory of regulation. *Journal of Law and Economics* 14:109–48.

Perry, M. K. 1984. Scale economies, imperfect competition and public policy. *Journal of Industrial Economics* 32:313–33.

Perry, M. K. 1989. Vertical integration: Determinants and effects. In Schmalensee and Willig, eds.

Phillips, A. 1991. Changing markets and institutional inertia—A review of US telecommunications policy. *Telecommunications Policy*: 49–61.

Porter, M. 1990. *The Competitive Advantage of Nations.* New York: Free Press.

Posner, R. 1971. Taxation by regulation. *Bell Journal of Economics* 2:22–50.

Posner, R. 1974. Theories of economic regulation. *Bell Journal of Economics* 5:335–58.

Powell, A. 1993. Trading forward in an imperfect market: The case of electricity in Britain. *Economic Journal* 103:444–53.

Price, C. 1989. Gas privatization: Effects on pricing policy. In Helm et al., eds.

Price, C. 1991a. Regulation of the UK gas industry, incentives and responses since privatisation. Department of Economics discussion paper no. 146. University of Leicester.

Price, C. 1991b. Privatisation and regulation—The effect on the UK gas industry. Department of Economics discussion paper no. 165. University of Leicester.

Price, J. 1992. Comparative competition in the water industry. Forthcoming in Bishop et al., eds.

Raja, N., and S. Smith. 1993. Distributional aspects of household water charges. *Fiscal Studies* 14(3):86–108.

Rand Journal. 1989. Symposium on price cap regulation. *Rand Journal of Economics* 20:369–472.

Rasmusen, E. B., J. M. Ramseyer, and J. S. Wiley, Jr. 1991. Naked exclusion. *American Economic Review* 81:1137–45.

Rees, R., and J. S. Vickers. 1992. RPI − X price cap regulation. Forthcoming in Bishop et al., eds.

Richardson, J. J., W. A. Maloney, and W. Rudig. 1992. The dynamics of policy change: Lobbying and water privatization. *Public Administration* 70:157–75.

Riordan, M. H. 1984. On delegating price authority to a regulated firm. *Rand Journal of Economics* 15:108–15.

Riordan, M. H., and D. Sappington. 1987. Awarding monopoly franchises. *American Economic Review* 77:375–87.

Röller, L. H. 1990. Proper quadratic cost functions with an application to the Bell system. *Review of Economics and Statistics* 72:202–10.

Rovizzi, L., and D. P. Thompson. 1992. The regulation of product quality in the public utilities and the Citizen's Charter. *Fiscal Studies* 13(3):74–95.

Salant, D. 1991. Behind the revolving door: A new view of public utility regulation. Mimeo. Boston University.

Salant, D., and G. Woroch. 1992. Trigger price regulation. *Rand Journal of Economics* 23:29–51.

Salop, S. C., and D. T. Scheffman. 1983. Raising rivals' costs. *American Economic Review Papers and Proceedings* 73:267–71.

Salop, S. C., and D. T. Scheffman. 1987. Cost-raising strategies. *Journal of Industrial Economics* 36:19–34.

Sappington, D. 1980. Strategic firm behavior under a dynamic regulatory adjustment process. *Bell Journal of Economics and Management Science* 11:360–72.

Sappington, D. 1983. Optimal regulation of a multiproduct monopoly with unknown technological capabilities. *Bell Journal of Economics* 14:453–63.

Sappington, D., and D. Sibley. 1988. Regulating without cost information: The incremental surplus subsidy scheme. *International Economic Review* 29:297–306.

Sappington, D., and D. Sibley. 1992. Strategic non-linear pricing under price-cap regulation. *Rand Journal of Economics* 23:1–19.

Scharfstein, D. 1988. Product market competition and managerial slack. *Rand Journal of Economics* 19:147–55.

Schmalensee, R. 1982. Product differentiation advantages of pioneering brands. *American Economic Review* 72:349–65.

Schmalensee, R. 1989. Good regulatory regimes. *Rand Journal of Economics* 20:417–36.

Schmalensee, R., and R. D. Willig, eds. 1989. *Handbook of Industrial Organization.* Amsterdam: North-Holland.

Schwartz, M. 1986. The nature and scope of contestability theory. *Oxford Economic Papers* (*supplement*) 38:37–57.

Seade, J. 1985. Profitable cost increases and the shifting of taxes in oligopoly. University of Warwick Research paper no. 260.

Sharkey, W. W. 1979. A decentralized method for utility regulation: A comment. *Journal of Law and Economics* 22:74–75.

Sharkey, W. W. 1982. *The Theory of Natural Monopoly*. Cambridge: Cambridge University Press.

Shaw, N. 1992. Fair competition and the incumbent. In Centre for the Study of Regulated Industries. (1992b).

Shepherd, W. 1984. Contestability vs. competition. *American Economic Review* 74:572–87.

Shin, R. T., and J. S. Ying. 1992. Unnatural monopolies in local telephone. *Rand Journal of Economics* 23:171–83.

Shleifer, A. 1985. A theory of yardstick competition. *Rand Journal of Economics* 16:319–27.

Slater, M., and G. Yarrow. 1983. Distortions in electricity pricing in the U.K. *Oxford Bulletin of Economics and Statistics* 45:317–38.

Spence, A. M. 1975. Monopoly, quality and regulation. *Bell Journal of Economics* 6:417–29.

Spence, M. 1983. Contestable markets and the theory of industry structure: A review article. *Journal of Economic Literature* 21:981–90.

Stigler, G. 1971. The theory of economic regulation. *Bell Journal of Economics* 2:3–21.

Stole, L. 1991. Mechanism design under common agency. Mimeo. MIT.

Suzumura, K., and K. Kiyono. 1987. Entry barriers and economic welfare. *Review of Economic Studies* 54:157–67.

Tirole, J. 1988. *The Theory of Industrial Organization*. Cambridge: MIT Press.

Varian, H. 1989. Price discrimination. In Schmalensee and Willig, eds.

Vickers, J. S. 1991. Privatization and the risk of expropriation. *Rivista di Politica Economia* 11:115–46.

Vickers, J. S. 1992. Competition and regulation in vertically related markets. Mimeo. Institute of Economics and Statistics, Oxford.

Vickers, J. S. 1993. Concepts of competition. Mimeo. Institute of Economics and Statistics, Oxford.

Vickers, J. S., and G. K. Yarrow. 1988. *Privatization: An Economic Analysis*. Cambridge: MIT Press.

Vickers, J. S., and G. K. Yarrow. 1991a. The British electricity experiment. *Economic Policy* 12:187–232.

Vickers, J. S., and G. K. Yarrow. 1991b. Reform of the electricity supply industry in Britain: An assessment of the development of public policy. *European Economic Review* 35:485–95.

Vives, X. 1988. Aggregation of information in large Cournot markets. *Econometrica* 56:851–76.

Vogelsang, I. 1989. Price cap regulation of telecommunications services: A long-run approach. In M. A. Crew, ed., *Price-Cap Regulation and Incentive Regulation in Telecommunications*. Amsterdam: Kluwer.

Vogelsang, I., and J. Finsinger. 1979. A regulatory adjustment process for optimal pricing by multiproduct monopoly firms. *Bell Journal of Economics* 10:157–71.

Waldman, M. 1987. Non-cooperative entry deterrence, uncertainty and the free-rider problem. *Review of Economic Studies* 54:301–10.

Walters, A. A. 1988. Arguing with success, without success (Review of Vickers and Yarrow 1988). *Regulation* 3:66–68.

Warford, J. J. 1966. Water "requirements"—The investment decision in the water supply industry. *The Manchester School of Economics and Social Studies* 34:87–106.

Water Services Association. 1990. *National Metering Trials: Second Interim Report.* London: Water Services Association.

Water Services Association and Water Companies Association. 1991. *The Cost of Capital in the Water Industry.* London: Water Services Association.

Water Services Association and Water Companies Association. 1993. *Assessing Capital Values at the Periodic Review.* London: Water Services Association.

Weitzman, M. 1974. Prices vs. quantities. *Review of Economic Studies* 41:477–91.

Weitzman, M. 1978. Optimal rewards for economic regulation. *American Economic Review* 68:683–91.

von Weizsäcker, C.-C. 1980. A welfare analysis of barriers to entry. *Bell Journal of Economics* 11:399–420.

Wigglesworth, W., and F. Barnes. 1992. UK policies and regulations. *Telecommunications Policy*: 721–25.

Williamson, O. E. 1975. *Markets and Hierarchies: Analysis and Antitrust Implications.* New York: Free Press.

Williamson, O. E. 1976. Franchising bidding for natural monopolies—In general and with respect to CATV. *Bell Journal of Economics* 7:73–104.

Willig, R. D. 1976. Consumer's surplus without apology. *American Economic Review* 66:589–97.

Willig, R. D. 1978. Pareto-superior nonlinear outlay schedules. *Bell Journal of Economics* 9:56–69.

Willig, R. D. 1979. The theory of network access pricing. In H. M. Trebing, ed., *Issues in Public Utility Regulation.* Michigan State University Public Utilities Papers.

Wilson, R. B. 1977. A bidding model of perfect competition. *Review of Economic Studies* 44:511–18.

Wilson, R. B. 1993. *Nonlinear Pricing.* Oxford: Oxford University Press.

Winston, C. 1993. Economic deregulation: Days of reckoning for microeconomists. *Journal of Economic Literature* 31:1263–89.

Yarrow, G. K. 1988. The price of nuclear power. *Economic Policy* 6:81–132.

Yarrow, G. K. 1991. Vertical supply arrangements: Issues and applications in the energy industries. *Oxford Review of Economic Policy* 7(2):35–53.

Name Index